T0371602

THE FINANCIAL CRISIS OF 2008

Supported by ten years of research, Wigmore has gathered extensive data covering the 2008 financial crisis and subsequent recovery to provide the first comprehensive history of the period. Financial crises cannot occur unless institutional investors finance the bubbles that created them. Wigmore follows the trail of data putting pressure on institutional investors to achieve higher levels of returns that led to over-leverage throughout the financial system and placed such a burden on recovery.

Here is a "very good picture – and painful reminder – of the crisis' evolution across multiple asset classes, structures, participants, and geographies." This is an important reference work for financial professionals, academics, investors, and students.

Barrie A. Wigmore is a retired partner of Goldman Sachs. He is a trustee of the Metropolitan Museum of Art, a member of the Investment Committee for its $3.5 billion endowment, and Chairman of the Trust for the Endowment of Worcester College Oxford. He is the author of *The Crash and Its Aftermath – Securities Markets in the United States 1929–1933* (1986), *Securities Markets in the 1980s* (1995), and a novel, *Morgenthal & Co. The Story of an Important Investment Bank 1972–2010* (2013).

STUDIES IN MACROECONOMIC HISTORY

Michael D. Bordo Rutgers University

EDITORS:

Owen F. Humpage, *Federal Reserve Bank of Cleveland*
Christopher M. Meissner, *University of California, Davis*
Kris James Mitchener, *Santa Clara University*
David C. Wheelock, *Federal Reserve Bank of St. Louis*

The titles in this series investigate themes of interest to economists and economic historians in the rapidly developing field of macroeconomic history. The four areas covered include the application of monetary and finance theory, international economics, and quantitative methods to historical problems; the historical application of growth and development theory and theories of business fluctuations; the history of domestic and international monetary, financial, and other macroeconomic institutions; and the history of international monetary and financial systems. The series amalgamates the former Cambridge University Press series Studies in Monetary and Financial History and Studies in Quantitative Economic History.

Other Books in the Series:

Max Harris, *Monetary War and Peace: London, Washington, Paris, and the Tripartite Agreement of 1936* (2021)

Kenneth D. Garbade, *After the Accord: A History of Federal Reserve Open Market Operations, the US Government Securities Market, and Treasury Debt Management from 1951 to 1979* (2020)

Harold James, *Making a Modern Central Bank: The Bank of England 1979–2003* (2020)

Claudio Borio, Stijn Claessens, Piet Clement, Robert N. McCauley, and Hyun Song Shin, Editors, *Promoting Global Monetary and Financial Stability: The Bank for International Settlements after Bretton Woods, 1973–2020* (2020)

Patrick Honohan, *Currency, Credit and Crisis: Central Banking in Ireland and Europe* (2019)

(continued after Index)

The Financial Crisis of 2008

A History of US Financial Markets 2000–2012

BARRIE A. WIGMORE

CAMBRIDGE
UNIVERSITY PRESS

CAMBRIDGE
UNIVERSITY PRESS

University Printing House, Cambridge CB2 8BS, United Kingdom

One Liberty Plaza, 20th Floor, New York, NY 10006, USA

477 Williamstown Road, Port Melbourne, VIC 3207, Australia

314–321, 3rd Floor, Plot 3, Splendor Forum, Jasola District Centre,
New Delhi – 110025, India

103 Penang Road, #05–06/07, Visioncrest Commercial, Singapore 238467

Cambridge University Press is part of the University of Cambridge.

It furthers the University's mission by disseminating knowledge in the pursuit of
education, learning, and research at the highest international levels of excellence.

www.cambridge.org
Information on this title: www.cambridge.org/9781108837637
DOI: 10.1017/9781108946872

First published 2024 (version 2, September 2024)

Printed in the United Kingdom by TJ Books Limited, Padstow Cornwall

A catalogue record for this publication is available from the British Library.

Library of Congress Cataloging-in-Publication Data
Names: Wigmore, Barrie A., author.
Title: The financial crisis of 2008: a history of US financial markets
2000–2012 / Barrie A. Wigmore.
Description: Cambridge, UK; New York, NY: Cambridge University Press, 2021. | Series:
Studies in macroeconomic history | Includes bibliographical references and index.
Identifiers: LCCN 2020041272 (print) | LCCN 2020041273 (ebook) | ISBN 9781108837637
(hardback) | ISBN 9781108946872 (ebook)
Subjects: LCSH: Global Financial Crisis, 2008–2009. | Financial crises – United States –
History – 21st century. | Capital market – United States – History – 21st century.
Classification: LCC HB3717 2008 .W54 2021 (print) | LCC HB3717 2008 (ebook) | DDC
330.973/0931–dc23
LC record available at https://lccn.loc.gov/2020041272
LC ebook record available at https://lccn.loc.gov/2020041273

ISBN 978-1-108-83763-7 Hardback

For Deedee

Contents

The plate section can be found between pp. 238 and 239.

Introduction

There can be few fields of human endeavor in which history counts for so little as in the world of finance.

John Kenneth Galbraith

The financial crisis of 2008 was initially seen by journalists, popular writers, the media, and some economists as the result of a housing bubble and subprime lending, funded by ill-structured private residential mortgage-backed securities (RMBS) that were exploitive of low-income mortgage borrowers.[1] In fact, the crisis was the product of multiple exaggerated financial developments. The private RMBS that funded the housing bubble included borrowers at all income levels and was only part of a massive increase in securitization that included commercial mortgage-backed securities (CMBS), collateralized debt obligations (CDOs), collateralized loan obligations (CLOs), and asset-backed commercial paper (ABCP). The housing bubble also facilitated an unprecedented increase in consumer borrowing that Mian and Sufi (2014) have documented and that I emphasize. The role of commercial real estate in the crisis has been little recognized and was mostly funded by institutional capital flows. There has been better recognition of the exaggerated increase in highly leveraged corporate debt, but its scale has been understated as has its unprecedented subordinated quotient. This expansion, too, was funded by institutional capital flows.

An important question is why the government-sponsored housing agencies – the Federal National Mortgage Association (Fannie Mae) and the Federal Home Loan Mortgage Corporation (Freddie Mac) – the state and local government pension funds, the corporate pension funds, the

---

[1] Reinhart (2009); Sorkin (2009); Tett (2009); Zuckerman (2009); Lewis (2010); McLean (2010); Morgenson (2011); Blinder (2013); Shiller (2013); Mian (2014).

1

insurance companies, and the commercial and investment banking intermediaries that serviced these institutions went along with these unusual
capital flows and their deteriorating credit quality. Why did these parties
fund them when they had unlimited information resources, paid constant
attention to financial markets, and had their own stakes in the outcomes?
Why weren't they worried? What were their regulators doing?

This book follows a systematic pattern of study through the pre-crisis
and crisis years to explore these questions of investors, their financial
intermediaries, and their regulators. Each chapter examines the consumer and housing, the economy, fiscal and monetary policy, and the
various investment markets – the stock market, mortgage-backed securities markets, commercial real estate, highly leveraged corporate debt,
private equity, mergers and acquisitions, hedge funds, derivatives, and
commercial paper. It is similarly systematic in examining the institutions
(especially state and local retirement funds) that drive these markets, and
the financial firms that intermediate them. These intermediaries include
Fannie Mae and Freddie Mac, commercial banks, investment banks,
insurance companies, and European banks. The book studies the investment pressures and modern portfolio practices that pushed institutional
investors into accepting greater leverage and risk and how difficult it was
for them and their regulators to grasp what the weaknesses were with so
many sectors in play.

The financing of the housing bubble needs to be looked at comprehen-
sively rather than focusing on subprime mortgages. Between 2002–07, $18
trillion in residential mortgages was securitized, 38% of which were privately securitized. Fannie Mae and Freddie Mac securitized most of the
balance. Thirteen percent of the private securitizations were subprime, but
many securitizations had credit flaws whether they were based on subprime, Alt-A, jumbo, or conventional mortgages. The riskiest sectors of the
mortgage expansion were financed under the belief that higher rates
compensated for higher risks, even after allowing for higher defaults,
a practice that often had produced superior returns in the past.

Households increased their mortgage debt by $5.4 trillion between
2002–07, of which $2.7 trillion was to take out appreciated equity for
consumption, and they did it at increasingly higher house prices. People
also invested aggressively in housing as 35+% of housing sales were
for second or investment homes financed with unusual leverage.

Many economists and prominent authorities have seen the crisis as a run
on the big banks as well as a quasi-bank run on the shadow banking system
(weakly defined). The implication is that there were corresponding failures

in monetary policy and financial regulation (Krugman, 2009; Eichengreen, 2016; Ball, 2018; Bernanke, 2019). Attention has been paid mostly to commercial and investment banks, asset-backed commercial paper, structured investment vehicles, and residential mortgages. Information about securities markets other than private RMBS has been highly generalized in these analyses.

Treating the crisis as a bank run is a familiar theoretical avenue for economists. It places the burden of policy response on the Federal Reserve as the lender of last resort and on regulation and reform to prevent recurrence. Aspects of the crisis resembled a bank run, such as the redemptions from the private RMBS funds sponsored by Bear Stearns, BNP-Paribas, and numerous other European banks, the loss of repo financing by Bear Stearns and Lehman Brothers, the inability to roll over some types of ABCP, the run on money market mutual funds, and the collateral demands on AIG. But broken business models shouldn't be treated as synonymous with bank runs. The failed RMBS funds were invested in the junior tranches of securitized mortgages and leveraged to improve returns. Bear Stearns and Lehman Brothers had stretched to extremes in commercial real estate and highly leveraged corporate debt. AIG was tripped up by an undisciplined financial operation in a London subsidiary. European banks and Citigroup set up structured investment vehicles that held long-term assets funded with ABCP to arbitrage interest rates. These vehicles' assets did not provide current cash flows to repay the commercial paper if it couldn't be rolled over. The repo markets were fundamentally unstable because the largest investing institutions were lending out 20–30% of their portfolios and reinvesting the cash collateral in the repo market or with money market mutual funds.

When broken business models threaten the whole economy it is central governments that step in rather than central banks. The Bank for International Settlements (the BIS) in December 2008 identified governments in sixteen developed countries that had guaranteed new bank debt or injected new capital into their banks (Domanski, 2008). The USA was a leader in this respect, nationalizing Fannie Mae and Freddie Mac, virtually taking over AIG, using the Troubled Asset Relief Program (TARP) to strengthen the banks' equity, guaranteeing all money market mutual funds, all business bank deposits, and new long-term debt for all of the major financial firms, and back-stopping huge pools of risky assets at Citigroup and Bank of America.

The bank run analogy has two problems. It does not explain the biggest failures of all – Fannie Mae and Freddie Mac with $5 trillion of debt and guaranteed mortgage obligations. Bank runs had nothing to do with the collapse in housing prices and commercial real estate, nor with the prices of private RMBS, CMBS, and highly leveraged corporate debt. These problems caused dramatic losses at Bear Stearns, Washington Mutual, Countrywide, Merrill Lynch, Morgan Stanley, AIG, Citigroup, and Wachovia before Lehman Brothers' bankruptcy created the impression of a bank run.

Nor does analyzing the crisis as a bank run help us to understand why the largest, most sophisticated investors and their equally sophisticated financial intermediaries participated in the bubbles mentioned above. The answers lie in 1) modern portfolio practices and 2) inadequate conventional investment returns following the collapse of the dot.com bubble and the terrorist attacks of 9/11. Modern portfolio theory established the virtue of diversification to reduce risk and the Sharpe ratio that measured reward relative to risk, but these theories were turned on their head as institutions justified greater risk, particularly greater leverage, and greater illiquidity in a stretch for higher returns. The best performing institutional investor in the last thirty years, David Swensen at the Yale University endowment, strongly advocated investments in hedge funds, private equity, commercial real estate, and real assets (timber, farms, and oil & gas) (Swensen, 2009). These investments usually involved high degrees of leverage and illiquidity. Readers will have to weigh this interpretation of the crisis against claims that investors' are perennially unable to rationally evaluate financial risks (Shiller, 2013; Gennaioli, 2018).

The major investors in 2006 were state and local government and corporate pension funds overseeing $9 trillion of assets, insurance companies overseeing $6 trillion, and banks $3 trillion (Table 2.6).[2] Foundations and endowments were aggressive investors but only oversaw $0.5 trillion. All of these institutions generally required 7–8% returns on their investments to maintain their solvency (pensions), to sustain their spending habits (foundations), or for pricing their products and achieving earnings growth (insurance companies and banks). University endowments required similar returns to fund 30% of their institutions' budgets (Harvard, Yale, Princeton, and Stanford). But these returns did not appear available in conventional bond and stock investments after the hi-tech bubble and 9/11.

---

[2] Federal Reserve (Financial Accounts of the United States), L.109, L.116–119. Individual investors were minor. The Forbes 400 Richest Americans had an aggregate net worth of only $1.5 trillion in 2006 and the bulk of that was tied up in companies that they or their forebears founded.

These various institutions and the commercial and investment bank intermediaries serving them increased their highly leveraged investments by almost $11 trillion between 2002–06 in a stretch for higher returns (Table 2.5). The $1.65 trillion increase in private RMBS was the largest percentage increase at 303%; but the $2.4 trillion increase in conforming mortgages was larger. So were the increase in commercial real estate if mortgages and equity are combined ($2.5 trillion) and the increase in combined private equity and highly leveraged corporate debt ($2.5 trillion). Hedge funds were the other fast-growing area at almost $1 trillion.

By the end of 2006, consumers were so extended in their debts and the institutional investment community and its financial intermediaries so imbedded in highly leveraged illiquid investments that it was impossible to reverse the situation without causing a major economic contraction. It would take five or six years for the situation to get resolved.

This history aims to contribute to our understanding of the crisis of 2008 and to provide insight into the behavior of financial markets between 2000–12. The nearest I come to theory is that leverage was the common denominator in most of the problems. Reinhart (2009) cites leverage as the common factor historically and in this crisis, but I describe leverage more broadly. Individuals increased their mortgages to draw out appreciated home equity and to purchase second/investment homes. Fannie Mae and Freddie Mac operated with leverage of 100 to 1 and were the largest subprime and Alt-A RMBS investors. The largest state and local retirement funds sought out the hidden leverage in commercial real estate, private equity, and hedge funds. Banks couldn't resist taking risks in these areas as the savvy intermediaries to the largest institutions. The leading US and European commercial banks accepted the leverage in private residential and commercial mortgages and the hidden leverage in the derivatives markets. Private equity funds induced record prices in the merger and acquisition market and funded their purchases with $2 trillion of highly leveraged corporate debt. In the aftermath of the crisis, much of the preceding leverage had to be unwound, especially among homeowners, commercial real estate, and highly leveraged corporate borrowers that, along with the huge wealth losses, stunted economic recovery.

There is a price, however, in being too theoretical. You miss things. The critical problem in the crisis was the decline in banks' asset quality and liquidity rather than their regulatory leverage. It is not incidental that the stock market gave strong approval to the accumulation of these assets until 2007 and that regulators had no ability to evaluate their quality. Poor management and weak corporate cultures were at fault at Bear Stearns,

Lehman Brothers, Merrill Lynch, AIG, Citigroup, Wachovia, Countrywide, Washington Mutual, and General Motors. The leadership of Hank Paulson, Tim Geithner, Ben Bernanke, and Barack Obama was vital to ultimately restoring financial markets (Warren Buffett called their presence "luck"). There were numerous other nontheoretical factors. Fannie Mae and Freddie Mac were among the largest individual buyers of subprime RMBS, partly due to government regulations. The European banks were a large class of buyers of subprime RMBS because their home markets lacked similar medium-term instruments. AIG was a phenomenon of its own struggling to perform, driven by a once-charismatic CEO, Hank Greenberg. I am also struck by the very human belief in 2007 throughout the financial and regulatory communities that the myriad problems of the housing market, corporate leverage, and investment banking illiquidity could be contained.

Nor does theory answer why regulators were inactive as the excesses developed. There was a maze of regulators overseeing the various participants. The Office of Federal Housing Enterprise Oversight oversaw Fannie Mae and Freddie Mac; the Federal Reserve oversaw banks and financial holding companies; the Comptroller of the Currency oversaw national banks; the Federal Deposit Insurance Corporation oversaw banks at all levels; the Office of Thrift Supervision oversaw savings and loans (of which Washington Mutual, Countrywide, and IndyMac were prominent examples); the SEC oversaw investment banks, their holding companies, and mutual funds; the Department of Labor oversaw corporate pension funds; state Treasurers oversaw state and local government pension funds; state Attorney Generals oversaw not-for-profits and endowments; state insurance departments oversaw insurance companies. The only preemptive actions were by a number of state Attorney Generals who attacked predatory and discriminatory mortgage lending (Totten, 2015). There were no actions related to investment practices. Surely this inaction reflected that regulators did not have the resources to understand the complexities of modern finance, although it may have also reflected belief in the self-governing powers of free markets. Other possibilities are that regulators had been "captured" by the regulated; some doubted their authority, as Christopher Cox, Chairman of the SEC, claimed in the middle of the crisis.[3]

There are indications that many regulatory changes in this period helped foster the trends leading to the crisis:

---

[3] Cox, Christopher, testimony before the House Committee on Oversight and Government Reform, 10/23/08.

- The federal government made a bipartisan push on Fannie Mae and Freddie Mac to assist low-income home ownership and their federal monitor thought they were well capitalized just as Hank Paulson was about to nationalize them.
- The Gramm-Leach-Bliley Act of 1999 dissolved the historic Glass-Steagall separation of commercial and investment banks and facilitated the growth in financial holding companies until the four largest had over 2,000 subsidiaries around the world.
- FDIC staff was reduced from 12,000 in 1995 to 4,500 in 2006, its bank inspections minimized, and its morale badly hurt.[4]
- The Commodities Futures Act of 2000 gave credit default swaps preference over traditional debts in bankruptcy making them a preferred speculative tool.
- The transition to Basel II international capital rules that allowed the major banks to internally calculate their own risk-weighted exposure led to capital arbitrage away from the common loans of the past into publicly rated asset-backed securities and highly leveraged off-balance sheet vehicles. Widespread acceptance of Basel II capital rules created a false image of safety because they failed to capture the deterioration in asset quality.
- The SEC amended the rules for broker-dealers' capital requirements in 2004 to include regulation at the holding company level, but with self-defined risk levels and vague enforcement. Christopher Cox, the SEC Chairman, eventually claimed that the SEC was not the regulator for 193 of the 200+ Lehman Brothers subsidiaries.

There was widespread dissatisfaction with the efforts of federal authorities during the crisis and the scale of the eventual economic recovery, but I disagree. There was unprecedented financial remediation (to fix or save the financial system as distinct from monetary, fiscal, or regulatory policy) during the crisis by the Bush administration and the Federal Reserve amounting to almost $14 trillion, equal to 100% of GDP. This remediation included $5 trillion in assumed obligations when the federal government took over Fannie Mae and Freddie Mac, over $5 trillion in guarantees for money market mutual funds, banks' commercial deposits, and financial institutions' bonds, and $750 billion for the Troubled Asset Relief Program (TARP). The Obama administration provided $1.5 trillion in fiscal stimulation, mostly in 2009 and 2010 when federal deficits were over 8% of GDP.

---

[4] Bair (2012), pp. 16–19.

The Federal Reserve undertook $3.65 trillion in unusual monetary initiatives to stimulate the economy, expanding its balance sheet by $1.4 trillion in the crisis (QE-1), and by $750 billion in the second program of Quantitative Easing (QE-2). In the absence of further fiscal stimulus, the Federal Reserve initiated its third purchase program in 2013 (QE-3), adding another $1.5 trillion to its balance sheet.

These actions by the Bush and Obama administrations and the Federal Reserve produced historic recovery in the securities markets and 2% economic growth, but they could not overcome three overwhelming burdens:

1. Incremental debt of almost $10 trillion incurred by consumers and business between 2002–08, the largest elements of which were $5 trillion of home mortgage debt, $2 trillion of commercial real estate debt, $1.4 trillion of highly leveraged corporate debt, and $0.5 trillion of student debt (Tables 6.3 and 6.5).
2. The $23 trillion in lost wealth equal to over 200% of Personal Disposable Income, the largest elements of which were $10 trillion lost in stocks, almost $5 trillion lost on residential mortgages of all types, $4 trillion in highly leveraged corporate debt, including commercial real estate, and $3.5 trillion in housing (Table 6.2).
3. The stimulus efforts were unable to reach small business as measured by profits and confidence so that this sector representing half of the economy remained depressed.

It was not clear that even the US government could deploy enough resources to quickly overcome these millstones.

1

The Heritage of the Hi-Tech Bubble 2000–2004

1.1 The End of the Millennium

Investors in 2000 looking back at the 1990s could have been pardoned for feeling euphoric. The S&P 500 (Chart 1.1) had risen 237% since 1992 – a compound annual rate of 16.4%. This gain followed a plethora of troubles at the end of the 1980s – the savings and loan crisis that corresponded with widespread commercial real estate problems; the collapse of the nascent junk bond market; the bankruptcy of Drexel Burnham, and the jailing of its hero, Michael Milken; and the military downsizing that followed the end of the Cold War. Anticipated earnings for the S&P 500 companies in the next year began to rise steadily in 1994 after a five-year hiatus, doubling during the rest of the decade (Chart 1.2) (more on the source of these estimates and their importance in conjunction with Chart 1.14).

The USA appeared to have a "Goldilocks" economy. Real GDP growth hovered around 4% with few hiccups. There was not a single quarter of GDP decline between 1992–9. The Federal Reserve opened its annual reports in the late 1990s with statements such as the following:

- "The economy performed reasonably well in 1995,"
- "The economy performed impressively in 1996,"
- "The US economy turned in another excellent performance in 1997,"
- "In 1998 the US economy again performed impressively,"
- "The US economy posted another exceptional performance in 1999."

Inflation appeared well managed as it dropped to 2%, having been the scourge of the two prior decades when it reached a peak of 17% in March 1980. The Federal Reserve in 1995 claimed that CPI inflation was "... less than 3 percent for the third consecutive year, the first such occurrence in thirty years," and proudly emphasized that "... there is no

Chart 1.1

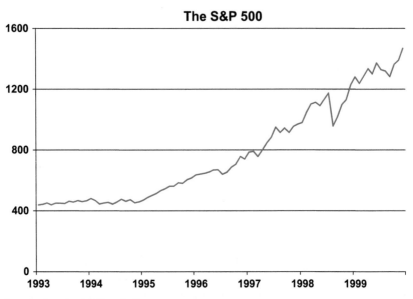

Source: Standard & Poor's Corp.

Chart 1.2

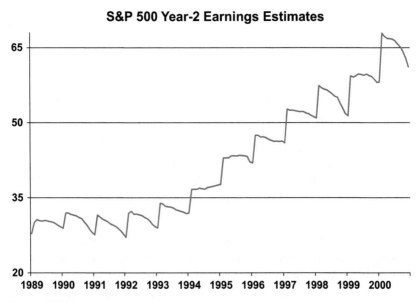

Source: IBES.

trade-off in the long run between the monetary policy goals of maximum employment and stable prices …."[1] Unemployment was down to 4% in 1999 while inflation was still under 2%.

There were many factors vying for the credit for this happy confluence. The federal government consistently balanced its budget for the first time since 1969 because of higher taxes on the wealthy, high capital gains tax revenues, and a "peace dividend" from the end of the Cold War. Federal deficits shifted from 1½% of GDP in 1993–5 to 1½% surplus by the end of the decade. Alan Greenspan was also given credit for accomplished leadership at the Federal Reserve. The close relationship between 2-year and 10-year treasury rates after 1994 (Chart 1.3) indicated how little volatility there was in monetary policy. He had a consultant's understanding of the US economy and appeared to pay no attention to money supply as M1 money supply and M2 behaved contrarily (Chart 1.4).

Some of the good results were inherited from the Reagan administration – its attack on inflation that stabilized around 4% after 1983, its emphasis on deregulation and free markets, and its Cold War "victory" over the Soviet

Chart 1.3

U.S. Treasury Rates
(percent)

Source: Federal Reserve.

[1] Federal Reserve (Annual Report 1995), "Introduction."

Chart 1.4

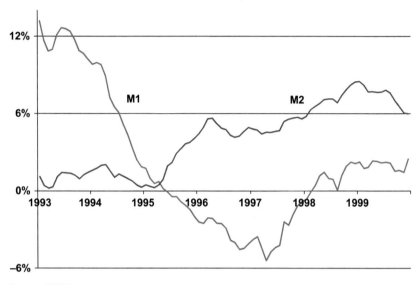

M1 & M2 Growth Rates
(year-on-year)

Source: FRED.

Union. There was also an end to labor strife as man-days lost to strikes dropped to insignificance (Chart 1.5). Other important factors included the prolonged 30% annual growth in computer use (Chart 1.6) and a 50% increase in FDA approval of new molecular entities in the 1990s, including drugs for high cholesterol, high blood pressure, lymphoma, breast cancer, psychoses, rheumatoid arthritis, asthma, diabetes, blood clotting, heartburn, allergies, erectile dysfunction, baldness, and fungus infections.

The 1990s were a far cry from the dismal atmosphere of the 1970s when there were two oil crises, the Vietnam War, record inflation and interest rates, attempts at centralized wage and price controls by both political parties, an impeached president, US hostages in Iran, struggles over integration, and a breakdown of many civil norms. The S&P 500 dropped 58% in real terms between the end of 1972 and mid-1982 (Chart 1.7).

Financial problems in the 1990s appeared to be foreign rather than domestic. There was a financial crisis in Mexico in early 1995. Brazil floundered throughout the decade. There was an Asian financial crisis in 1997 that involved Thailand, South Korea, Indonesia, Malaysia, and the Philippines (less in China, Hong Kong, and Taiwan). Russia defaulted on its external

Chart 1.5

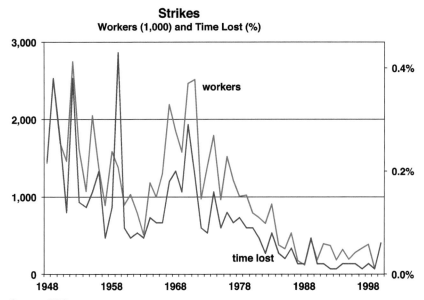

Strikes
Workers (1,000) and Time Lost (%)

Source: BLS.

Chart 1.6

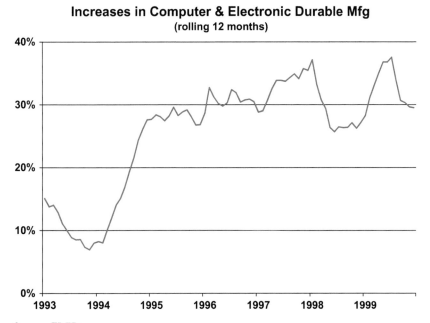

Increases in Computer & Electronic Durable Mfg
(rolling 12 months)

Source: FRED.

Chart 1.7

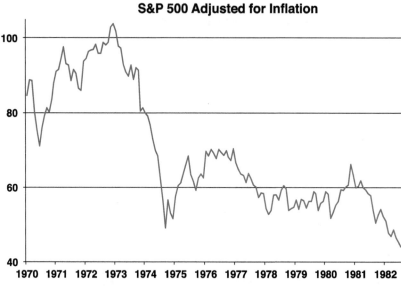

S&P 500 Adjusted for Inflation

Sources: Standard & Poor's Corp. and author's calculations.

debts in 1998, contributing to a mini-crisis in the USA in which the Federal Reserve Bank of New York arranged a Wall Street consortium to take over the liquidation of Long-Term Capital Management, a highly leveraged hedge fund speculating in government bonds. Turkey had to be bailed out by the IMF and the World Bank in late 2000. Japan appeared unable to escape perpetual economic stagnation after decades of admired growth. The Euro was launched on January 1, 1999 only to decline 25% in the next two years.

Oil prices were unthreatening, having dropped to between $10–20 between 1993–4 and again in 1997–9. Buying gold (a traditional safe haven) looked like "dead money" as it declined by 25% between 1996–9 (Chart 1.8).

The only apparent weaknesses on the horizon were an over-valued stock market and the worsening of the trade deficit as it rose to almost 3.5% of GDP.

1.2 The Hi-Tech Bubble Bursts

Investors' good times in the 1990s led to high stock market valuations. In 1999, the S&P 500 reached twenty-five times expected earnings for 2000 (Chart 1.9) – double the early 1990s. And while the S&P 500 had risen 237% since 1993, hi-tech stocks had risen 700% (Chart 1.10).

The euphoria came to an abrupt end in the middle of 2000. The collapse began on the NASDAQ (over the counter) market where most technology

Chart 1.8

Source: FRED.

stocks traded. The NASDAQ index fell 25% in just one week in April 2000 as analysts lowered their earnings estimates for Microsoft, the software favorite, and Motorola, a dominant cell phone manufacturer. Initial public offerings were down 26% in that quarter.[2] A debate raged over whether residential demand for desktop computers could make up for saturated business demand; but by the 4th quarter of 2000 it was clear that computer sales were lagging badly. Technology spending overall dropped from a 45% growth rate to only 6%. In September, Intel and Dell warned they would not meet their earlier projections. Apple's revenues dropped from $2.3 billion in the 4th quarter of 1999 to only $1 billion in the 4th quarter of 2000, producing a 4th quarter loss of $250 million for its recently reinstated CEO, Steve Jobs. By the end of 2000, the NASDAQ index was down 50%, erasing its gains of the past two years. The volatility was frightening as the NASDAQ index moved over 5% on twenty-seven days versus only seven such days in the prior decade (in one sense, a 3,850% increase in volatility). By the end of 2002, technology stocks were down 75% (Chart 1.11).

---

[2] Hershey, Robert T., Jr., *New York Times*, 7/1/2000.

Chart 1.9

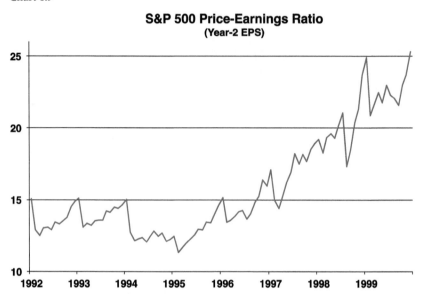

S&P 500 Price-Earnings Ratio
(Year-2 EPS)

Sources: Standard & Poor's Corp.; IBES; author's calculations.

Chart 1.10

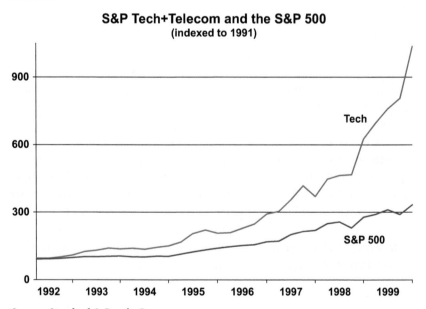

S&P Tech+Telecom and the S&P 500
(indexed to 1991)

Source: Standard & Poor's Corp.

Chart 1.11

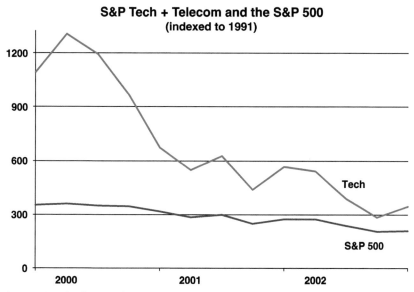

Source: Standard & Poor's Corp.

There were also problems in the telecommunications industry. The opportunities had appeared wondrous as the technological possibilities of fiber-optic cable, mobile phones, and the internet converged with government deregulation. Both conventional and mobile phones were effectively deregulated by the Telecommunications Act of 1996, and the Balanced Budget Act of 1997 required open auctions of the telecommunications spectrum. The result was a frenzy of new companies, and huge bids for the spectrum. Companies paid $37 billion at FCC spectrum auctions between 1994–2001 and laid eighteen million miles of long-haul fiber-optic cable. This resulted in as much as two-thirds excess capacity. Prices to use or rent fiber-optic capacity plunged 80% in 2000–01, and 118 independent carriers went bankrupt. The four largest independent fiber-optic carriers lost billions of dollars in 2000–01.[3]

The telecom frenzy also carried over into unrealistic merger and acquisition transactions:

- In 1996, AT&T spun off Western Electric, its telephone equipment manufacturing subsidiary, home of the venerable Bell Labs that started the semiconductor revolution. Renamed Lucent Technologies, the company made half a dozen acquisitions in short order totaling about

---

[3] Telegeography (2002), pp. 29, 46; Shampine (2006), pp. 2–3.

$6 billion. It achieved a peak stock price in 1998 of $84 and a market capitalization of $270 billion; but its revenues of $29 billion in 2000 shrunk to $12 billion in 2002. It lost $25 billion in 2001–02, ending up with $5 billion of debt and negative equity of $5 billion (versus $26 billion of equity in 2000). Its stock price dropped to 76¢ and its bond ratings suggested it might go bankrupt (Moody's Caa1, S&P B-).[4] It limped along until it was merged into Alcatel SA of France in 2006.

- Bell Canada spun off its manufacturing analog, Northern Electric, renamed Nortel Networks, in 2000. It reached a market capitalization of $400 billion (Canadian) despite that it had virtually no pre-tax profits in 1998–2000. The excess capacity among its customers crippled its business. In 2002, its stock dropped to 47¢ versus a high of $125 in 2000.[5] It, too, limped along until it was liquidated in 2009.
- Global Crossing acquired Rochester Telephone for $11 billion and laid fiber-optic cable to 200 major cities on 4 continents in an expansion that included 14,000 employees by the end of 1999. However, it had three CEOs in two years and was bankrupt by the end of 2001.
- Deutsche Telekom offered $51 billion for Voicestream before it ever made a profit.
- Qwest International, a much-hyped start-up in western data services using fiber-optic cable laid along railroad rights of way, acquired US West (a former AT&T subsidiary serving fourteen northwestern states) in a stock transaction valued at $34 billion. By 2002 the company's market capitalization had dropped to $1 billion and it was hovering on bankruptcy. It had $25 billion of debt and took a $23 billion write-off that left the company with no remaining equity. An SEC lawsuit accused the original Qwest of fraud, and a criminal lawsuit was begun by the Colorado Attorney General.[6]

These excesses brought about a permanent destruction in the value of the once mighty telephone stocks as their share of S&P 500 market capitalization shrunk from 8½% to 4% (Chart 1.12). The communications industry dominated defaults in 2000–02. Recoveries in reorganization were only 16¢ on the dollar.[7]

---

[4] Lucent Technologies 2000 10-K, p. 22; 2002 10-K frontal page and p. 20.
[5] Nortel Networks Corp 2001 10-K, pp. 23, 26, 36.
[6] Qwest 1999 10-K, pp. F2-5, F-26; 2002 10-K, pp. 48–9; District of Colorado, SEC Plaintiff, Qwest Communications International, Defendant, Complaint, pp. 2–3, www .sec.gov/ . . . /comp18936.pdf.
[7] Altman (2005), p. 24.

Chart 1.12

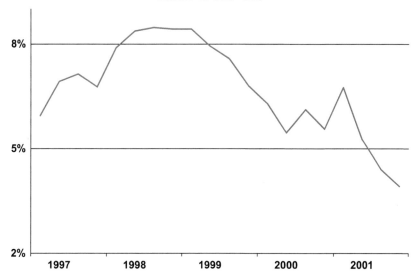

**Telephone Index
Share of S&P 500**

Source: Standard & Poor's Corp.

The shock of the downturn in technology and telecommunications was so severe that it cut real GDP growth to almost zero in the eighteen months from mid-2000 through 2001. Business spending on technology equipment and software dropped 9% in 2001 after growing 30% for many years (Chart 1.13). Industrial production stalled in mid-2000 and dropped 4% by August 2001 (before the attack on the World Trade Center). Consumer Confidence dropped from 110 in May 2000 to 88 in April 2001 (again, before the attack on the World Trade Center).

By the end of 2000 (six months after hi-tech earnings estimates were initially cut), analysts' earnings expectations for the S&P 500 in 2001 had dropped from $67 to $60. Hopes that 2002 would be better disappeared as the 2002 earnings estimates dropped from $68 to $60 in August (again, before the attack on the World Trade Center) and $52 after the attack (Chart 1.14). This represented a 23% decline in earnings expectations.

These earnings estimates are an especially useful indication of equity market expectations and the economic outlook. They have been gathered monthly since 1978 from over 15,000 analysts following individual companies in the S&P 500 Index. Their originator, Institutional Brokers' Estimate

Chart 1.13

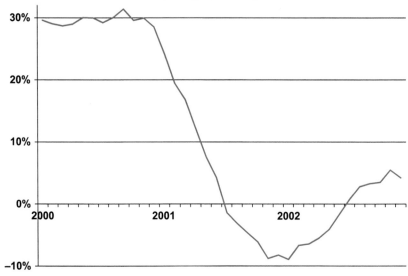

Increases in Computer & Electronic Durable Mfg
(rolling 12 months)

Source: FRED.

System (IBES), weighted the estimates by the size of each company to create aggregate estimates for the whole index. The format is estimates for the current calendar year (year-1) and the next year (year-2). The estimates were influenced by companies' indications of their expected earnings, by analysts' own research (into competition, costs, changing tastes, regulation, management), by macroeconomic and financial trends, and by company-specific events. These estimates are a felicitous proxy for anticipated profits and economic growth. They incorporate more variables than most forecast models – the consumer, industrial output, commodities prices, business competition, productivity, technology, public policy, fiscal policy, monetary policy, taxes, regulation, foreign trade, industry differences, management, pricing power, and much more. These estimates form a rich sample of informed opinion on individual companies. The estimates capture turning points in anticipated growth quickly and translate current events into quantified future expectations. It should be noted that these projections differ from reported earnings. They are based on non-GAAP results or "adjusted earnings" that companies and analysts commonly relied upon to eliminate one-time costs or gains and unusual events.

Chart 1.14

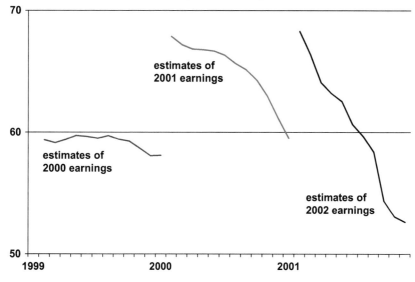

S&P 500 Next-year Earnings Estimates

estimates of 2001 earnings

estimates of 2000 earnings

estimates of 2002 earnings

Source: IBES.

The decline in earnings estimates illustrated in Chart 1.14 reflected the economic decline reverberating from the collapse of the hi-tech bubble and a litany of other shocks:

- The attack on the World Trade Towers in September 2001. The stock market was closed for the ensuing week and the S&P 500 dropped 11% for the month. Consumer Confidence, already down from 105 to 91, plunged to 82, the lowest it had been since 1993.
- California had an electricity crisis in mid-2001 as an outgrowth of the state's poorly structured utility deregulation effort. Pacific Gas & Electric filed for bankruptcy, Southern California Edison narrowly avoided bankruptcy, and shortages of electricity led to multiple black-outs and widespread business problems.
- Enron went bankrupt in December 2001 with debts of $10 billion, but $20 billion of liabilities under derivatives contracts and $20 billion of liabilities in unconsolidated subsidiaries.[8] Arthur Andersen, one of the big five accounting firms, went out of business in 2002 after being found guilty of obstruction of justice related to its role in Enron's

---

[8] Enron Annual Report 2000, pp. 33, 39, 42.

bankruptcy (the verdict was ultimately reversed but not Arthur Andersen going out of business).

- WorldCom, the second largest long-distance carrier after it bought MCI in 1998, technically broke Enron's record in July 2002, filing for bankruptcy with $31 billion of debt and $10 billion of other liabilities, although it had nothing like Enron's web of off-balance sheet and derivatives liabilities.[9]
- The dollar rose 18% between 1999 and 2002 as the euro (introduced in 1999) dropped from $1.10 in early 2001 to $0.88 in early 2003.
- There were recurring financial crises in less-developed countries as the IMF had to rescue Turkey and Argentina in 2000 and Brazil in 2002.
- The SARS respiratory virus epidemic occurred in 2003 when over 8,000 cases caused 775 deaths in 37 different countries. Although deaths were mostly in Hong Kong, the fright was widespread, particularly when there was a SARS outbreak in Toronto that resulted in 257 cases and 33 deaths and it was deemed to be spread mostly by hospitals themselves.[10]

1.3 Monetary and Fiscal Policies

The Federal Reserve raised the federal funds rate by 175 basis points to 6½% between mid-1999 and May 2000. The increase reflected concerns about overheating as unemployment fell below 4% and oil prices tripled (Chart 1.15).[11] However, once the hi-tech bubble burst, the Federal Reserve cut the federal funds rate seven times until it was 3¾% in the first half of 2001 (before 9/11) and then six more times after 9/11 until it was just above 1% by the end of 2002 (Chart 1.16). This was the lowest rate since Eisenhower was President. Treasury rates followed suit as the 2-year rate dropped from 6¾% to only 1¾% and the 10-year rate from 6% to 4% (Chart 1.17). Such aggressiveness would have inspired fears of inflation in the past, but the consumer price index not only stayed low, it declined sharply throughout 2002–03 to almost 1%.

The new Bush administration made a conscious shift in foreign policy, fiscal policy, and regulation. A discretionary war in Iraq was begun. Budgets shifted from four years of balance to projected deficits of 3% of GDP. Congress cut the lowest individual tax rate from 15% to 10%,

---

[9] WorldCom Inc. 2002 10-K, p. F-6.
[10] Center for Disease Control, MMWR weekly, June 13, 2003, pp. 547–50.
[11] Federal Reserve (Annual Report 2000), pp. 18–19.

Chart 1.15

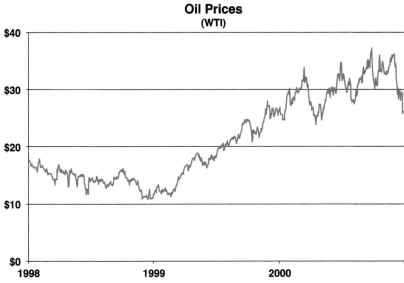

Source: FRED.

Chart 1.16

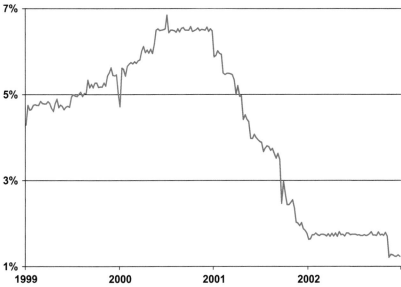

Source: FRED.

Chart 1.17

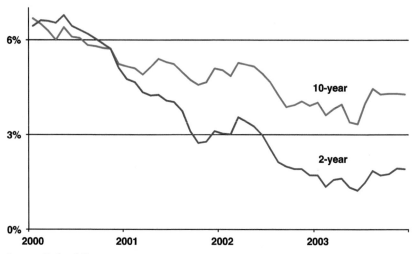

US Treasury Rates

Source: Federal Reserve.

resulting in $36 billion of tax refunds to 85 million taxpayers and author-
ized increased defense spending for the war in Iraq, a $60 billion transpor-
tation bill (including homeland security) and a $250 billion farm bill. The
Budget Enforcement Act of 1990 was allowed to expire in September 2002,
opening the way for $1 trillion of tax cuts over ten years – across the board tax
reductions, reduced dividend and capital gains tax rates, and repeal of estate
taxes.[12] There was a symbolic act of reducing regulation in a 2003 photo op of
agency heads cutting up stacks of regulations. There were real rather than
symbolic changes in the financial sphere as the SEC allowed investment banks
to calculate their own capital requirements at the holding company level;
derivatives were put in a preferential position in bankruptcies and their
regulation was ensured in the market-friendly hands of the Commodities
Futures Trading Commission; and the Federal Reserve shifted the emphasis in
bank inspections to minority lending and other social issues rather than
assessing banks' asset quality.

These monetary, fiscal, and regulatory policies had an immediate impact
on economic activity. Consumer Confidence rose from around 80 to
a more normal 95. Home prices, reflecting lower mortgage rates, increased

[12] Greenspan (2007), pp. 233–40.

Chart 1.18

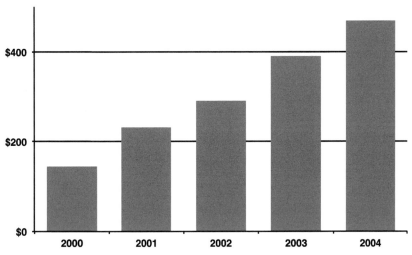

Home Equity Withdrawal Through Refinancing
(GS estimates--$ billions)

Source: Goldman Sachs.

45% between 2001 and 2004. All forms of consumer borrowing accelerated. Credit card and home equity loans rose 21% in 2002 and 33% in 2004. Home equity withdrawal tripled to over $450 billion in 2004 as people refinanced their mortgages (Chart 1.18). Consumer spending, the bedrock of the US economy, reversed the slowdown in 2001–02, and grew expansively. Retail sales were growing at 6% by 2004.

On the industrial side of the economy, the low level of interest rates resulted in a 20% reduction in the dollar exchange rate (Chart 1.19) that abetted a rise in oil prices from $30 to $50. Industrial production picked up, buoyed by the mix of increased consumer spending, a weak dollar, and higher oil prices. Capital spending by business followed, rising over 5% in 2003–04. Oil industry capital spending particularly picked up as technological advances in horizontal drilling, fracking, and geophysical mapping allowed the industry to exploit hitherto uneconomic oil and gas reserves. The stock market response was quite cautious, however.

1.4 Securities Markets

Investment returns in 2000–03, outlined in Table 1.1, placed institutional investors in a quandary. Returns were negative for stocks, but dramatic in

Chart 1.19

US $ Exchange Rate
(trade-weighted)

Source: FRED.

fixed income as the decline in rates on 10-year treasuries from 6% to 4% produced a total return of 39%. Once the effects of the Enron and telecom troubles washed out, high yield spreads dropped sharply creating total returns of 28% in 2003. Commodities returns were even higher at 63% because of the rise in oil prices. The problem for bond investors at this point was that *prospective* returns could not meet the 7–8% that pension funds, insurance companies, and endowments needed for financial stability or to continue their established spending levels. The 10-year US treasury rates were barely over 4%. Baa-rated corporate bonds had rates only 2% over US treasuries (Chart 1.20). High yield rates were 4% over US treasuries, but one had to assume there would be losses to subtract from this (Chart 1.21).

The stock market was unattractive as it reacted weakly to the fiscal and monetary stimulus. Total returns for the S&P 500 were negative from 2000 to 2002, and in 2004 it was still down 27% from its peak in 2000 (Chart 1.22). This occurred even while projected earnings for the S&P 500 were up 17% in 2004 to a record $74 – 10% above 2000 (Chart 1.23). This dichotomy reflected that the price-earnings ratio on projected earnings for the next year declined steadily from a peak of 25 during the hi-tech bubble to a more normal 16 times earnings in 2003–04 (Chart 1.24).

Table 1.1

	S&P 500	MSCI EAFE	Emerging Mkts	U.S. Bonds	High Yield	Commodities	Cash
RETURNS FOR VARIOUS INVESTMENT SECTORS							
2000	–9%	–14%	–31%	20%	–5%	50%	6%
2001	–12%	–21%	–2%	4%	4%	–32%	4%
2002	–22%	–16%	–6%	17%	–2%	32%	2%
2003	29%	39%	56%	2%	28%	21%	1%
1999–2003	–20%	–21%	0%	50%	25%	63%	14%

Sources: Standard & Poor's Corp.; MSCI-EAFE; MSCI-EM; Barclays; Bank of America ML; GSCI.

Chart 1.20

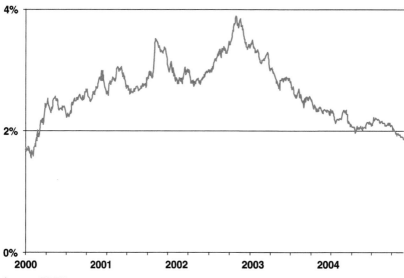

Moody's Baa Spread vs 10-year US Treasuries

Source: FRED.

However, this comparison takes no account of the dramatic decline in interest rates that conventionally would have raised price-earnings ratios and boosted stock prices. Instead, the opposite happened. The yield for projected earnings on the S&P 500 rose to over 150% of the yield on

Chart 1.21

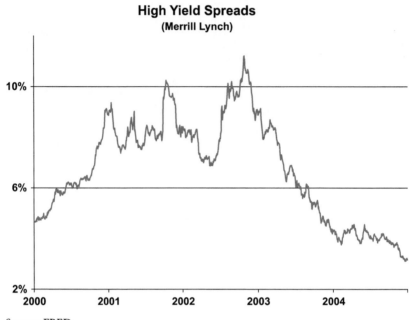

Source: FRED.

10-year treasuries compared with around 100% that had prevailed since the 1970s (Chart 1.25).[13]

The potential explanations were that stock market investors treated the low 10-year treasury rate as artificial because it was depressed by the Federal Reserve or that investors had a new higher level of risk aversion (required a higher risk premium) following the hi-tech bubble and 9/11; but another factor was that stocks were strong in industries with historically higher earnings yields (lower-than-average price-earnings ratios) such as tobacco, textiles, freight, durable goods, and banking (Table 1.2). Technology and telecommunications stocks still dominated the worst performing industries at the end of 2004.

---

[13] This was a favorite metric of Alan Greenspan's because it combined earnings growth and a discount rate in the form of 10-year treasury rates (there were many other possible rates). I have used the furthest forward projection of analysts' earnings estimates – the year-2 estimate. Greenspan and many strategists used a rolling twelve months earnings estimate that combined rolling fractions of the year-1 and year-2 estimates depending upon how many months remained in year-1. This resulted in smoother graphs but at the expense of not using all of the available information.

Chart 1.22

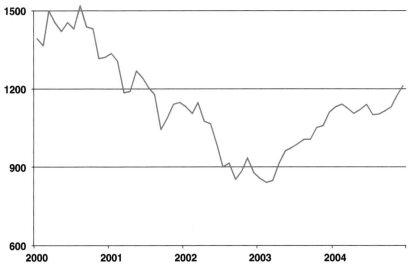

The S&P 500

Source: Standard & Poor's Corp.

Chart 1.23

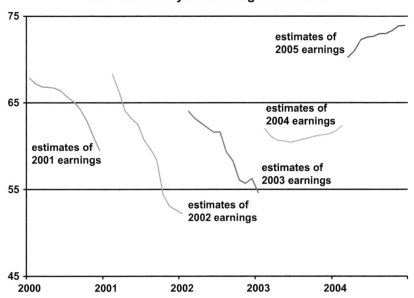

S&P 500 Next-year Earnings Estimates

Source: IBES.

Chart 1.24

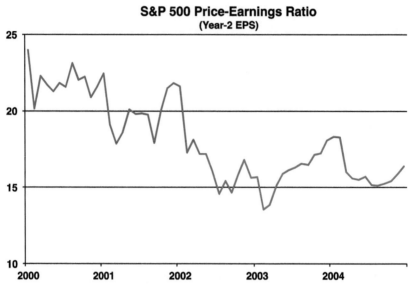

Sources: Standard & Poor's Corp.; IBES.

Chart 1.25

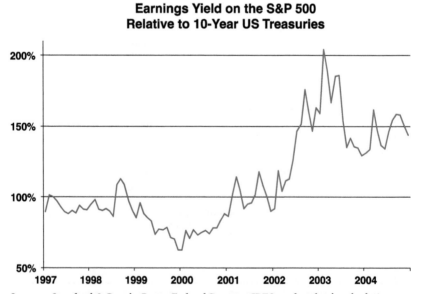

Sources: Standard & Poor's Corp.; Federal Reserve; IBES; and author's calculations.

Table 1.2

THE WORST AND BEST PERFORMING S&P INDUSTRIES 2000–2004	
WORST:	
Multi-utilities industry	−82%
Communications equipment	−77%
Electronics, instruments, components	−68%
Telecom services	−62%
Wireless telecommunications	−62%
Software	−51%
Semiconductors	−50%
Computers & peripherals	−42%
Media	−41%
Automobiles	−36%
Airlines	−36%
BEST:	
Internet & catalog retail	340%
Tobacco	158%
Healthcare providers	121%
Textiles & apparel	91%
Road & rail	75%
Machinery	70%
Airfreight	68%
Household durables	64%
Construction & engineering	57%
Food products	54%
Commercial banks	51%

Source: Standard & Poor's Corp.

Indications of higher risk aversion were contradictory. There was a dramatic decline in high yield interest rate spreads off US treasuries and funds flows were strong into hedge funds and private equity, as we shall see in Chapter 2. However, gold prices climbed from $300 in 2002 to $450 in 2004 (Chart 1.26) and there was a decline of almost 50% in merger and acquisition activity from $1.4 trillion in 1999 to $750 billion in 2004 (Chart 1.27).

Thus, a dramatic shift in investors' perspectives took place between the end of the 1990s and 2002–04. The 1990s had produced record returns in the S&P

Chart 1.26

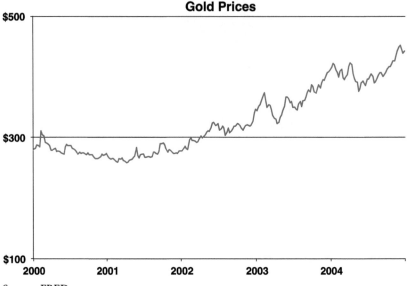

Source: FRED.

500 on the back of strong earnings growth, federal budget surpluses, labor peace, stable interest rates, and dramatic innovations in technology and communications. Unfortunately, the fervor for the latter created a hi-tech and telecommunications bubble that led to a sharp downturn in tech/telecom sales, capital spending, and stock market valuations in 2000. A recession followed that was exacerbated by the terrorist attacks of 9/11, record bankruptcies by Enron and WorldCom, and the SARS epidemic in 2003.

Fiscal and monetary policies responded aggressively to this turmoil. The federal government cut personal, capital gains, dividend, and estate taxes even while it had begun a war in Iraq. The Federal Reserve cut the federal funds rate to 1¼% by 2002, the lowest since Eisenhower was president. Baa and high yield corporate bond rates followed treasury rates down.

Consumer spending and the economy recovered but there were unanticipated financial effects. Analysts' anticipations for S&P 500 earnings reached record levels, but the S&P 500 did not recover to the levels of the late 1990s. Price-earnings ratios were only 2/3 of the level in 2000. The earnings yield jumped to 250% of 10-year treasuries after hovering around 100% since the 1970s. Gold prices rose from $300 to $450. Merger activity dropped in half. The stocks that did do well – financials, tobacco, transportation, and construction – were too narrow a focus for institutional investors.

Chart 1.27

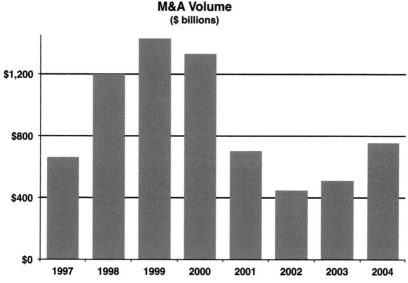

M&A Volume
($ billions)

Source: Mergerstat Review (2012).

Monetary policy turned out to be a blunt instrument. Lower interest rates produced 30% gains in long-term US treasury and corporate bond prices, but left them at interest rates so low that they were uninviting investments looking forward. Such low rates were intended to induce real spending in the general economy facilitated by greater risk-taking as investors moved further out the yield curve and into equities, but in a highly securitized financial system the effects turned out to be different. Stock prices and capital expenditures didn't respond but housing prices did, becoming a source of incremental borrowing for consumers and an attractive, highly leveraged investment.

Large institutional investors that needed 7–8% investment returns to sustain their current activities were forced to stretch for yield in a broad range of alternative investments such as private equity, hedge funds, highly leveraged corporate debt, commercial real estate, and real assets (forestry, oil and gas, farmland).

Financial intermediaries that restricted themselves to fixed income would fund the rapidly growing market for privately securitized residential and commercial mortgage-backed securities, highly leveraged corporate debt, and commercial real estate debt.

These trends would gather dramatic momentum in the next few years.

2

The Stretch for Higher Returns 2004–2006

Any chance of remembering tends to be erased by the promise of easy money.
Howard Marks

In the years between 2002–06, especially in 2004–06 as the economy recovered, institutional investors expanded their "alternative investments" by $7.7 trillion, most notably in commercial real estate ($2.6 trillion), private residential mortgage-backed securities (RMBS) ($1.6 trillion), high yield corporate debt and leveraged loans ($1.1 trillion), private equity ($0.9 trillion), and hedge funds ($0.8 trillion). In many respects, this was a reaction to an unrewarding stock market and monetary policy that brought interest rates too low to meet the returns that institutional investors needed.

Pension funds were the best illustration of the needed returns. The adequacy of the funding for their liabilities was reported annually based on actuarial calculations and their prospective investment returns. State and local government pension funds were both the largest and most vulnerable in this respect because they all had defined *benefit* plans, whereas by 2000, 56% of corporate pension assets were in defined *contribution* plans where the beneficiaries took the risk on investment returns. Table 2.1 illustrates the assumed investment returns for the four largest state retirement funds and the defined benefit pension funds of six prominent US corporations. They can be generalized as 8%. If state and local governments failed to meet these returns it meant some mix of higher taxes, laying off employees, lower services, or a growing pension liability that could lower their debt ratings and threaten their ability to pay pensions (the equivalent of bankruptcy). Failure for corporations meant some mix of lower earnings, the need to raise prices, cost-cutting, lower debt ratings, and also bankruptcy (General Motors in 2009).

Table 2.1

MAJOR RETIREMENT FUNDS' ACTUARIAL ASSUMPTIONS	
	Assumed returns
CALPERS	7.25%
Teachers' Retirement System–Texas	8.00%
New York State & Local Employees	7.00%
Florida Retirement System	7.75%
Teachers' Retirement System–Ohio	8.00%
General Motors–U.S.	8.40%
AT&T	8.50%
General Electric	8.50%
IBM–U.S.	8.00%
Lockheed–Martin	8.50%
DuPont	8.75%

Source: Annual Reports.

Insurance companies faced similar pressures as their return on assets dropped from 8% in 2000 to under 6% in 2004 (Chart 2.1). Low returns affected overall earnings, insurance rates, credit ratings, and employment.

Universities relied on the investment earnings of their endowments to fund a significant part of their budgets, including salaries, amenities, scholarships, and educational activities. Harvard, Yale, Princeton, and Stanford depended upon their endowment income to provide 31% of their budgets in 2004.

With 10-year treasury rates at 4%, there was a search for higher returns in alternative investments. An unattractive stock market still suffering from the hi-tech bubble was not one of them. The compound annual return on the S&P 500 from 2000 to 2006 was zero. Instead, institutional investors followed a strategy of taking higher risks in search of higher returns and did not seem to give regard to the leverage and illiquidity involved. All of the leading sectors of institutional investors, as well as major US and European commercial banks, investment banks, and Fannie Mae and Freddie Mac followed some variation on this strategy.

Table 2.2 outlines the investors in the private funds of Blackstone Group, one of the leading alternative asset managers. It illustrates how institutional investors dominated the growth in alternative investments. State and local

Table 2.2

INVESTORS IN BLACKSTONE GROUP'S PRIVATE FUNDS (% of $102 billion)	
Public pensions	34%
Corporate pensions	13%
Insurance companies	9%
Funds of funds	8%
Blackstone employees	7%
Individuals	7%
Foundations/endowments	6%
Financial institutions	6%
Sovereign wealth funds	5%
Other	5%
Total	100%

Source: The Blackstone Group 2007 Annual Report.

Chart 2.1

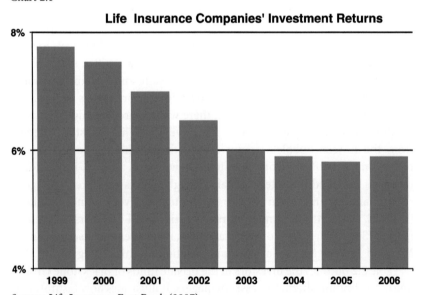

Life Insurance Companies' Investment Returns

Source: Life Insurance Fact Book (2007).

government and corporate pensions, insurance companies, and funds of funds (that were in effect the same investors) accounted for 64% of Blackstone's investors.

The economic background was a significant recovery in 2004–06. Retail sales, always an important engine for the economy, recovered to steady 6+% growth. Housing starts rose from an annual rate of 1.6 million units to 2.3 million by the end of 2005. Manufacturing had steady growth. Real GDP grew 3+% annually.

Oil and gas was especially strong as oil prices rose to over $70 a barrel. Worldwide oil consumption had been growing steadily, but the war in Iraq took a major oil-producing country out of world supply, Russian production was declining due to incompetence, and the Gulf of Mexico was disrupted in 2005 by the worst hurricane season on record as hurricanes Katrina (category 5), Rita (category 5), and Wilma (category 3) left behind 3,900 dead and $159 billion in property damage. At the same time, social turmoil threatened Nigerian production and Iran became increasingly improbable as a world supplier because of rising controversy over its secretive efforts to develop nuclear capability. In 2006, the UN declared Iran in violation of the Nuclear Proliferation Treaty and the world further tightened sanctions on it.

Inflation also picked up, rising from 1% in 2003 to 3% by the end of 2006. In response, the Federal Reserve began raising the federal funds rate until it reached 5¼% in 2006 (Chart 2.2). The Federal Reserve described this as "removing monetary policy accommodation." However, almost all of the effect was confined to the short end of the yield curve as 2-year treasury rates rose 300 basis points but 10-year rates only rose marginally (Chart 2.3).

The economic outlook did not overly concern the Federal Reserve. It expected 3% GDP growth in 2007, stabilized oil prices, and thought that the inflated housing market had "lost steam."[1]

The stock market had an ambiguous response to the economic recovery. The S&P 500 rose 50% by the end of 2006 from its low point in late 2002, but it was still below its 2000 peak (Chart 2.4). This was even though earnings estimates for 2007 were 40% above the peak estimates of 2000 (Chart 2.5). The price-earnings ratio on year-2 earnings estimates dropped from 22+ in 1999–2000 to only 14 by 2006 (Chart 2.6), and the earnings yield (based on year-2 estimates) relative to 10-year treasuries stayed stuck at 150% versus the 100% level that had prevailed since the 1970s (Chart 2.7).

This apparent under-valuation in part reflected the market rotation toward the finance, tobacco, transportation, and energy industries that carried

---

[1] Board of Governors of the Federal Reserve, Annual Report, 2006, pp. 11–12, 38.

Chart 2.2

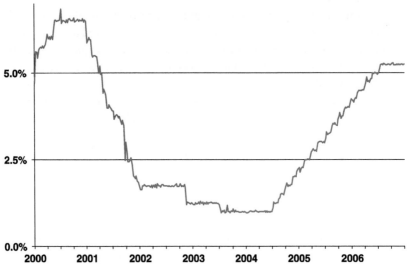

Federal Funds Rates

Source: FRED.

Chart 2.3

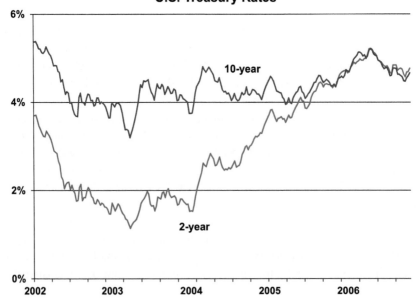

U.S. Treasury Rates

Source: Federal Reserve.

Chart 2.4

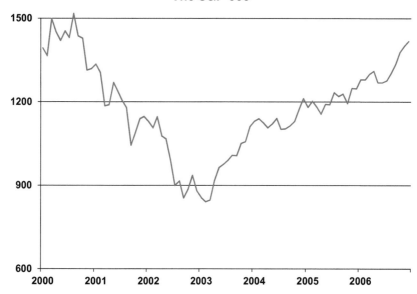

The S&P 500

Source: Standard & Poor's Corp.

Chart 2.5

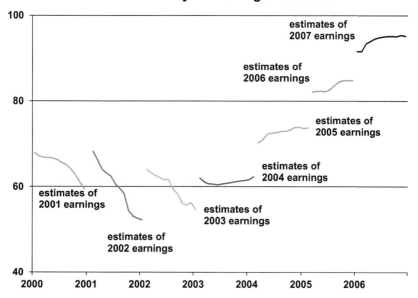

S&P 500 Next-year Earnings Estimates

Sources: IBES; Goldman Sachs.

Chart 2.6

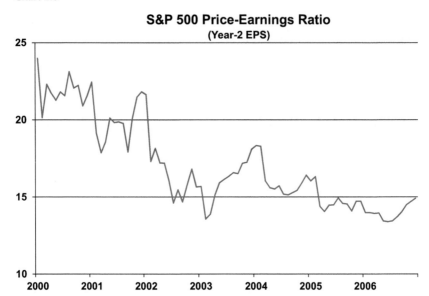

Sources: Standard & Poor's Corp.; IBES; Goldman Sachs; and author's calculations.

Chart 2.7

Sources: Standard & Poor's Corp.; IBES; Federal Reserve; Goldman Sachs; and author's calculations.

lower price-earnings ratios because of their cyclicality and leverage versus tech, telecom, and media stocks. Prices for the latter group were still 30–50% below their peaks of six years ago. Between 2000–06 Energy, Utilities, and Finance increased their weights in the S&P 500 39%, 76%, and 26%, respectively, while Healthcare, Telecommunications, and Technology weights were reduced 21%, 38%, and 32% (Table 2.3). Table 2.4 illustrates the dichotomy in stock performance for all S&P 500 sectors between 2000–06.

There was no increase in traditional risk measures to explain the S&P 500's low valuations. Volatility declined all through 2004–06 (Chart 2.8). Rates on the weakest Caa-rated high yield bonds dropped from 25% to 12%. Merger and acquisition activity recovered strongly, especially companies going private. The 50% rise in gold prices in 2006 (Chart 2.9) did suggest that some investors thought there was increased risk in some form. Stock valuations may also have reflected public dissatisfaction with the direction of the country. Dissatisfaction in Gallup polls rose from 30% of the public in 2000 to 70% by 2006. At this level, money managers had to be dissatisfied as well.

Thus, institutional investors faced a dilemma with low interest rates and a poorly performing stock market. The traditional fixed income alternatives offered prospective returns too low to fund their return requirements and if interest rates rose they would face losses (and ultimately did – corporate bond losses were about 1% annually 2004–07). The stock market had not performed well since the hi-tech bubble broke and there was undesirable risk in it because, what growth it had came from the cyclical energy and finance sectors.

As a result, institutional investors substantially altered their investment practices in the next few years in search of higher returns, putting almost $11 trillion of new funds into alternative investments between 2002 and

Table 2.3

SECTOR SHIFTS IN THE S&P 500						
	Energy	Utilities	Financial	Healthcare	Telecoms	Infotech
2000	6.9%	3.4%	17.5%	14.8%	5.5%	21.2%
2006	9.6%	6.0%	22.0%	11.7%	3.4%	14.4%
Change	39%	76%	26%	−21%	−38%	−32%

Source: Standard & Poor's Corp.

Table 2.4

S&P INDUSTRY INDICES CHANGE 2000–2006	
Healthcare equipment & services	124%
Energy	114%
Consumer services	69%
Food, beverages & tobacco	61%
Diversified financials	60%
Banks	57%
Transportation	55%
Consumer durables & appliances	50%
Insurance	41%
Materials	35%
Commercial & professional services	31%
Utilities	31%
Retailing	27%
Household & personal products	25%
Capital goods	13%
Pharmacy, biotech & life sciences	–5%
Food & staples	–14%
Media	–34%
Autos & components	–42%
Software & services	–51%
Telecommunications	–52%
Hi-tech hardware & equipment	–53%

Source: Standard & Poor's Corp.

2006 (Table 2.5). The largest percentage increase was 300% for the $1.65 trillion increase in private RMBS; but the $2.4 trillion increase in conforming mortgages was larger. So was the increase in commercial real estate if mortgages and equity are combined ($2.5 trillion) and the increase in combined private equity and highly leveraged corporate debt ($2.2 trillion). Hedge funds were the other fast-growing sector at almost $1 trillion – a 200% increase over 2002.

2.1 High Yield Bonds

The high yield bond market did not grow exceptionally between 2002–06, but it is a good place to begin the exploration of the stretch for yield because higher leverage and risk were explicit in the sector's bond

Chart 2.8

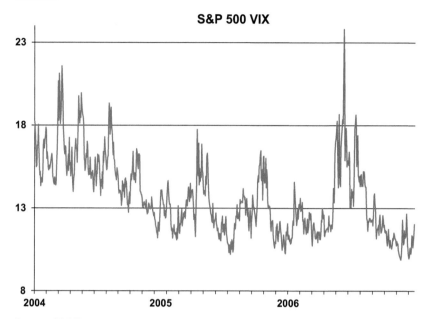

Source: CBOE.

Chart 2.9

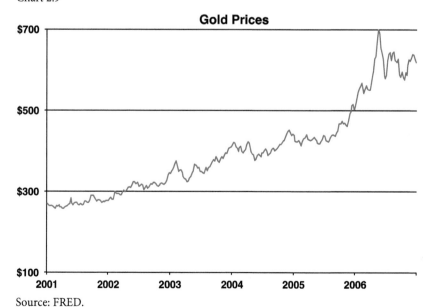

Source: FRED.

Table 2.5

	$ billions	increase
INVESTORS' STRETCH FOR YIELD (INCREASE IN OUTSTANDINGS 2002–2006)		
Private RMBS	1,651	303%
Conforming and non-sec'd mortgages	2,447	42%
Commercial real estate mortgages	1,465	64%
Commercial real estate equity	1,000	50%
Private equity (2007)*	882	135%
Highly leveraged corporate loans (2007)	1,350	106%
Hedge funds	966	197%
Asset-backed commercial paper	425	63%
High yield bonds	285	54%
Banks' home equity loans	256	121%
Total	**10,727**	
*capital committed vs 1998–2002		

Sources: Federal Reserve (mortgage debt outstanding); Federal Reserve (Financial Accounts of the United States); FRED; BIS (2008); Edelman (2013); Cambridge Associates (2006, 2011); Reilly (2009).

ratings.[2] Bonds rated below investment grade were never considered acceptable or legal investments by pension funds, mutual funds, insurance and bank regulators, or trustees prior to the 1980s. Most individual investors had never heard of them. In the 1980s, Michael Milken at Drexel Burnham popularized what were then known as "junk bonds." They grew from almost nothing in 1980 to $1 trillion in 2006 as junk bonds became a staple of portfolio management, approved by institutional investors, pension sponsors, regulators, investment strategists, and academics. Chart 2.10 illustrates this growth, but also the risk as market values periodically diverged sharply from par values.[3]

[2] "High Yield" refers to bonds rated below investment grade that were rated BB, B, CCC, CC, or C by Standard & Poor's and Ba, B, Caa, Ca, or C by Moody's.

[3] The amounts of high yield bonds outstanding can be confusing. Some studies cite par values, others market values, and yet others may include highly leveraged loans. For example for 2009, Altman (2012) reports $1.15 trillion outstanding, Black Rock cites

Chart 2.10

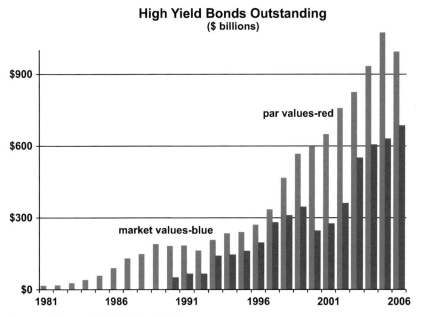

High Yield Bonds Outstanding
($ billions)

Sources: Altman (2012); Reilly (2009).

High yield bonds carried more explicit risk than investment-grade bonds. They had more debt relative to cash flow (Earnings Before Interest, Taxes, Depreciation, and Amortization – EBITDA) than investment-grade issues and lower earnings coverage of their annual interest (Earnings Before Interest and Taxes – EBIT). They were also more prone to default and the variability of their returns (two year trailing standard deviation of interest plus capital gains or losses) varied by large multiples of the variability on bonds with investment-grade ratings. The approximate measures for these credit variables during the years 2000–05 are outlined in Table 2.6.

The appeal of high yield bonds revolved around an expectation of superior returns based on a calculation of higher yields, default rates, and recovery rates in default (defaulted bonds rarely traded down to zero because of anticipation that the creditor company would be restructured or liquidated). A simplified calculation for Ba bonds two years after issuance for vintages 1997–2006 looked like the data in Table 2.7 with the emphasis on the last column.[4]

Merrill Lynch and S&P Capital IQ as reporting $810 billion outstanding, and Reilly (2009), working with Merrill Lynch data, cites $520 billion market value.

[4] "Simplified" because default rates included new issues rated from BB to CCC and recovery rates applied to all defaulted issues, not just issues originally rated below investment grade.

Table 2.6

	Debt x EBITDA	Net debt % of assets	EBIT/ interest	Defaults in 4 years	Std dev'n of returns (bp)
HIGH YIELD vs INVESTMENT-GRADE BOND CREDIT PARAMETERS 2000–2005 AVERAGES					
Investment grade	2.0	20%	16.0	5%	150
All high yield	3.5	30%	4.0		
Rated Ba				9%	332
B				24%	523
Caa				45%	965

Sources: Reilly (2009); Goldman Sachs (2016–1); Goldman Sachs (2016–2); Altman (2012).

High yield bond returns were cyclical as can be seen by the default and net return rates in Table 2.7, but the variability extended further. Whenever defaults dropped, there was a dramatic increase in default-prone new issues (Chart 2.11). The default-prone industries also varied over time from miscellaneous industrials and manufacturers in 1990–91 to telecommunications and entertainment companies in 1999–2002. Issue purposes changed over time from acquisitions in the 1980s, to hi-tech and communications funding in the 1990s, to private equity transactions in 2002–06. The proportion of Caa-rated bonds in the market also varied from 15% in 1986 to 3% in 1993 to 21% in 2007.[5] The rating agencies during the beginning junk bond years of the 1980s proved slow to react to these shifts as they allowed progressive credit deterioration while maintaining ratings (Wigmore, 1990). This phenomenon would reappear for private RMBS in 2004–07.

High yield bonds did not appear to be an attractive investment in 2001–02 in light of the Enron and Worldcom bankruptcies, but demand increased in 2003 when 10-year treasury rates fell below 4%. Such low treasury returns made the argument more persuasive that the default rates on high yield bonds in 2000–02 were unusual (i.e. fraud at Enron and Worldcom) and that high coupons on a diversified high yield portfolio more than compensated for defaults. Subsequent results fortified these beliefs as default rates dropped

[5] Reilly (2009), exhibit 2, p. 66.

Table 2.7

	Ba coupon	Default rates	Recovery rates	Net loss[1]	Net return
AN EXAMPLE OF HIGH YIELD RETURN CALCULATIONS					
1997	8%	2%	58%	1%	7%
1998	8%	3%	41%	2%	6%
1999	9%	5%	28%	4%	5%
2000	10%	7%	27%	5%	5%
2001	9%	10%	26%	7%	2%
2002	10%	9%	25%	7%	3%
2003	7%	6%	45%	3%	4%
2004	6%	3%	58%	1%	5%
2005	7%	4%	61%	2%	5%
2006	7%	1%	65%	0%	7%

[1] losses are 2 years after issue.

Sources: FRED and Altman (2012).

from 10% in 2001 to 1% in 2006 (Table 2.7 above). Investors' stretch for yield pushed Ba rates down 400 basis points and Caa rates down 1400 basis points in 2003 (Chart 2.12). In response, new issues of high yield bonds rose from $60 billion in 2000 to $155 billion in 2006.

It will be helpful to understanding the roles of various sectors of the securities markets in the crisis of 2008 if we can identify the investors in them. In many cases, the data is poor and we need to generalize based on the largest investors. In some cases, particularly before accounting changes in 2009 required more disclosure, we have to make inferences from data that becomes available after 2008.

The influence of different investors begins with their relative scale, outlined in Table 2.8. Mutual funds, corporate pension funds, state and local pension funds, life insurance companies, and banks dominated the markets with $22 trillion in investment assets at the end of 2006. There is some

Chart 2.11

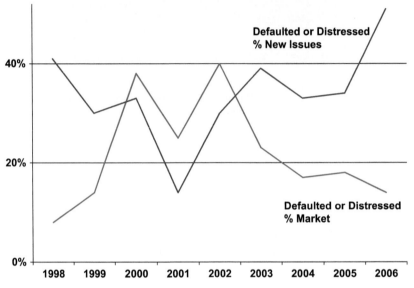

Defaulted or Distressed High Yield Issues

Source: Altman (2012).

Chart 2.12

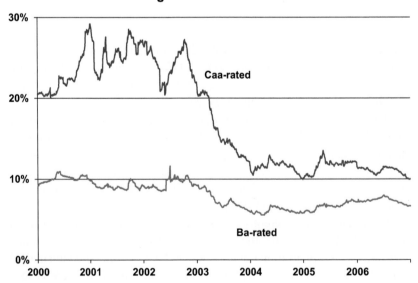

High Yield Bond Rates

Source: FRED.

Table 2.8

INVESTMENT ASSETS IN 2006	
	($ billions)
Mutual funds*	7,068
Corporate pension funds	5,558
Life insurance companies	4,709
State & local pension funds	2,978
Commercial banks	2,244
Casualty insurance companies	1,365
Investment banks + brokers	769
Universities	225
Foundations	220
Total	25,136
* excludes money market mutual funds	

Source: Federal Reserve (Financial Accounts of the United States).

double counting in so far as pension funds and insurance companies invested in mutual funds. The table does not show individuals' investments but 90% of their financial assets were intermediated through these institutions. The Forbes 400 Richest Americans were only worth $1.5 trillion and not a large influence.[6] Much of their wealth was as founders of companies or heirs of founders so that their shareholdings were often inert. Individuals' share of stock market trading was less than 10% despite the rise of online brokerage companies. A few universities with reputations for sophisticated investment practices (Harvard, Yale, Princeton, and Stanford) did not represent a significant share of institutional wealth. The data underestimates the influence of state and local pension funds because it does not include their commercial real estate investments that approximated 10+% of investments. The influence of corporate pension funds is overestimated because 56% of assets were in defined contribution plans that followed relatively confined investment choices given to employees.

Table 2.9 makes broad estimates of the dominant investors in high yield bonds. It suggests that mutual funds, banks, and insurance companies

[6] Forbes (2007), 400 Richest Americans.

dominated the market and that there was insignificant participation by state and local retirement funds. There was virtually no direct retail participation. The attributions in Table 2.9 accounted for the market value of all high yield bonds in 2006.[7]

Mutual funds were mostly driven by retail investors and participants in defined contribution pension plans seeking higher interest rates. These investors were uncharitably characterized as "dumb money." It would take additional research to determine whether life insurance companies were investing to meet their own investment needs or for customers' variable accounts, the latter amounting to the same retail demand as mutual funds. AIG was the largest insurance investor in high yield bonds ($29 billion in 2006). However, insurance companies' holdings were only 6% of their total investment assets which the companies may have perceived as a prudent allocation.

Table 2.9

HIGH YIELD INSTITUTIONAL INVESTORS 2006			
	Corp & fgn bonds ($ billions)	Percentage high yield	Estimated high yield ($ billions)
Mutual funds	813	29%	234
Commercial banks	572	33%	189
Insurance companies	1,882	6%	147
Investment banks	398	33%	131
Distress hedge funds	57	100%	57
Corporate pension funds	285	5%	14
State & local pension funds	211	1%	2
Totals	**4,218**		**775**

Sources: Federal Reserve (Financial Accounts of the United States); Investment Co. Institute (2016); Cambridge Associates (2006); NAIC (2016); pension fund annual reports.

[7] JP Morgan/BlackRock estimated non-high yield and balanced mutual funds held 29% high yield; Goldman Sachs example of high yield holdings (33%) is assigned to all banks.

Investment and commercial banks' high yield holdings may have been as high as 45% of the market. This is an estimate based on Goldman Sachs holding 33% of their corporate bond inventory in high yield bonds, but it may also involve some mixing of high yield bonds and highly leveraged corporate loans. In any event, banks held large inventories of high yield bonds. Some of this inventory was related to making markets and underwriting, but the size of the inventory suggests banks were using it to generate positive carry over short-term borrowing costs and in some cases to speculate in distressed bonds. To the extent that high yield bond prices were driven by "dumb money" going into mutual funds, the banks were playing a dangerous game of musical chairs because there were invariable reversals.

There should be a distinction in the high yield market between highly leveraged companies rated Ba because that was their financing strategy and the remaining 60% of the market represented by issues rated B or lower because of financial problems. The investment results in the two sectors were different. Default rates for B and Caa-rated new issues were three to five times those of Ba-rated new issues. Ba-rated new issues over 1985–2009 provided a 1+% higher return than investment-grade Baa corporate bonds with 4 percentage points higher standard deviation, whereas B-rated new issues incurred ½% lower returns and 7 percentage points higher standard deviation. Caa-rated new issues had 2% lower returns with 20 percentage points higher standard deviation.[8] This distinction is rarely made in mutual fund reports, or in descriptions of investment alternatives in defined contribution plans, or when investment strategists recommend buying high yield bonds.[9]

Obviously, from these large holdings, mutual funds and most insurance companies were heavily invested in distressed securities even though they did not have the expertise of bankruptcy investors. That expertise involved unique focus, years of experience, high-priced lawyers, and hardball negotiating tactics. It primarily existed among the investment banks and hedge funds investing in distressed assets (and they bought bank loans and creditors' claims as well as high yield bonds).

2.2 Residential Mortgage-Backed Securities

Low interest rates in 2001–04 led to a number of distortions in the housing market – rising house prices, increased consumer borrowing, booming

---

[8] Reilly (2009), exhibit 3, p. 67.
[9] After 2009 a ratings breakdown for bond investments was required in the footnotes to financial statements.

housing construction, investment in second and investment homes, the growth of substantial businesses originating residential mortgages and mortgage-backed securities, and widespread fraud and abuse.

Residential mortgage-backed securities (RMBS) were 80% of a larger market of securitized assets (Table 2.10) and it was in RMBS markets that most of the problems arose in the crisis of 2008. Outstanding RMBS

Table 2.10

SECURITIZED ASSETS OUTSTANDING						
($ billions)						
	Agency RMBS	Private RMBS	Comm'l MBS	Asset-backed	Total	RMBS %
1997	1,795	253	75	441	2,565	80%
1998	1,979	321	125	538	2,964	78%
1999	2,248	353	158	622	3,381	77%
2000	2,442	377	191	604	3,614	78%
2001	2,788	463	225	697	4,173	78%
2002	2,965	544	250	727	4,486	78%
2003	3,244	666	295	694	4,899	80%
2004	3,329	1,051	323	675	5,378	81%
2005	3,506	1,624	420	710	6,261	82%
2006	3,811	2,144	523	769	7,248	82%
2007	4,436	2,184	650	796	8,066	82%
2008	4,954	1,872	620	746	8,193	83%

Sources: Inside Mortgage Finance (2012); Federal Reserve (Financial Accounts of the United States).

guaranteed by Fannie Mae and Freddie Mac (Agency RMBS) rose $2 trillion between 2000–07 and private RMBS, securitized by investment and commercial banks, rose $1.8 trillion, while commercial mortgage-backed securities (CMBS) rose $0.45 trillion and asset-backed securitizations (ABS), mostly for credit card or similar receivables, rose $0.2 trillion.

This overall growth was a reflection of the decline in treasury bill rates from 6% to 1% between 2000–04, conventional thirty-year mortgage rates from 8% to 5½%, and floating rate mortgages to 3½% (Chart 2.13). Single-family mortgage debt doubled from $5 trillion to $10 trillion between 2000–06, an annual growth rate of 13%. New mortgage originations rose from $1 trillion in 2000 to between $3–4 trillion in 2003–06, with both refinancing and Adjustable Rate Mortgages (ARMs) consistently accounting for over 50% of volume (Table 2.11). If one used an ARM in 2004 to refinance a traditional thirty-year fixed rate mortgage incurred in 2000, the savings were almost 4 percentage points or $8,000 annually on a $200,000 mortgage – 18% of the median household income.

The decline in interest rates and the corresponding mortgage payments contributed to a 40% rise in house prices nationwide between 2002 and 2006, but speculation also raised house prices. In the metro areas of San Francisco, Las Vegas, Los Angeles, Miami, and Phoenix, housing prices rose 70–125% (Chart 2.14).

Chart 2.13

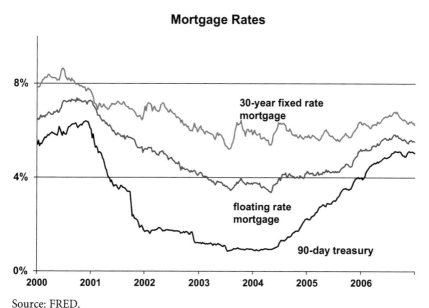

Mortgage Rates

Source: FRED.

Table 2.11

MORTGAGE ORIGINATIONS (ALL TYPES)			
	Originations ($ billions)	Refinancing	ARMs
2000	1,048	44%	31%
2001	2,215	59%	17%
2002	2,885	63%	25%
2003	3,945	72%	28%
2004	2,920	52%	57%
2005	3,120	50%	54%
2006	2,980	49%	53%

Source: Inside Mortgage Finance (2012).

Housing speculation was at work in various forms. People bought second homes as a good investment for their weekends and vacations, as an eventual retirement home, to rent, or to flip. Surveys by the National Association of Realtors suggested that 40% of sales was for investment or vacation purposes in 2005 (Chart 2.15). This was a big jump from Census estimates in 2002 that only 11% of housing was "occasional," "seasonal," or "off market" (not the same definition, as the National Association of Realtors measured flow and the Census measured stock).[10] DeFusco (2017) documented that 42% of the increase in housing sales between 2000–05 in 140 Metropolitan Statistical Areas was accounted for by sales of homes held less than three years, suggesting quick flips by investors.[11] At the extreme, real estate agents put together portfolios of homes that they managed and traded for groups of limited partners.

Homeowners aggressively used higher house prices and lower interest rates to take out cash. Annual cash out in mortgage refinancings rose from

[10] US Bureau of the Census, "Quarterly Residential Vacancies and Home Ownership," table 4.
[11] DeFusco (2017), p. 3.

Chart 2.14

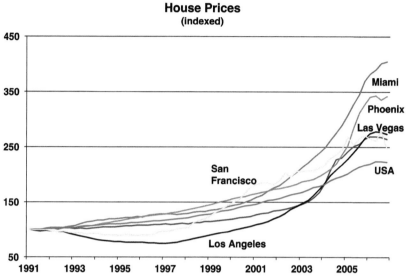

Source: FHFA (house price index datasets).

Chart 2.15

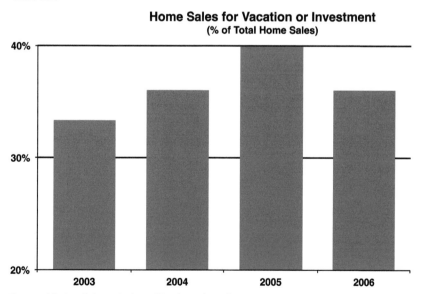

Source: National Association of Realtors (2017).

$50 billion in the 1990s to almost $500 billion in 2005. The cumulative withdrawal reached $2.4 trillion between 2001–06 (Chart 2.16) broadly fueling increased consumption.[12]

In this atmosphere of rising prices, investor speculation, and equity withdrawal the mortgage market underwent a shift to a higher proportion of nonconforming residential mortgages ineligible for Fannie Mae or Freddie Mac guarantees (Chart 2.17). The shift was not simply to subprime mortgages, but also to jumbo mortgages (above the maximum allowed for Fannie/Freddie guarantees) and Alt-A mortgages (where disclosure was weak, a second/rental/speculative home was involved, or appraisals were low relative to the loan amount). Subprime, jumbo, and Alt-A mortgages collectively doubled from 30% to 60% of originations by 2006 (Chart 2.18).

Securitization of subprime and Alt-A originations rose from 40% in 2000 to 80% in 2006 (Chart 2.18). Jumbo securitizations rose from under 20% in 2000 to 45% in 2005 (Chart 2.19), although the creditworthiness of jumbo residential mortgages was more variable because in some cases they represented borrowing by the wealthy. Private securitizations (as distinct from originations) based on non-conforming mortgages rose from 20% of

Chart 2.16

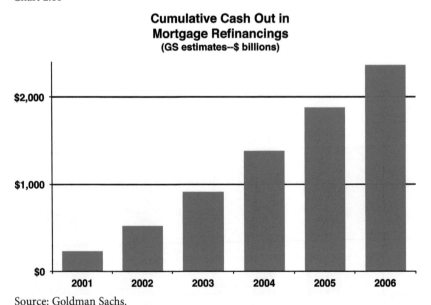

**Cumulative Cash Out in
Mortgage Refinancings**
(GS estimates–$ billions)

Source: Goldman Sachs.

[12] Goldman Sachs estimates.

Chart 2.17

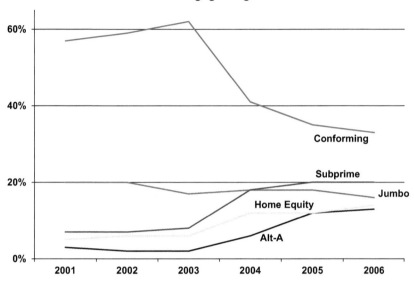

Source: Greenlaw (2008).

Chart 2.18

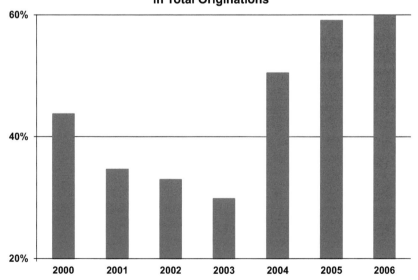

Source: Inside Mortgage Finance (2012).

Chart 2.19

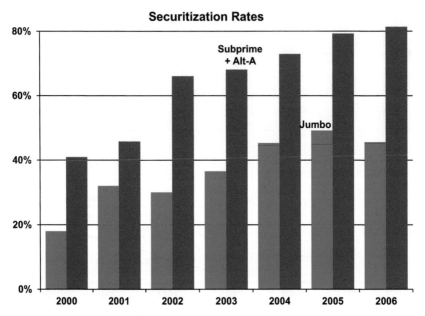

Securitization Rates

Source: Inside Mortgage Finance (2012).

the RMBS market in 2000–03 to 55% in 2005–06 (Chart 2.20). Fannie Mae and Freddie Mac securitizations accounted for the balance.

New issues of collateralized debt obligations (CDOs) tripled in late 2005 and 2006 in conjunction with the rise in private RMBS issues (Chart 2.21). The cumulative total in 2005–06 was $550 billion compared with $2.1 trillion of outstanding private RMBS. CDO issues originally packaged other collateral besides private RMBS, such as corporate bonds, home-equity loans, and derivatives, but private RMBS collateral grew from under 20% in 2001 to 80% in 2006 as CDO volume grew (Chart 2.22). The private RMBS collateral tended to be lower-rated tranches that were difficult for underwriters to sell. These RMBS had an average rating of only A/A. Synthetic CDOs based simply on derivatives amounted to approximately 15% of CDO issues in the high volume of 2006. CDOs (other than synthetic CDOs based on derivatives) did not increase the volume of outstanding private RMBS since the collateral was taken out of the market thereby. The stretch for yield in CDOs was apparent from the low-rated collateral and as only 34% of the initial tranches were rated Aaa.[13] CDOs would show up as trouble in the crisis.

[13] Benmelech (2009), table 8, p. 183; Owusu-Anah (2013), pp. 9, 13, 17.

Chart 2.20

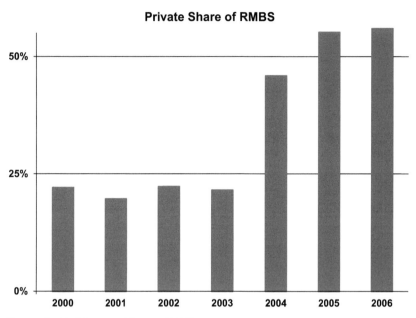

Source: Inside Mortgage Finance (2012).

Chart 2.21

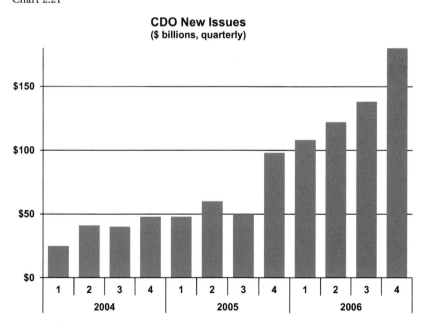

Source: SIFMA Research Quarterlies.

Chart 2.22

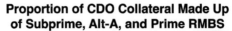

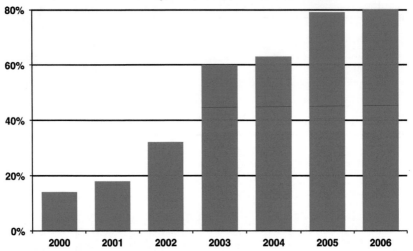

Source: SIFMA Research Quarterlies.

Investors in private RMBS made similar calculations to those in high yield bonds in that investors assumed more risk in return for a higher coupon that allowed for expected defaults. Professional investors in private RMBS knew from data routinely reported by Inside Mortgage Finance that this was not their grandparents' residential mortgage market. California and Florida (two states with highly volatile real estate markets) accounted for over 30% of all new residential mortgages between 2002–06.[14] Delinquency rates were steadily over 5% and often over 15% for some of the largest mortgage servicing companies (Table 2.12). Servicers were not necessarily originators or underwriters, but repeat appearances over the years for servicers with the worst records such as Ocwen, Option One (an H&R Block subsidiary), Washington Mutual, US Bank, and NetBank indicated that this was a consistent factor in private RMBS returns.

Elaborate models were used to illustrate how higher interest rates could more than compensate for higher default rates. Countrywide Financial exemplified a simplified version of this thinking when it was flying high. Countrywide's 2006 10-K outlined its delinquency rates as follows (percentages rounded):

[14] Inside Mortgage Finance (2012), volume 1, pp. 26–30.

Delinquent Mortgage Loans (%)

	2006	2005	2004	2003
Conventional	3	3	2	2
Nonprime mortgage	19	15	11	12
Prime home equity	3	2	1	1
Government	14	15	13	13
Total delinquent loans	5	5	4	4

Note: "Government" loans are for FHA and VA guaranteed mortgages.

Table 2.12

LOAN SERVICERS WITH THE HIGHEST DELINQUENCY RATES

2003		2004	
Ocwen	13%	Ocwen	15%
Union Federal (Indpls)	9%	Aurora	14%
Option One	9%	Option One	8%
GMAC	7%	Waterfield	8%
U.S. Bank	6%	U.S. Bank	8%
Homecomings	6%	Flagstar	7%
Washington Mutual	6%	Net Bank	6%
Greenpoint	5%	Wells Fargo	5%
		Washington Mutual	5%
2005		**2006**	
Select Portfolio	27%	Option One	21%
Ocwen	20%	Ocwen	20%
Litton	15%	Net Bank	17%
Option One	8%	Litton	16%
HSBC Consumer	6%	New Century	15%
Aurora	6%	Aurora	10%
Washington Mutual	5%	EMC/Bear Stearns	10%
First Horizon	4%	Flagstar	7%
National City	4%	Residential Capital	6%
Wells Fargo	4%	Countrywide	6%
		IndyMac	6%

Source: Inside Mortgage Finance (2012).

Similarly, Warren Buffet's Berkshire Hathaway had a $10 billion mobile home lending operation through its Clayton Homes subsidiary that was described as follows in its 2005 annual report:

In this brutal (for mobile homes) environment Clayton has bought a large amount of manufactured-housing loans from major banks that found them unprofitable and difficult to service. Clayton's operating expertise and Berkshire's financial resources have made this an excellent business for us and one in which we are preeminent. We presently service $17 billion of loans, compared to $5.4 billion at the time of our purchase (of Clayton Homes). Moreover, Clayton now owns $9.6 billion of its servicing portfolio, a position built up almost entirely since Berkshire entered the picture.

Subprime lending was not only considered good business; it had a democratic appeal. Federal government policy was to extend home ownership to low-income buyers, and Fannie Mae and Freddie Mac were mandated to make a proportion of low-income, high loan-to-value loans. Finance companies, credit card companies, and auto finance companies believed that they were saving low-income borrowers from loan sharks and payday loans at much higher rates. In other words, higher default rates – even surges in default rates – were expected in the subprime lending business.

However, lenders also knew that private RMBS were more complicated than high yield bonds or credit cards (where the regular percentage write-off factor also existed). Not only was every mortgage pool different, lenders and the rating agencies relied on a long list of general parameters designed to assess creditworthiness – FICO scores, borrower's income, loan-to-value ratios, owner occupancy, prior price increases for the homes, levels of borrower documentation, existence of second mortgages, regional diversification, "excess spread" that provided a cushion for the RMBS versus the underlying pool of mortgages, and third party insurance/guarantees of a layer of the bonds. Analysts drilled down to the zip codes of mortgages to assign Census and other variables to individual mortgages. People with the interest and ability to explore all of these details were mostly limited to the sponsors of new issues, the rating agencies, and eventually a few short sellers.

Investors also knew it was difficult to track yields on private RMBS because each mortgage pool was different and the bonds were illiquid. Privately issued RMBS had about 25% of the daily turnover of high yield bonds and about 3% of Agency RMBS.[15] There were no public reference

---

[15] Goldman Sachs (2016–2).

prices until the ABX indices were introduced in 2006 for bonds backed by subprime mortgages.

Despite the complexities and illiquidity of private RMBS, investors' stretch for yield led to rising risk in new issues in 2004–06. Subprime loan-to-value ratios (including junior liens) rose from 87% in 2003 to 97% in 2007; low or no documentation loans rose from 25% in 2001 to 46% in 2006; home price appreciation in the prior twelve months rose from 8% in 2002 to 18% in 2005. The pattern was similar in the Alt-A mortgage market. Low or no documentation loans (always high in Alt-A loans) rose from 63% in 2002 to 79% in 2007; home price appreciation in the prior twelve months rose from 9% in 2002 to 18% in 2005; and the proportion of Alt-A loans with a loan-to-value ratio between 90–100% rose from 8% to 33%.[16]

The credit structure of private RMBS loan pools also worsened. The fraction of subprime mortgages that had bond insurance dropped from 40% in 2001 to 6% in 2006; the proportion of interest-only mortgages rose from zero in 2001 to 28% in 2005; the "excess spread" that served as a cushion for bond holders dropped from 6.3% in 2002 to 2.7% in 2007; and one-third of all loans were in California and Florida in 2004–06. Forty-five percent of all jumbo loans were originated in California in 2006.[17] For Alt-A RMBS, bond insurance fell from 29% to 5%; interest-only loans rose from 0% to 62%; and excess spread dropped from 2.4% to 1%.

The rise in mortgage volume made mortgages look like a good business. The most aggressive players had high performing stocks in a market where the S&P 500 performed poorly. Countrywide's stock rose from $15 in 2001–03 to $45 in 2006; Washington Mutual's from $35 to $45; Indy Mac's from $12 to $45; Ocwen's from $3 to $16; and New Century's from under $20 to over $60, although it was one of the first to fail in early 2007.

Major banks were anxious to expand their mortgage business. Jamie Dimon, CEO of JP Morgan Chase, bemoaned his bank's lack of market share in 2005 and declared improving it a major priority.[18] Robert Rubin pushed an in-house committee at Citigroup to improve their position in structured securities. Wachovia acquired Golden West Financial, a leading California originator, in May 2006. Merrill Lynch acquired another leading California originator, First Franklin Financial, in December 2006. Bear

---

[16] Ashcraft (2010), table 3.
[17] Ashcraft (2010), table 3; Inside Mortgage Finance (2012), vol. 1, p. 26.
[18] Tett (2009), pp. 120–1.

Stearns, Lehman Brothers, and Morgan Stanley also had subsidiaries originating mortgages. Bank of America was pursuing Countrywide and JP Morgan was pursuing Washington Mutual, as was Wells Fargo although it would eventually decide on buying Wachovia.

As with high yield bonds, it is helpful to understand who was investing in private RMBS. Table 2.13 outlines estimated holdings of the largest investors in 2006, accounting for over 90% of the private RMBS outstanding. These are rough estimates because of weak disclosure. The estimates are not helped by the absence of private RMBS investors in the Federal Reserve's Financial Accounts of the United States. Better US disclosure began in 2007 but was limited to subprime exposure with no reference to Alt-A and jumbo mortgages. Even the subprime disclosure did not always include 2006 exposure. Off-balance sheet reporting was also difficult to interpret and differed from bank to bank. European disclosure remained poor and also emphasized subprime exposure. European banks' private RMBS exposure has been estimated based on subsequent write-offs and delayed disclosures and restatements.

Citigroup was in a class by itself among commercial and investment banks as the largest private RMBS investor at $274 billion – 13% of total private RMBS. The largest part of this was in off-balance sheet vehicles of $120 billion where liability is difficult to untangle. It was certainly material as Citigroup had to take over $50 billion onto its balance sheet in 2007. Much of the off-balance sheet exposure related to collateralized debt obligations that Citigroup sponsored to market the lower-rated tranches of its securitizations. Citigroup had a large trading operation domestically and internationally inherited from its acquisition of Salomon Brothers in 1998. It was a leader in assembling CDOs and SIVs.

American commercial and investment banks, excluding Citigroup, only held 21% of outstanding private RMBS, but their risks are understated because they were left with unwanted tranches as underwriters and market makers. In general, these banks were the best informed about the market.

Freddie Mac and Fannie Mae combined were much larger than Citigroup, holding 18% of the total private RMBS outstanding. They had to make subprime mortgage loans or hold private RMBS to satisfy US Department of Housing and Urban Development (HUD) mandates for low-income lending. The mandates evolved out of a long-standing bipartisan political effort to increase the number of low-income home-owners, beginning with the Community Reinvestment Act in 1992. In 1994 Fannie Mae announced a "Trillion Dollar Commitment" for afford-able housing over the next six years (matching President Clinton's

Table 2.13

LARGEST INVESTORS IN PRIVATE RMBS IN 2006	
($ billions)	
Citigroup	274
FHLMC	243
FNMA	146
AIG	111
ING	110
UBS	100
Credit Agricole	100
Merrill Lynch	82
Bank of America	77
Banque Nationale de Paris	71
Fortis Bank	59
Lehman Brothers	58
BlackRock	58
Metropolitan Life	52
JP Morgan	47
Commerzbank	45
Morgan Stanley	44
HSBC	43
Bear Stearns	43
Goldman Sachs	41
Wells Fargo	37
Deutsche Bank	36
Barclays	33
Wachovia	23
Royal Bank of Scotland	22
Pimco	9
Norway Pension Fund	8
Total	**1,972**
European banks	29%
FNMA/FHLMC	18%
American banks	34%
Total Private RMBS	2,145
Total Represented	92%

Sources: Annual Reports; author's estimates; Inside Mortgage Finance (2012).

remaining term in office).[19] In 1995, President Clinton announced The National Homeownership Strategy: Partners in the American Dream with a target of 8 million new homeowners by the year 2000. His plan included "... financing strategies fueled by creativity to help home buyers who lacked the cash to buy a home . . .." In 2002, President George W. Bush announced his own Blueprint for the American Dream, promising 5.5 million new minority homeowners by 2010. In 2003, Barney Frank declared of low-income borrowers, "I believe there has been more alarm raised about potential unsafety (*sic*) and unsoundness than, in fact, exists . . .. I want to roll the dice a little bit more in this situation towards subsidized housing."[20] New York Senator Charles Shumer expressed support.

In November 2004, HUD set higher low-income lending goals for Fannie Mae and Freddie Mac outlined in Table 2.14. The categories were overlapping and the percentages were based on the number of borrowers so the percentages based on dollar values would have been lower, but the goals inherently promised credit problems. Fannie Mae was explicit in 2006 about the risks of these goals and that it was achieving them by buying private mortgage-backed securities:

We have made significant adjustments to our mortgage loan sourcing and purchase strategies in an effort to meet the increased housing goals and sub-goals.

Table 2.14

HUD 2004 GOALS FOR FANNIE MAE AND FREDDIE MAC				
Financing[1]	2005 goals	FNMA results	2006 goals	FNMA results
Low & moderate income	52%	55%	53%	57%
Underserved areas	37%	41%	38%	44%
Special affordable housing	22%	26%	23%	28%
[1] There were also slightly lower home purchase goals.				

Source: Fannie Mae 2006 10-K.

[19] Morgenson (2011), p. 59.   [20] Zuckerman (2009), p. 46.

These strategies include entering into some purchase and securitization transactions with lower expected economic returns than our typical transactions. We have also relaxed some of our underwriting criteria to obtain goals-qualifying mortgage loans and increased our investments in higher-risk mortgage loan products that are more likely to serve the borrowers targeted by HUD's goals and sub-goals, which could further increase our credit losses.[21]

However, Fannie Mae and Freddie Mac were exposed to the weakest credit sectors beyond HUD's dictates. Consider the following risk items in Fannie Mae's "credit book" (retained mortgages, securitized conforming mortgages, and private RMBS investments) that it cited in its 2006 10-K:

- 10% was for loans greater than 80% of appraised value.
- 6% was for negative amortization ARMs or interest-only ARMs.
- 12% was for Alt-A mortgages,
- 2% was in subprime mortgages.
- 19% relied on mortgage insurance or lender recourse, and
- 26% of its business was with Countrywide Financial.[22]

These numbers were not additive (75%), but despite double counting there was a looming problem for a company that had tangible equity capital equal to only 1% of its mortgage guarantees plus its debt. Freddie Mac was in an even worse position with tangible equity equal to only 0.4% of its guarantees plus debt.

The European banks held 29% of the private RMBS outstanding. They also set up off-balance sheet highly leveraged special purpose corporations holding private RMBS. Federal Reserve Chairman Ben Bernanke described the flow of international money into US mortgage-backed securities after the Asian crisis of 1999 as one of the causes of the housing bubble.[23] The European banks are the best candidates for the assertion by Blundell-Wignall (2008) that the growth in private RMBS was stimulated by banks arbitraging the reduced capital requirements under the proposed Basel II rules. AAA ratings from the rating agencies were fundamental to this arbitrage.

The European banks originated mortgages, serviced them, securitized them (i.e. as US underwriters), made markets in them, and held them in SIVs for off-balance sheet interest rate arbitrage. European banks provided less disclosure than American banks and held asset-backed securities that were originated in Europe as well as the USA, but Barclays, Credit Suisse,

---

[21] Fannie Mae 2006 10-K, p. 16. [22] Fannie Mae 2006 10-K, pp. 23–4, 123.
[23] Bernanke (2013), p. 53.

Deutsche Bank, HSBC, ING, and UBS had significant US trading operations. Other large participants in the US market included ABN AMRO, BNP-Paribas, Commerzbank, Crédit Agricole, ING, and Royal Bank of Scotland.

The largest sovereign and foreign exchange funds are missing from Table 2.14 although they held assets of $5 trillion that were mostly invested in fixed income.[24] The Norway Pension Fund (based on its North Sea oil revenues) was the only such fund to detail its holdings. It held a wide array of securitized debt on residential and commercial mortgages, home-equity loans, credit cards, car loans, and receivables. These investments included substantial holdings from originators and servicers with the worst default records – Countrywide, WAMU, Fremont, Option One, Long Beach, First Franklin (Merrill Lynch), Household Finance (HSBC), Greenpoint Mortgage (Capital One), Thornburg Mortgage, Ownit (H&R Block), and IndyMac. The other large sovereign funds (the Abu Dhabi Investment Authority, China's SAFE Investment Company, the China Investment Corporation, and the Saudi Arabian Monetary Authority) provided no disclosure. The huge foreign exchange funds of Japan and China also offered no disclosure. These various state funds probably followed the practices of the Norway Pension Fund to some degree.

The investors in Table 2.14 were different from those driving other areas of financial growth at this time. The growth in hedge funds and private equity funds was driven by pension funds, endowment funds, and very wealthy individuals whereas the institutional investors buying private RMBS were restricted in whole or part to fixed income securities – Fannie Mae, Freddie Mac, US and European banks, investment managers, mutual funds, credit hedge funds, insurance companies, and savings banks.[25] Here was the most direct stretch for yield in reaction to low interest rates. These investors were the opposite of the "dumb money" flowing into high yield mutual funds. This was a sophisticated group stretching for yield with knowledge of the increased risk. They had access to information, knowledge of securities markets, significant resources spent on analysis, transparency, and active governance. Fannie Mae and Freddie Mac, commercial banks, savings banks, and investment banks

---

[24] Blundell-Wignall (2008), table 1.

[25] I don't give attention to savings banks, but between 2002 and 2007 they increased their investment in private RMBS from $11 billion to $112 billion (5% of the market, a sum that collectively ranked them with the largest individual RMBS investors other than Citigroup and Fannie Mae/Freddie Mac). Source: Board of Governors of the Federal Reserve, Financial Accounts of the United States.

were eating their own cooking. Fixed income managers such as BlackRock and Pimco were among the most sophisticated investors in the world.[26]

The reader should be aware that the data in Table 2.14 is roughly double that reported by Inside Mortgage Finance's Mortgage Market Statistical Annual 2012, Volume II. It reported that the top twenty-five commercial banks held only $137 billion of non-agency RMBS and Citigroup only $11 billion. It reported that all foreign investors held only $266 billion.[27]

Private RMBS holdings are open to interpretation for many reasons:

1. Reporting improved in subsequent years as troubles developed.
2. Subprime RMBS was a reporting focus rather than all private RMBS.
3. CDOs funding substantial private RMBS holdings could get grouped under "Other" securities holdings in financial reports. Banks did not report CDOs consistently, facilitated by the Federal Reserve's practice of reporting CDO funding other than with ABCP as "corporate debt" in the Financial Accounts of the United States.
4. Some banks (especially Citigroup) had substantial off-balance sheet private RMBS holdings as well as conduit exposures and contingent bank line commitments.
5. Credit default swaps on private RMBS could appear under Derivatives, in CDOs, or off-balance sheet in SIVs.

I try to resolve these differences by making numerous judgment calls and examining individual annual reports with a one- or two-year lag to catch disclosure improvements.

2.3 Commercial Banks

Domestic commercial banks faced the same pressure to stretch for yield as large institutional investors. They held $1.6 trillion of mostly short-term fixed income investments (22% of total financial assets) at the end of 2002, the returns on which fell as interest rates declined.[28] In response, commercial banks increased their risk assets by $2.25 trillion in just four years – a growth rate of 13% per annum (Table 2.15). The dollar amounts were similar, around $500 billion in each of residential mortgages, home equity

---

[26] Perhaps State Street Bank & Trust should be on this list. It held $34 billion of ABS and CMOs of which $30 billion had maturities over five years (2006 10-K, p. 44).
[27] Inside Mortgage Finance (2012), volume II, pp. 275, 282.
[28] Federal Reserve (Financial Accounts of the United States), L.109.

Table 2.15

COMMERCIAL BANKS' GROWTH IN RISK ASSETS 2002-2006			
($ billions)			
	2002	2006	Growth
Residential mortgages	919	1,428	509
Home equity + consumer credit	890	1,395	505
Commercial mortgages	798	1,281	483
Highly leveraged loans	850	1,343	493
Top 5 private RMBS, SIVs, etc.	196	458	262
Totals	3,653	5,905	2,252

Note: leveraged loans assume that banks held 2/3 of outstanding.
Sources: Federal Reserve (Financial Accounts of the United States); BIS (2008); Annual Reports; and author's calculations.

and consumer credit, commercial real estate mortgages, and highly leveraged loans.

The largest commercial banks tended to hold their 1–4 family mortgages rather than securitize them which is at odds with the public (and academic) perception. Their combined first mortgages and home-equity loans grew at a 16% compound annual rate between 2002–06. The two most active, Bank of America and Wells Fargo, only securitized 17% of their own loans in 2005. The big players in the originate-to-distribute business were Countrywide and Washington Mutual as can be seen in Table 2.16. Neither was a commercial bank.

The growth in commercial mortgages highlights an area that has not been well recognized as contributing to the eventual crisis. Banks' risks in commercial real estate were also rising because loans were made on rapidly rising property prices and also funded developers, accumulations of land, construction of office and apartment buildings, and resorts. Involvement was skewed as Wells Fargo, Bank of America, and Wachovia had a combined $211 billion of commercial real estate loans in 2007 versus only $36 billion at JP Morgan Chase and Citigroup.

Real estate involvement was rewarding for the banks most involved in it. The stocks of Wells Fargo, Bank of America, and Wachovia were up 50% in 2002–05, while Citigroup and JP Morgan, were flat (Chart 2.23).

Table 2.16

LARGEST ISSUERS OF PRIVATE RMBS 2002–2006						
($ billions)						
	2002	2003	2004	2005	2006	Aggregate
Countrywide	45	59	118	167	154	543
Washington Mutual	49	42	37	74	73	275
Wells Fargo	15	22	34	49	60	180
Bank of America	25	26	28	34	25	138
JP Morgan	7			23	33	63
Citigroup	5	6	9	18	20	58

Source: Inside Mortgage Finance (2012).

The pressure on JP Morgan Chase and Citigroup to get further into the mortgage market was obvious. Citigroup, JP Morgan, and European banks played leading roles in creating off-balance sheet vehicles that used asset-backed commercial paper (ABCP) to arbitrage short-term interest rates against longer-term investments. These structured investment vehicles (SIVs) financed private RMBS inventories prior to securitization as well as portfolios of mortgage-backed securities, collateralized debt obligations (CDOs), and collateralized loan obligations (CLOs).[29] ABCP grew $400 billion or 60% between 2004–06 while traditional commercial paper volume was flat (Chart 2.24). ABCP structures where the creditworthiness depended upon the market values of long-term portfolios contrasted with structures using credit cards, auto loans, and corporate receivables that had immediate cash flows to service their ABCP. The former became a problem in the crisis when the prices for their underlying collateral fell and there was no cash flow to pay off the ABCP. Funding student loans with ABCP was a prominent victim of this problem.

[29] CDOs were bonds issued against collateral packages of private RMBS and other debt securities such as CMBS, corporate bonds, shorter-term asset-backed securities, and derivative equivalents of these. CLOs were notes issued against packages of (usually) highly leveraged corporate loans with floating rates and intermediate maturities. Both CDOs and CLOs were issued in tranches of descending seniority.

Chart 2.23

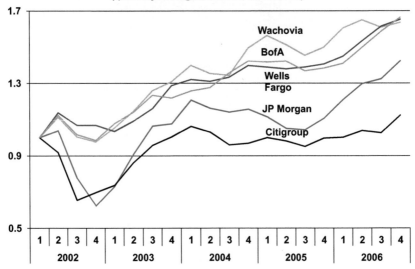

Commercial Banks' Stocks
(quarterly averages, indexed 1Q2002=1.0)

Source: Annual Reports.

Chart 2.24

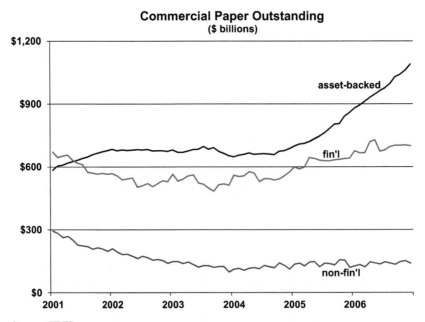

Commercial Paper Outstanding
($ billions)

Source: FRED.

Citigroup was the most active US bank in setting up off-balance sheet ABCP conduits for itself and customers, but European banks accounted for over half of the ABCP conduits and SIVs at the end of 2006 (Table 2.17).[30] While interest rates in Europe were similar to those in the USA, the European banks' home markets did not have similar volumes of higher

Table 2.17

ASSET BACKED COMMERCIAL PAPER, SIVs, AND STRUCTURED NOTE VEHICLES 2006	
($ billions)	
Citigroup	180
JP Morgan	111
HSBC*	104
Barclays*	78
Fortis Bank*	59
Bank of America	59
ABN-Amro	54
Deutsche Bank	52
Credit Suisse	40
Wachovia	38
IKB Deutsche Industriebank	19
Royal Bank of Scotland	16
Countrywide Financial	8
Total	**818**
European share	422
	52%
*2007 due to change in reporting	

Source: Annual Reports.

[30] It would be a useful project to determine the exact breakdowns of the issuers, collateral, and financing structures of these conduits and SIVs. The information is in Moody's and S&P's quarterly ABCP reports.

yielding investment alternatives such as private RMBS, CDOs, and highly leveraged loans. Investment banks did not participate in SIVs in a meaningful way.

Investors bought ABCP in their own stretch for yield because the rates were higher than other short-term instruments. Money market mutual funds were prominent buyers as they competed to advertise higher rates. The Reserve Primary Fund, one of the largest money market funds and the first to "break the buck" after Lehman Brothers failed, initially bought ABCP in 2006 because of the competition. Corporations, state and local retirement funds, some corporations, and assorted money managers made up the bulk of the other investors.[31]

Commercial banks occupied a complex position in the increase in investment risks between 2002–06 because while their mortgages and loans were not securities and not marked-to-market, securitization brought residential and commercial mortgages and highly leveraged corporate loans into the realm of securities that were marked-to-market. As the crisis developed, investors naturally assigned market values to the banks' various loans despite the accounting.

One of the least understood aspects of the banks' stretch for yield was the derivatives market. Derivatives are an old financial product. Foreign exchange futures have been traded for centuries. Commodities exchanges were founded to trade cash farm products as well as futures and options in the nineteenth century in Chicago (1864), New York (1870), and Kansas City (1876). The Chicago Mercantile Exchange was spun off from the Chicago Board of Trade in 1919 exclusively to trade futures. The first exchange-traded petroleum futures were in London in 1980.

The Chicago Board of Trade established the first futures contract on government-guaranteed Government National Mortgage Association mortgage-backed securities in 1975. By 1989, interest rate futures were 50% of all futures contracts. By 2000 they were 70%, but the shift to interest rate swaps rather than futures moved this trading from the exchanges to commercial banks operating in the over-the-counter markets.

Derivatives volume accelerated after the Commodities Futures Modernization Act (CFMA) was passed in late 2000. The CFMA placed derivatives under the jurisdiction of the (friendly) Commodities Futures Trading Commission rather than the SEC and also established the priority of derivatives over most other forms of debt in bankruptcy (Bolton, 2011).

[31] I am grateful to Ira Powell and Nick Cancro, both formerly of Goldman Sachs' commercial paper department, for their help on this topic.

Chart 2.25

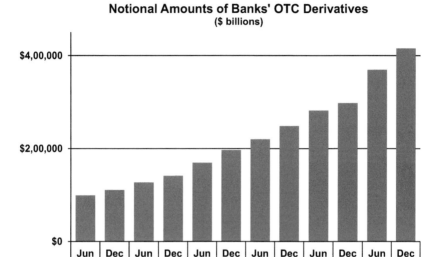

Notional Amounts of Banks' OTC Derivatives
($ billions)

Source: BIS (derivatives).

Banks worldwide increased their notional contracts $300 trillion (yes, "trillion") between 2001 and 2006 to over $400 trillion (Chart 2.25). Seventy percent of the $400 trillion was interest rate swaps, but transaction volumes grew in credit guarantees, natural gas, electricity, and European carbon instruments. Both US and European banks were active in the derivatives markets as European banks acquired prominent US dealers.[32]

Only the **net** market value of derivative assets and liabilities appeared on banks' balance sheets. Table 2.18 outlines how JP Morgan Chase, the largest dealer in derivatives, reported its derivatives business in 2007 (only part of this information was available in its 2006 Annual Report). Its notional derivatives of $77 trillion went through three shrinkages:

1. Down to a gross asset value of $1 trillion,
2. but net asset value shrunk to $122 billion after netting out $833 billion according to FIN 39 (an accounting rule permitting netting where there was "... a legally enforceable master netting agreement ... between the Firm and a derivative counterparty") and $62 billion of collateral.

---

[32] Credit Suisse acquired First Boston in 1988 and Deutsche Bank acquired Bankers Trust in 1999. UBS acquired Paine Webber and Credit Suisse added DLJ in 2000.

3. On the liability side its notional derivatives of $937 billion shrunk to a net liability of $92 billion after netting out $822 billion under FIN 39 and $23 billion of collateral it had posted with counterparties. Thus, $77 trillion of notional derivatives with an asset value of almost $1 trillion shrunk to a net positive position of only $30 billion ($122 billion of net assets minus $92 billion of net liabilities). At $30 billion, the regulatory implications for required capital and oversight were minimized.

Table 2.18

JP MORGAN DERIVATIVES REPORTING IN 2007	
	($ billions)
Notional amount	77,249
Gross Assets	1,017
Netting (FIN 39)	–833
Collateral netted	–62
Net assets (reported)	122
Gross liabilities	937
Netting (FIN 39)	–822
Collateral netted	–23
Net liabilities (reported)	92
Net position (reported)	30

Source: JP Morgan Annual Report, 2007.

Notional values were inflated in various ways and therefore not representative of risks. Contracts for interest rate swaps simply reflected the notional value on which interest rate payments were made or received. However, for credit default contracts notional values represented the amount insured collateral could be required if the price of the insured bonds declined. The notional amount could become due in the case of default. A more complicated factor inflating notional values was that dealers didn't actually resell contracts, but "novated" them, with a new contract offsetting an existing one, so that notional values kept increasing even if economic exposure did not.

The **market value** of all derivatives contracts was only 3–4% of the notional value, but nonetheless tripled to $10 trillion between 2001–05 (Chart 2.26).

The banks justified net treatment based on Master Netting Agreements that governed most contracts by 2006, but the real objective was to hold down regulatory capital requirements and thereby get leverage. This was implicit in their reporting. They consigned derivatives to a late footnote in their financial statements. Until 2007, Citigroup reported only net assets and net liabilities without mentioning notional amounts or categorizing the types of derivatives. No bank reported profits or losses for derivatives, blending them instead with fixed income, equity, or other sectoral results.

In fact, neither netting nor collateral requirements were solidly in place to justify the high leverage implicit in the differences between notional values and market values. Collateral requirements only existed on 30% of derivatives contracts in 2003 and 63% in 2007.[33] When Lehman Brothers filed for bankruptcy, only fifteen of its top twenty-five counterparties had the necessary Credit Support Agreements.[34]

In practice, there was a great deal about derivatives contracts that did not net out. Interest rate contracts were the most standardized of the derivatives

Chart 2.26

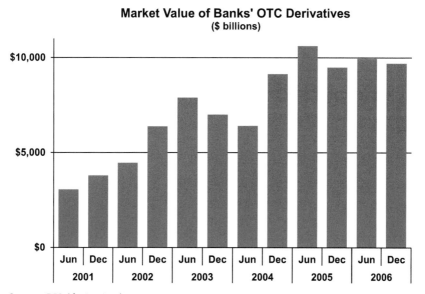

Market Value of Banks' OTC Derivatives
($ billions)

Source: BIS (derivatives).

[33] Stulz (2010), p. 81.   [34] Valukas (2010), pp. 575–6.

contracts, but earlier contracts did not have Master Netting Agreement language, many were individualized with floors and ceilings, and collateral requirements were negotiable or nonexistent. Importantly, novating contracts created counterparty risks that were difficult to evaluate as the expected financial exposure passed from one counterparty to another.

The relationship between notional and market values, in other words the leverage, could shift significantly. For interest rate swaps, the ratio of notional amount to market value was cut in half in 2002–03 in the aftermath of the Enron and telecommunications credit collapses before rising again in 2006 (Chart 2.27).[35] Fannie Mae, one of the larger nonbank counterparties with notional contracts of $745 billion, estimated in 2006 that a 1% increase in interest rates would increase the fair market value of its derivatives by 110%.[36] Only 14% of derivatives volume was with non-financial customers so it was an intra-bank trading activity with all the

Chart 2.27

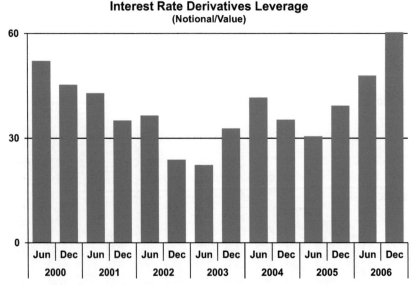

Source: BIS (derivatives).

---

[35] This swing could reflect many factors, most of them related to credit risk – balance/imbalance of market-makers' books, contract maturity, variation in the parameters being swapped, counter-party creditworthiness, currencies, option aspects, and margin requirements.
[36] Fannie Mae 2006 10-K, p. 146.

limitations of an over-the-counter market – weak disclosure, uncertain margin requirements, disputes over valuation, counterparty credit risks, and unknown risks as transaction volume grew in complex mortgage-backed and asset-backed securities and new virtual securities.

Derivatives represented significant market risks for the five US and European banks. The largest had gross derivatives assets ranging from $400 billion to $1 trillion in 2007 (more complete reporting than 2006) (Table 2.19).[37] These commitments ranged from seven to twenty-seven times tangible common equity (book equity minus goodwill and intangibles) before netting reductions for counterparty agreements and collateral. Credit Suisse and Deutsche Bank were the extreme at twenty-seven and twenty-five times tangible common equity. Deutsche Bank reflected the aggressive derivatives business that came with its acquisition of Bankers Trust in 1999.

Interest rate swaps were the largest part of the banks' derivatives business and did not subsequently become a problem, but problems arose in the newer credit default swaps market. The BIS did not collect data on credit default

Table 2.19

MAJOR BANKS' 2007 DERIVATIVES ASSETS			
	Derivatives gross assets (billions)	Tangible common equity (billions)	Derivatives/ tangible equity (times)
Citigroup ($)	467	70	7
Credit Suisse (chf)	877	32	27
Deutsche Bank (€)	606	24	25
JP Morgan ($)	1,017	64	16
UBS (chf)	444	41	11

Sources: 10-K and Form 20-F filed by foreign banks.

[37] Investment banks' derivative books were much smaller than the major banks. The 2007 market value of Goldman Sachs' gross derivative assets was only 13% of JP Morgan's.

swaps until the second half of 2004, after which they expanded to almost $30 trillion notional value in 2006 (Chart 2.28). Credit default "swaps" were not swaps at all, but credit guarantees, mostly of private RMBS (sometimes in CDOs), and also of faltering industrial and financial companies.

Credit default swaps assumed unusual hedging and speculative attractiveness after the Commodities Futures Modernization Act was passed in 2000 giving them exemption from stays in bankruptcy and thus making their position superior to normal debts (Bolton, 2011).

Credit default swaps initially had notional value fifty times market value and almost seventy times in early 2006 (Chart 2.29). JP Morgan, Credit Suisse, and UBS had notional exposure around sixty-five times their tangible common equity (Table 2.20). Citigroup's exposure was only 28 times and Deutsche Bank again was an outlier at 132 times tangible common equity. By comparison, AIG had notional exposure only five times its tangible common equity.[38] These two forms of leverage (versus market value and tangible common equity) would contract sharply in 2008.

Chart 2.28

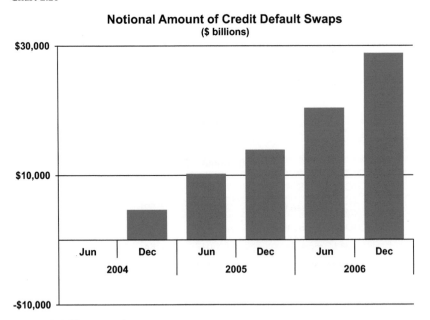

Source: BIS (derivatives).

[38] International Swaps & Derivatives Association (2004, 2006, 2010).

Table 2.20

MAJOR BANKS' CREDIT DERIVATIVES EXPOSURE			
2006			
	Notional credit derivatives (billions)	Tangible common equity (billions)	Notional/ tangible equity (times)
Citigroup ($)	1,945	70	28
Credit Suisse (chf)	2,088	32	65
Deutsche Bank (€)	3,173	24	132
JP Morgan ($)	4,619	64	72
UBS (chf)	2,640	41	64
AIG ($)	483	94	5

Sources: Annual Reports and author's calculations.

Chart 2.29

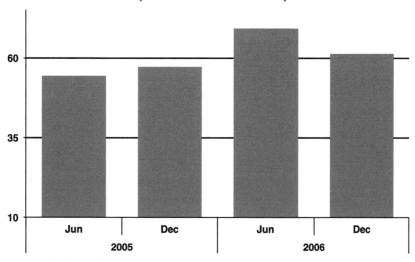

Source: BIS (derivatives).

2.4 Investment Banks

Investment banks added significant highly leveraged and illiquid investments by 2006 as the intermediaries underwriting private RMBS, sponsoring hedge funds and private equity funds, and providing merger and acquisition advice. Almost everything they did required that they put up some amount of money to inventory what could not be sold, to align their interests with investors, and as a commitment of sincerity. For example:

- Securitization involved the investment banks in accumulating assets for eventual securitization, market-making positions, and accumulation of unsold, lower-rated tranches.
- Sponsoring hedge funds required putting up significant seed money, lending to them on margin, clearing for them, and often providing derivatives transactions.
- Sponsoring private equity funds required putting up significant seed money as well as making highly leveraged loans for their acquisitions.
- Bear Stearns, Goldman Sachs, and Lehman Brothers sponsored commercial real estate investment vehicles that required seed money, and substantial loans.
- Advising on mergers and acquisitions led the banks to make bridge loan commitments, highly leveraged loans, and high yield bond commitments as part of the competition for clients.

Goldman Sachs described borrowing against such investments in its 2006 annual report:[39]

Certain financial instruments may be more difficult to fund on a secured basis during times of market stress. Accordingly, we generally hold higher levels of total capital for these assets than more liquid types of financial instruments. The table below sets forth our aggregate holdings in these categories of financial instruments (billions):

Mortgage whole loans and CDOs	$41
Bank loans	$28
High yield securities	$11
Emerging market debt securities	$2
SMFG convertible preferred stock	$5
Other corporate principal investments	$4
Other private equity and restricted securities	$4
Real estate principal investments	$1

[39] Goldman Sachs, 2006 Annual Report, p. 66.

In the past, as private partnerships, the investment banks would have avoided such investments because the banks had small equity bases and almost all of their borrowing was collateralized. However, they became more aggressive as they went public (Bear Stearns in 1985, Morgan Stanley in 1986, Lehman Brothers in 1994, and Goldman Sachs in 1999) substantially increasing their equity bases and their access to unsecured debt financing. They were also given new freedom when the SEC approved its "consolidated supervised entities program" in 2004 under which investment banks were able to make their own risk assessments and appropriate capital requirements (leverage ratios) in return for submitting their holding companies to SEC supervision.

By 2006, the leading investment banks' illiquid assets constituted 37% of their financial instruments and significant multiples of their tangible common equity (Table 2.21).[40] Merrill Lynch was particularly illiquid at almost eight times its tangible common equity. Unlike commercial banks that were funded with deposits, the investment banks collateralized a substantial portion of their borrowing and such illiquidity made them vulnerable in a crisis.

Table 2.21

INVESTMENT BANKS' ILLIQUID ASSETS IN 2006

($ billions)					
	Illiquid assets	Financial instruments	Illiquid % financial instruments	Tangible common equity	Illiquid x tangible common equity
Bear Stearns	42	125	34%	11	3.8
Goldman Sachs	107	335	32%	36	3.0
Lehman Brothers	91	227	40%	19	4.9
Merrill Lynch	213	360	59%	27	7.9
Morgan Stanley	84	381	22%	31	2.7

Sources: 2006 and 2007 10-Ks.

[40] Goldman Sachs disclosed its illiquid assets. The other investment banks provided only partial disclosure. Table 2.21 represents best efforts to calculate their illiquid investments.

Chart 2.30

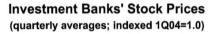

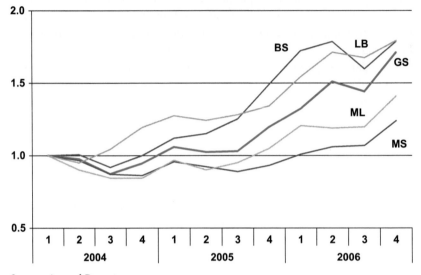

Source: Annual Reports.

For the time being, however, these illiquid assets were making money and the investment banks that accumulated them were rewarded with superior stock performance, especially Bear Stearns, Lehman Brothers, and Goldman Sachs (Chart 2.30). It is easy to infer from the weaker performance of Merrill Lynch and Morgan Stanley that they would feel pressure to take on more such risk.

2.5 Private Equity

Private equity fundraising began to grow again in 2003–06 after substantially under-performing the S&P 500 in the last half of the 1990s (Chart 2.31).[41] Private equity reported 10–20% returns from 2000 to 2002 while the S&P 500 was down each year. However, published returns are complicated for private equity because they are internal rates of return over the lifetime of "vintage" funds (i.e. the year the fund was raised) unlike the calendar year returns for most other investment vehicles. However, quarterly returns for

---

[41] For a description of the private equity "industry" as of 2008 see Kaplan (2009), pp. 121–46.

Chart 2.31

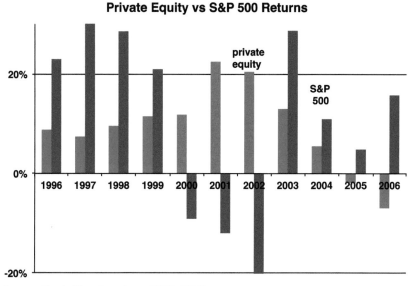

Private Equity vs S&P 500 Returns

Source: Cambridge Associates (2006, 2011).

the 2000–02 funds were known by their investors and helped private equity sponsors to raise cumulative commitments of $1.4 trillion in 2004–07 compared to under $400 billion in 2000–03 (Chart 2.32).[42] Assuming this $1.4 trillion could be leveraged 2-to-1, it represented over $4 trillion of investment capital and would reverberate throughout the securities markets in 2007–09 in terms of merger and acquisitions volumes and prices, highly leveraged corporate loans, high yield bonds, banks' illiquidity, and unfortunately timed capital calls on investors.

Private equity funds offered institutional investors several attractive features:

- High unreported leverage without recourse to the investor;
- Exposure to the low interest rates and market tolerance for highly leveraged corporate borrowing; and
- Investments that only marked-to-market quarterly and then with considerable leeway.

The largest institutional investors in private equity are outlined in Table 2.22. These nineteen institutions had $144 billion invested in private equity

---

[42] Cambridge Associates (2006), p. 72; (2011), p. 101. It is appropriate to stretch this analysis to 2007 because there was a long lag between when funds began to raise money and closed.

Chart 2.32

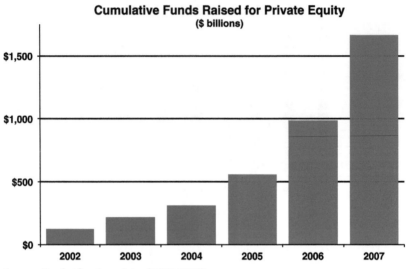

Cumulative Funds Raised for Private Equity
($ billions)

Source: Cambridge Associates (2006, 2011).

in 2006/2007 (state and local retirement funds had June 30 fiscal year-ends). State retirement funds were the largest with $64 billion. AIG and Metropolitan Life accounted for most of the insurance industry's $27 billion in 2006.[43] We have limited data for corporate pension funds, but their commitments do not appear to have been large, partly because the majority of their pension plans were defined contribution plans that did not offer private equity alternatives. The leading investment and commercial banks were a focus of private equity because of their own investments and their sponsorship of private equity funds.

Table 2.23 outlines the alternative assets under management at the largest banks and the author's estimates of the private equity portion ($117 billion). Combined with the banks' own investments, this was $145 billion. For most of these banks private equity was an important source of profits but it was virtually a condition that they had to invest 10–20% of the capital they raised so that their incentives were aligned with their clients. In the crisis of 2008, it was difficult to borrow against these private equity interests because of the leverage on the portfolio companies and the illiquidity of the limited partnership interests.

There were other funds managed by independent firms such as Kohlberg Kravis Roberts, Bain Capital, Blackstone Group, Apollo Global Management,

[43] NAIC, Capital Markets Special Report (2011–12), table 1.

Table 2.22

MAJOR PRIVATE EQUITY INVESTORS IN 2006/2007	
($ billions)	
California State Teachers	25
NY State Common Fund	15
California Public Employees	13
Teacher Ret't System of Texas	<u>11</u>
sub-total	**64**
AIG	18
AT&T pension*	5
Met Life	5
GE pension	<u>4</u>
sub-total	**32**
Citigroup	11
JP Morgan	6
Merrill Lynch	5
Goldman Sachs	3
Lehman Brothers	2
Morgan Stanley	<u>2</u>
sub-total	**28**
University of Texas*	6
Harvard	4
Princeton	4
Yale	4
Stanford	<u>3</u>
sub-total	**<u>21</u>**
Grand-Total	**144**
* estimated from later reports	

Source: Annual Reports

Carlyle Group, Cerberus Capital Management, Forstmann Little, Fortress Investment, Oaktree Capital, Silver Lake Partners, Thomas Lee Partners, and TPG Capital.

Table 2.23

BANKS' PRIVATE EQUITY UNDER MANAGEMENT			
	2006		
	Total AUM $ billions	Private equity proportion *	Private equity $ billions
Goldman Sachs	145	35%	51
Morgan Stanley	61	35%	21
JP Morgan	100	20%	20
Citigroup	39	35%	13
Blackrock (acqu'd ML assets)	48	20%	10
Lehman Brothers	23	10%	2
Totals	417		117
*author's estimates			

Source: Annual Reports.

The funds raised in 2004–07 were drawn down slowly. Cambridge Associates calculated that half of the commitments raised in 2007 were still uncalled in 2010.[44] Because of this, the major public pension funds and university endowments were more heavily invested in private equity than their financial reports suggested. The amount drawn down as of 2006/2007 represented 10–20% of their aggregate portfolios (Table 2.24). The undrawn amount was rarely disclosed, but the New York State Teachers Retirement System revealed that it was committed to $9.6 billion beyond $4.3 billion carried in its financial statements.[45] The private equity commitments of the state funds and university endowments may have amounted to 20–30% of their pre-crisis portfolios.

There has been debate about the returns achieved in private equity because of the drawn-out timing of investments and the leverage applied to acquired companies. Analysis has been based on the vintage of funds

[44] Cambridge Associates (2011), exhibit 1.
[45] New York State Teachers' Retirement System Annual Report 2007, p. 50.

Table 2.24

PRIVATE EQUITY ALLOCATIONS (2006/2007)	
Public Pension Funds:	
Washington State Investment Board	18%
California State Teachers	17%
NY State Common Fund	10%
Teacher Ret't System of Texas	10%
New York State Teachers Retirement	10%
California Public Employees	5%
New Your City Retirement	4%
Florida Retirement System	3%
average	**10%**
Universities:	
Princeton	25%
Yale	15%
Texas (2012)	15%
Stanford	12%
Harvard	10%
average	**15%**

Source: Annual Reports.

raised. Academics have created "public market equivalents" matching public equity prices against the timing of private equity inflows and return of funds to investors over the years of each vintage fund. L'Her (2016), the most recent evolution of this methodology, used data for over 200 investment programs that Burgiss Group LLC administered and that represented over $1 trillion in committed capital. L'Her adjusted this data over 1986–2008 for leverage, high yield interest rates, industry concentration, and small company size and found that there was no outperformance by private equity versus public markets.

Such comparisons miss the basic point that institutions used private equity to take on high leverage without recourse and without disclosing it – higher risk for higher returns. The risks behind this strategy defy measurement:

- Private equity acquisitions resulted in leverage eight times the small-cap S&P 600. This ratio was typically misrepresented in comparisons with the leverage of the small-cap S&P 600. Debt ratios for private equity companies are based on post-acquisition debt and equity while small-cap companies' ratios are based on historic book values. If leverage calculations were based on tangible common equity, this difference would immediately be apparent.

- Investors committed fixed amounts when a fund was raised, but were uncertain when the amounts would be drawn down. The drawdown period usually extended over five years. In the early years, the proportion of undrawn funds could exceed 75%. Sometimes the funds were never fully drawn upon, but fund sponsors borrowed against the commitments. Undrawn funds had an up-front option value that might have exceeded 30% (average drawdown life three years, small-cap investment premium of 2%, 8% conventional equity returns). If the option value were charged it would have made private equity returns uncompetitive. Many institutions did not reserve against this option aspect and found themselves in a liquidity squeeze when funds were called during 2007–09 (notably Harvard). Efforts to off-load these commitments generally failed as low secondary market prices substantiated that the option value was indeed high.

- Investors committed to a "black box" because they did not know what companies the sponsors would acquire or at what valuations. There were few constraints on sponsors "jumping the tracks" except to the extent a fund had a specialty focus (i.e. energy, healthcare, finance, technology, etc.). A surge to $500 billion of large public company leveraged buyouts between 2005 and mid-2007 compared to $260 billion in the prior decade suggests that some funds did "jump the tracks."[46]

- Exits for acquired companies were limited to going public or sale to strategic buyers. The latter was dependent upon antitrust freedom. Sales to strategic buyers and to other private equity firms (increasing concentration) accounted for 2/3 of sales from 1995 to 2005.[47]

- Other risks that were difficult to measure included investors' inability to control the timing of sales (especially for tax purposes), the illiquidity of private equity investments, and the burden of unsalable stub investments.

---

[46] Kaplan (2009), pp. 121–46.   [47] Kaplan (2009), table 2.

Investors knew these risks. They accepted them in pursuit of higher returns from unreported higher leverage.

2.6 Mergers and Acquisitions

The scale of private equity fundraising was reflected in the mergers and acquisitions market. Mergerstat Review for 2006 editorialized that:

> The transformational deal making of private equity groups (PEGs) played an important role in making 2006 one of the best markets ever in M&A history. PEGs helped to push up deal multiples to record levels, clubbed together to pursue mega deals, and took a record number of public companies private.

The rebound in merger and acquisition activity in 2005–06 (Chart 2.33) corresponded to the surge in private equity fundraising as firms going private rose to over 40% of all merger and acquisition transactions (Chart 2.34). Seventeen of the twenty largest "going private" deals since 1998 were in 2005–06 with the most prominent being HCA, Clear Channel, Harrah's, Freescale Semiconductor, Kinder Morgan Energy, Univision, Biomet,

Chart 2.33

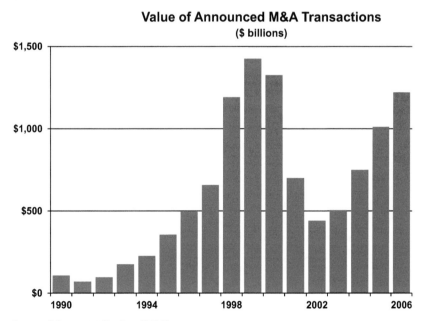

Source: Mergerstat Review (2012).

Chart 2.34

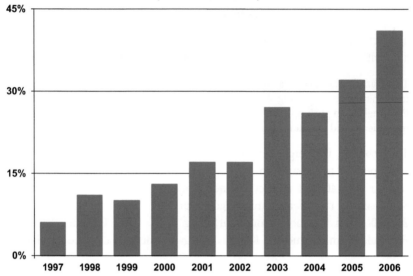

Public M&A Transactions Going Private
(No. of Transactions)

Source: Mergerstat Review (2012).

Albertson's, Cablevision, Realogy, ARAMARK, Michael's Stores, and Advanced Semiconductor.[48] Worldwide, going private deals were six times their level in 2003 as US firms carried their practices abroad or were copied (Chart 2.35).

Half of the ten most active acquirors in 2006 were private equity sponsors (Table 2.25), as were half of the top ten buyers of foreign companies – Morgan Stanley, Carlyle Group, Riverside Co., Goldman Sachs, and Blackstone Group.[49]

The capital commanded by private equity firms loomed over all merger and acquisition transactions because of its massive scale. Assuming that private equity firms could add debt equivalent to twice the equity they raised, the capital available to 2007 vintage funds was over 100% of all announced merger and acquisition transactions (Chart 2.36). This inexorably pushed private equity firms into bigger deals than their average acquisition of $250 million. Private equity firms did 19 acquisitions over

---

[48] Mergerstat Review (2006), table 1–42.   [49] Mergerstat Review (2006), table 1–53.

Table 2.25

THE TEN LARGEST ACQUIRORS IN 2006	
	No. of deals
General Electric	30
Wolseley PLC	29
Morgan Stanley*	28
Carlyle Group*	26
Riverside Co.*	24
CRH PLC	21
Goldman Sachs*	19
3M Co.	18
Illinois Tool Works	18
Blackstone Group*	18
* private equity sponsor	

Source: Mergerstat Review (2007).

Chart 2.35

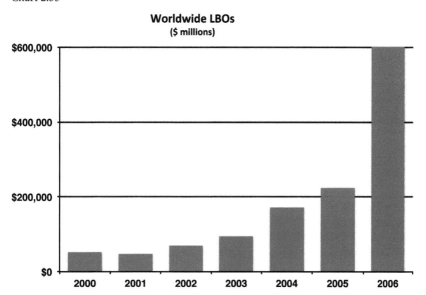

Source: Mergerstat Review (2012).

Chart 2.36

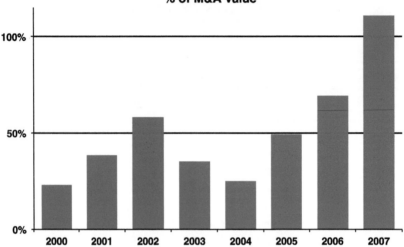

Private Equity New Leveraged Capital
% of M&A Value

Note: funds raised multiplied by 2.
Sources: Mergerstat Review (2012); Cambridge Associates (2006, 2011).

$4 billion in 2006 for a total of $179 billion (Table 2.26) and 75 of the 216 deals over $1 billion for a total of $291 billion.[50]

The growth in private equity acquisitions resulted in highly leveraged corporate loans growing $700 billion between 2002–06. The Bank for International Settlements (BIS) provided the best analysis of this sector. It reported that annual issues of highly leveraged US corporate loans rose from $450 billion to $900 billion between 2002–06 (Chart 2.37).

Investment banks played the leading role in this loan expansion and their distribution to nonbank investors such as fixed income mutual funds, credit hedge funds, CLO and CDO aggregators, investment managers, and insurance companies. Even on loans led by commercial banks the lead banks retained less than 10% of the loans while nonbank investors' participation rose from 30% in 2000–01 to over 50% in 2003–06 (Chart 2.38).[51] This aspect of the shadow banking system received little notice from US regulators and was weakly followed in general. It represented a large and risky diversion from traditional bank term loans.

Highly leveraged loans were thought to have less risk than high yield bonds because they were collateralized and had floating interest rates, but the

[50] Mergerstat Review (2006), pp. 197–216.   [51] Bord (2012), charts 6, 8.

Table 2.26

THE LARGEST PRIVATE EQUITY DEALS IN 2006		
Buyers:	**Acquired:**	**$ billions**
Bain, KKR et al	HCA	21
Thomas H. Lee	Clear Channel	19
Texas Pacific Group	Harrah's	17
Blackstone, Carlyle et al	Freescale Semiconductor	16
Kinder Morgan et al	Kinder Morgan Inc	14
Madison Dearborn et al	Univision	11
KKR et al	Biomet Inc	11
Super Value, Cerberus	Albertson's	10
Dolan family et al	Cablevision	9
Cerberus	GMAC	7
Apollo Mgt	Realogy Corp	6
Joseph Neubauer et al	ARAMARK	6
Bain, Blackstone et al	Michaels Stores	6
Carlyle Group	Advanced Semiconductor	5
Goldman Sachs, KKR	Linde AG	5
Silver Lake, Texas Pacific	Sabre Holdings	4
Blackstone Group	Cendant Corp	4
Goldman Sachs, KKR	Pages-Jaunes Groupe	4
Apollo Mgt	GE Advanced Materials	4
	Total	**179**

Source: Mergerstat Review (2006).

stretch for yield in this market was clear when 75–80% of new-issue volume was rated below BB and there were significant subordinated tranches.

Based on BIS data, highly leveraged loans outstanding rose from $1 trillion in 2000 to $2 trillion in 2006 (Chart 2.39). This is an estimate in a field full of ambiguity and with widely different estimates. There is abundant proprietary information on the origination (flow) of syndicated bank loans and highly leveraged loans from Dealscan, Dealogic, and the rating agencies; but there is no adequate information on the amount (stock) of highly leveraged loans outstanding. There is also differentiation between syndicated bank loans and

Chart 2.37

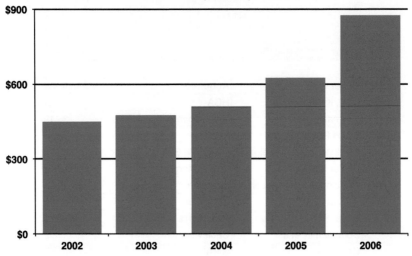

US Highly Leveraged Loan Issues
($ billions)

Source: BIS (2008).

Chart 2.38

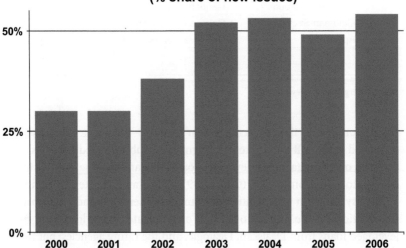

Non-bank Investors in Term Loans
(% share of new issues)

Source: Bord (2012).

Chart 2.39

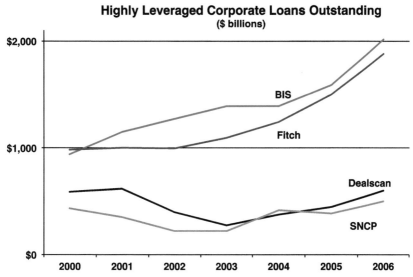

Highly Leveraged Corporate Loans Outstanding
($ billions)

Sources: BIS (2008); Cambridge Associates (2006, 2011); Fitch Ratings; and author's calculations.

highly leveraged loans that have been largely distributed by investment bankers (two-thirds market share). The best flow data was produced by the BIS in 2008 because it adjusted Dealogic annual issuance data whether managed by commercial or investment banks to isolate highly leveraged loans based on pricing irrespective of ratings (BIS, 2008).

Chart 2.39 illustrates the wide divergence in my estimates of highly leveraged loans outstanding based on data variously from the BIS, Fitch Ratings, Dealscan, and the Shared National Credit Program (SNCP) run by the FDIC.[52] My estimates based on the BIS, Fitch, and Dealscan data assume that loans had an average life of four years – an approximation from Fitch Ratings (2016) that reflects both refunding and repayments when companies were acquired or went public. The SNCP data needs no assumptions as it tracks actual amounts outstanding when held by banks. The Fitch estimates are lower than the BIS's because Fitch data did not include investment-grade loan issues that had non-investment-grade pricing. The Dealscan and SNCP estimates reflect just bank-managed syndicated loans and miss the two-thirds of the leveraged loan market managed by investment banks. The Dealscan and SNCP approaches correspond to

[52] SNCP data is from Bord (2012).

the Federal Reserve's Financial Accounts of the United States that indicate that only \$832 billion of nonfinancial corporate loans were outstanding at the end of 2006.[53]

The BIS estimates of highly leveraged loans are much higher than oft-quoted references to the underlying debt in S&P's LSTA leveraged loan index launched in 10/20/2008. The LSTA index has limited relevance to estimates of the total highly leveraged loans outstanding because it included only \$500 billion of loans, followed only the 100 largest loans outstanding (not new each year), and included only senior secured loans. It also had other restrictions on loans included in the index such as a publicly assigned CUSIP. As the BIS (2008) said of its own estimates, it found leveraged loan ".... Volumes that are far higher than estimates published by some vendors, notably S&P LCD." The BIS did not criticize the Federal Reserve's data.

The securitization of many loans as Collateralized Loan Obligations (CLOs) with public ratings turned what had been indistinguishable corporate loans for which banks and other lenders could use discretionary valuations into securities with public market values. This was not important prior to 2007 because CLO prices were close to par, but in 2008 they dropped sharply.

2.7 Commercial Real Estate

Awareness of commercial real estate's role in the crisis of 2008 is only developing slowly despite that real estate equity was 10–20% of the largest investors' assets and that commercial real estate loans were the largest share of banks' loans nationwide. Commercial real estate had an exceptional run in popularity between 2000–06, attracting huge unprecedented institutional capital flows that led to record prices and record levels of construction. Bank of America, Wells Fargo, Wachovia Corp., Goldman Sachs, Lehman Brothers, and Bear Stearns were all involved in it. Its post-crisis problems were also a significant hindrance to a stronger recovery There is only modest academic research on commercial real estate. The Federal Reserve does not treat its ownership as a security and collects limited data on its funding, possibly missing subordinated debt and debt provided by unconventional sources. There is no national database of ownership.

Commercial real estate is notable for its leverage and has been a focus of financial problems in the past, especially in the 1970s when many REITs went

---

[53] Federal Reserve (Financial Accounts of the United States), combining direct bank loans (L.102) and "other loans and advances" (L.216).

bankrupt, in the late 1980s when the savings and loan industry collapsed, and in 1992 when Olympia & York, the largest developer in the world, went bankrupt.

Commercial real estate investments have come to be treated much like securities. The National Council of Real Estate Investment Fiduciaries (NCREIF) publishes quarterly price indices for various classes of commercial real estate. Commercial real estate is an established part of private equity fundraising. Institutions expect to realize a total return composed of current rental flows plus capital appreciation. Real estate funds are expected to sell their properties regularly to establish values and to return the proceeds to their investors.

Commercial real estate found widespread favor post-9/11 because of its investment performance. Prices for apartment and retail buildings rose 75–90% between 2001–06 and office buildings by just as much although not as steadily (Chart 2.40).

Returns published by the NCREIF for a composite of institutionally owned properties increased 10–20% annually over the same period.

Prices were influenced by a decline in cap rates from 9% to 6% (the discount rate for rent rolls and anticipated resale value) (Chart 2.41). This was not due to declining interest rates as ten-year treasury rates rose 50 basis points between 2002–06. Prices reflected strong demand as commercial real estate transactions rose from $100 billion in 2002 to $365 billion in

Chart 2.40

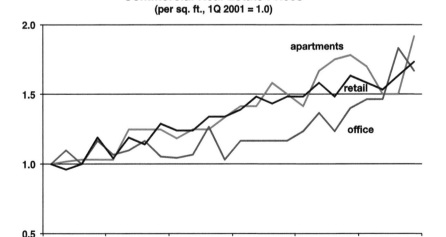

Commercial Real Estate Prices
(per sq. ft., 1Q 2001 = 1.0)

Source: Mortgage Bankers Association (2010).

Chart 2.41

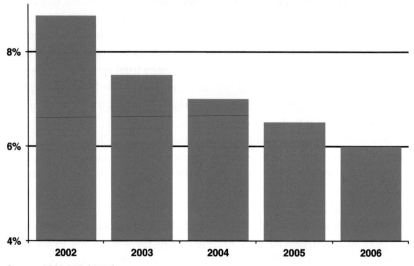

Cap Rates for Commercial Real Estate Sales

Source: NCREIF (2018).

2006 (Chart 2.42) – over $1 trillion cumulatively in four years. The demand came from institutional investors, including REITs. Transactions reached $500 billion in 2007. Duca (2020) provides extensive econometric evidence that a significant factor in the decline in cap rates arose out of the availability of funds.

REITs were another way for institutions to participate in commercial real estate. Total returns for the NAREIT Composite Index were over 30% for three of the four years 2003–06 (Chart 2.43). REITs were also highly leveraged. Simon Property, the largest REIT in the retail sector, had 70% leverage between 2001–06. Vornado, a large but more diversified REIT, had leverage of 83%.

There are no national records of commercial real estate ownership, but a broad estimate of institutional ownership is $3 trillion in 2006. This is based on $0.5 trillion in state and local retirement funds, assuming they allocated 15% to commercial real estate (the California funds were over 20%), $0.5 trillion in private pension funds, assuming they allocated 10%, and REITs owning $2 trillion. The growth between 2002–06 appears to have been in the area of $1 trillion based on the volume of public transactions.

Commercial real estate also attracted lenders stretching for yield. Commercial mortgages grew $1 trillion to almost $3 trillion between

Chart 2.42

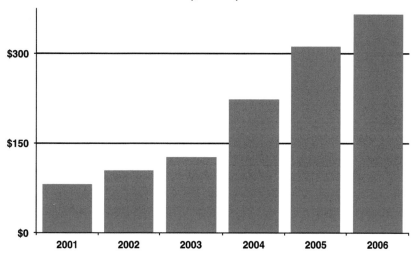

Source: Business Insider (2010).

Chart 2.43

Composite REIT Index Total Returns

Source: NAREIT, ReitWatch.

2002–06, their growth rate steadily escalating to 13% in 2005–06.[54] This may understate the total debt expansion if the Federal Reserve's data does not include subordinated debt. Subordinated debt was popular in commercial real estate, just as it was for highly leveraged corporate loans.[55]

Banks' commercial mortgages grew almost $600 billion (12% per annum) between 2002–06. They lent up to 75% of value on floating rate loans and increasingly took construction risks. Our focus has been on the largest banks and investment institutions, but smaller banks had 36% of their total assets exposed to commercial real estate.

Commercial mortgage-backed securities (CMBS) doubled to $600 billion between 2002–06 (Chart 2.44). The stretch for yield in CMBS was obvious. They offered higher loan-to-value ratios than banks and at the peak in 2007–08 were mostly interest-only or even negative amortization (i.e. capitalizing interest). They also had mezzanine and equity tranches popular with life insurance companies and hedge funds. Life insurance companies owned $215 billion or 30% of the outstanding CMBS issues in 2006 and Fannie Mae/Freddie Mac owned $87 billion, repeating their appetite for private RMBS.

Chart 2.44

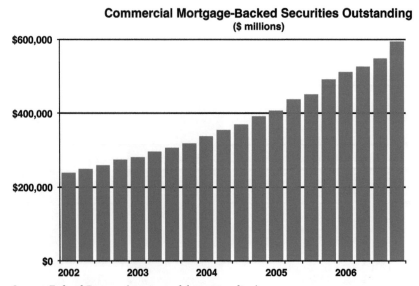

Source: Federal Reserve (mortgage debt outstanding).

[54] Federal Reserve (mortgage debt outstanding).
[55] Commercial real estate mortgages, as referred to here, include multifamily apartment building loans and private commercial mortgage-backed securities (CMBS), but exclude mortgages with government departments or GSEs (small).

2.8 Hedge Funds

Hedge fund assets tripled from $0.6 to $1.2 trillion between 2002–06 (Chart 2.45). The hedge fund category included different strategies that became increasingly specialized over time. The classic hedge funds aimed to protect capital while achieving equity returns by being both long and short (hedging) at the same time. The ten largest in 2006, accounting for about 17% of the business, are outlined in Table 2.27.

The prominent universities were among the most aggressive investors in hedge funds with Harvard allocating 35% of its endowment and Princeton 28% (Chart 2.46).

The fund types at the core of the industry were long-short equity, global macroeconomic strategy, and multi-strategy funds. The latter two also invested in fixed income, commodities, and currencies at times. These were 50% of the funds in 2002. Their strategies protected capital in 2002 as can be seen in Table 2.28 (+5% versus –22% for the S&P 500), and their aggregate return over the period 2002–06 was double the S&P 500 (71% versus 35%). However, the differentiation after 2002 favored the S&P 500. It is possible that hedge fund returns in 1999–2002 simply reflected return dispersions 100% higher and volatility 50% higher than average since 1980

Chart 2.45

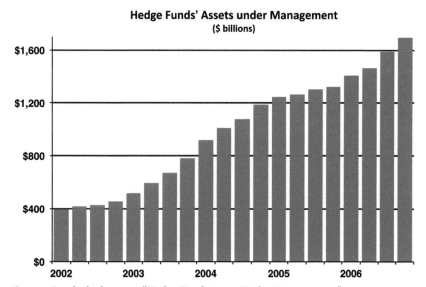

Hedge Funds' Assets under Management
($ billions)

Source: Barclayhedge.com, "Hedge Fund Assets Under Management."

Table 2.27

THE LARGEST HEDGE FUNDS IN 2006	
($ billions)	
Highbridge (JP Morgan)	33
Goldman Sachs	33
Bridgewater	30
D.E. Shaw	27
Farallon Capital	26
Renaissance Technologies	26
Och-Ziff Capital	21
Barclays Global Investors	19
Man Investments	19
ESL Investments	18
Total	252

Source: Investors' Alpha Magazine, June 2007.

Chart 2.46

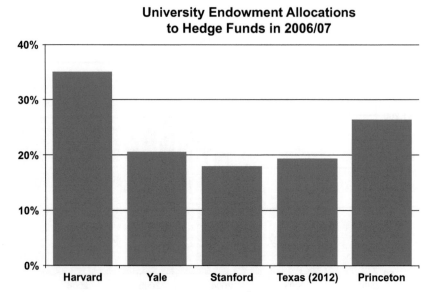

University Endowment Allocations to Hedge Funds in 2006/07

Source: Pension & Investment Age, December 2006.

Table 2.28

AVERAGE RETURNS FOR BROAD EQUITY HEDGE FUNDS 2002–2006				
	Hedge funds	Indexed	S&P 500	Indexed
2001		1.00		1.00
2002	5%	1.05	−22%	0.78
2003	19%	1.25	29%	1.00
2004	10%	1.39	11%	1.11
2005	10%	1.52	5%	1.17
2006	12%	1.71	16%	1.35

Source: Cambridge Associates (2006).

due to the hi-tech bubble. Once volatility and dispersion became below average in 2003–06, hedge fund returns were below the S&P 500.[56]

The same hedge fund strategies were also applied in Europe, Asia, and Emerging Markets, although hedging was difficult in many of these markets because of illiquidity and social norms against shorting securities. Returns in the Emerging Markets sector of hedge funds from 2001 to 2006 were more than double broad hedge funds as can be seen in Table 2.29 (up 164% versus 71%).

There may be a question whether investors were "stretching for yield" in the classic hedge funds. To some degree, investors simply followed the migration of the best investment managers to the hedge fund structure where the managers could charge more. Also, the moderation of losses in 2002 suggested that hedging offered a reduced risk profile. Commercial hedge fund data sources claim that the standard deviations of hedge fund returns were lower than the S&P 500, but this is based on monthly data that averages out daily fluctuations and self-pricing for illiquid investments.

It is difficult to analyze hedge fund risk broadly because the best data is only available by commercial subscription, there is a broad range of strategies, and there is no data on leverage and other forms of risk (derivatives, illiquid securities, sidecar investments, concentration). Investment

[56] Goldman Sachs (2014), p. 10.

Table 2.29

	Emerging markets	Indexed	Asia Pacific	Indexed	Broad hedge	S&P 500
	HEDGE FUND RETURNS IN ASIA AND EMERGING MARKETS					
2001		1.00		1.00	1.00	1.00
2002	12%	1.12	1%	1.01	1.05	0.78
2003	45%	1.62	25%	1.26	1.25	1.00
2004	14%	1.85	10%	1.39	1.39	1.11
2005	17%	2.17	16%	1.61	1.52	1.17
2006	22%	2.64	13%	1.82	1.71	1.35

Source: Cambridge Associates (2006, 2011).

services such as Cambridge Associates had detailed information on individual funds as part of their evaluations for institutional clients, but their data only covered about 2/3 of the hedge fund universe and their function as an investment advisor led them to focus on the most successful funds.

We are not able to make a risk analysis of hedge funds that is comparable to that for public equity portfolios. The best we can offer is generalizations. All of the following aspects of hedge funds suggest high risks. Investors knew these risks, but as with private equity, they were seeking better performance through leverage without liability or having to report it in their financial statements.

- The classic hedge funds of the 1980s and 1990s run by investors such as George Soros, Julian Robertson, Michael Steinhardt, Leon Cooperman, Arthur Samberg, and Paul Tudor Jones bought on margin, moved opportunistically among fixed income, equity, commodity, and currency markets, used futures aggressively, concentrated their positions, and did not concern themselves with balance between long and short positions.
- Long-Term Capital Management borrowed $125 billion – over twenty-five times its capital of $4.7 billion – to speculate in worldwide government bond markets. It failed in 1998 during the Russian and Asian credit crises and was liquidated under a settlement organized by the Federal Reserve Bank of New York.

- In 2002 when there was considerable divergence among hedge funds' performance Institutional Investor had the following to say about the four top performing funds:

With some variation in timing and allocation, all four investors played the same trends. Tropin (a manager) says he got almost 19 percentage points of his nearly 44 percent gain from fixed income futures, cashing in on the global decline in rates; an additional 15 or so percentage points from the foreign exchange market, especially during the dollar's sharp decline against the euro last summer; a further 6 to 8 percentage points from shorting stock index futures in France, Germany and the USA; and the remainder from bullish plays on grains.[57]

All of these transactions represented dramatic leverage.

- John Paulson's group of hedge funds that made spectacular returns in the crisis of 2008 held $25 billion of credit default swaps on private RMBS. This was like putting all of one's money into options and over ten times the equity in the funds.[58]
- Contrary to Paulson's success, Amaranth Advisors (Greenwich, CT) lost $5 billion trading natural gas and folded.
- Hedge fund risks in emerging markets went beyond standard risk measures of volatility, leverage, and illiquidity to include lack of disclosure, respect for private capital, rule of law, and social stability.
- Funds exploiting bankruptcies and credit problems were by definition taking risks beyond standard measures.
- Hedge fund returns suggested that investors were "swinging for the fences." Chart 2.47 shows the highest, median, and lowest returns for "broad hedge funds." Any investment strategy is risky when the highest returns are five times the median and the lowest persistently lose money. However, the highest returns illustrate the attraction of hedge funds if one could find the best.

All hedge funds were leveraged in the sense that their combined long and short positions ("gross positions") usually exceeded 100% of capital – at times over 200%. The proceeds of short sales were used to make larger (thereby leveraged) long investments.

2.9 Foreign Equities

Investors' foreign equity assets grew $2.6 trillion (202%) between 2002–06 to $4 trillion (Chart 2.48), but this growth did not reflect an increased flow of

[57] Institutional Investor (2003).   [58] Zuckerman (2009), pp. 199–200.

Chart 2.47

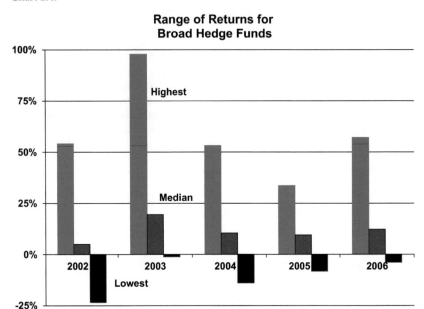

Source: Cambridge Associates (2011).

Chart 2.48

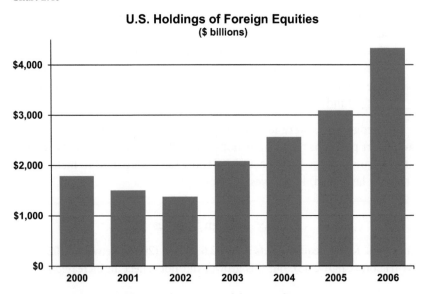

Source: Federal Reserve (Financial Accounts of the United States).

funds into the sector and thus cannot be considered part of the general stretch for yield. Part of the growth (25%) was depreciation of the US dollar (Chart 2.49). The greater part of the growth was the rise in stock prices in both foreign developed and emerging markets as the MSCI–EAFE index (developed country markets outside the USA and Canada) rose 143% between 2002–06 (Chart 2.50) and the MSCI–Emerging Markets Index rose 250% (Chart 2.51).

It is tempting to view the increase in foreign equity holdings as another example of stretching for returns since foreign holdings introduce currency risk, informational disadvantages, weaker disclosure, exposure to corruption and government interference, less respect for intellectual and property rights, industry concentration, illiquidity, restrictive social norms, and lower corporate returns on equity.

The largest public pension funds provide the best disclosure in this respect, and their foreign equity holdings only grew from $87 billion to $176 billion – $100 billion less than they would have from appreciation alone if their 2002 investments held constant (Table 2.30). They must have withdrawn foreign funds in reaction to their high performance to avoid being over-allocated.

Chart 2.49

Note: trade-weighted index.
Source: FRED.

Chart 2.50

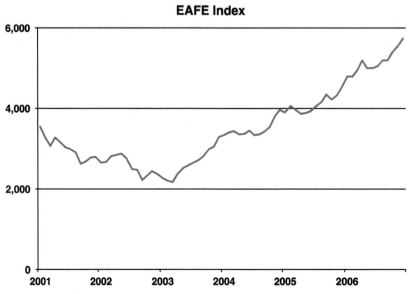

Source: MSCI Inc.

Chart 2.51

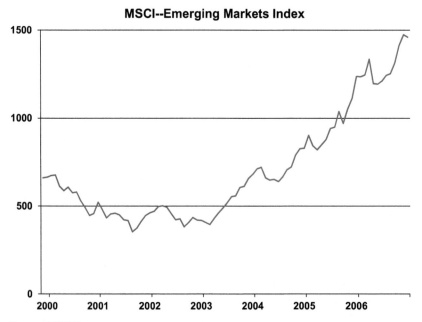

Source: MSCI Inc.

Table 2.30

PUBLIC PENSION FUNDS' FOREIGN EQUITIES HOLDINGS				
	2006/2007		**2001/2002**	
	$ billions	**% allocation**	**$ billions**	**% allocation**
California Public Employees	56	23%	27	19%
California State Teachers	36.6	21%	21.2	22%
Florida Retirement System	22.3	16%	11.5	13%
NY State Common Fund	24.8	16%	9.8	10%
New York City Retirement	8	16%	4	18%
Teacher Ret't System of Texas	27.8	25%	13	13%
Washington State Investment Board	15.2	24%	5.8	15%
Totals	**176**	**20%**	**87**	**16%**

Source: Annual Reports.

2.10 Securities Lending

Lending portfolio securities was a little noticed indication of the institutional stretch for yield that got AIG into serious trouble and undoubtedly played a role in the contraction of the repo market in the crisis. Securities lending grew out of short sellers' need to borrow securities. In a simple model, short sellers would post cash plus a margin for safety with the lender and sometimes pay a small percentage fee as well, depending upon the difficulty of borrowing the securities. For the lenders, it was a way to increase portfolio returns, especially on stocks and low-yielding debt obligations such as US treasuries, if they relent the collateral funds in the repo market. JP Morgan Chase and Bank of New York Mellon acted as brokers, lending the securities, collecting the cash, and reinvesting it in the repo market against appropriate collateral (usually US treasuries, agencies, or AAA or AA-rated corporate bonds), segregating collateral, assigning values to it, and setting any margins required for safety. This was the oft-referenced tri-party repo market.

Participation in the tri-party repo market by nonbanks grew from $500 billion to $2 trillion between 2000–07 and from 29% to 45% of the total (Chart 2.52). Volume almost doubled between 2004–07 in response to the Bankruptcy Abuse Prevention and Consumer Protection Act of 2005 in

Chart 2.52

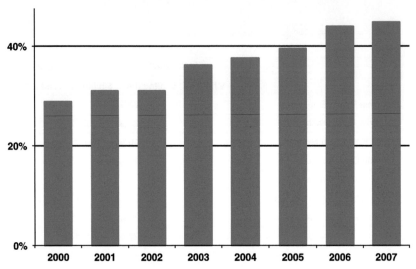

Nonbank Share of the Tri-Party Repo Market

Source: Federal Reserve (Financial Accounts of the United States).

which a wide range of repo collateral was given exemption from a stay in bankruptcy and could thereby be converted preemptively to cash if a borrower appeared to be in trouble.

Repo market collateral also expanded with the expansion in asset-backed and mortgage-backed securities because of higher returns if asset-backed securities were accepted as collateral. These were generally not accepted in the tri-party repo market but were in the dealer market along with other assets of lower credit standing such as whole mortgages, RMBS residuals, CMBS, CDOs, CLOs, subordinated securities, bridge loans, etc.

Stretching for yield in this fashion could tip securities lending over into margin borrowing. AIG used the cash collateral to buy subprime RMBS and CDOs. Harvard was even more aggressive in 2004–05, borrowing $29 billion versus only $24 billion in its investment portfolio. This was frankly described as an "arbitrage account" although that doesn't tell us what securities the university was buying or what its returns were. The arbitrage ceased when Jack Meyer and his fixed income team left in 2006 to set up their own firm.[59]

Securities lending by the largest state pension funds and endowments approached 20% of their investments (Table 2.31). Their reporting does

[59] Financial Report to the Board of Overseers of Harvard College, 2004–05, p. 57.

Table 2.31 *Securities Lending ($ billions)*

SECURITIES LENDING			
($ billions)			
	fiscal 2006/2007		
	Investments	**Securities loaned**	**Percent**
AIG	791	70	9%
Metropolitan Life	325	46	14%
California Public Employees	304	46	15%
NY State Common Fund	184	25	14%
Florida State Board	184	18	10%
California State Teachers	173	28	16%
Texas Teachers	168	29	17%
NYC Retirement	138	18	13%
New York State Teachers	105	13	12%
New Jersey Div. Pensions & Benefits	86	18	21%
Wisconsin Investment Board	71	6	8%
Ohio Public Employees	70	11	16%
Harvard University*	30	20	67%
Gates Foundation	29	5	17%
	1,542	**237**	**19%**
*2005/2006			

Source: Annual Reports.

not enable us to differentiate what types of securities they were lending or how they were deploying the cash received. They had repo loans of $237 billion, but the Federal Reserve only reported them as having $3 billion in the tri-party repo market (Financial Accounts of the United States, Z.1). In 2011, the life insurance industry was reported as lending $80 billion, half corporate bonds and $31 billion in treasuries and agencies (NAIC, 2011–1); but the Federal Reserve only reported $7 billion of this in the tri-party repo market. Both state and local pensions and the life insurance companies were deploying the balance in a stretch for yield in the dealer repo market. Comparable information is not available for corporate pension funds.

Securities lending was open to any endowment, foundation, pension fund, money manager, mutual fund, or insurance company. The New York Federal Reserve estimated that 4,000 institutions provided loans in the tri-party repo market and that those reinvesting cash from lending securities accounted for 25% of the $2.8 trillion total in 2008.[60] We do not know what risks these institutions were taking other than the highly public case of AIG in 2008–09 and the large balances that state and local pension funds and life insurance companies placed in the dealer market.

2.11 Damage Done

Between 2002 and 2006 the largest US investors added almost $11 trillion of alternative investments with higher credit risks and leverage (Table 2.5). The investors were principally state and local government pension funds, corporate pension funds, insurance companies, banks, Fannie Mae and Freddie Mac, and endowments. I attribute this massive investment flow to the low interest rates created by monetary policy, the unrewarding equities market of 2002–06, and the difficulty in meeting the 7–8% returns these institutions needed to continue their operating practices.

At the same time, the consuming public engaged in a massive debt expansion, thanks to a 45% rise in home prices, lower interest rates, and a surge in housing speculation. This debt expansion (which included conventional mortgage borrowers just as much as those taking out non-conforming mortgages) only got financed because major institutional investors restricted to fixed income were interested in taking more risk on the theory that they could thereby get greater returns. These investors had no illusions about the risks they were taking. Bear Stearns, Countrywide, Washington Mutual, Fannie Mae, Freddie Mac, AIG, Citigroup, Wachovia, and General Motors pushed this risk-taking to extremes and were rewarded for it in the stock market.

By the end of 2006 the level of borrowing had become irreversible without a major contraction. Institutions and individuals could withdraw from the securities markets and leverage conditions, but someone else had to buy their positions. The situation could only have been averted if the following exposures had not occurred in the first place:

- The public took out $1.5 trillion for consumption through mortgage refinancing ("equity withdrawal").

---

[60] Copeland (2010), pp. 6–7.

- 35+% of all home sales were for second or investment homes using unprecedented investment leverage.
- Privately originated RMBS based on subprime, Alt-A, and jumbo mortgages with substantial credit flaws expanded by $1.7 trillion.
- Fannie Mae and Freddie Mac held almost $400 billion of private RMBS and had debt plus mortgage guarantees of $5.5 trillion supported by less than 1% tangible equity.
- Commercial mortgages grew by $1 trillion and institutional property ownership by $1 trillion.
- Commercial banks increased their lending in mortgage-related products by $1.5 trillion.
- Institutional investors increased their investments in private equity by $900 billion that led to private equity firms dominating the merger market and increasing the amount of highly leveraged corporate debt by $1.7 trillion.
- Institutional investors increased their investments in hedge funds by $1 trillion.
- Commercial banks' OTC derivatives grew to notional exposure over $400 trillion, including notional credit default swaps of $29 trillion. Banks' derivatives had a market value of $10 trillion.
- Citigroup, JP Morgan, and the major European banks built up over $800 billion of off-balance sheet ABCP conduits and structured investment vehicles.
- Securities lending grew to 25% of the repo market, leading some lenders such as AIG to use it as an arbitrage vehicle to invest in private RMBS and CDOs.

The only question was what damage would be done as these excesses were worked out (or not).

3

The Impending Storm – 2007

3.1 Housing and the Economy

Housing and the economy began to show obvious problems in the second half of 2007. Housing prices nationally leveled off after their 45% run from 2002 and declined 11–14% in the high growth areas of Los Angeles, Phoenix, and Las Vegas. While Miami declined just 5% in 2007, six months later it was down 24%. New home sales in 2007 dropped 50% from 2005. In California, housing starts fell by two-thirds from 2005.

The Federal Reserve wasn't worried, reporting in mid-2007:

Although the contraction in homebuilding has been a drag on growth, that restraint seems likely to diminish over 2007. Further gains in real wages as well as ongoing increases in employment should support a solid rise in consumer spending.[1]

The Federal Reserve was not wrong. GDP growth was still 3% in the 2nd quarter of 2007. Retail sales were still growing 3% at the end of 2007. Manufacturing continued to grow around 4%. Private nonresidential fixed investment was particularly strong, growing over 8%, in part because oil prices rose to $100 a barrel and natural gas prices were at $7/mcf (under $2.00 today). The weak dollar, down 35% from its peak in 2002, also stimulated growth.

Based on this outlook, Federal Reserve monetary policy favored continued tightening. The federal funds rate had risen from 4% at the end of 2005 to 5¼% in June 2007. At that time, the Federal Open Market Committee (the FOMC) reported:

The economy was expected to expand over coming quarters at a rate close to or a little below its long-run sustainable pace. At the same time, FOMC members noted that, even though core inflation had slowed from the very rapid rates of the spring and summer, current rates remained undesirably high. The central

---

[1] Federal Reserve (Annual Report 2006), p. 3.

tendency of the FOMC participants' forecasts for the increase in real GDP is 2½ percent to 3 percent over the four quarters of 2007 and 2¾ percent to 3 percent over the four quarters of 2008.[2]

However, problems in the consumer sector soon disrupted this sunny outlook. Consumer confidence took a sharp fall in the second half of 2007 from 90 to 75. The Gallup organization found 75% of the public dissatisfied with the direction of the country.

Consumers' debt situation was worse than the traditional debt service ratio published by the Federal Reserve which was 18% of Personal Disposable Income at the time.[3] Adjusted for taxpayers with income greater than $200,000 whose financial obligations were a constant 4% of disposable income, the remaining population (98%) had financial obligations equal to 22% of disposable income.[4] Taking account of the low level of interest rates and the recent tax cuts, this reflected an unusual debt load.

It was popular at the time to focus on the increase in consumers' net worth as an offset to their increasing debt. The Federal Reserve reported:

... at the beginning of 2007, households' balance sheets appeared to be in good shape. Whereas gains in home prices slowed last year, household net worth increased moderately as stock market wealth grew and households lessened their accumulation of debt. Delinquency rates on consumer loans and on most types of mortgages remained low, although they increased markedly for subprime mortgages ....[5]

The 2006 Economic Report of the President cited a rise in consumers' net worth to 6.5 times disposable personal income vs 4.5 from 1952 to 1997 as a safety feature in the general economic outlook.[6] But both arguments were propaganda. Consumers' liabilities rose from 15% to 22% of net worth between 2000–07 and home values had risen from 15% to 21% of net worth in the same period. As home prices began to decline in 2007 home equity made a sharp decline to 15% of household net worth.

The only way to understand rapidly growing credit markets is to analyze annual (or more frequent) cohorts. This revealed that defaults on subprime mortgages originated in 2004 began to escalate in late 2005 when 16% defaulted after eighteen months. By 2007, subprime mortgages originated in 2006 were defaulting at a 35% rate. Prime mortgages originated in 2006

[2] Federal Reserve (Annual Report 2006), pp. 6–7.
[3] The Federal Reserve eventually revised this ratio to 19%.
[4] IRS, Statistics of Income, table 1. Individual Income Tax Returns: Selected Income and Tax Items for Tax Years 1999–2013.
[5] Federal Reserve (Annual Report 2006), p. 4.
[6] Council of Economic Advisors, Economic Report of the President 2006, p. 30, citing the Bureau of Economic Analysis.

Table 3.1

PRIME AND SUBPRIME MORTGAGE DEFAULT RATES				
	Year originated-prime			
	2004	2005	2006	2007
% default in first 12 months	2%	2%	4%	5%
% default in 18 months	4%	4%	8%	7%
cash out in refinancing loans	12%	21%	21%	21%
	Year originated-subprime			
	2004	2005	2006	2007
% default in first 12 months	11%	16%	24%	25%
% default in 18 months	16%	23%	35%	34%
cash out in refinancing loans	35%	43%	47%	57%

Source: Amromin (2010).

were defaulting in 2007 at double the rate of earlier originations (4% vs 2%) and would double again to 8% after eighteen months (Table 3.1). These escalating defaults reflected the general expansion of household debt as 20+% of prime mortgage and 45+% of subprime mortgage refinancings took cash out between 2004–07. Cash out in refinancings was running at $80–90 billion per quarter from late 2005 to early 2007 and aggregated $2.6 trillion between 2001–07 (Chart 3.1). But this was the end of the line.

3.2 Securities Markets

Private RMBS

The decline in home prices and rising mortgage defaults disrupted their corresponding securities markets in a steady progression throughout 2007. The most quoted measure of the mortgage market's problems was the Markit Group's ABX indices, originated in 2006, for subprime mortgage-backed bonds. These indices were based on market prices for semiannual cohorts of subprime RMBS originations, such as the first half of 2005, second half of 2005, etc. In August and September 2007, these indices began a disconcerting double deterioration (Chart 3.2). The rule of thumb was that the later mortgages were originated in this cycle, the worse the credit.

Chart 3.1

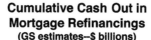

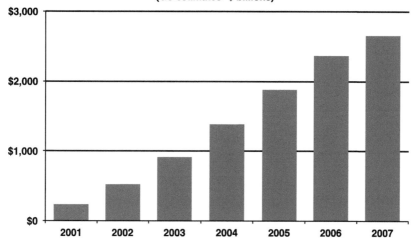

Source: Goldman Sachs.

Thus, the AAA-rated 2006–1 index that represented the senior tranche of RMBS issued on subprime mortgages originated in the second half of 2005 traded down to 90 while the AAA-rated 2007–1 index traded down to 70 and the AAA 2007–2 index traded down to 60. More disturbing was the decline to 60 and 40 in the A-rated 2006–1 and 2006–2 indices representing the junior credit tranches (Chart 3.3). As ratings were cut, more and more bonds were A-rated. Often these lower-rated tranches represented the tag ends of earlier issues that underwriters had been unable to sell. A popular course of action was to repackage them into collateralized debt obligations (CDOs), the senior portion of which could be rated AAA because of the presumed benefits of diversification. We do not have an index like the ABX for CDOs, but given the average A/A rating of underlying CDO collateral in CDOs we can assume their prices performed much like the A-rated ABX indices. CDOs made up approximately 25% of the private RMBS market.

ABCP

The other disrupted market was asset-backed commercial paper (ABCP). It fell by one-third ($400 billion) in the last half of 2007 (Chart 3.4). The decline was concentrated in SIV programs collateralized by private RMBS, CMBS,

Chart 3.2

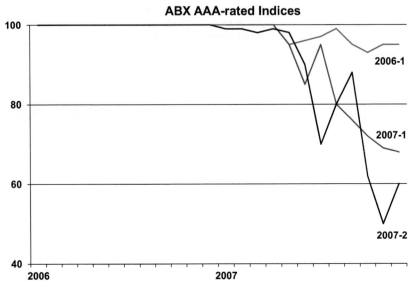

Sources: Stanton (2008, 2011).

Chart 3.3

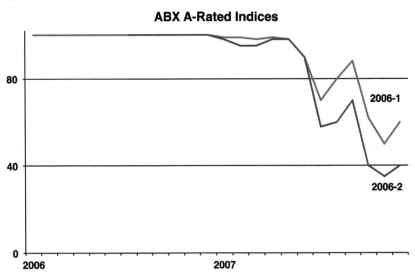

Source: Stanton (2008, 2011).

Chart 3.4

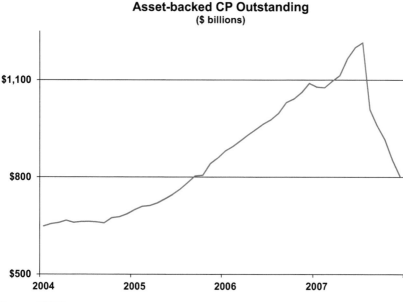

Asset-backed CP Outstanding
($ billions)

Source: FRED.

CDOs, CLOs, and warehoused mortgages, the values of which were declining sharply and for which liquidity was questionable. Citigroup and European banks in particular had set up arbitrage SIV vehicles that used ABCP. These vehicles had a maturity mismatch and lacked regular cash flows. If they needed liquidity they were reliant upon selling their assets into markets that were falling sharply or frozen. As these vehicles failed to roll over their funding, the sponsor banks, especially Citigroup, had to take them on to their balance sheets because of backup lines of credit they had provided or for reputational reasons. By contrast, ABCP funding auto loans, credit cards, and commercial receivables that had regular cash flows continued to be viable.[7]

The student loan program was thrown into disarray at this point. Student debt had grown $200 billion between 2002 and 2007 (Chart 3.5). In an unfortunate convergence, the federal government passed the College Cost Reduction & Access Act in September 2007, reducing lenders' profitability on student loans just when the lenders' cost of money was rising due to the disruptions in the ABCP market. Eighty percent of US government

---

[7] Thanks to Nick Cancro and Ira Powell, both formerly of Goldman Sachs' commercial paper department, for their insight into this market.

Chart 3.5

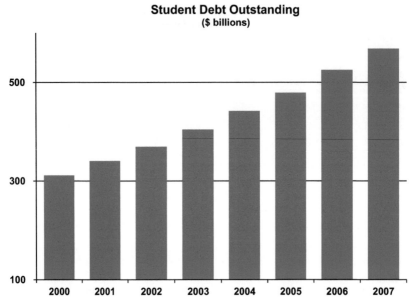

Student Debt Outstanding
($ billions)

Source: Yannelis (2018).

guaranteed student loans was provided by private lenders and 160 of them quit the program. Sallie Mae (originally the Student Loan Marketing Association), the largest lender, was borrowing heavily in the ABCP market with just the sort of collateral the market was rejecting. Sallie Mae's costs rose sharply and a proposed acquisition by J.C. Flowers & Co. at $60 per share was cancelled. Sallie Mae's stock sunk to $19, and it had to rearrange $31 billion of backup bank financing because it broke the covenants. In February 2008, Standard & Poor's cut Sallie Mae's rating to A-3 with a negative further outlook. All of Sallie Mae's interest rate hedges were threatened with cancellation if its rating fell to BBB.[8]

Mortgage Intermediaries and the Big Banks

Escalating mortgage delinquencies and falling private RMBS prices translated into a steady string of problems for mortgage intermediaries. Option One, an H&R Block subsidiary, was forced to take back mortgages that had been securitized in July 2006 because debtors were failing to make their

[8] Sallie Mae 2007 10-K, 2008 10-K.

first payment.[9] New Century Financial began to have problems in the second half of 2006, when it reported 3rd-quarter income was down 50%. New Century was a California based mortgage broker of some prominence as a prime NASCAR sponsor that used Bob Vila as its spokesman (host of This Old House). It ranked second in the nation in origination of subprime and Alt-A mortgages and had over $17 billion in lines of credit with Bank of America, Barclays, Citigroup, Deutsche Bank, State Street Bank & Trust, UBS, Bear Stearns, Credit Suisse-First Boston, Goldman Sachs, and Morgan Stanley. Morgan Stanley and Bear Stearns were able to sell $100 million of subordinated notes and preferred stock to prop it up.[10] One looked in vain through the company's eighty-five-page 3rd quarter 10-Q for any indication that it was in trouble, although its stock had declined from a high of $64 in 2004 to $35 at the beginning of 2007. In February 2007, its stock dropped suddenly to $2 after several subprime mortgage brokers declared bankruptcy and Hong Kong & Shanghai Bank (HSBC) announced that it was taking a $10.5 billion write-off in its Household Finance subsidiary and exiting the US subprime mortgage business. HSBC's write-off was the first large-scale recognition of subprime mortgage problems. New Century promptly lost half its lenders. In March, it announced that it was considering bankruptcy and was the subject of a criminal investigation. Its stock was de-listed by the NYSE. In subsequent lawsuits, it admitted that it "probably" did not accurately report its earnings for 2005 and 2006. Its apparent profitability was destroyed by escalating mortgage default rates in the early months following origination, demands that it repurchase mortgages previously securitized, write-offs in its own portfolio, and recalculation of the value of its mortgage residuals and mortgage servicing rights. Its sophisticated lenders had missed or ignored all of this.

Early in 2007, Fremont General, one of the five largest originators of subprime mortgages, went through similar travails. Its stock dropped 60% when it announced that it could not file its 2006 10-K with the SEC on time. Shortly thereafter, the FDIC ordered Fremont to stop making subprime loans. It tried a series of rescue efforts, but its stock was down 88% by the end of 2007 and its business in tatters. Its 2,200 employees involved in subprime lending were laid off.

In June 2007, it became apparent that subprime problems were also affecting the larger institutions when Bear Stearns announced that two of its sponsored private RMBS funds could not meet redemption demands

---

[9] Zuckerman (2009), p. 157.   [10] Tett (2009), pp. 170–4.

Chart 3.6

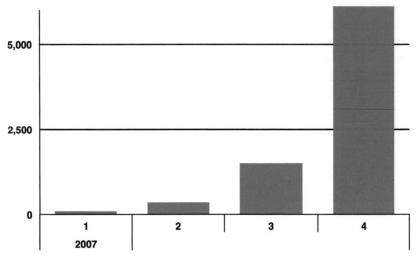

**Moody's Downgrades of RMBS Tranches
in 2007**

Source: ESF Quarterly Securitisation Data Reports.

because of market illiquidity. They had lost 19% in April and the more
leveraged of the two funds lost a further 23% in May. They had built up
$20 billion in assets on just $2 billion of equity before repo lenders forced
Bear Stearns to inject $3.2 billion of additional capital. The two funds filed
for bankruptcy on July 31.[11] Bear Stearns' attitude was that the investors in
its funds were professionals and could accept the losses. Bear Stearns' stock
dropped by one-third.

The turmoil was raised a notch in July when Moody's announced tougher
criteria for ratings on ABS, private RMBS, and CDOs, and said they expected
a 10% decline in housing prices. They downgraded 399 private RMBS
tranches, two-thirds of which were issues sold by New Century,
Washington Mutual, Long Beach Savings, and Fremont Savings – all subprime and low documentation lenders. In the 3rd quarter it downgraded 1,500
private RMBS and 6,000 in the 4th quarter (Chart 3.6). By year-end Moody's
had downgraded 8,000 private RMBS tranches and 1,500 CDO tranches.

The timing of the change in Moody's criteria may not have been due
simply to their evaluation of housing prices. Housing sales and starts had
been declining for eighteen months. House prices in the "sand states"

[11] Zuckerman (2009), pp. 205–6.

where there was the most speculative buying had been declining for at least six months. Regulation may have been the stimulating factor. The Credit Reform Act of 2006 required the three nationally recognized rating agencies to register with the SEC and submit to its regulation. In the summer of 2007, the SEC promulgated a rule requiring them to eliminate conflicts of interest and "unfair rating practices." Michael Lewis in *The Big Short* suggested that Moody's reconsideration of ratings began at this time.[12]

Coincident with Moody's announcement, mortgage problems began to cascade for European banks. Industriekreditbank (IKB), a small German bank headquartered in Dusseldorf that had been arbitraging US subprime RMBS in an SIV that issued ABCP, announced losses that required a $5 billion bailout (versus only $21 billion of assets). On August 7, Banque Nationale de Paris et Pays Bas (Paribas), suspended redemptions in three mortgage funds totaling $2 billion because of a run that depleted 20% of their assets in two weeks. The funds had one-third of their assets in subprime mortgage bonds. Paribas said in a statement, "The complete evaporation of liquidity in certain segments of the US securitization market has made it impossible to value certain assets fairly regardless of their quality or credit rating." Two German banks also stopped redemptions of their bond funds and the Dutch investment bank NIBC Holding (backed by J.C. Flowers & Co.) announced it had lost $200 million on subprime investments (Boyd, 2008).

Lehman Brothers came under increasing criticism at this time. David Einhorn of Greenlight Capital was aggressively shorting the stock, criticizing the firm at investment conferences, and plaguing it with questions on quarterly conference calls. Andres Barry was criticizing it in Barron's, as were Jesse Eisinger at Portfolio and Jonathan Weil at Bloomberg. The Wall Street Journal repeatedly criticized Lehman Brother's deal to buy Archstone, an apartment REIT, recommending that Lehman Brothers back out of the deal. Standard & Poor's in September said that Lehman Brothers' Archstone equity value was zero at a 7% cap rate.[13]

In August, Goldman Sachs demanded $1.5 billion in collateral from AIG on its credit default swaps. This was not made public.

Mortgage problems began cascading through the major US mortgage intermediaries in the second half of 2007. Countrywide Financial said "unprecedented disruptions" in the mortgage markets could affect its financial condition as it reported a 3rd quarter loss of $1.2 billion, but

[12] Lewis (2011), p. 167.   [13] Valukas (2010), pp. 368–9, 380.

Bank of America came up with a lifeline investment of $2 billion for 16% of the company's equity.

Thornburg Realty, a REIT lender on wholesale jumbo mortgages whose stock had been a darling in 2006 (up 84%), developed problems. It was arbitraging $35 billion of jumbo ARMS on $2 billion of equity with almost 100% short-term borrowing. It was forced out of the ABCP market and sold $600 million of preferred stock and $50 million of common equity to bolster its credit. However, it lost $875 million in 2007 and was subject to repeated collateral calls from its lenders – Bear Stearns, Citigroup, Credit Suisse, Royal Bank of Scotland, and UBS. Its stock dropped from $27 to $8 in the 3rd quarter and it cut its dividend 60%.[14]

IndyMac, another large originator of non-qualifying mortgages was in deep trouble by the 4th quarter of 2007. Virtually all of its mortgage portfolio was subprime or Alt-A. Forty-three percent of its portfolio was in California and it was also a big lender to homebuilders, 56% of whose loans were in arrears at year-end. The trustees for its RMBS were demanding that it repurchase loans because they were defaulting so quickly that they didn't meet IndyMac's representations when they were securitized. IndyMac had losses of $334 million in the 3rd quarter of 2007 and $616 million in the fourth. Its ratings were cut to BB with a negative outlook. Its stock had been as high as $46 early in 2007 but dropped to $6 in the 4th quarter. It withdrew from making non-qualifying mortgages – markets for which had "ceased to exist." It cut staff 24% staff in January 2008.

Washington Mutual (WAMU), another of the largest mortgage originators, had serious troubles by the 4th quarter of 2007. It had expanded across the country through numerous bank acquisitions and by opening "loan stores." Forty-eight percent of its loans were in California, 10% in Florida, and it had been a leader in limited documentation option ARMs with a "pick your payment" offering that allowed an increase in principal (i.e. less than full interest payments). The rating agencies assigned a negative outlook to WAMU's Baa1/A- ratings in October that disrupted its access to funds. Its earnings dropped over 75% in the 3rd quarter and it lost $2.4 billion pre-tax in the 4th as it took almost $4 billion in write-offs. It held $13 billion of mortgages that were on nonaccrual status (52% of stockholders' equity). It had lost $30 billion of deposits since the end of 2006 (15% of total deposits) and was borrowing $64 billion from the Federal Home Loan Bank Board. In November, New York Attorney General Andrew Cuomo filed a complaint accusing WAMU of appraisal

[14] Thornburg Mortgage Inc. 2007 10-K.

Table 3.2

BANKS' QUARTERLY PRE-TAX INCOME				
($ millions)				
	1Q2007	2Q2007	3Q2007	4Q2007
AIG	6,172	6,328	4,879	−8,436
Bank of America	7,823	8,660	5,356	−915
Bear Stearns	835	554	175	−1,371
Citigroup	6,715	8,782	261	−17,342
Goldman Sachs	4,859	3,439	4,259	5,055
Lehman Brothers	1,699	1,879	1,205	1,230
JP Morgan	7,332	6,351	5,000	4,122
Merrill Lynch	2,901	2,826	−3,638	−14,920
Morgan Stanley	3,430	3,504	2,246	−5,786
Wachovia	3,300	3,481	2,362	−16
Wells Fargo	3,200	3,444	3,289	1,693

Sources: 10-Ks and 10-Qs.

fraud. In December, it closed half of its home loan offices, cut 22% of its staff, and quit making subprime mortgages. Its stock fell from $44 in September to $13 by year-end. The company was nonetheless able to issue $3 billion of convertible preferred stock in December.[15]

In the 4th quarter of 2007, even some of the most established institutions began to suffer large losses (Table 3.2). Bear Stearns discovered that it too was one of the pros that had to accept losses. It wrote off $2.6 billion in the second half of 2007, lost $1.2 billion, and its stock dropped to $91 versus its high of $172. Moody's and S&P lowered its ratings slightly to A2/A with the latter leaving the outlook "negative."[16]

AIG wrote off $15 billion in the 4th quarter of 2007 and had a pre-tax loss of over $8 billion. Goldman Sachs asked it for another $3 billion of collateral on its credit default swaps at this time.[17]

---

[15] Washington Mutual 2007 10-K, pp. 135, 182, 204 and 10-K/A, p. 76.
[16] Bear Stearns 2007 10-K, p. 35.   [17] AIG 2007 10-K, p. 34.

Merrill Lynch, in October, announced that it would take an $8 billion write-off on its asset-backed inventory.[18] Its stock dropped to $51, down from a record high of $98 at the beginning of the year. It lost over $18 billion pre-tax in the second half of 2007. Stan O'Neal, its CEO who had encouraged the asset-backed buildup, suppressing all dissent, resigned and was replaced by John Thain, ex-CEO of the NYSE and ex-President of Goldman Sachs. Merrill Lynch's ratings were downgraded slightly to A1/ A+ with further negative expectations. It initiated what would become a rash of equity sales by investment banks to Asian sovereign funds, selling $6 billion of common stock to Temasek (Singapore) and $7 billion of convertible preferred stock to Korea Investment Corporation, Kuwait Investment Authority, and Mizuho Corporate Bank. Merrill Lynch ended up writing off $23 billion on fixed income investments in 2007.

The venerable Morgan Stanley came under suspicion late in the year. The firm dramatically increased its trading positions after John Mack became CEO in 2005. He was under unusual pressure to perform because he came in as part of a unique change of CEO orchestrated by disgruntled retired executives. Mack expanded the balance sheet by 50%, including a big push in private RMBS. This was not part of the firm's historic expertise, and it expanded in the weakest parts of the market – CDOs, private RMBS, credit guarantees, ABS, and SIVs. Plus, late in the year two lawsuits were filed against it related to its underwritings for Countrywide Financial and New Century Financial. Morgan Stanley had a $9 billion write-off in the 4th quarter of 2007 that led to a pre-tax loss of almost $6 billion. The majority of the write-off was on synthetic CDOs that tracked bundles of the lowest rated RMBS. The write-off was not surprising given the 50% decline in the A-rated ABX indices in the last half of 2007. The rating agencies put the firm's AA ratings on credit watch with negative expectations. Its stock dropped from a high of $91 in the 3rd quarter of 2007 to only $48 three months later. Just before the end of the year, the company sold $5.6 billion of equity to the China Investment Corporation to bolster its capital.[19]

The pain among investment bankers was not universal. Lehman Brothers reported $1.2 billion pre-tax income in the 4th quarter and Goldman Sachs reported record $5 billion pre-tax income.

Citigroup emerged as a special case of having overstretched in all of the markets. It lost $17 billion pre-tax in the 4th quarter of 2007. It took a $20 billion write-off on its subprime holdings and still had a remaining

[18] Merrill Lynch "News," October 24, 2007.   [19] Morgan Stanley 2007 10-K, pp. 29, 52–5.

exposure of $37 billion. It had $259 billion of ABCP, SIV financing, CDOs, CLOs, and euphemistic "asset-based financing" that was about to unravel. It was stuck with $43 billion of highly leveraged loan commitments that it couldn't remarket and also had over $3 trillion notional amount of credit and equity derivative liabilities where margin requirements were rising steeply.

Citigroup's funding was dangerously short-term. Ninety percent of its deposits were interest-bearing (wholesale funding rather than customer deposits). It was sourcing $450 billion short-term, and $190 billion of its long-term debt was due in the next two years. Charles Prince, its CEO, resigned November 4 and the stock dropped to $29 from $48 just a few months previously. Moody's cut its bond ratings to Aa- in December with a "negative outlook." Standard & Poor's followed suit in January, even though the company raised $30 billion of new preferred equity. Citigroup cut its common dividend 40% in January.[20]

Wachovia Corp, once a conservative pillar of business in the southeast, saw its stock drop from $52 to $38 in the 4th quarter and serious questions arise about its credit. It had morphed into a real estate bank after merging with First Union Corporation, a North Carolina competitor, and acquiring California's Golden West Financial in 2006. Over 60% of its loans were related to real estate, not counting aggressive off-balance sheet loans and guarantees. It errantly increased its dividend during the summer of 2007, but took $2 billion in write-offs in the second half and reported a narrow loss in the 4th quarter. It sold $600 million of preferred stock to bolster its capital.[21]

Northern Rock Bank, a British mortgage lender, had to ask the Bank of England for emergency support in September which led to a run on its deposits and government takeover in early 2008.

A troubling question arose at this time as to whether things were out of control. Citigroup's 3rd quarter write-off of $11 billion was seven times what it predicted just three weeks previously. Earlier in 2007, the Bear Stearns RMBS funds said their April loss was 6½%, but it was revised to 19%. Tim Geithner, then President of the New York Federal Reserve, estimated that subprime and near subprime mortgages were three-quarters of Bear Stearns' mortgage book versus the firms' AAA claims.[22] Goldman Sachs and AIG had disputes throughout the second half of

---

[20] Citigroup 2007 10-K, pp. 48, 57, 69, 84, 86, 92, 96.
[21] Wachovia Corporation 2007 Annual Report, p. 53.
[22] McLean (2010), p. 293; Geithner (2014), p. 154; Bernanke (2015), pp. 179, 195.

Table 3.3

BANKS' 4TH QUARTER 2007 STOCK PRICES	
	% decline
Morgan Stanley	47%
Bear Stearns	47%
Citigroup	47%
Merrill Lynch	46%
Lehman Brothers	43%
Goldman Sachs	37%
Wachovia Corp	35%
JP Morgan	25%
Bank of America	24%
Wells Fargo	23%

Source: Annual Reports.

the year over the appropriate prices for various AIG liabilities because they were almost 50% apart.[23] Morgan Stanley's pre-announced year-end write-off of $3.7 billion changed to $9.4 billion. Merrill Lynch's October estimate of a $5.5 billion write-off turned into $8.4 billion two weeks later. UBS's similar estimate of a $3.5 billion write-off turned into $13 billion.[24] In January 2008, Société Générale discovered that Jerome Kerviel, a futures trader, had lost $7 billion in unsupervised trades. Société Générale lied to the Federal Reserve and kept the loss secret for a week until it had unwound Kerviel's positions.[25] Lehman Brothers began hiding $50 billion in assets in "Repo 105" financings to reduce its apparent leverage.[26]

These problems were reflected in investment banks' stock prices. They dropped 45% in the 4th quarter from their previous highs (Table 3.3). The decline was less for the big commercial bank stocks (with the exception of Citigroup) as they mostly dropped around 25%.

[23] Fcic-static.law.stanford.edu.cdn_media/fcic-testimony/2010–0701-Goldman-AIG-collateral-timeline.pdf, table 18.
[24] Tett (2009), p. 206.　[25] Bernanke (2015), pp. 195–6.　[26] Valukas (2010), p. 6.

Fannie Mae and Freddie Mac

Fannie Mae and Freddie Mac began to suffer even though their stocks ran up earlier in 2007. The companies had been forced to restate their earnings for the first part of the decade by their regulator, the Office of Federal Housing Enterprise Oversight (OFHEO), and it had taken three years to do the job. Their $3.5 trillion of mortgage guarantees now included $500 billion with FICO scores below 660 (14%), $600 billion with loan-to-value ratios over 80% (17%), and $200 billion of interest-only or negative amortization loans (6%).[27] This $1.3 billion of low-quality mortgages was supported by the two companies' combined common equity base of only $40 billion. Their equity would be wiped out by a 3% decline in value, let alone what was happening in the better-quality mortgages.

Fannie Mae's first timely report was its 3Q 2007 10-Q in which it reported $4 billion in write-offs. Write-offs rose to $7 billion for the second half of 2007 and it cut its dividend 50%. Its stock dropped from an all-time high of $71 early in 2007 to $26 in December. But FNMA was still rated Aaa/AAA and early in 2008 it sold $9 billion of preferred stock to build up its equity.[28]

Freddie Mac was doing no better. It had raised its dividend at the end of 2006 pushing its stock to an all-time high of $72, but the company took $9 billion in write-offs in 2007 and had a $6 billion pre-tax loss.[29] It halved its dividend at the end of 2007, and its stock sank to $23 – down two-thirds. Freddie Mac was also still rated Aaa/AAA and it sold $6 billion of preferred stock in November.

Monoline Insurance Companies

There was a general collapse of the monoline insurance companies in the second half of 2007. Nonconforming mortgages had opened the door to companies offering mortgage guarantees. Fannie Mae and Freddie Mac had long histories of accepting residential mortgage guarantees when a borrower's loan-to-value ratio exceeded 80%, but bulk guarantees for mortgage pools amounted to 50–70% of mortgage guarantees in 2004–06 – a faster way to expand business with lower administrative costs than insuring one mortgage at a time. The monoline insurers' annual guarantees extended for subprime and Alt-A mortgages grew 4-fold between 2001 and

[27] Acharya (2011), p. 81.   [28] Fannie Mae Annual Report 2007, p. 106.
[29] Freddie Mac Annual Report 2007, pp. 93–5, 114.

Table 3.4

GUARANTEES OF SUBPRIME & ALT-A MORTGAGES	
	($ billions)
2001	15
2002	26
2003	31
2004	65
2005	53
2006	34

Source: derived from Ashcraft (2010) data.

2004, although these volumes are not additive because up to 50% was for refundings (Table 3.4).

It is surprising that the monoline insurance companies received AAA ratings. The original business of guaranteeing municipal bonds played upon the tendency of state governments to backstop municipalities that got in trouble, but residential nonconforming mortgage pools had no backstops and the monoline insurers' capacity to pay claims (common equity plus investments) only amounted to 3% of all guarantees in force. As an active participant in municipal finance in the 1980s, I know that the bonds the monoline insurers guaranteed traded as if they had A ratings. The AAA rating was mostly a lure to retail investors.

AMBAC, one of the original monoline insurance companies, began as a guarantor of municipal bonds in 1971 and experienced few defaults aside from the Washington Public Power Supply System failure in 1983. AMBAC began guaranteeing residential mortgage pools in the 1980s. The business became highly competitive with many other firms writing guarantees, especially MGIC. Between 2000 and 2006 AMBAC tripled its "guarantees in force" on asset-backed securities to over $170 billion with $55 billion in the form of credit derivatives.[30] These guarantees were virtually all related to nonconforming mortgages, home equity loans, or international residential mortgages. Investors approved, pushing AMBAC's stock from $60 in 2002 to $85 in 2006; but by 2006 the monoline insurance companies had become a target of short sellers, notably of William Ackman's Pershing Square Capital Management.

AIG also entered the guarantee market through its UK Financial Products subsidiary, taking advantage of AIG's AAA ratings to sell credit default swaps guaranteeing asset-backed securities. It was purposely obscure about its guarantees of various asset-backed securities, debt pools, and asset-backed commercial paper until 2007 when its guarantees were revealed to be $155 billion, up from insignificance in 2002.[31]

AMBAC had a 4th quarter 2007 loss of $5 billion, eliminated its dividend, and virtually ceased writing new guarantees. Its stock dropped from a high of $96 in the 2nd quarter of 2007 to a low of $21 in the 4th quarter. Guarantees of private RMBS pools and other mortgage derivatives constituted half of its liabilities. It had $525 billion in guarantees backed by only $18 billion in investments and $6 billion in common equity. Half of these guarantees were on 2005–07 mortgage vintages. It was liable for collateral calls as high as $8 billion if its ratings dropped to A/A2 (which they soon did). Its protective measures increased its risks rather than diversifying them. Seven billion of its $18 billion in investments was in ABS, including over one-third guaranteed by itself or its competitors, and most of its reinsurance of $88 billion (almost one-third of its business) was with similar monoline companies – Assured Guaranty, Radian Insurance, and RAM Reinsurance.[32]

MGIC, another pioneer, similarly guaranteed subprime bonds and invested in two subprime loan companies. It had $3 billion in write-offs in 2007, reported a pre-tax loss of $2.2 billion, most of it in the 4th quarter,

---

[30] AMBAC 2006 10-K, p. 117.

[31] AIG 2007 10-K, note 8 to the financial statements. It also had a guarantee program for banks in Europe to reduce their capital requirements, but this program did not become a problem. GE Credit also took advantage of its parent's AAA ratings to offer mortgage guarantees on a scale that made it the 5th largest such insurer in the country; but GE spun the business off as Genworth Financial in 2004. Genworth in 2007 had $31 billion of mortgage guarantees at risk, virtually all on mortgages that were greater than 80% loan-to-value, but only 2% of this was bulk insurance. The portfolio was 87% prime mortgages, 90% of which were fixed rate, and only 14% in the high-risk states of Florida and California. It appeared to be an appropriately managed business.

[32] AMBAC 2007 10-K, pp. 44, 47, 50, 56, 60, 78, 80, 89, 148.

Chart 3.7

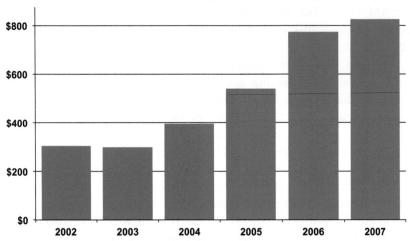

Estimated Private Equity Acquisitions
(Public Go-private plus Non-public M&A Sellers)
($ billions)

Sources: Mergerstat Review (2007, 2012).

and eliminated its dividend. It reported that the number of mortgage delinquencies in California in the second half of 2007 was up 130% and twice the dollar average per mortgage. In Florida, delinquencies were up 175%. MGIC's ratings were cut from Aaa/AAA to Aa2/AA- but with negative indications that they could be cut further which would end its ability to do business. Its stock fell from a high of $73 in 2006 to $16 in the 4th quarter of 2007. Nonetheless, it was able to sell $835 million in stock and subordinated debentures to bolster its capital in early 2008.[33]

Mergers and Acquisitions and Highly Leveraged Loans

The merger market had developed its own level of excess and fears. Private equity acquisitions swelled to over $800 billion in 2007 (Chart 3.7) with a quarter of the volume fueled by unusually large public acquisitions. Private equity funds were paying record prices, up from four times EBITDA (Earnings Before Interest, Taxes, Depreciation, and Amortization) in 2003 to six times in 2007. The price-earnings ratios paid for these deals averaged a premium of 69% to that of the S&P 500 compared to 25% in 2004 (Chart 3.8).

[33] MGIC Annual Report 2007, pp. 2, 4, 80, 83.

Chart 3.8

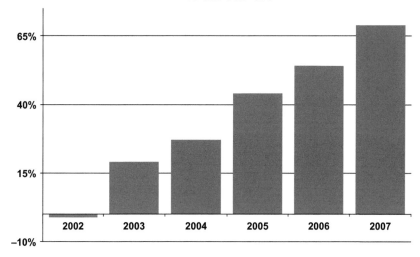

Source: Mergerstat Review (2007, 2012).

New issues of highly leveraged loans doubled to $1.1 trillion versus 2005 (Chart 3.9). B-rated loans rose to 40% of volume (Chart 3.10) and were "covenant lite," catering to aggressive nonbank lenders stretching for yield. Nonbank lenders were 57% of commercial bank syndicated loans, and undoubtedly much higher for the loans led by investment banks.[34] The stretch for yield was even greater in new issues of high yield bonds as the proportion of issues rated lower than B (i.e. already in distress) rose to over 50% (Chart 3.11).

But highly leveraged acquisitions dropped from 40% of transactions to less than 10% in the second half of 2007 (Chart 3.12) and prices of collateralized loan obligations dropped to 93, making new leveraged loans difficult to market.[35] The Federal Reserve estimated that at the end of the year lead banks held $250 billion of highly leveraged loans that had not been successfully syndicated.[36] It is not clear whether this estimate included loans led by investment banks.

[34] BIS (2008), graph 3.4; Moody's Analytics, CLO Vintage Analysis (2015), p. 7.
[35] SIFMA Research Report, February 2008, p. 16.
[36] Federal Reserve (Annual Report 2007), pp. 30, 34.

Chart 3.9

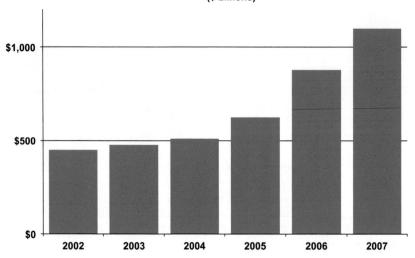

U.S. Leveraged Loan Issues
($ billions)

Source: BIS (2008).

Chart 3.10

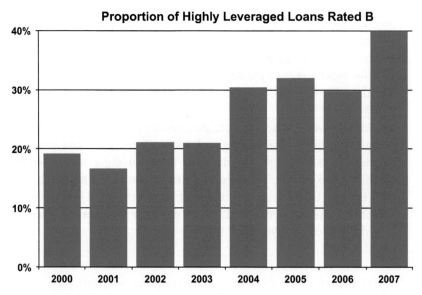

Proportion of Highly Leveraged Loans Rated B

Source: BIS (2008).

Chart 3.11

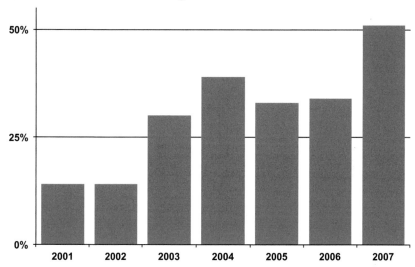

New Issues of High Yield Bonds Rated Below B

Source: Altman (2012).

Chart 3.12

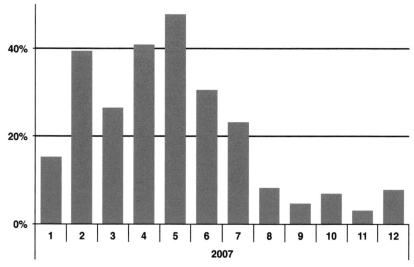

Highly Leveraged Mergers as % of US Total

Source: Dealogic.

Commercial Real Estate

Prices for apartment buildings, office buildings, and retail properties peaked between 4Q 2006–2Q 2007, and then fell by approximately 15% in the second half of 2007 (Chart 3.13). Institutional investors nonetheless continued their aggressive pursuit of commercial real estate. Transactions grew 43% in 2007 (Chart 3.13) as cap rates declined further to 6.5%.

Both bank loans and new issues of CMBS continued their strong growth rates (Chart 3.15). Wells Fargo's commercial real estate loans grew from $61 billion in 2006 to $95 billion in 2007; Bank of America's from $36 billion to $61 billion; Wachovia's from $36 billion to $42 billion. Lehman Brothers' commercial real estate grew from $11 billion to $36 billion. Life insurance companies made 15% of their direct commercial real estate loans in 2007 – triple that of 2004. Life insurance companies' commercial real estate commitments, counting direct loans, CMBS, outright real estate, and REIT investments, were $545 billion, 18% of investment assets.[37] Blackstone Group reported in its first annual report after

Chart 3.13

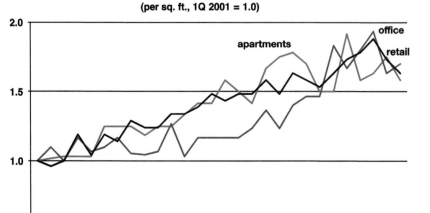

Commercial Real Estate Prices
(per sq. ft., 1Q 2001 = 1.0)

Source: MBA (2010).

---

[37] NAIC (2012), the total was for 2010, but there is no reason to expect much difference from 2007.

Chart 3.14

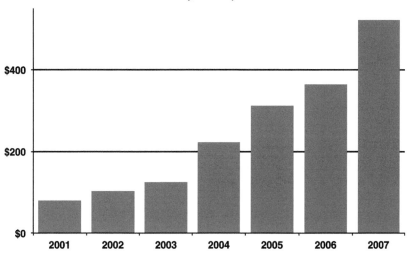

Commercial Real Estate Transactions
(\$ billions)

Source: Moody's/Real Capital Analytics.

Chart 3.15

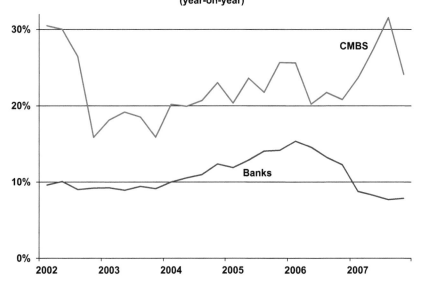

Growth in Commercial Real Estate Mortgages
(year-on-year)

Source: Federal Reserve (mortgage debt outstanding).

Table 3.5

LARGE INVESTORS in COMMERCIAL REAL ESTATE in 2008		
	$ billions*	% allocation
California Public Employees	40	20%
California State Teachers	35	22%
NY State Retirement System	15	14%
NY State Teachers	12	13%
Wisconsin Investment Board**	10	12%
Florida Retirement System**	10	8%
Ohio Public Employees**	5	6%
GE Pension**+	5	9%
IBM (U.S.)	3	9%

* includes commitments.
** commitments not available.
+ December 2007.
Source: Annual Reports.

going public that it owned 615,000 hotel and resort rooms – the riskiest sector of commercial real estate.[38]

By 2008, large pension funds' commercial real estate commitments had risen to the mid-teens as a percentage of investment assets with California Public Employees Retirement System (CALPERS) over 20% (Table 3.5). 2008 is an appropriate date to reflect 2007 asset values because most public funds had June 30 fiscal year-ends plus there was a long lead-time between commitments and cash calls. It should be remembered that these commitments were levered approximately 2 or 3 to 1, although the debt was nonrecourse to investors and not on their balance sheets.

This continuing institutional flow into commercial real estate contrasted with price-sensitive public markets. REIT prices deteriorated all through 2007 until they were down almost 20% by year-end (Chart 3.16). Public markets for CMBS similarly deteriorated as A-rated spreads rose from 25 basis points in the summer to over 500 basis points in November (Chart 3.17).

---

[38] "riskiest" in the sense of having the highest cap rates and as Barry Sternlicht CEO of Starwood Capital Group, once said, "The leases are for only a few days."

Chart 3.16

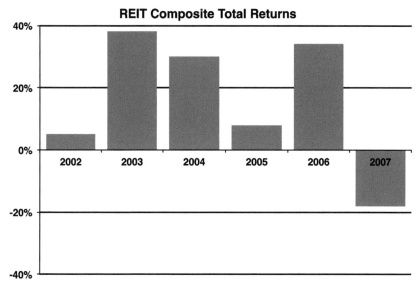

REIT Composite Total Returns

Source: NAREIT, REITWatch.

Chart 3.17

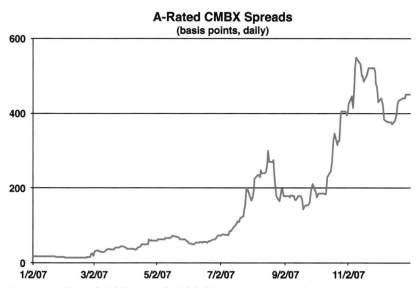

A-Rated CMBX Spreads
(basis points, daily)

Source: Markit and Goldman Sachs Global Investment Research.

Credit Default Swaps

Derivatives markets (which were opaque except to active professionals) also indicated credit concerns. The notional value of credit default swaps doubled in 2007 to almost $60 trillion (Chart 3.18) and their market value quadrupled to $2 trillion (Chart 3.19). This cut the leverage of credit default swaps from sixty to thirty times (Chart 3.20) which meant huge margin calls on the providers of credit protection. The leading recipients of the calls were AIG, Morgan Stanley, Citigroup, UBS, and the monoline insurance companies.

3.3 The Belief in Containment

There was still a conviction at the end of 2007 that the problems in the housing market could be contained. Across the board, the Federal Reserve, the Council of Economic Advisors, Treasury Secretary Hank Paulson, the OECD, the IMF, the rating agencies, Fannie Mae, and the largest banks claimed that these problems could be contained. The New York Federal Reserve told bankers in August, "This is a correction, but it is not dramatic in light of history. . . .. It

Chart 3.18

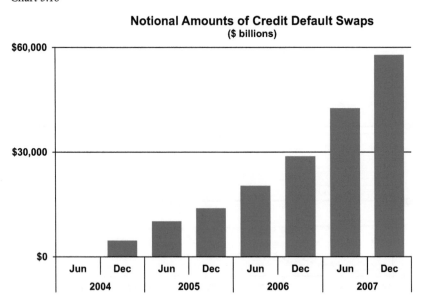

Notional Amounts of Credit Default Swaps
(\$ billions)

Source: BIS (derivatives).

Chart 3.19

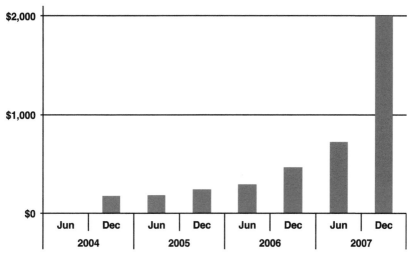

Source: BIS (derivatives).

Chart 3.20

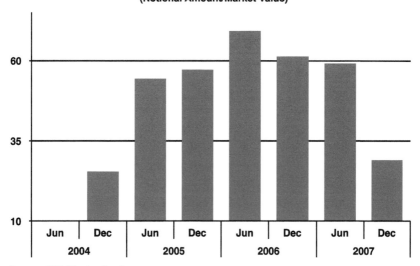

Source: BIS (derivatives).

could be over in a matter of weeks."[39] Opinion at the October Federal Open
Market Committee (FOMC) meeting was that 3rd quarter 2007 economic
growth had been solid and that ". . . spillovers from the turmoil in the housing
and financial markets had been limited at that point." It was not until the
FOMC's December meeting that committee members believed ". . . that
spillovers from housing to other parts of the economy had begun to emerge."
At the FOMC meeting at the end of January 2008 participants expected
economic growth would be weak in the first half of 2008 ". . . before picking
up strength in the second half."[40] The Annual Report of the Council of
Economic Advisors began with the statement:

Economic growth is expected to continue in 2008. Most market forecasts suggest
a slower pace in the first half followed by strengthened growth in the second half of
the year.[41]

Hank Paulson, as Treasury Secretary and one of the best informed
financial people in the world, was telling China's leaders that he expected
the economy to ". . . rebound in the second half . . ."[42] The OECD Annual
Report for 2007 didn't think that housing was important enough to
address, instead choosing to emphasize health, environment, trade, and
human rights. The IMF's Annual Report focused on its own activities, such
as governance, aid to developed countries, and "surveillance." The rating
agencies also expected that the problems would get sorted out. Fannie Mae
and Freddie Mac retained their AAA/Aaa ratings. Lehman Brothers was
upgraded by two of the agencies.

Fannie Mae's annual housing report for 2007 noted the rise in early
delinquencies for mortgages originated in 2005 but thought delinquencies
were coming down for 2006 originations.[43] Lehman Brothers consciously
raised its risks and leverage in 2006, and in 2007 it doubled down on
subprime mortgages and mortgage residuals because it thought investors
were overly negative.[44] Peloton Partners (London, UK) had a sensational
2007 when it bet against subprime RMBS but it collapsed in February 2008
after it decided they were oversold and began buying them.[45]

Consumer spending was still growing, as were commercial real estate
sales, capital spending, and industrial production. Oil was at $100. Merger
and acquisition activity was at record levels.

[39] Tett (2009), p. 182.
[40] Federal Reserve (Annual Report 2007), "Monetary Policy in 2007 and Early 2008."
[41] The Annual Report of the Council of Economic Advisors 2008, p. 17.
[42] Paulson (2010), p. 242.   [43] FNMA Annual Housing Report 2007, p. 26.
[44] Valukas (2010), p. 4.   [45] Boyd (2008).

Segmenting the decline in the stock market suggested that containment could be achieved. There was an ordered progression of deterioration from industries that were the most involved with housing to those least involved (Table 3.6). The S&P 500 was only down 11% (less excluding financial stocks) while the stocks of subprime lenders and monoline insurers were down 84%, homebuilders and Fannie Mae and Freddie Mac 65%, investment bankers 42%, and commercial banks 29%.

There was also a sharp contrast in the stocks of industries still expected to do well such as construction, internet retail, technology, machinery, and commodities that were up 25–100% (Table 3.7).

The stock market in general gave no warning signs. The S&P 500 was back to record levels in late 2007 (Chart 3.21). Analysts still expected earnings to be up 10% in 2008 (Chart 3.22). There was no sign that the stock market was overvalued as the earnings yield on the S&P 500 was 175% of 10-year treasuries – well above the norm of 110% from 1979 to 1996.

There were warning signs related to real estate, as was to be expected. Consumer sentiment was bad, but blamed on housing prices. Margin calls were rising on credit default swaps, mostly related to subprime RMBS. REIT prices were down 15%. Spreads on A-rated CMBS rose, but only to 200 basis points in October.

Among non-real estate signals, stock market volatility was up from 10 to 25 (and briefly higher). CLOs had become unsalable. There were signs of a flight to cash as money market mutual fund assets grew 66% from mid-2005 to $3.2 trillion (Chart 3.23) and gold rose from $600 to over $800. But the classic indicator of financial market stress – the spread between Baa-rated corporate bonds and 10-year treasuries – was consistent with a belief in containment. The spread rose from 1.6% to 2.6%, but this was only in the 4th quarter and was still well below the peak spread of 3.9% in 2002. Rates on BB-rated corporate bonds rose from 6½% to 8¼% and C-rated bonds from 9% to 12½% throughout the last half of the year. These were signs of nervousness, but all of them were consistent with containment and it was uncommon for investors, government, and regulators to emphasize narrow indicators rather than broad, general factors.

The Federal Reserve was anxious not to overreact because of the dichotomy between housing and the rest of the economy. Real GDP growth was almost 3% in the 2nd and 3rd quarters of 2007 and 1.4% in the 4th quarter. The weak dollar was providing stimulus, dropping 20% from 2006 and it was contributing to inflation concerns because CPI had reached 3% in 2006. Although inflation came down to 2% in early 2007, it was headed

Table 3.6

DECLINES IN FINANCIAL STOCKS IN 2007			
	High	Low	% Decline
Subprime focus:			
New Century Financial	35	0	100%
Fremont General	16	2	88%
IndyMac	46	6	87%
Countrywide Financial	45	8	82%
AMBAC	96	21	78%
MGIC	73	16	78%
WAMU	46	12	74%
		average	**84%**
Homebuilders index[1]	5,003	1,703	**66%**
Government-sponsored enterprises:			
Freddie Mac	69	23	67%
Fannie Mae	71	26	63%
		average	**65%**
Investment banks:			
Merrill Lynch	98	51	48%
Bear Stearns	172	91	47%
Morgan Stanley	91	48	47%
Lehman Brothers	85	52	39%
Goldman Sachs	251	175	30%
average			**42%**
Commercial banks & AIG:			
Citigroup	48	29	40%
Wachovia Corp	59	38	36%
AIG	73	51	30%
JP Morgan	53	40	25%
Bank of America	54	41	24%
Wells Fargo	38	30	21%
		average	**29%**
S&P 500	1,576	1,406	**11%**
[1] from 2006 high price			

Source: Annual Reports.

Table 3.7

THE BEST PERFORMING S&P INDUSTRIES 2007	
Construction & engineering	101%
Internet & catalog retail	70%
Energy equipment & services	45%
Machinery	32%
Oil and gas	30%
Metals & mining	30%
Computers & peripherals	29%
Automobile components	27%
Trading & distributing	25%

Source: Standard & Poor's Corp.

Chart 3.21

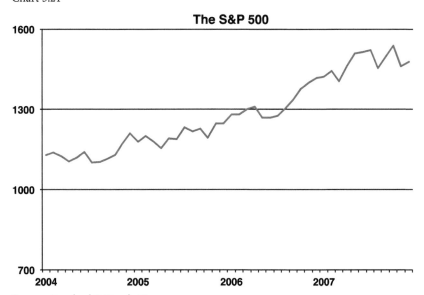

Source: Standard & Poor's Corp.

back up in the second half. M2 money supply growth was also up sharply throughout 2006–07 to almost 7% in mid-2007.

The Federal Reserve made only traditional monetary moves focused on financial markets because of the belief in containment. In August, it

Chart 3.22

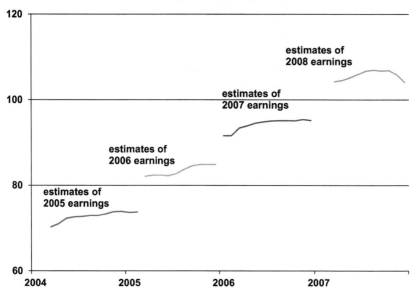

S&P 500 Next-year Earnings Estimates

Sources: IBES; Goldman Sachs.

Chart 3.23

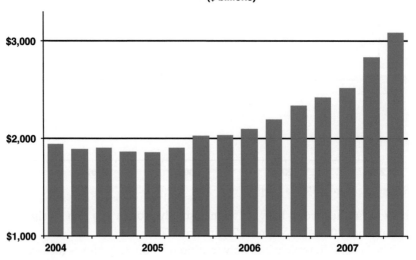

Money Market Mutual Fund Assets
($ billions)

Source: FRED.

Chart 3.24

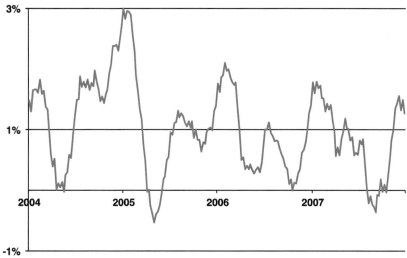

Growth in Federal Reserve Assets
(year on year quarterly average)

Source: FRED.

introduced numerous changes to make borrowing easier from its discount window. Between September 2007–January 2008 it cut the federal funds rate 200 basis points to 3%. In December, it announced coordinated moves with various central banks to ease banks' funding, as part of which it set up $160 billion of Term Auction Facilities (TAF) for borrowing at the discount window against a broad range of collateral. Over 90% of TAF funds went to European, mostly German, banks.[46] At the same time, the Federal Reserve set up $24 billion of currency swaps with the European Central Bank and Swiss National Bank to ease dollar funding for European banks active in the USA. This seemed to take care of the banking system.

There was no impression that the Federal Reserve was preparing for a crisis. It made no move to expand its assets. They persisted in a downward trend from 2% and 3% growth in 2004–05 to 0% in mid-2007 and only 1% at the end of the year (Chart 3.24). Ben Bernanke wrote that the Federal Reserve was gun-shy because it believed it had overreacted in the Russian Crisis of 1998.[47]

Nor was the federal government inclined to undertake any broad fiscal measures. It was busy negotiating foreign trade agreements. The Economic

[46] Bernanke (2015), p. 185.   [47] Bernanke (2015), pp. 160–2.

Report of the President in February 2008 recognized the disruptions in the financial markets and outlined efforts that had been made to ease distress among low-income borrowers, but published the following detached conclusion:

Beyond such targeted responses, the best course of action is often to simply allow markets to adjust.

Policies that attempt to protect market participants from the discipline of the market risk delaying necessary adjustments and creating a potential moral hazard problem by giving lenders and borrowers less incentive to make prudent financial decisions in the future.[48]

Large banks saw the mortgage market troubles of 2007 as an opportunity to buy into the mortgage business on the cheap. In December 2006, Morgan Stanley purchased Saxon Capital, an originator and servicer of home mortgages. Barclays acquired Equifirst Corporation, an originator of subprime mortgages, in March 2007. Merrill Lynch acquired the First Franklin mortgage origination franchise in 2007 for $1.3 billion and First Republic Bank for $1.8 billion. Citigroup acquired ABN AMRO Mortgage Group, an originator and servicer of prime mortgages, from LaSalle Bank for $12 billion. In December 2007, Goldman Sachs paid $1.4 billion for Litton Mortgage, a loan servicer with one of the worst records for defaulting borrowers. Bank of America acquired Countrywide in January 2008 and Wells Fargo began circling Wachovia Corp.

Investors were also willing to provide new capital. Financial firms raised over $90 billion in equity between September 2007 and March 2008 (Table 3.8). Citigroup raised $30 billion. UBS, Lehman Brothers, Merrill Lynch, and Morgan Stanley collectively raised almost $22 billion. Fannie Mae and Freddie Mac raised over $15 billion. Wachovia Corp. raised almost $7 billion.

There were some market participants that began to prepare for trouble. Goldman Sachs' chief financial officer, David Viniar, convened a committee in December 2006 to evaluate exposure to the US residential market. In 2007, Goldman Sachs was able to establish a short position in private RMBS, although it got reversed in 2008.[49] Goldman Sachs also bought credit default swaps from AIG that led Goldman Sachs to demand $2 billion of collateral by the end of 2007.[50] JP Morgan Chase forecast

---

[48] Council of Economic Advisors, Economic Report of the President 2008, pp. 76–7.
[49] Viniar (2010).
[50] Fcic-static.law.stanford.edu.cdn_media/fcic-testimony/2010–0701-Goldman-AIG-collateral-timeline.pdf, table 32.

Table 3.8

FINANCIAL SECTOR EQUITY NEW ISSUES OR ACQUISITIONS IN LATE 2007-EARLY 2008				
Issuers or Acquired Companies	Investors or Acquirors	Amount ($ millions)	Date	Cumulative ($ millions)
Fannie Mae	public	1,000	Sep-07	1,000
Freddie Mac	public	500	Sep-07	1,500
Thornburg Realty	public	674	Sep-07	2,174
Fannie Mae	public	375	Oct-07	2,549
Citigroup	public	788	Nov-07	3,337
Citigroup	Abu Dhabi	7,500	Nov-07	10,837
UBS	Singapore	10,000	Nov-07	20,837
Fannie Mae	public	530	Nov-07	21,367
Freddie Mac	public	6,000	Nov-07	27,367
Morgan Stanley	China	5,600	Dec-07	32,967
Merrill Lynch	Temasek (Singapore) et al	5,600	Dec-07	38,567
Citigroup	public	3,500	Dec-07	42,067
Fannie Mae	public	7,000	Dec-07	49,067
WAMU	various	3,000	Dec-07	52,067
Wachovia	public	2,300	Dec-07	54,367
Wachovia	public	838	Dec-07	55,205
Merrill Lynch	Korea, Kuwait, etc.	6,600	Jan-08	61,805
Citigroup	Singapore, Kuwait, et al	12,500	Jan-08	74,305
Citigroup	public	3,200	Jan-08	77,505
Citigroup	public	3,700	Jan-08	81,205
Countrywide acquisition	Bank of America	4,100	Jan-08	85,305
Wachovia	public	3,500	Feb-08	88,805
Lehman Bros	unknown	4,000	Mar-08	92,805

Source: author's compilation.

trouble in its 2006 Annual Report and tightened its underwriting of subprime loans six times in 2007. The bank also minimized its exposure to CDOs and cut back home equity loans originated by brokers.[51] HSBC ceased subprime lending at its Household Finance subsidiary in 2007.

[51] JP Morgan Chase 2007 Annual Report, pp. 10–11.

Various small investors outlined in Michael Lewis' *The Big Short* saw the problems. In 2006, John Paulson organized his Paulson Credit Opportunity Fund to bet against the subprime securities market. In 2007 he worked with Goldman Sachs and Dusseldorf-based Industriekreditbank (IKB) to create the toxic subprime Abacus 2007AC1 deal that eventually involved Goldman Sachs in a $550 million penalty and long-lasting image problems. Lehman Brothers closed BNC Mortgage, their platform to originate subprime mortgages, in 2007 and in January 2008 suspended wholesale and correspondent mortgage lending at its Aurora Loan Servicing subsidiary.[52] But the system as a whole could not avoid the looming problems even if some market participants could bet against them.

The President's Working Group on Financial Markets, composed of the US Treasury Secretary, the Chair of the Federal Reserve Board, the Chair of the SEC, and the Chair of the Commodities Futures Trading Commission (or their designees), assembled in late 2007 and reported in March 2008 that market troubles were caused by subprime mortgages, the whole pipeline that generated residential mortgages, highly leveraged corporate loans, investors' efforts to maintain higher returns, inadequate risk discipline, failings of the rating agencies, erosion of market discipline, and investors' overreliance on the rating agencies. They missed commercial real estate and only obliquely dealt with credit default swaps. The Working Group recommended that the whole process of residential mortgage finance be reformed, that risk management and capital assessment be improved in financial institutions, their off-balance sheet obligations be better disclosed, that weak management practices be corrected, that large investors do more of their own risk assessment, that there be greater consumer protection, that disclosure be stronger, that state regulators be more active, and that over-the-counter derivatives be centrally cleared.[53] Their policy statement was at least two years late and had no prescription as to how to do these things.

The year 2007 closed amidst mixed expectations. Early in the year the problem had appeared confined to housing when prices began to decline and recent mortgage cohorts – conventional and nonconforming – had elevated default rates. This threatened lower level mortgage originators such as Option One, New Century, HSBC's Household Finance, Indy Mac,

---

[52] Lehman Brothers 2007 10-K, p. 46.
[53] The President's Working Group on Financial Markets (2008), "Policy Statement on Financial Market Developments," March.

Countrywide, and Washington Mutual. Bear Stearns had two highly lever-aged RMBS hedge funds that folded. A number of British, French, German, and Dutch banks had troubles related to their US subprime activities.

Things were more serious in the second half when Moody's cut 8,000 ratings for private RMBS, and their prices collapsed. The collapse rever-berated in CDOs and credit default swaps that were weakly understood by regulators and the investors themselves. Commercial real estate prices began to decline for the first time in years. Private equity firms' domination of the merger and acquisition market came to an end after they had made unusually large acquisitions at record prices. The highly leveraged loans that had funded these acquisitions had become unsalable.

In this atmosphere, the problems escalated to the big financial firms. Bear Stearns had losses, Fannie Mae and Freddie Mac reported losses and cut their dividends. Stan O'Neal resigned as CEO of Merrill Lynch because of heavy losses in mortgage-backed securities. Chuck Prince, CEO of Citigroup, also resigned because of losses and troubled off-balance sheet vehicles. Short sellers began to focus on Lehman Brothers, and even Morgan Stanley's credit came under suspicion.

Still the belief persisted that the stress would be contained to housing and the financial sector. The Federal Reserve, Hank Paulson, Fannie Mae, and financial forecasters in general expected growth to pick up in the second half of 2008. The Council of Economic Advisors thought it was inadvisable to interfere with "market discipline." Analysts' earnings expectations for the S&P 500 in 2008 only dipped slightly. Lehman Brothers decided to take on more risk in the belief that fears were over-done. The Federal Reserve let its assets stop growing. Financial companies were able to raise $93 billion of new equity. Many of the big banks thought the stress in mortgage markets represented an opportunity to buy into the mortgage business cheaply.

Only a few saw ahead. Goldman Sachs got short subprime exposure and partially insured itself with credit default swaps with AIG. Household Finance quit making subprime loans. JP Morgan cut back on subprime loans and quit buying brokered loans. Several small hedge funds made big bets against the subprime market. Gold rose to $800.

4

The Crisis – 2008

Hello, I'm from the government and I'm here to help you.
A saying that used to be accompanied by laughter

4.1 The First Half of 2008

Housing problems escalated in the first half of 2008. The decline in prices that began in 2007 accelerated to over 5% nationally in mid-2008 (Chart 4.1). Housing prices in the exuberant markets of Los Angeles, Las Vegas, Miami, and Phoenix dropped 20–30% (Chart 4.2). The ABX AAA 2006–2 index (for subprime mortgages originated in the first half of 2006) was down 20% and ABX AAA 2007–2 (mortgages originated in the first half of 2007) was down 60% (Chart 4.3). Default rates on subprime mortgages originated in 2006 soared to 35% after just two years and to 11% on prime mortgages.

Lack of discipline in nonconforming mortgage originations was coming home to roost. Loan-to-value ratios at origination had risen to 100% for subprime borrowers in 2005–07 and 95% for Alt-A borrowers. Borrowers for over 1/3 of all subprime loans and 80% of all Alt-A loans didn't provide proof of income or financial assets.[1] The scale was huge. $1.6 trillion of nonconforming residential mortgages were originated in each of 2005 and 2006.[2]

All indications were that the consumer (70% of the economy) was in trouble. Fifty-seven percent of subprime borrowers in California/Florida/Arizona/Nevada had negative equity in their homes. Alt-A borrowers in the same states, many of whom had bought homes for investment purposes, had similar negative equity. Housing starts nationwide dropped to only 26% of their 2005 peak. The Consumer Confidence Index dropped

[1] Mayer (2008), chart 3 and table 2. [2] Inside Mortgage Finance (2012), volume 1, p. 17.

154

Chart 4.1

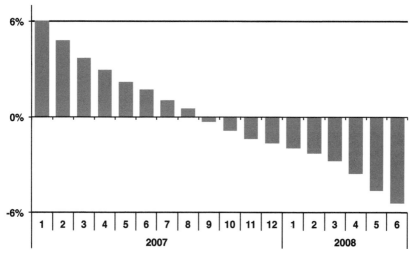

Source: Shiller (home page).

Chart 4.2

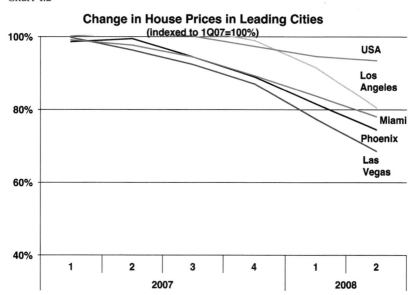

Source: FHFA (house price index datasets).

Chart 4.3

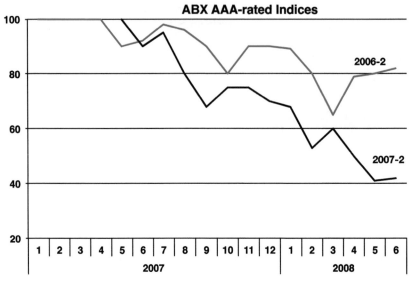

Source: Stanton (2008, 2011).

from 95 to 56 – a level not seen since the 1970s. Retail sales growth approached zero for the first time since 1990.

Faced with consumer credit deterioration on many fronts, Moody's downgraded 13,000 RMBS tranches in the 2nd quarter of 2008, more than doubling all of the previous downgrades (Chart 4.4). Suddenly market prices for A-rated RMBS became vitally important as Aaa ratings turned into A ratings. Even the prices for the earlier 2006–1 and 2006–2 A-rated cohorts were down below $25 (Chart 4.5). New issues of private RMBS and CDOs that incorporated them disappeared.

Commercial real estate prices told a mixed story as the prices for apartment buildings dropped 20% in sympathy with housing and prices for office buildings briefly dropped similarly. Retail property prices were remarkable, edging to a new record despite the obvious consumer problems and the Amazon juggernaut (Chart 4.6). But the general interruption was ominous after almost a decade of high gains. Eighty percent of banks were tightening their standards for commercial real estate loans (Chart 4.7).

The market value of credit default swaps (heavily made on private RMBS) continued to escalate to over $3 trillion by June (Chart 4.8), shrinking the leverage from sixty times to sixteen (Chart 4.9) and increasing collateral requirements dramatically.

Chart 4.4

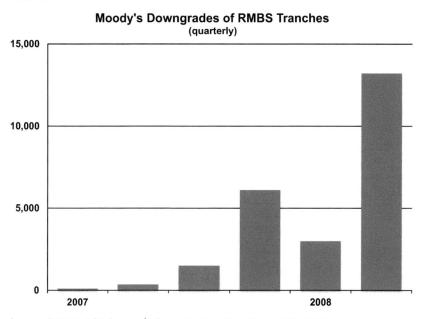

Source: SIFMA, ESF Quarterly Securitisation Data Report Q2: 2009.

Chart 4.5

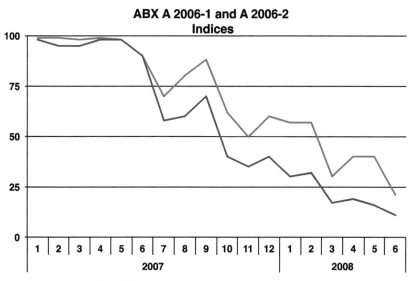

Sources: Stanton (2008, 2011).

Chart 4.6

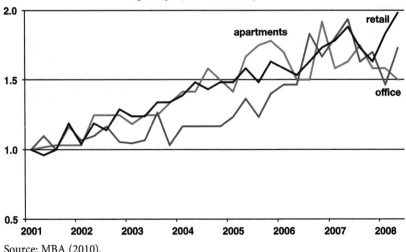

Commercial Real Estate Prices
(per sq. ft., 1Q 2001 = 1.0)

Source: MBA (2010).

Chart 4.7

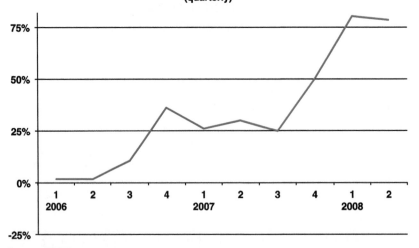

**Banks Tightening Terms for
Commercial Real Estate Loans**
(quarterly)

Source: FRED.

Chart 4.8

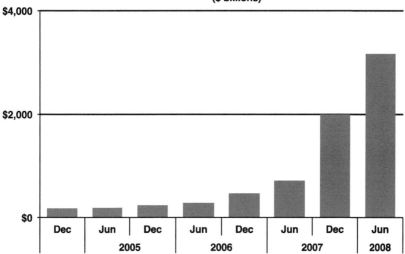

Source: BIS (derivatives).

Chart 4.9

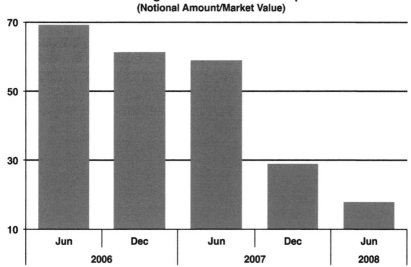

Source: BIS (derivatives); author's calculations.

Chart 4.10

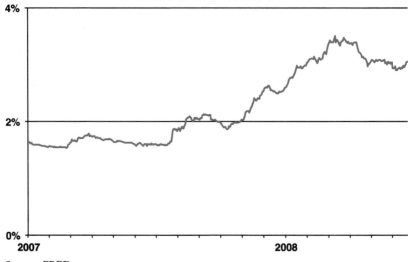

**Moody's Baa Spread
off 10-year US Treasuries**

Source: FRED.

Baa corporate bond spreads rose from under 2% to almost 3½% (Chart 4.10) and high yield bond spreads doubled to 8% (Chart 4.11), flashing traditional signs of credit market troubles.

Credit concerns remained intensive in the asset-backed commercial paper (ABCP) market. The main decline in ABCP was in 2007, but it continued to decline through mid-2008 (Chart 4.12). ABCP was unsalable for the weaker structures that relied on the market value of their assets for their creditworthiness rather than regular cash flows.

The belief in containment began to waiver as a number of serious financial problems arose. In February, Westdeutsche Landesbank failed because of investments in US private RMBS, but the German government bailed it out. AIG's bond ratings were cut to Aa/AA with a "negative" outlook in February after disclosing an $11 billion 4th quarter write-off on its credit default swaps and a citation from its accountants that it had ". . . a material weakness in internal control over financial reporting and over-sight relating to the AIGFP (AIG Financial Products in London) subsidiary's valuation of its super senior credit default swap portfolio . . .."[3] UBS, an important US market participant after its acquisition of Paine Webber,

---

[3] AIG 2007 10-K, pp. 19, 122.

Chart 4.11

Source: FRED.

Chart 4.12

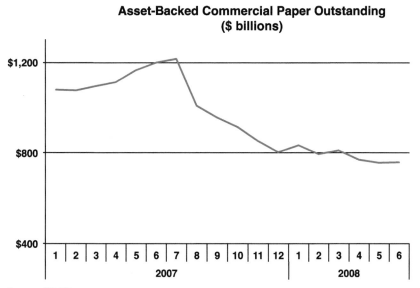

Source: FRED.

Chart 4.13

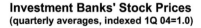

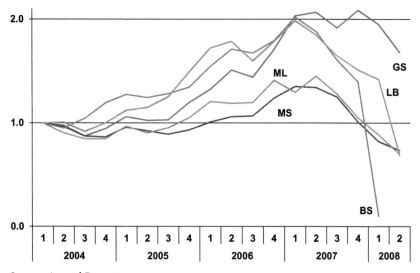

Source: Annual Reports.

Dillon Read, and Warburg Pincus, reported an $11 billion loss for the 4th quarter of 2007. In March, Bear Stearns collapsed and was taken over by JP Morgan with the Federal Reserve Bank of New York guaranteeing $30 billion of Bear Stearns' weakest mortgage assets. JP Morgan paid just 6% of Bear Stearns' peak stock price in 2007. Other financial firms were building up startling losses in the first half as AIG lost $19 billion pre-tax, Citigroup lost $14 billion, Wachovia $11 billion, and Merrill Lynch $11 billion. Lehman Brothers had a second quarter loss of $4 billion.

Investment banking stocks (with the exception of Goldman Sachs) converged on just one-third of their 2007 peaks (Chart 4.13), as did Citigroup, Wachovia, and AIG.

Fannie Mae lost $5.1 billion pre-tax in the 1st quarter of 2008 and $2.7 billion in the 2nd as it boosted its loan loss estimates to almost $9 billion. It cut its dividend 90% and its stock dropped from a high of $70 in 2007 to $19. Analysts and financial newspapers began to report that Fannie Mae and Freddie Mac might fail. Fannie Mae had $3 trillion in combined mortgage guarantees and debt but only $20 billion in common equity against losses that were accumulating at $15 billion a year. Freddie Mac's condition was similar. In response, Congress in July passed the

Housing and Economic Recovery Act (HERA) that authorized the US Treasury to inject capital into the two companies if necessary.

Congress handed off substantial executive power in HERA. The bill dealt with everything from establishing a new oversight agency for Fannie Mae and Freddie Mac to affordable housing and Hawaiian homelands; but vital wording in Section 117 provided that in an emergency situation the funds necessary to bail out Fannie Mae and Freddie Mac were deemed appropriated (in red below – author's addition) so that the Treasury did not have to come back to Congress for approval:

(3) FUNDING. For the purpose of the authorities granted in this subsection, the Secretary of the Treasury may use the proceeds of the sale of any securities issued under chapter 31 of Title 31, and the purposes for which securities may be issued under chapter 31 of Title 31 are extended to include such purchases and the exercise of any rights in connection with such purchases. Any funds expended for the purchase of, or modifications to, obligations and securities, or the exercise of any rights received in connection with such purchases under this subsection shall be deemed appropriated at the time of such purchase, modification, or exercise.[4]

Hank Paulson would use this power shortly.

The auto industry was also in distress. US vehicle sales were down almost 10% in 2007 and 24% by mid-2008. General Motors, Ford, and Chrysler were plagued by design problems, high labor costs, and a persistent loss in market share. They had eliminated their dividends and their unsecured debt ratings were down to Caa1/B (GM) and Caa1/B1 (Ford). GM had been dismembering itself, spinning-off Delphi, its parts division, in 1999, selling 51% of GMAC in 2006, and selling its Allison Transmission division in 2007. Ford sold Jaguar, Land Rover, and Volvo. Daimler Chrysler sold 80% of Chrysler to Cerberus Capital in 2007.

GM's cumulative pre-tax losses were $12 billion in 2006–07 (excluding a 3Q 2007 charge of $39 billion to write off deferred tax assets) despite its leading 23% US market share. It had a loss on continuing operations of $3 billion in the first quarter of 2008 and $15 billion in the second. GM's 2007 debt of $44 billion (excluding GMAC's debt) was built on a negative net worth of $37 billion. GMAC, its finance subsidiary, had an ill-timed investment of $168 billion in residential mortgages.[5]

Ford lost $15 billion in 2006–07 and had a $9 billion loss in the 2nd quarter of 2008. It gave up second place in the US auto market to Toyota.

---

[4] Public Law 110–289 – 110th Congress, July 30, 2008/H.R. 3221, "Housing and Economic Recovery Act of 2008," 42 USC 4501 note.

[5] General Motors 2008 10-K, pp. 6, 55, 245, note 9 on p. II-85.

Its debt of $170 billion (including Ford Motor Credit) compared with equity of just $3.6 billion, but at least it still had $29 billion of cash.[6]

Nonetheless, there was still indecision among federal authorities. The Federal Reserve's Open Market Committee was still projecting slow growth for the balance of the year and "... a gradual strengthening of economic growth over coming quarters ...."[7] The Bureau of Economic Research's advance estimate of 2nd quarter GDP growth was +1.9%. The Blue Chip Economic Consensus in July was for slight growth in the rest of 2008 and a pickup in 2009. The Federal Reserve's own econometric models projected similar results.[8] The mid-year outlook at the Securities Industry and Financial Markets Association (SIFMA) Economic Advisory Roundtable was for anemic GDP growth for the balance of the year and 1.9% growth in 2009.[9] Electricity production hit repeated records through July. Oil prices were particularly strong as they hit $145 in July. The dollar was stable. Manufacturers' new orders were growing 4–5%, particularly for oil and gas machinery. There was still 6% growth in nonresidential fixed investment. Orders for computers and other electronic equipment were still growing 10–15%. Corporate R&D spending was a record. Truck tonnage was back up to record levels after a dip in 2007. Monthly jobless claims only rose from 349,250 in December 2007 to 372,750 in June 2008.

The broad financial markets also indicated that things would be okay after Bear Stearns was rescued. The S&P 500, after dropping 11% in the 1st quarter, recovered 7% by May. Analysts' as late as June were forecasting a new peak in earnings in 2009 for the S&P 500. Stock market volatility came down from 32 early in the year to 16 in May. Merger and acquisition volume was back near the record levels in 2007 despite the decline in highly leveraged transactions to insignificance (Chart 4.14).

Traditional stress indicators, such as Baa and high yield corporate bond spreads came down slightly in mid-summer. ABCP rates came down sharply from 5% to 2½% and could even be seen as a flight to quality. Credit default spreads for major bank holding companies had risen during the Bear Stearns crisis but were trending back down. Gold prices came down 10%.

The Federal Reserve lowered the federal funds rate 225 basis points in the first half of 2008 (Chart 4.15). In response to the Bear Stearns collapse, it worked to make dealer borrowing easier. It initiated the Primary Dealer

[6] Ford Motor Company 2007 10-K, p. FS-4; 2Q 2008 10-Q, pp. 2, 4–5.
[7] Federal Reserve Annual Report 2008, "Monetary Policy Report of July 2008," part 1.
[8] Federal Reserve Bank of New York, "Liberty Street Economics," "Forecasting the Great Recession: DSGE vs Blue Chip," April 16, 2012.
[9] SIFMA, "US Economic Outlook Mid-Year 2008."

Chart 4.14

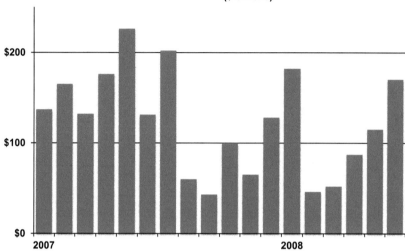

U.S. Merger & Acquisition Volume
(\$ billions)

Source: Dealogic.

Chart 4.15

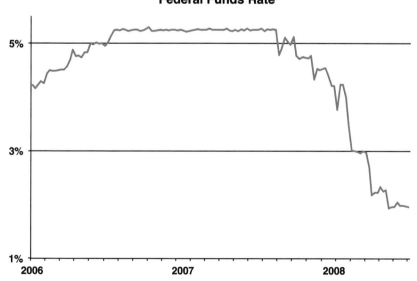

Federal Funds Rate

Source: FRED.

Chart 4.16

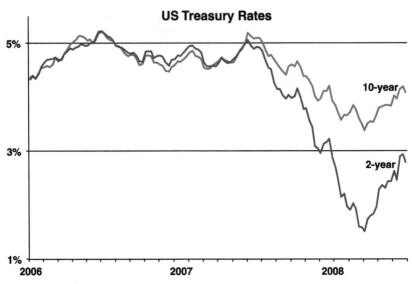

Source: Federal Reserve.

Credit Facility against asset-backed securities. It expanded its Term Securities Lending whereby it lent out US treasuries (to be further repledged by the borrower) against investment grade collateral. And it set up its Term Auction Facilities for multi-month loans. But these facilities were directed at financial market liquidity rather than the economy. The FOMC still expected the economy to resume growth in the second half of 2008 and fully in 2009.

Contrary to the decline in the federal funds rate, the Federal Reserve did nothing to try to stem a rise in 2- and 10-year treasury rates by 75–100 basis points as events built toward the crisis (Chart 4.16). Federal Reserve assets through April grew at the slowest rate in the last five years (Chart 4.17). There was no effort to control money supply growth as M1 money supply and M2 followed divergent courses throughout 2007 and early 2008 (Chart 4.18), but M1 and M2 did rise in the 2nd quarter as if in accord with an easing policy.

But the Federal Reserve was operating with unreliable data that left it well behind events. GDP growth estimates became volatile in 2007–08 as can be seen in Chart 4.19. In the 3rd quarter of 2007 the initial estimates were high by 2 percentage points, in the 1st quarter of 2008 by 4 percentage points, and in the 3rd quarter of 2008 by almost 4 percentage points. In GDP terms these misestimates were horrendous. Members of the Fed's Open Market Committee were also still concerned about inflation, especially with oil at $140, and because the CPI had been over 4% for eight

Chart 4.17

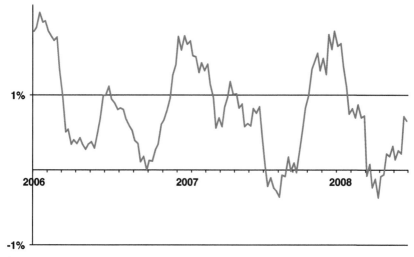

Growth in Federal Reserve Assets
(year on year quarterly average)

Source: FRED.

Chart 4.18

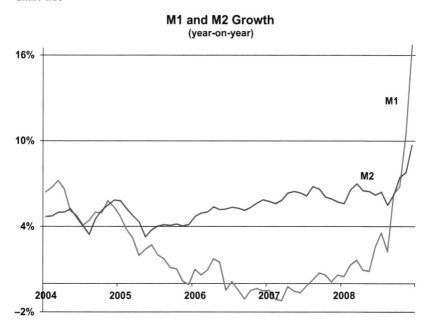

M1 and M2 Growth
(year-on-year)

Source: FRED.

Chart 4.19

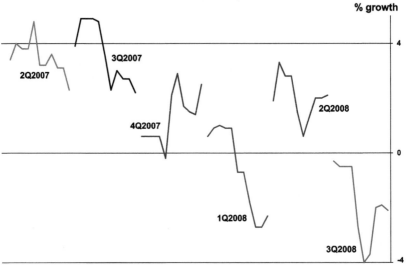

Revisions to 2007 and 2008 GDP Growth Estimates
(annual % rates)
(each data point represents a subsequent quarter)

Source: BEA (Vintage History).

months.[10] In July, it hit 5½%, although ex-food and energy it was stable around 2½%.

The one fiscal policy step in the first half of 2008 was in January/ February, before the Bear Stearns failure, when Congress passed the Economic Stimulus Act of 2008 – a temporary tax cut that mailed out checks of $300 ($600 for couples) to low- and middle-income taxpayers. The Act also allowed businesses to immediately expense 50% of equipment expenditures. The measure's cost of $113 billion was 0.8% of GDP but the effects were minimal because of the subsequent crisis.

4.2 The Crisis – Phase 1

Crises began to cascade in the second half of 2008. At the end of June, Senator Charles Schumer (NY), Chairman of the Joint Economic Committee, publicly criticized IndyMac, an aggressive California savings and loan that was the ninth largest mortgage originator in the nation and

---

[10] Federal Reserve, Annual Report 2008, "Part 3 Monetary Policy Over the First Half of 2008," pp. 88–92.

a leader in "no-docs," Alt-A, and Option ARMs mortgages. It quickly lost 8% of its deposits. It also announced that it had received notice from the Federal Deposit Insurance Corporation (the FDIC) that it was no longer "adequately capitalized." On July 11, the FDIC put it into conservatorship.

The ratings agencies lowered AIG's ratings in mid-2008 to Aa3/AA- in anticipation of AIG's pre-tax loss of $20 billion for the first half of 2008. It had received $16 billion in collateral calls on its credit default swaps on as of June 30, and it reported that if its ratings dropped to A2/A demands would be for $15 billion more. Its stock, which was $70 in mid-2007, was down to $26 at the end of June. Its CEO was forced out and succeeded by Robert Willumstad, a seasoned Citigroup executive. He immediately began alerting the New York Federal Reserve that the company was in crisis.[11]

In August, Hank Paulson began building support for a federal takeover of Fannie Mae and Freddie Mac. A Morgan Stanley team under Co-President Robert Scully was brought in to examine all the mortgages that FNMA and FHLMC had guaranteed. The two companies probably thought they had protected their independence in the July enactment of the Housing and Economic Recovery Act since injecting capital into them required their consent and the preservation of their "... status as a private shareholder-owned company ...," but they hadn't reckoned on Hank Paulson "persuading" the Federal Housing Finance Agency that Fannie and Freddie were insolvent.[12]

Paulson and the Federal Reserve were pressing Lehman Brothers at the same time to raise $15 billion after reporting a $2.8 billion 2nd quarter loss.[13] The firm spent the summer shopping for new capital even as its stock dropped from $45 in May to only $15 in August.

When the crisis came it appeared endless. Basis Yield Fund in Australia had to liquidate. First Magnus Alt-A, a $17 billion RMBS fund, collapsed overnight. Cheyne Capital, a $7 billion SIV, breached its covenants and began winding down. Citigroup had to absorb $58 billion of SIVs that couldn't find funding.[14] The media was widely discussing whether Fannie Mae and Freddie Mac were insolvent. Although nominally involved in conforming mortgages, Fannie Mae and Freddie Mac held subprime and Alt-A mortgages over thirty times their common equity. Their recently issued preferred stocks had dropped from $25 to $10 and Fannie Mae's common stock (and Freddie Mac's similarly) had dropped from $70 in 2007

---

[11] AIG 2Q 2008 10-Q, p. 101; Geithner (2014), p. 184; McDonald (2015), p. 91.
[12] Paulson (2010), pp. 161–70.   [13] Bernanke (2015), p. 253.
[14] McLean (2010), pp. 301–5.

Table 4.1

FINANCIAL STOCKS IN THE CRISIS			
	2007 high	2008 low	decline
AIG	$73	$1	−98%
Wachovia	53	2	−97%
Lehman Bros	86	5	−94%
Citigroup	55	4	−93%
Morgan Stanley	91	7	−93%
Merrill Lynch	98	17	−83%
Goldman Sachs	251	47	−81%
Bank of America	54	11	−79%
JP Morgan	53	20	−63%
Wells Fargo	38	20	−48%

Source: Annual Reports.

to as low as $5 in August. Hank Paulson put Fannie Mae and Freddie Mac into federal conservatorship on the Labor Day weekend of September 5–7 (to the agencies' surprise) on the grounds that they were insolvent.

Other financial stocks plunged to levels that seemed inconceivable (Table 4.1). AIG dropped 98% from its 2007 high, Wachovia 97%, Lehman Brothers 94%, and Citigroup and Morgan Stanley 93%. Wells Fargo stood out because its stock only dropped 48%.

On the heels of the nationalization of Fannie Mae and Freddie Mac, Hank Paulson became adamant that there would be no further federal assistance to the financial community. This was vital to Lehman Brothers that had struggled all summer to find a rescuer. Just after Labor Day, it announced write-offs of $8 billion and a $6 billion pre-tax quarterly loss. Gregory Zuckerman in his book, *The Greatest Trade Ever,* declared that "... so many hedge funds pulled money from their accounts at Lehman that the firm couldn't properly process the requests ...."[15] Lehman

[15] Zuckerman (2009), p. 259.

Brothers proposed to spin off its commercial real estate business (and thereby avoid mark-to-market accounting) and to sell its Neuberger Berman investment advisory business; but this was too little too late. Lehman Brothers held $85 billion of suspect real estate, high yield debt, and highly leveraged acquisition loans versus its tangible common equity of $15 billion.[16] Its stock had fallen from over $80 in 2007 to $5. On September 9, Korea Development Bank revealed it would not invest in Lehman after its regulator protested. The next weekend, a large group of Wall Street firms agreed to take on $40 billion of Lehman Brothers' weakest assets to facilitate its acquisition by Barclays Bank, but the Bank of England blocked the deal when it wouldn't allow it to go through without a shareholders' meeting. On Monday, September 15 Lehman Brothers was forced to file for bankruptcy.[17]

At the same time, under heavy prodding from Hank Paulson, Bank of America took over Merrill Lynch. Losses on its CDOs and other related private RMBS assets had destroyed its access to funding. It had sold $30 billion of CDOs for $6.7 billion at the end of July and $2.5 billion of Alt-A-backed RMBS at 40 cents on the dollar on September 12.[18]

AIG was downgraded again by the rating agencies and needed $85 billion the next day for collateral calls, commercial paper it could not roll over, and other cash shortfalls.[19] Its stock dropped to less than $5. AIG's probable failure on top of Lehman Brothers' changed the thinking of both Hank Paulson and Tim Geithner, President of The Federal Reserve Bank of New York. The New York Federal Reserve lent AIG $85 billion to avoid bankruptcy in what was to become the most controversial of all the authorities' remediation efforts aimed at restoring financial firms' credit. Geithner only went forward after Paulson promised to seek legislation that would protect the Federal Reserve against out-sized losses (it turned out to be Troubled Asset Relief Program [TARP]).[20]

On Tuesday, September 16, The Reserve Primary Fund, a prominent money market fund with $62 billion in assets, announced that it could not redeem investors at par because it held almost $800 million of Lehman Brothers' commercial paper. Redemption requests had reached $40 billion.

---

[16] Lehman Brothers Press Release, Sept 10, 2008. $85 billion assumes Lehman still held the $24 billion of highly leveraged corporate debt that was on its May 2008 balance sheet. This was not addressed in the press release.
[17] See Chapter 5 for the issue of whether Lehman Brothers should have been "saved."
[18] Farrell (2010), pp. 216–18, 257.
[19] Paulson (2010), p. 229; AIG 3Q–10Q 2008, pp. 49–52.
[20] Paulson (2010), p. 229; Geithner (2014), p. 193.

State Street Bank and Trust had stopped funding redemption requests for the fund the day before and suspended its overdraft privileges. The fund had doubled in size since January 1 and held a lot of ABCP, having begun to invest in it during 2007 because of competitive pressures. Management had tried to sell the fund without success earlier in the year.[21] In response to its collapse, the Treasury moved further away from its refusal to assist Wall Street and guaranteed all money market funds (except The Reserve Primary Fund) with the unconventional technique of using the Exchange Stabilization Fund.[22]

At this point in the crisis, the stretch for yield came home to roost in the repo markets as overnight financing on weaker assets contracted. The dealer market where much of the collateral is not eligible for discount at the Federal Reserve contracted sharply. Large state and local pension funds and insurance companies that had been lending out their securities resisted reinvesting except against treasuries. Margin requirements ("haircuts") on high-grade corporate bonds rose from 5% to 15% and on conforming RMBS (i.e. guaranteed by Fannie Mae or Freddie Mac) from 17% to 33%. Gorton (2010–2) published the "Haircut index" below rising to 45% for a variety of securitized products (Chart 4.20). Repo lending disappeared for subprime RMBS, subprime ABS, CDOs, CLOs, and CMBS that were not rated AA or AAA (and few were) that were included in the Gorton index.[23]

This index understates the contraction in repo lending because it does not capture the comprehensive downgrades to A and BBB ratings that most securitized products experienced, nor does it include the multitude of riskier assets that had come to dominate investment banks' balance sheets such as high yield bonds, highly leveraged corporate loans, commercial real estate mortgages, real estate whole loans, RMBS and CMBS residuals, and private equity and hedge fund participations. The problem in these markets was not excessive selling but rather that markets disappeared, a complaint that had already been heard from suffering bond funds, AIG, Citigroup, and Lehman Brothers.

The $2.5 trillion tri-party repo market that mostly involves collateral eligible for discount at the Federal Reserve only contracted slightly and margin requirements on collateral only rose slightly, in part because the Federal Reserve expanded the eligible collateral under the Primary Dealer

---

[21] Complaint no. 08-CV-08060-PGG, 1/05/2010, SOUTHERN DISTRICT OF NEW YORK. Also, SEC Plaintiff, Case 1:09-md-02011-PGG, filed 11/25/09 and The Wall Street Journal, 10/12/2012.

[22] Robert Rubin previously used it in 1994 to assist Mexico in a currency crisis.

[23] Gorton (2010–1), Chart 2, and Gorton (2010–2), p. 20, Chart 4, and Table II.

Chart 4.20

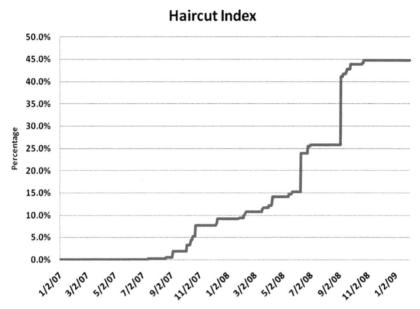

Haircut Index

Source: Gorton (2010–2).

Credit Facility to include any collateral acceptable in the tri-party repo market.

Lehman Brothers was especially exposed to the dealer repo market because of $85 billion it had accumulated in commercial real estate, highly leveraged corporate debt, whole mortgages, private RMBS and CMBS residuals, and mortgage servicing rights.[24] JP Morgan demanded $10 billion additional collateral from Lehman Brothers as intraday margin (protection for JP Morgan's clearing function for repo borrowings) just before Lehman Brothers failed – a huge demand versus its tangible common equity of only $15 billion.[25]

Lehman Brothers was not alone. Clients pulled $32 billion out of Morgan Stanley in one day, September 18, and its liquidity pool shrank from $130 billion to $50 billion that week. Goldman Sachs's liquidity pool shrank $60 billion. Much of this was hedge funds moving money in their accounts to safer venues. The Federal Reserve responded by allowing both

[24] This number could be over $125 billion based on residential $25, commercial $29, other $6, real estate owned $10, lending including undrawn $39, and one-third of $50 level 2 and 3 corporate debt. See 2Q 2008–1Q.

[25] Zuckerman (2009), p. 259.

firms to become bank holding companies on condition that they raise emergency equity capital.[26] Goldman Sachs raised $10 billion from a combination of Warren Buffet and a simultaneous public offering while Morgan Stanley raised $9 billion from Mitsubishi Financial.

The two firms' transition to bank holding companies was both more complicated and more advantageous than appeared on the surface, per the following from Morgan Stanley's 2008 Annual Report:

On September 23, 2008, the Office of the Comptroller of the Currency (the OCC) authorized Morgan Stanley Bank to commence business as a national bank, operating as Morgan Stanley Bank, N.A. Concurrent with this conversion, the Company became a financial holding company under the Bank Holding Company Act of 1956, as amended (the BHC Act). As a result of becoming a financial holding company, the Company gained additional access to various government lending programs and facilities including the Commercial Paper Funding Facility (CPFF), the Temporary Liquidity Guarantee Program (TLGP), the Term Securities Lending Facility (TSLF) and the Primary Dealer Credit Facility (PDCF).[27]

Economists have interpreted the squeeze in the repo markets as a bank run following Lehman Brothers' bankruptcy, but the tri-party repo market actually benefited from a flight to quality because of the preponderance of collateral eligible for discount at the Federal Reserve. Tri-party collateral not eligible for Federal Reserve discounting only dropped from $700B to $500B by September 30, mostly due to Lehman Brothers' and AIG's absence. Ineligible collateral dropped further after Citigroup's rescue at the end of November, falling to $150 billion at year-end.[28] The role ascribed to the repo markets in the crisis appears exaggerated as the four leading investment banks had only $1.2 trillion in financial instruments in mid-2008 (Table 4.2) and long-term debt equal to 50% of that. Gorton (2010–2) estimated they only financed $600 billion of their own assets in the repo markets versus a total market of $10 trillion.[29] It appears that the large institutional investors had the largest reduction in repo loans, and they were neither leveraged nor banks.

Washington Mutual Bank's (WAMU) collapse quickly followed that of Lehman Brothers. It experienced a rapid run on its deposits because of a ratings downgrade and its concentration in subprime and option-ARM lending. On September 25, the Office of Thrift Supervision and the FDIC stripped the holding company of its subsidiary bank and sold it to JP Morgan for $2 billion, leaving the parent to file for bankruptcy the next day. WAMU was the sixth largest bank in the country and the largest

---

[26] Geithner (2014), pp. 198–9, 203–5.   [27] Morgan Stanley 2008 Annual Report, p. 113.
[28] Copeland (2010), chart 6.   [29] Gorton (2010–2), p. 12 and table 1.

Table 4.2

INVESTMENT BANKS' FINANCIAL INSTRUMENTS IN 2Q 2008	
	($ billions)
Goldman Sachs	291
Lehman Brothers	222
Merrill Lynch*	340
Morgan Stanley	303
Total	1,156
* year-end 2007	

*year-end 2007.
Note: excludes derivate assets.
Sources: Annual 10-Ks.

bank failure in history. The holding company's stock and bond obligations became valueless, creating doubts about the viability of all bank holding companies.

On September 29, the FDIC announced that it was helping Citigroup take over troubled Wachovia Corp., the sixth largest bank holding company. Wachovia had plunged deeply into subprime lending when it acquired Golden West Financial in 2006 and had also leveraged itself for other diversification efforts. Controversially, Wells Fargo interceded and took over Wachovia without government help, raising $12 billion of new equity to do it.

The cascading failures created an intense focus on counterparty risks throughout the system that is not widely appreciated. Banks routinely have credit limits on counterparties in derivatives contracts, trading commitments, brokerage transactions, foreign exchange dealings, and similar business commitments. However, counterparty considerations attract much less attention than loan portfolios, and rarely show up in financial reports or enter into outside credit evaluations of banks. Transactions normally operate routinely in the context of trading or transferring

Table 4.3

LEADING TRADING FIRMS' COUNTERPARTY RISK			
($ billions)			
	Receivables	Tangible equity	Receivables % tangible equity
	2008	2007	
Citigroup	189	50	378%
Goldman Sachs	214	32	669%
Lehman Brothers	75	16	469%
Merrill Lynch	139	14	993%
JP Morgan	321	63	510%
Morgan Stanley	138	25	552%

Source: Company 10-Ks.

money. This changed, however when the creditworthiness of banks and their nonbank counterparties was thrown into doubt.

The leading trading banks' receivables from counterparties suddenly became a focal point. Receivables were between four to ten times the leading banks' tangible common equity, as can be seen in Table 4.3.

"Receivables" includes derivatives assets, claims on monoline insurers, and receivables from brokers and customers. It is not clear whether it includes foreign exchange contracts. It does not include intraday repo loans of as much as $700 billion on collateral not eligible for discount at the Federal Reserve that JP Morgan routinely cleared as one of two agents in the tri-party repo market or Citigroup's intraday receivables clearing foreign exchange in London. Nor does it reflect peak trading days and nontrading transactions.

Counterparty fears led to a spiral where banks cut credit limits or required more stringent collateral from counterparties who in turn had to reduce their inventories or find new capital. JP Morgan made progressively larger collateral claims on Lehman Brothers for intraday repo clearing throughout the summer, culminating in the $10 billion claim on the weekend that Lehman Brothers went bankrupt. Citigroup made a similar

Chart 4.21

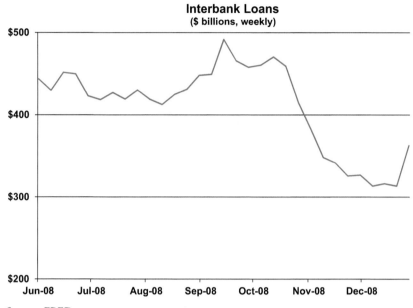

Interbank Loans
($ billions, weekly)

Source: FRED.

$5 billion claim for foreign exchange clearing. We do not know what claims were made on others. Banks had the same concerns about counterparty credit among themselves as inter-bank loans declined almost $150 billion in November when Citigroup had to be rescued (Chart 4.21). This aspect of the crisis does fit with interpretation as a bank run except it did not have to do only with banks.

The crisis forced the Federal Reserve to drop the relative passivity it had shown in the first half of 2008. Its initial actions tended toward structural remedies, beginning with the New York Federal Reserve rescuing AIG and allowing Goldman Sachs and Morgan Stanley to become bank holding companies. The Federal Reserve Board quickly broadened acceptable collateral at the discount window to any form that was acceptable to third-party repo lenders. It set up a facility to finance purchases of ABCP from money market funds. In October, it provided a $150 billion lending facility to relieve issuers of A1/P1 commercial paper as well as a facility to assist money market funds suffering redemptions.

The Federal Reserve also began a series of traditional monetary policy actions, cutting the federal funds rate from 2% to almost zero (Chart 4.22) which drove the 2-year treasury rate to under 1% (Chart 4.23).

Chart 4.22

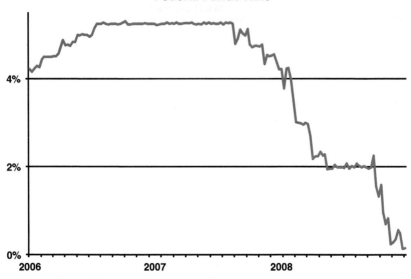

Source: FRED.

Chart 4.23

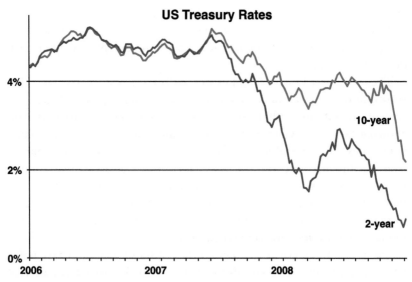

Source: Federal Reserve.

Chart 4.24

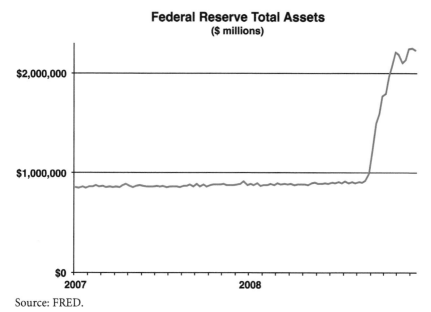

Source: FRED.

The mix of structural remedies and open market purchases expanded the Federal Reserve's balance sheet by $1.4 trillion (175%) in short order (Chart 4.24) which became known as Quantitative Easing One (QE-1). M1 money supply began to grow by over 16% and M2 growth jumped to over 10% (Chart 4.25).

The bankruptcy of Lehman Brothers has become a popular focal point in descriptions of the crisis, despite that Fannie Mae, Freddie Mac, AIG, Merrill Lynch, WAMU, Wachovia Corp. and the money market mutual fund industry needed rescuing simultaneously. Many economic indicators were sharply negative well before Lehman Brothers failed, reflecting housing prices and consumer credit and their impact on consumer confidence, housing starts, and consumer spending. Markets for housing-related securities had already dropped sharply as well as markets related to commercial real estate, highly leveraged corporate debt, and derivatives. Many of these markets had dried up and liquidity disappeared. Private A-rated RMBS, CMBS, and CDO prices were down to rock bottom. Commercial real estate prices were falling, reversing a 5-year up-trend, and bank lending for commercial real estate had tightened severely. Prices on collateralized leveraged loans that were supposed to be solid because they were senior debt and had floating rates were down to 65. The unanticipated risks in credit

Chart 4.25

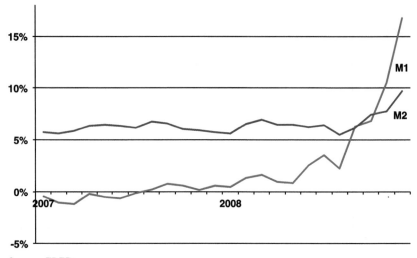

M1 and M2 Growth
(year-on-year)

Source: FRED.

default swaps had already shrunk their leverage and caused critical collateral calls at AIG, Merrill Lynch, Morgan Stanley, and UBS. The leading commercial and investment banks had also developed shocking illiquidity as we shall see in Chapter 6 and their stock prices had dropped to only 10–20% of their high prices in 2007. All of these troubles had the same causes.

Nor was the crisis resolved by the many remedial actions following Lehman Brothers' collapse – the passage of TARP, the aid to AIG and Citigroup, the guarantees of money market mutual funds and business bank accounts, the guarantees of new bank unsecured debt, making Morgan Stanley and Goldman Sachs banks, and the Federal Reserves' efforts to resolve the stress in repo markets. Six months after Lehman Brothers' failure, the crisis was still at hand. Economic and financial declines had continued for nine months as the economy nosedived, AIG, Citigroup, Merrill Lynch, and Bank of America floundered, and the world waited to see what would happen under a new president and an incensed, Democratic Congress.

I have marked the convulsive month of September in the charts in the rest of this chapter and in Chapter 5 to give the reader perspective on what surrounded these multiple failures. It will be up to econometricians to sort out the impact of earlier and later factors and the feedback effects.

4.3 The Crisis – Phase 2

The crisis continued on Monday, September 28 as only 1/3 of House Republicans and 2/3 of Democrats supported Hank Paulson's initial request to Congress for a $700 billion TARP. Two hundred and thirty economists signed a public letter opposing it. The S&P 500 and the NASDAQ Composite dropped 9%.[30] The administration was put in the unusual position of appealing to a Democratic House of Representatives to pass the bill. It only passed when the sense of emergency became so palpable that Hank Paulson publicly begged Speaker Pelosi on bended knee to pass it. It was three weeks after Lehman Brothers' failure on October 3 that President Bush signed the Emergency Economic Stabilization Act that included TARP. Even then, only $350 billion was available initially and the continuing controversy over limiting bank executives' compensation made its effectiveness uncertain.

Nor was there any assurance that $700 billion would be enough. The Federal Reserve had estimated during the summer that financial companies had written down $300 billion of assets, that $650 billion in write-downs were still to come, and possibly $1.5 trillion.[31] It was not until October 14 that Hank Paulson forced the nine largest banks to accept $125 billion in new equity from the Treasury as a stabilization move. Just as important, as part of the Emergency Economic Stabilization Act, the FDIC provided a guarantee to banks and bank holding companies (now including Goldman Sachs and Morgan Stanley) to issue new unsecured debt. The FDIC ultimately guaranteed $618 billion.[32] Making the guarantee available for bank holding companies was important to stability as aiding bank holding companies had long been controversial. In the resolution of Continental Illinois Bank & Trust in 1984, the stockholders lost everything. The same was true in the savings and loans crisis of 1990. Bear Stearns' stockholders were initially due to get only $2 per share in JP Morgan's takeover, and the stockholders in Washington Mutual's holding company lost everything in September.

In November, market problems built up into an ominous situation at Citigroup which had a $32 billion 4th quarter loss in the making. It laid off 52,000 workers worldwide. Moody's and S&P downgraded it to A2/A in mid-December. To stay afloat, it needed a second $20 billion infusion of equity from TARP plus a "ring fence" guarantee built around $300 billion of its worst assets. With Citigroup's stock down to $4, its ability to raise capital was gone. The stress the authorities were under was reflected in the

---

[30] CNN Money, "Bailout Plan Rejected – Supporters Scramble" and "Stocks Crushed," 9/29/08.
[31] Geithner (2014), p. 172.   [32] FDIC 2009 Annual Report, p. 15.

fractured nature of Citigroup's support from a combination of TARP, the FDIC, and the New York Federal Reserve.[33]

In December, the auto companies needed TARP capital to get them through the next months until the Obama administration could deal with them more thoroughly. GM and Chrysler got loans of $25 billion and a clear message that the Obama administration was going to restructure them. Ford refused the help.

At the end of 2008 just as power was being passed to the Obama administration, Bank of America sought to cancel its acquisition of Merrill Lynch on the grounds that a "material adverse change" had occurred. There was ample justification as Merrill Lynch reported a $22 billion pre-tax loss for the 4th quarter. Bank of America only agreed to go forward under intense pressure from Hank Paulson and the Federal Reserve that included the threat to remove management and the board of directors. The merger closed with an understanding that the authorities would give Bank of America capital support if needed.[34] In January, the US Treasury (the Obama administration) purchased $10 billion of Bank of America preferred stock along with 10-year warrants to purchase 49 million common shares at $31 per share. Federal authorities also ring-fenced $118 billion of Merrill Lynch assets to give Bank of America protection against "unusually large losses." This was described in Bank of America's 2008 annual report:

Also in January 2009, the US Treasury, the FDIC and the Federal Reserve agreed in principle to provide protection against the possibility of unusually large losses on an asset pool of approximately $118.0 billion of financial instruments comprised of $81.0 billion of derivative assets and $37.0 billion of other financial assets. The assets that would be protected under this agreement are expected generally to be domestic, pre-market disruption (i.e. originated prior to September 30, 2007) leveraged and commercial real estate loans, CDOs, financial guarantor counterparty exposure, certain trading counterparty exposure, and certain investment securities. These protected assets would be expected to exclude certain foreign assets and assets originated or issued on or after March 14, 2008. The majority of the protected assets were added by the Corporation as a result of its acquisition of Merrill Lynch. This guarantee is expected to be in place for 10 years for residential assets and five years for nonresidential assets unless the guarantee is terminated by the Corporation at an earlier date. It is expected that the Corporation will absorb the first $10.0 billion of losses related to the assets while any additional losses will be shared between the Corporation (10 percent) and the US government (90 percent). These assets would remain on the Corporation's balance sheet and the Corporation would continue to manage these assets in the ordinary course of business as well as retain the associated income.[35]

---

[33] Federal Reserve Annual Report 2008, p. 57; Geithner (2014), pp. 252–4.
[34] Paulson (2010), pp. 425–30.
[35] Bank of America 2008 Annual Report, note 25 – Subsequent Events, p. 190.

Chart 4.26

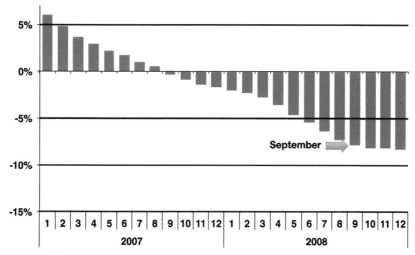

Change in Housing Prices
(year-on-year)

Source: Shiller (home page).

The economic outlook in the 4th quarter was so dire that it invariably led to comparisons with the Great Depression. House prices were down 8% nationally (Chart 4.26) and 25–35% in Phoenix, Los Angeles, Miami, and Las Vegas (Chart 4.27).[36] Moody's downgraded the ratings on 16,000 RMBS tranches in the 4th quarter (Chart 4.28). The ABX AAA index for subprime mortgages issued in the first half of 2006 (2006–2) dropped to 50, while those issued in the second half and the first half of 2007 (2007–1, 2007–2) dropped to 40 (Chart 4.29).[37] Only the ABX A-rated indices didn't fall further. They had already collapsed to between 10–20 (Chart 4.30). A-rated prices were the best indication of private RMBS values since so many issues had been downgraded.[38] These values were also indicative of the pricing for the $550 billion of CDOs outstanding since their original collateral averaged an A rating.

---

[36] Federal Housing Finance Agency, house price index datasets.
[37] Repeating an earlier footnote, each ABX index tracks bonds issued in the prior ½ year. Thus AAA 06–1 refers to bonds issued in the last half of 2005, and AAA 06–2 refers to bonds issued in the first ½ of 2006, etc.
[38] Fender (2008), table 1.

Chart 4.27

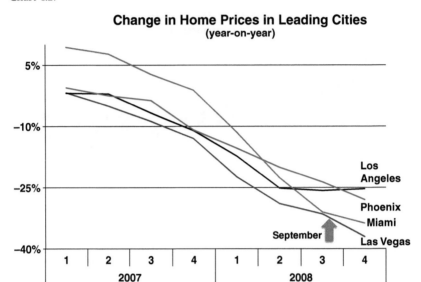

Source: FHFA (house price index datasets).

Chart 4.28

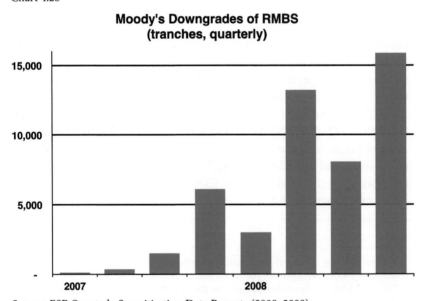

Source: ESF Quarterly Securitisation Data Reports (2008, 2009).

Chart 4.29

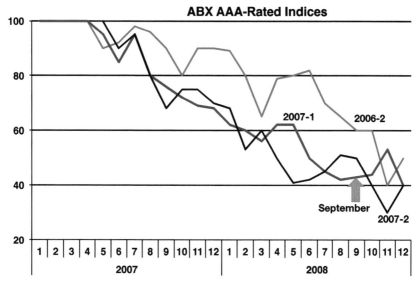

Sources: Stanton (2008, 2011).

Chart 4.30

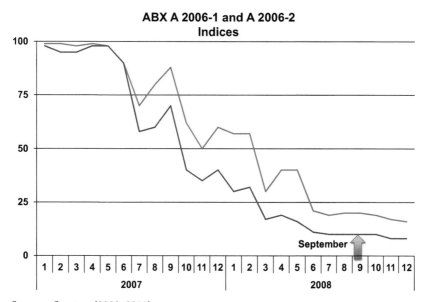

Sources: Stanton (2008, 2011).

The Crisis – 2008

Chart 4.31

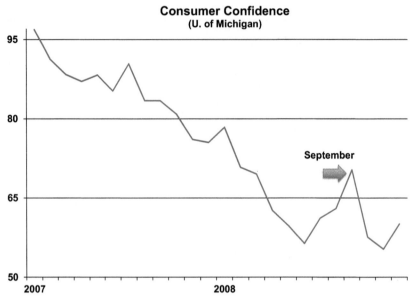

Consumer Confidence
(U. of Michigan)

Source: FRED.

Economic indicators continued to fall. Consumer confidence reversed an uptick in its 2-year decline and dropped back to its previous low of 57 (Chart 4.31). Retail sales declined 11% versus 3–4% growth earlier in the year (Chart 4.32). Vehicle sales extended a 20% drop to 35% (Chart 4.33).

Manufacturers' new orders for capital goods (excluding defense and aircraft) fell 17% in the 4th quarter (Chart 4.34); orders for computer equipment and electronics shifted from slowing growth to a sudden drop of 11% (Chart 4.35); total capital spending that had been down 6%, dropped 10% (Chart 4.36); and industrial production accelerated a drop of 8% to 12% (Chart 4.37). Oil prices dropped 30% to $100 in September, then in October began a shocking decline to $30 by the end of the year (Chart 4.38). The index of small business optimism dropped to a new low (Chart 4.39) as did small business earnings – down 40% (Chart 4.40) (this should be thought of as an index despite its title). Both had been in steep decline for two years. The importance of small business is not well recognized despite representing 50% of both GDP and job creation.[39] Real GDP shrunk at an 8% rate in the 4th quarter (Chart 4.41).

---

[39] Atkinson (2019).

Chart 4.32

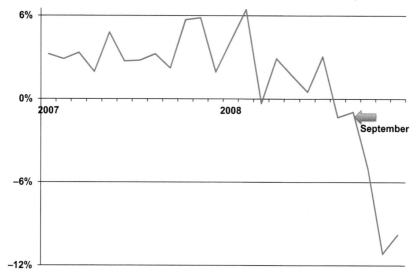

Source: Census Retail Trade Survey.

Chart 4.33

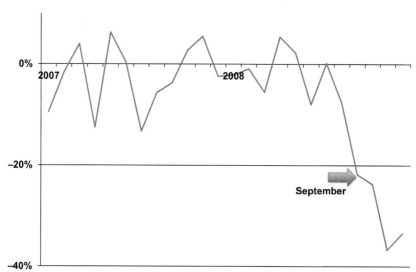

Source: FRED.

Chart 4.34

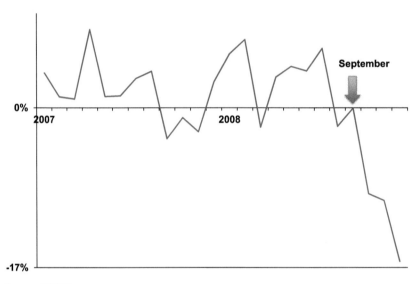

Source: FRED.

Chart 4.35

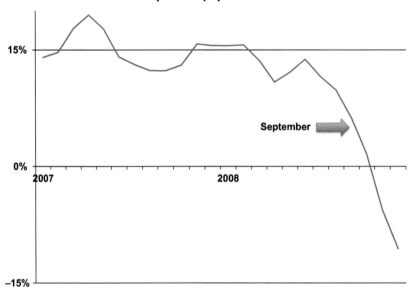

Source: FRED.

Chart 4.36

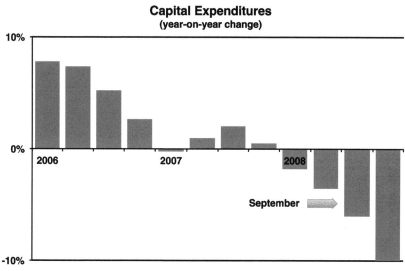

Source: FRED.

Chart 4.37

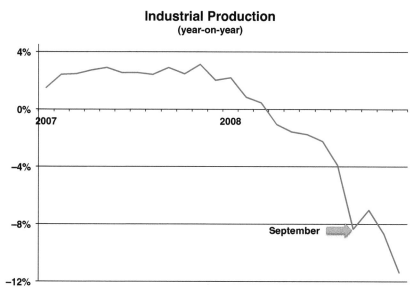

Source: FRED.

Chart 4.38

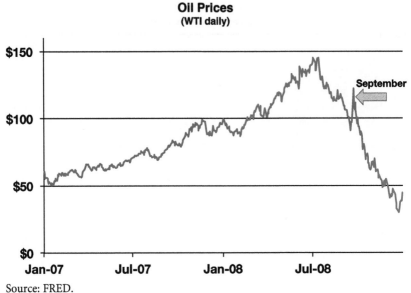

Source: FRED.

Chart 4.39

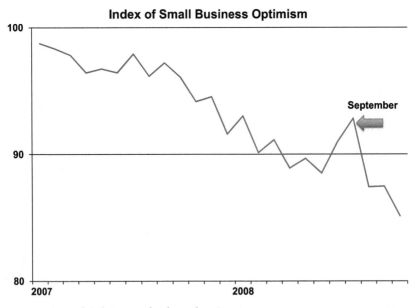

Source: National Federation of Independent Businesses.

Chart 4.40

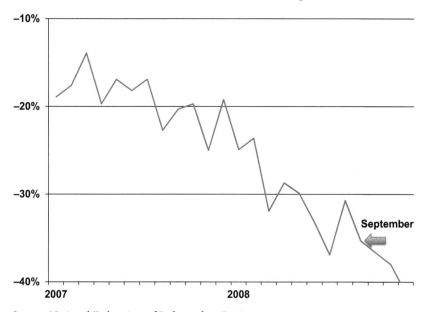

Decline in Small Business Earnings

Source: National Federation of Independent Businesses.

Chart 4.41

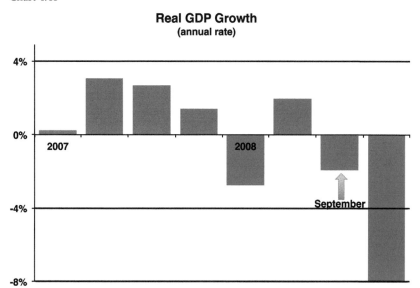

Real GDP Growth
(annual rate)

Source: FRED.

Chart 4.42

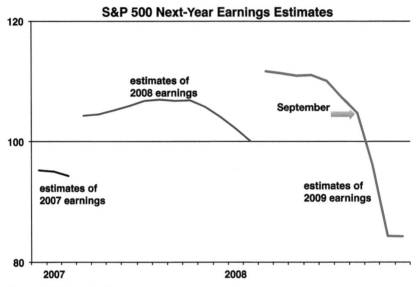

Source: Goldman Sachs.

Earnings estimates for the S&P 500 in 2009 had one of the strongest links to the convulsions of September, as estimates dropped abruptly from modest growth to down 18% (Chart 4.42). The S&P 500, already down 20% from its peak in 2007 by August, actually rose after FNMA and FHLMC were taken over, but then lost 27% in thirty days (Chart 4.43). It was down 40% briefly in mid-November when Citigroup's troubles erupted.

Volatility (the VIX index) had been high since the second half of 2007 around 25, but it soared to 70 in October and November (Chart 4.44). Weekly outflows from domestic equity mutual funds rose from $75 billion to over $150 billion in December (Chart 4.45).

Traditional bond market indicators of stress surged. The spread on Baa-rated corporate bonds rose from 3% to 6% between October and December (Chart 4.46). High yield bond spreads rose from 9% to 22% in December (Chart 4.47).[40]

Credit default markets went through a wrenching contraction. Notional amounts declined 29% to $41 trillion (Chart 4.48), but their market value rose to $5.6 trillion (Chart 4.49) which meant that the leverage on credit

---

[40] In such a chaotic market, the rates aggregated by information agents should be treated with some skepticism.

Chart 4.43

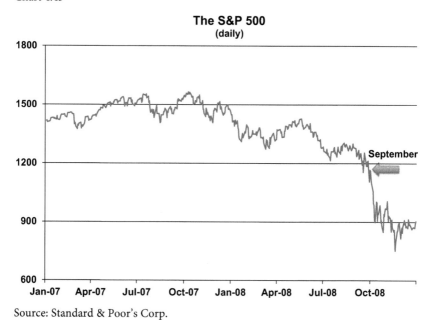

Source: Standard & Poor's Corp.

Chart 4.44

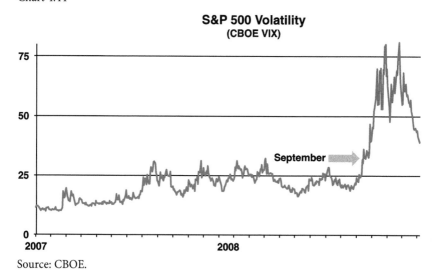

Source: CBOE.

The Crisis – 2008

Chart 4.45

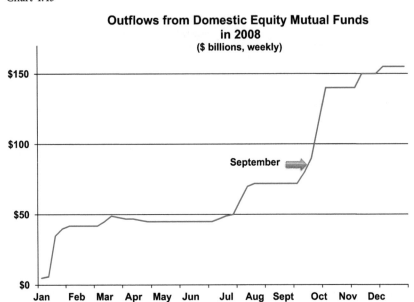

Source: Investment Company Institute.

Chart 4.46

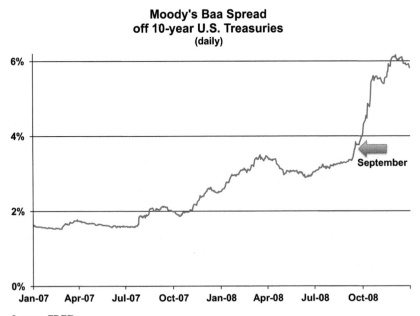

Source: FRED.

Chart 4.47

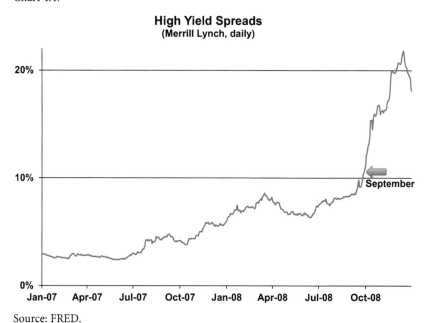

Source: FRED.

Chart 4.48

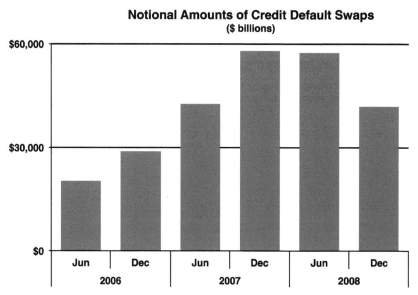

Source: BIS (derivatives).

Chart 4.49

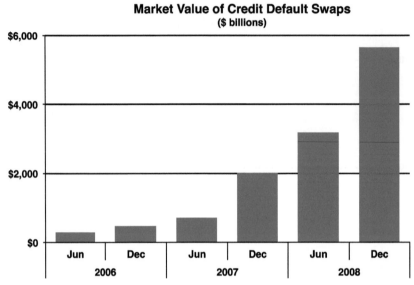

Market Value of Credit Default Swaps
($ billions)

Source: BIS (derivatives).

default swaps contracted from a high of around seventy in early-2006 to eight times at the end of 2008 (Chart 4.49). The contraction represented massive margin calls, not just for AIG. Some of the losses were in CDOs that used credit default swaps as part of the collateral, particularly at Merrill Lynch, Morgan Stanley, Citigroup, and UBS.[41] The market value of Morgan Stanley's derivatives obligations tripled.

Merger and acquisition activity disappeared except for the few banks being taken over (Chart 4.51). Highly leveraged corporate lending had declined sharply before the September convulsion (Chart 4.52) because prices for collateralized loan obligations (CLOs) were around ninety and banks and brokers had to mark these to market. In the 4th quarter, CLO prices fell to $65 (Chart 4.53). Default rates on highly leveraged corporate loans rose to 4% in the 4th quarter and the increase to 14% in the 1st quarter of 2009 was easily anticipated (Chart 4.54).

Commercial real estate developed its greatest problems since the savings and loans collapse at the end of the 1980s. REIT stocks signaled the likely future for commercial real estate prices as they dropped 45% in October–

---

[41] Zuckerman (2009), p. 212.

Chart 4.50

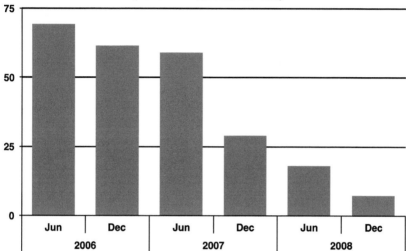

Source: BIS (derivatives).

Chart 4.51

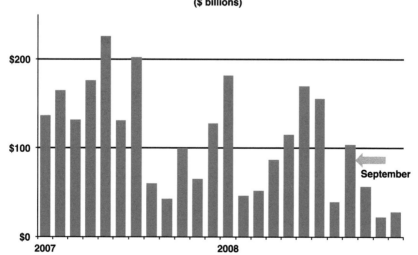

Source: Dealogic.

Chart 4.52

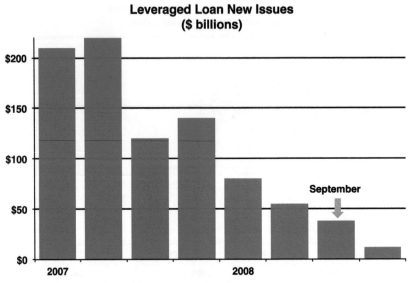

Source: European High Yield Association (2008).

Chart 4.53

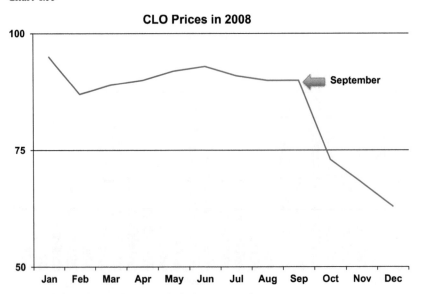

Source: SIFMA, Research Quarterly (February 2010).

Chart 4.54

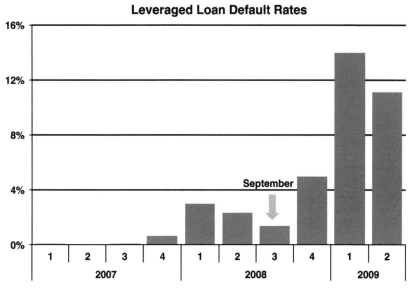

Leveraged Loan Default Rates

Source: Credit Suisse.

November, having already been down 25% from their peak (Chart 4.55). It makes sense to look at mid-2009 commercial real estate prices as a proxy for anticipated prices in 2008 because of the long lead times to sell commercial real estate. At that point, prices for apartment buildings were down 35% from their peak, office buildings 52%, and retail properties 30%, in line with earlier REIT prices (Chart 4.56). AAA-rated CMBX spreads didn't react to Septembers' convulsions, but rose to 800 basis points in November when Citigroup was in trouble (Chart 4.57). There was widespread fear of defaults on commercial real estate loans maturing in 2009–10.[42] Commercial real estate transactions in 4Q 2008 were less that 1/6th of their peak in 2007 (Chart 4.58), and markets knew they would be next to nothing in 2009 because of the long lead times.

Estimating the mark-to-market losses in commercial real estate is difficult because we don't know its scale nationally and price indices are only for properties of institutional quality. Based on Florance (2010), $9 trillion is a ballpark estimate of the value of all US commercial real estate in 2009 after $4 trillion of losses, but this includes specialty property for which institutional price indices would not apply as well as factories and older

---

[42] Longinetti (2009); Marsh (2011).

Chart 4.55

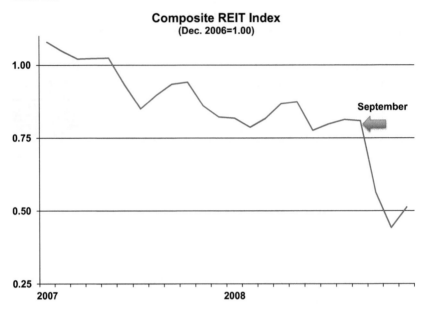

Source: NAREIT.

Chart 4.56

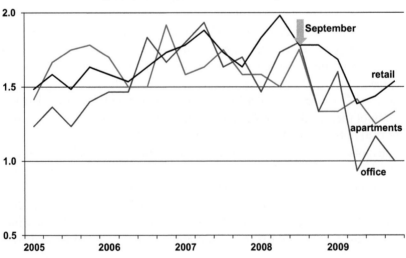

Source: MBA (2010).

Chart 4.57

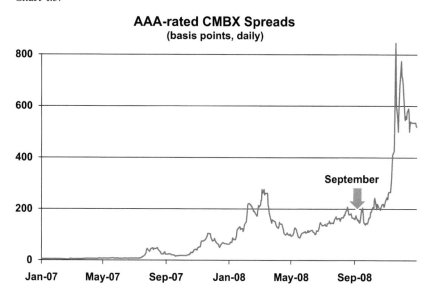

Source: Bloomberg/Goldman Sachs.

Chart 4.58

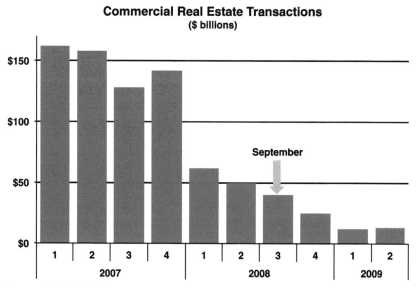

Source: NAIC (2012).

Table 4.4

COMMERCIAL MORTGAGE LOSSES IN 2008			
($ billions)			
	Outstanding	Pricing	Losses
CMBS	730	0.30	511
Mortgages	870	0.65	305
Subordinated	100	0.00	100
Totals	**1,700**		**916**

Source: Federal Reserve, mortgage debt outstanding; author's calculations.

properties that are privately owned.[43] Using some heroic assumptions, NCREIF price indices might apply to $2.5 trillion of office, retail, warehouse, hotel/resort, and apartment buildings as of 2007.[44] If equity was one-third of this value (two-thirds leverage), the average price decline of 39% in Chart 4.55 ($1 trillion) would have eliminated it on a mark-to-market basis. These losses were widely distributed among institutional investors, REITs, private owners, and foreign investors.

Mark-to-market losses on commercial real estate debt were approximately $900 billion (Table 4.4), again under heroic assumptions, assuming the $2.5 trillion of property above was leveraged with $1.7 trillion of debt (67%, composed of mortgage loans, CMBS, and subordinated debt). CMBS in Table 4.4 are priced midway between AAA-rated and A-rated prices of approximately $50 and $10, respectively. Subordinated debt equal to 12% of non-CMBS mortgages is priced at zero. "Mortgages," principally held by banks and life insurance companies, are assumed to have the same price as highly leveraged corporate loans.

We should not confuse the low losses ultimately booked on commercial mortgages by banks and insurance companies with the mark-to-market losses implied in 2008. Loans by banks and insurance companies were not

[43] Florance (2010), using CoStar data, estimated the value in mid-2009 of all commercial real estate was $9 trillion (Exhibit 3) and the loss since 2006 was $4 trillion. I have excluded specialty real estate of $2 trillion (prisons, libraries, parks, golf courses, sports facilities) and pro-rated the $4 trillion estimate of losses to get a 2007 estimate.

[44] Based on Bureau of Economic Research construction expenditures in these categories 1981–2008 adjusted each year for NCREIF price increases and prior properties equal to 40% of the total.

marked-to-market and accounting was lenient. "Extend and pretend" practices were common enough to earn that shorthand description.

Securities Prices

At the end of 2008, no matter where investors looked, the only shelter from the downdraft in securities markets was US treasuries. Even cash in banks was suspect. Declines in the S&P 500 sectors varied from 40% to 50% for Autos, Financials, Oil, Materials, and Semiconductors to under 15% throughout the consumer sector of Household Products, Pharmaceuticals, Consumer Services, Food, Beverages, and Tobacco (Table 4.5).

Losses were as great or greater in emerging markets, high yield bonds, and commodities (including oil) (Table 4.6).[45] Commodities lost 59% and emerging markets 52% versus 35% for the S&P 500. High yield bonds lost 32% through November, but recovered in December to only lose 27%. Long US treasuries, both a safe haven and a beneficiary of reduced interest rates, uniquely returned 24% by the end of the year.

Hedge funds were only down 11% because they could short stocks and many went to cash (Table 4.7). Private equity lost money throughout 2006–08 (Table 4.8), but these publicly available returns surely overstate private equity results for their active investments. The 37% decline in the S&P 500 would have eliminated investors' equity in most portfolio companies.

Private equity's troubles were reflected in the public stock prices of three of the prominent private equity firms – Blackstone Group, Apollo, and Kohlberg Kravis Roberts. Blackstone went public in 2007 and had a high price of $34, but was down to $4 in February 2009. Apollo Alternative Assets L.P. (Amsterdam) had a high price of $22 but sold as low as 75¢ in December 2008. KPE, Kohlberg Kravis's first public format, went public in 2006 at $25 but was down to $3 in December 2008. These were no more than option values on their private portfolios. The firms could report higher valuations to their investors than this implied for various reasons: 1) mark-to-market accounting accorded their companies a gain on their heavy debt loads (even though the companies had almost no cash flow to pay off their debt and would have to borrow again at the new high yield rates); 2) the sponsors could plead they had sales opportunities at higher prices; and 3) many sponsors had conserved cash that arguably could be used to buy back debt.

---

[45] MSCI-EM index, Merrill Lynch high yield index, Barclay's US long bond index, and Goldman Sachs Commodities Price Index.

Table 4.5

S&P SECTOR PERFORMANCE IN THE SECOND HALF OF 2008	
Autos	−51%
Materials	−47%
Insurance	−43%
Real estate	−42%
Diversified financials	−41%
Energy	−41%
Semiconductors	−40%
Hi-tech hardware & equipment	−35%
Capital goods	−34%
Software & services	−33%
Media	−30%
Utilities	−28%
Consumer durables	−26%
Commercial & professional services	−24%
Transportation	−24%
Heating & cooling equipment	−24%
Retailing	−21%
Banks	−20%
Telecommunications	−18%
Food & specialty retail	−14%
Food, beverages & tobacco	−11%
Consumer services	−9%
Pharmacy & biotech	−7%
Household products	−2%

Source: Standard & Poor's Corp.

Gold, which had been as high as $980 in July dropped to $790 in mid-August (Chart 4.59), offering no safe harbor at all. It must have reflected investors' liquidity pressures.

Table 4.6

RETURNS JUNE-DECEMBER 2008 (INDEXED)					
	S&P 500	MSCI-EM	Long UST	Hi yield	Comm'ties
June	0.92	0.90	1.02	0.97	1.09
July	0.91	0.87	1.02	0.96	0.96
August	0.92	0.80	1.04	0.96	0.89
September	0.84	0.66	1.05	0.88	0.78
October	0.70	0.48	1.01	0.74	0.56
November	0.65	0.44	1.14	0.68	0.48
December	0.65	0.48	1.24	0.73	0.41

Note: returns are indexed to May 2008.
Sources: Standard & Poor's Corp.; MSCI EAFE; MSCI-EM; Barclays; Bank of America ML; Goldman Sachs Commodities Index.

Table 4.7

AVERAGE RETURNS FOR BROAD EQUITY HEDGE FUNDS 2006–2008				
	Funds	Indexed	S&P 500	Indexed
2006	12%	1.12	16%	1.16
2007	14%	1.28	6%	1.23
2008	−11%	1.14	−37%	0.77

Source: Cambridge Associates (2006, 2011).

Financial Sector Losses

Financial markets foresaw shocking losses for AIG and the largest commercial and investment banks in the 4th quarter of 2008. AIG, Citigroup, and Merrill Lynch continued their succession of quarterly

Table 4.8

RETURNS FOR PRIVATE EQUITY FUNDS 2006–2008				
	Private equity	Indexed	S&P 500	Indexed
2006	−7%	0.93	16%	1.16
2007	−11%	0.83	6%	1.22
2008	−18%	0.68	−37%	0.77

Note: median returns, vintage years.
Source: Cambridge Associates (2006, 2011).

Chart 4.59

Source: FRED.

losses that had begun in 2007 (Table 4.9 in red). The elite banks – Bank of America, Goldman Sachs, JP Morgan, Morgan Stanley, and Wells Fargo – suddenly had losses ranging from $1 billion (JP Morgan) to almost $5 billion (Wells Fargo).

Table 4.9

BANKS' QUARTERLY PRE-TAX INCOME				
($ millions)				
	1Q2008	**2Q2008**	**3Q2008**	**4Q2008**
AIG	−11,264	−8,756	−28,185	−60,556
Bank of America	1,798	4,921	1,511	−3,802
Bear Stearns	153	n.a.	n.a.	n.a.
Citigroup	−9,186	−4,667	−6,812	−32,390
Goldman Sachs	2,143	2,832	960	−3,599
Lehman Brothers	663	−4,087	−5,824	n.a.
JP Morgan	3,535	2,767	−2,187	−1,342
Merrill Lynch	−3,301	−8,111	−8,251	−22,168
Morgan Stanley	2,216	1,465	1,057	−3,350
Wachovia	−898	−10,824	−26,345	n.a.
Wells Fargo	3,073	2,587	2,367	−4,770

Source: Companies' 10-Ks and 10-Qs.

Reported pre-tax losses for the top ten commercial and investment banks between mid-2007 and the 4th quarter of 2008 accumulated to $322 billion, approximating their total 2007 tangible common equity (Table 4.10).

Stocks of the five largest commercial banks lost $769 billion in market value as they fell 78% from their 2007 highs (Table 4.11) while stocks of the five largest investment banks lost $319 billion, falling 93%, (Table 4.12).

The aggregate loss in stock market value between 2007 and the end of 2008 among the ten largest commercial and investment banks, AIG, Fannie Mae, and Freddie Mac was $1.4 trillion. Fannie Mae and Freddie Mac were gone as public companies. AIG was a ward of the state. Lehman Brothers was gone. Bear Stearns, Merrill Lynch, and Wachovia were taken over at scrap prices. So were WAMU and Countrywide. Most of the lesser mortgage banks and the monoline insurance companies were out of business.

Table 4.10

BANKS' QUARTERLY PRE-TAX LOSSES						
($ millions)						
	3Q2007	4Q2007	1Q2008	2Q2008	3Q2008	4Q2008
Losses only	−3,638	−47,415	−24,649	36,445	−77,604	−131,977
Cumulative	−3,638	−51,053	−75,702	−112,147	−189,751	−321,728

Source: Annual Reports.

Table 4.11

COMMERCIAL BANKS' STOCK MARKET CAPITALIZATION			
($ billions)			
	2007 high	2008 low	Loss
Citigroup	303	21	282
Bank of America	240	50	190
JP Morgan	195	72	123
Wells Fargo	132	69	63
Wachovia	115	4	111
Totals	985	216	769

Source: Annual Reports.

As David Greenlaw and Jan Hatzius outlined at the US Monetary Policy Forum in early 2008, banks' losses were a leveraged blow that threatened their capital.[46] As the crisis progressed, financial market participants had to calibrate losses for the leading commercial and investment banks for their own protection. These participants included counterparties on

[46] Greenlaw (2008).

Table 4.12

INVESTMENT BANKS' STOCK MARKET CAPITALIZATION			
($ billions)			
	2007 high	2008 low	Loss
Goldman Sachs	109	21	88
Morgan Stanley	96	6	90
Merrill Lynch	88	11	77
Bear Stearns	19	1	18
Lehman Brothers	46	0	46
Average	358	39	319

Source: Annual Reports.

conventional transactions, repo lenders, derivatives counterparties, depositors, clearing customers, custodial accounts, margin borrowers, portfolio clients, and equity and bond investors. But these bank counterparties had to go further than Greenlaw and Hatzius did and evaluate the losses on all residential mortgages, commercial mortgages, highly leveraged corporate debt, SIVs, equities, and various illiquid assets. Some calculations were sophisticated; some were on narrow asset classes that were then extrapolated; some were based on word-of-mouth. Calculations reflected that financial market participants' interests and insight varied widely. Their calculations were by necessity simplistic because of the wide range of banks' asset exposures, banks' accounting for most loans at cost, and the differing fair value disclosures based on whether loans and securities were for trading, investment, or "available for sale."

In April 2009, the IMF estimated that "gross financial sector" write-offs in the USA as a result of the crisis would be $1.6 trillion for all banks. The report considered virtually all types of mortgages and loans, including consumer loans, and all forms of securities including municipals, but not common equities for some reason. The IMF's loss rates were surprisingly low – 10% for commercial mortgages, 5% for corporate loans, and 14% for RMBS[47] versus mid-crisis prices down 35% on senior CMBS and highly

[47] IMF (2009), table 1.3, p. 35.

Table 4.13

	Private RMBS, CDOs, MSRs, etc.	Home equity + conventional mortgages	Highly leveraged corp. debt incl. 50% of commit'ts	Commercial real estate incl. commitments	Public equities	Total	Tangible common equity
COMMERCIAL BANKS' POSSIBLE 2008 LOSSES (2007 investment assets)							
($ billions)							
Bank of America	91	390	154	113	23	771	54
Citigroup	274	268	165	87	107	901	50
JP Morgan	91	150	131	39	91	502	63
Wachovia	69	228	86	92	4	479	30
Wells Fargo	58	155	58	74	3	348	34
Totals	583	1,191	594	405	228	3,001	231
Crisis prices*	0.25	0.75	0.65	0.67	0.55		
Losses	437	298	208	134	103	1,179	
*Pricing	A-rated ABX prices	1/2 sand state decline of 40%	CLO pricing of 60% and 85% for commitments	See Table 5.4 discussion	S&P 500 decline		

* Pricing A-rated ABX prices 1/2 sand state decline of 40% CLO pricing of 60% and 85% for commitments. See Table 5.4 discussion S&P 500 decline
Sources: Annual Reports; public indices; author's calculations.

leveraged corporate debt and 80–90% on A-rated private RMBS (which is where most ratings were). The IMF used models rather than market prices. When market prices were used, as in Tables 4.13 and 4.14 below, the losses for just the five leading commercial banks and four remaining prominent investment banks were $1.7 trillion.

Sophisticated financial market participants applying current market prices to the investment assets held by just the five largest commercial banks were looking at losses of almost $1.2 trillion, distributed across a broad range of investments (Table 4.13). Losses, rounded off, were largest in investments related to private RMBS ($437 billion), second in conventional mortgage lending ($298 billion), and significant for highly leveraged corporate lending ($208 billion), commercial real estate ($134 billion), and public equities ($103 billion). Every category was a threat to their tangible common equity of $231 billion. In aggregate, mark-to-market losses appeared to be five times tangible common equity.

Losses for the four largest investment banks appeared to be $677 billion with a heavy concentration in investments related to private RMBS

Table 4.14

INVESTMENT BANKS' POSSIBLE 2008 LOSSES (2007 investment assets)							
($ billions)							
	Private RMBS, CDOs, mtges, MSRs, etc.	Highly leveraged corporate debt	Comm'l real estate incl. commit's	Private investments	Public equities	Totals	Tangible equity
Goldman Sachs	87	115	20	19	122	363	35
Lehman Brothers	97	95	22	7	51	272	17
Merrill Lynch	207	120	11	34	11	383	23
Morgan Stanley	75	112	23	6	87	303	26
Totals	466	442	76	66	271	1,321	101
Crisis prices*	0.25	0.65	0.67	0.20	0.55		
Losses	350	155	25	26	122	677	101
Pricing	A-rated ABX prices	CLO pricing of 60% and 85% for commitments	See Table 5.4 discussion	Excludes Merrill Lynch	S&P 500 decline		

* Pricing A-rated ABX prices CLO pricing of 60% and 85% for commitments. See Table 5.4 discussion Excludes Merrill Lynch S&P 500 decline
Source: Annual Reports; public indices; author's calculations.

($350 billion), but there were other large losses in highly leveraged corporate debt ($155 billion) and public equities ($122 billion) (Table 4.14). Here, too, most categories were a threat to the investment banks' tangible common equity of $101 billion. Even in categories where the totals looked modest, such as commercial real estate and private investments, there were individual concentrations greater than the bank's tangible common equity. The aggregate apparent losses were almost seven times the four banks' tangible common equity.

Tables 4.13 and 4.14 use 4th quarter 2008 public market prices for private RMBS, highly leveraged corporate loans, and the S&P 500. Most prices incorporated the negative projections of the moment, but the table also uses prices that became available later in 2009 to capture projections for highly illiquid investments lacking public indices, such as private equity and commercial real estate. The assumption is that sophisticated market participants were projecting these prices in late 2008. Investment assets are as of year-end 2007, the last audited accounts available to contemporaries. There is no effort to reflect hedging which was common for common equities. In most other categories, one financial firm's hedge was another financial firm's liability. There is no effort to include derivatives losses although they were significant for Merrill Lynch, Morgan Stanley, and Citigroup. They are difficult to trace because the banks spread derivative losses among different functions. Because banks included many highly leveraged loans as part of their general corporate loans that were not marked-to-market, 50% of their corporate loans are treated as highly leveraged. Private investments are assumed to be reduced to option values because of their leverage except no loss is attributed to Merrill Lynch's investments in Bloomberg and BlackRock.

Senior finance executives who have read this section have argued that the portrayal of these mark-to-market losses is extreme, claiming that their firms never reported losses approximating these, that their firms reduced inventories after 2007, that many investments were hedged, that the crisis prices didn't last, that some were patently unreasonable, and that many assets did not have to be marked-to-market such as conventional mortgages, highly leveraged loans, commercial mortgages, and unfunded loan commitments. Private equity accounting was flexible. Prices during the crisis appeared to make no provision for economic recovery or government intervention.

Such claims are true, but they don't rebut how market participants must have seen things during the crisis, applying mark-to-market valuations to everything. The $1.1 trillion decline in the leading commercial and investment banks' stock market value at the depth of the crisis gives some verity to the $1.7 trillion of mark-to-market losses in Tables 4.13 and 4.14. The tangible common equity of the leading commercial and investment banks' was severely compromised even if the mark-to-market estimates were double reality.

In order to estimate market participants' judgments in September, it is important to realize that they were dealing with quarterly financial reports for April or May, that these were unaudited, and that there was a high level of distrust because of reporting problems at Lehman Brothers, AIG, Merrill Lynch, Morgan Stanley, and Citigroup. The latest audited financial statements were for 2007. Outsiders could not interpret hedges and who knew how good they were? John Breit, a Merrill Lynch risk executive, told then CEO Stan O'Neal in late 2007 that theirs were worthless.[48] Many credit default swaps were with monoline insurers that were going bankrupt. Larry Fink, CEO of BlackRock, when he considered acquiring Merrill Lynch in the heat of the crisis, would not assign any value to the company other than its holdings in his own company.[49] AIG could not have paid out $62 billion

[48] Farrell (2010), pp. 71–2.   [49] Farrell (2010), p. 358.

on its credit default swaps if it had not been rescued. What was the credit of those providing other hedges? Merrill Lynch? Lehman Brothers? Citigroup? Royal Bank of Scotland? Société Générale? Swiss banks? All were in need of rescue. What if unused commitments for highly leveraged corporate loans and commercial real estate were suddenly used? How long would it take for "reasonable" prices to be restored? Would the government continue to provide support to the financial system?

The one sure thing that market participants had was current prices.

The "mark-to-market" pricing in Tables 4.13 and 4.14 affected markets in multiple ways:

- Credit ratings were reduced.
- Banks borrowing short-term faced demands for increased collateral.
- Questions arose whether elements of previous collateral were appropriate for collateralized borrowing at all, such as private RMBS, residual interests in securitized asset pools, CDOs, real estate, whole commercial and residential mortgages, mortgage servicing rights, highly leveraged loans, high yield bonds, private equity holdings, general partner interests, and derivative assets.
- Large collateral demands arose in credit derivatives contracts.
- SIV vehicles that were funded in the ABCP market lost access and additional collateral was required for any collateralized borrowing.
- CLOs and CDOs that used credit derivatives in their asset pools had to put up increased collateral.
- Brokerage clients, especially hedge funds, pulled their accounts from commercial and investment banks in pursuit of safe havens, depriving the banks of working capital.
- Rules got stricter for asset pricing, margin accounts, clearing arrangements, access to credit lines, securities lending, financial statements, documentary representations, loan covenant enforcement, and all the other details of day-to-day transactions.
- The largest institutional investors suddenly reverted to more conservative policies across the board.

The Large European Banks

The large European banks doing business in the USA were not spared in the crisis. UBS owned what had been Paine Webber, Dillon Read, and Warburg Pincus. Credit Suisse owned what had been First Boston Corporation and Donaldson, Lufkin, and Jenrette. Deutsche Bank owned

Table 4.15

PRE-TAX INCOME OF EUROPEAN BANKS		
(billions)		
	2007	2008
Barclays £	7	6
BNP Paribas €	11	4
Commerzbank €	4	−1
Credit Agricole €	8	4
Credit Suisse chf	14	−15
Deutsche Bank €	9	−6
HSBC $	24	9
Royal Bank of Scotland £	7	−7
UBS chf	-4	−27

Source: Annual Reports.

what had been Bankers Trust. These banks were active in the private RMBS, CDO, and derivatives markets. They were among the largest users of SIVs. They all participated in highly leveraged corporate and commercial real estate lending.

There were concomitant problems at Credit Suisse, UBS, Deutsche Bank, and Royal Bank of Scotland, but in general the European banks' losses lagged behind their US counterparts in terms of early onset and scale. Their earnings held up in 2007. Losses only got large at Royal Bank of Scotland that had taken the high risk/high reward strategy to heart and was taken over by the UK government and at Credit Suisse and UBS (Table 4.15). UBS was a prominent case having replaced its CEO in 2007 after a $10 billion write-off on US subprime mortgages. Its new CEO, Marcel Rohner, took a $19 billion write-off in 2008 on US real estate. However, the European bank stocks in general did as poorly as the big US banks, falling 75% (Chart 4.60).

Equity bases for most of the big European banks' were sounder than the US banks (Table 4.16) because of fewer mergers. Only Credit Suisse and Deutsche Bank had negative tangible common equity under the severe test of subtracting "other assets." But the Europeans were on a delayed fuse

Table 4.16

EUROPEAN BANKS' TANGIBLE EQUITY NET OF "OTHER ASSETS"		
(billions)		
	2007	**2008**
Barclays £	28	30
BNP Paribas €	28	26
Commerzbank €	3	7
Credit Agricole €	45	40
Credit Suisse chf	8	−7
Deutsche Bank €	0	−15
HSBC $	51	28
Royal Bank of Scotland £	−19	23
UBS chf	9	9

Source: Annual Reports.

Chart 4.60

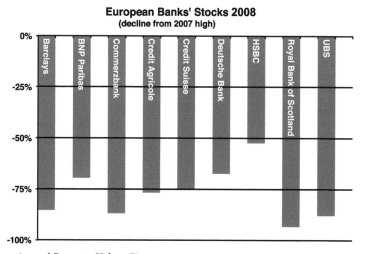

European Banks' Stocks 2008
(decline from 2007 high)

Source: Annual Reports; Yahoo Finance.

until they experienced their own problems with local real estate, weak countries such as Greece, Ireland, Spain, Portugal, and Italy, and obscure accounting.

Throughout the crisis, both the government and the Federal Reserve adopted ad hoc solutions that constituted remediation rather than policy. The most prominent example of this was the "conservation" of Fannie Mae and Freddie Mac. This was never debated publicly or approved as policy in any explicit manner. There had been debate for years about the structure of Fannie Mae and Freddie Mac, but in the end their fate was resolved by Treasury fiat. None of the other rescues followed previously settled policies – not the New York Federal Reserve's rescue of AIG; not the New York Federal Reserve's effort to engineer a deal with Wall Street that would facilitate Barclay's acquisition of Lehman Brothers; not Hank Paulson's pressure on Bank of America to acquire Merrill Lynch; not making Goldman Sachs and Morgan Stanley bank holding companies; not the use of TARP to inject equity into the big banks. Other ad hoc actions included using the Exchange Stability Account to guarantee mutual fund accounts after The Reserve Primary Fund "broke the buck" and the FDIC guaranteeing all business bank accounts. The one exception was the FDIC program to guarantee notes issued by banks. It was approved under the Emergency Economic Stabilization Act.[50]

The prevalence of Bush administration executive decisions in dealing with the crisis led to widespread uncertainty as to how the new Obama administration would deal with the continuing crisis. Treasury Secretary Hank Paulson's leadership had been critical thus far. He was the oldest of the Bush administration's leaders, independently wealthy, and he had spent his entire adult life at Goldman Sachs. Barack Obama himself was an unknown and his colleagues were not as familiar with the financial markets. Treasury Secretary designate, Tim Geithner, as strong as his performance had been as President of The Federal Reserve Bank of New York, had no other experience with US markets and no apparent political strength. Larry Summers, National Economic Counselor to the President, and Christina Romer, Chair of the Council of Economic Advisors, favored nationalization of troubled banks. Sheila Bair, Chair of the FDIC, wanted to punish the banks and was opposed to saving their holding companies. Geithner had to fight a widespread desire to punish the banks among colleagues, in Congress, and in the media, led by Paul

---

[50] Readers interested in a more detailed listing of Bush administration and Federal Reserve actions should refer to the Chapter Note at the end of this chapter.

Krugman, the left-wing *New York Times* columnist who had recently won the Nobel Prize in Economics.

A sense of futility prevailed as the Obama administration was about to take over. The authorities were looking into "no man's land" in dealing with US consumers' problems. US consumers had never led a recession. Traditional policies aimed at consumers were limited to tax cuts and lower interest rates; but consumers' debt built on housing had more than doubled since 2001, much of it for second or investment homes. Servicing it seemed insurmountable as housing prices fell. Home values fell $3.5 trillion in 2008. They would fall more in 2009. Unemployment was heading to 10% and consumer spending to its largest drop since WW II. Consumer confidence and dissatisfaction with the direction of the country were the worst since the 1970s. With consumers representing 70% of the economy, how and whether the authorities could deal with a problem on this scale was unknown.

Wealth losses were approaching $23 trillion – 154% of GDP and 208% of Disposable Personal Income – as we shall see in Chapter 6 (Table 6.2).

America's leading commercial and investment banks had suffered such extreme losses that it was unknown whether they could function. Bear Stearns, Lehman Brothers, Merrill Lynch, Wachovia Corp, WAMU, and Countrywide were gone. Fannie Mae, Freddie Mac, AIG, General Motors, and Chrysler Corp. were in the hands of the government.

Remediation had kept the financial system intact in a manner of speaking, but the economy was spiraling downward. Oil prices were down by two-thirds, small business earnings by 40%, vehicle sales by 35%, manufacturers' new orders by 30%, house prices in the most speculative states by 30%. Estimates for 2009 earnings for the S&P 500 were down 25%, orders for computer equipment and electronics by 25%, capital expenditures by 10% and headed for 18%, industrial production by 11%, and real GDP by 8%. Residential and commercial real estate markets were frozen. So was bank lending. An optimist would say that investors, too, were frozen. A realist would say they were terrified.

It would be up to the Obama administration to try to overcome the crisis the country was in.

4.4 Chapter Note on the Calendar of Remediation Efforts

For readers who wish more detail of the crisis, the remediation efforts by the Treasury, various other government agencies, and the Federal Reserve during the last four months of the Bush administration are listed below chronologically.

September

- The US Treasury put Fannie Mae and Freddie Mac into federal conservatorship (Labor Day weekend).
- The US Treasury guaranteed all money market funds following The Reserve Fund's announcement that it had "broken the buck" (September 16).
- The Federal Reserve accepted Goldman Sachs and Morgan Stanley as bank holding companies.
- The Federal Reserve agreed to accept any form of collateral acceptable to third-party repo lenders under the Primary Dealer Credit Facility.[51]
- The Federal Reserve established the ABCP Money Market Mutual Fund Liquidity Facility to finance purchases of ABCP from money market mutual funds.
- The Federal Reserve made all investment grade securities acceptable as collateral under its Term Securities Lending Facility.
- The Federal Reserve quickly expanded its balance sheet from $800 billion to $2 trillion (QE-1).[52]
- The Federal Reserve Bank of New York lent AIG $85 billion to avoid bankruptcy (September 16).
- The Federal Reserve agreed on unlimited foreign exchange swaps with the central banks of Europe, Britain, Switzerland, and Japan and added ten more central banks later.
- The Federal Reserve Open Market Trading Desk began purchasing secondary market federal agency notes (September 19).[53]
- The FDIC seized Washington Mutual Bank and sold it to JP Morgan.
- The SEC temporarily banned short selling in 799 financial stocks.
- Citigroup proposed to take over Wachovia Bank with the help of the FDIC (September 29).

October

- Congress passed the $700 billion TARP as part of the Emergency Economic Stabilization Act (October 3).

---

[51] Geithner (2014), p. 187.
[52] Council of Economic Advisors, Economic Report of the President 2010, p. 48; Federal Reserve, Factors Affecting Reserve Balances, H.4.1, table 1.
[53] Federal Reserve Annual Report, 2008, p. 55.

- TARP injected $125 billion of preferred stock capital into the nine largest banks (Bank of America, Bank of New York-Mellon, Citigroup, Goldman Sachs, Merrill Lynch, JP Morgan, Morgan Stanley, State Street Bank & Trust, and Wells Fargo,) (October 13).
- The FDIC created its TLGP that guaranteed all funds in bank checking and business transaction accounts (part of the TARP legislation).[54]
- The Federal Reserve Bank of New York lent AIG an additional $38 billion against investment grade bonds previously lent by AIG to third parties (October 8).[55]
- The Federal Reserve provided a Commercial Paper Funding Facility to issuers of commercial paper rated A-1/P-1 that lent $150 billion by the end of October (October 7 announcement).[56]
- The Group of Seven agreed that they would intervene to prevent failures of systemically important institutions in their various countries and they would protect ordinary bank depositors (October 10).
- The FDIC further offered a guarantee of new unsecured debt issued by banks and their holding companies (Columbus Day weekend, 2nd Monday of October).[57]
- The Federal Reserve Bank of New York announced a Money Market Investor Funding Facility to assist money market funds in handling redemptions (announced October 21).[58]

November

- The Treasury purchased $40 billion of AIG preferred stock (net $15 billion after the Federal Reserve reduced its commitment by $25 billion).[59]
- The Federal Reserve conducted two forward auctions of $150 billion each to cover the year-end under its Temporary Auction Facilities (TAF).
- The Federal Reserve announced its Term Asset-Backed Securities Loan Facility (TALF) for $200 billion (with support from TARP) that would lend without recourse against new AAA-rated asset-backed securities for everything from auto and credit card loans to student loans, small business loans, and equipment leases (November 25).[60]

---

[54] Geithner (2014), pp. 233–4.   [55] Federal Reserve Annual Report 2008, p. 57.
[56] Federal Reserve Annual Report 2008, p. 53; Geithner (2014), pp. 228–9.
[57] Geithner (2014), pp. 233–4.   [58] Federal Reserve Annual Report 2008, p. 54.
[59] Federal Reserve Annual Report 2008, p. 57.
[60] Federal Reserve Annual Report 2008, pp. 54–5; Geithner (2014), p. 280.

- After Citigroup announced the layoff of 52,000 workers and absorbed $17 billion in distressed assets from unconsolidated structured investment vehicles, it received another $20 billion of equity from TARP plus a "ring fence" guarantee was built around $300 billion of its worst assets by a combination of commitments from TARP, the FDIC, and the Federal Reserve.[61]

December

- TARP made loans of $25 billion to GM and Chrysler and their finance subsidiaries (December and early January).
- CIT Financial received $2.3 billion from TARP.

---

[61] Federal Reserve Annual Report 2008, p. 57; Geithner (2014), pp. 252–4.

5

What Caused the Crisis?

Never confuse wishes with facts.

Harry Truman

People date the financial crisis differently. The earliest dates look to 2007 when several fixed-income funds and mortgage banks failed or to early 2008 when Bear Stearns failed. Those focused on housing date it from early 2007 or even 2006 when housing prices began to decline and subprime mortgagees began to default in large numbers. There is little academic focus on when it ended, but Tim Geithner maintained that it did not end until May 2009 when the Treasury's stress tests of the major banks were resolved.[1] The stock market (and other markets) in early 2010 still felt as if the crisis had not ended. We will see that how long the crisis lasted is relevant to how the causes are evaluated.

There have been different approaches to explaining the crisis. Those involved in the heat of the action such at the Federal Reserve, the Treasury, and the FDIC tend to see the crisis as a bank run in which private RMBS and related problems led to the failure of Lehman Brothers and AIG, and froze the commercial paper, repo, money market mutual fund, and inter-bank markets. That interpretation fathered massive federal intervention such as Federal Reserve liquidity programs, central bank currency swaps, the rescue of AIG, TARP, guarantees of money market mutual fund obligations, guarantees of all business bank deposits, FDIC guarantees of new bank debt, and "ring fence" guarantees of dubious assets to rescue Citigroup and promote forced mergers of Merrill Lynch and Wachovia Corp. Many economists also see the crisis as a bank run (Gorton, 2010–1,

[1] Geithner (2014), pp. 353–5.

221

2010–2; Eichengreen, 2016; Ball, 2018). However, bank runs cannot explain the largest failures of all – those of Fannie Mae and Freddie Mac.

Some economists have focused on increased bank leverage (Reinhart, 2009; Eichengreen, 2016) and speculation by commercial and investment banks (Gennaioli, 2018) as the inevitable determinant of failure when markets declined significantly. They do not document the pervasiveness of high leverage, however, in Fannie Mae and Freddie Mac, highly leveraged corporate loans, commercial real estate, and derivatives. Nor do they distinguish between leverage and illiquidity.

Popular books and media as well as respected economists have focused on the problems in housing finance and the losses in housing wealth that resulted in the first consumer-led recession in modern US history (Shiller, 2013; Mian, 2014). Mortgage securitization was the channel that brought housing problems into the securities markets – a process that innumerable critics have faulted for unfair consumer lending practices, adverse selection, wrongful incentives at the rating agencies, inordinate complication, lying at all stages of the process, and the difficulty of resolving mortgage defaults.

There is no need here to choose a theory of financial crises. The object of this history is to describe the factors contributing to the crisis and the long, but muted recovery. While some of the factors in the crisis are obvious – home mortgage debt, faults in securitization, banking illiquidity – there are aspects of each that are surprises. For example, Alt-A and jumbo mortgages and home equity withdrawal through conventional mortgages were as troublesome as subprime mortgages. The biggest buyers of private RMBS were Fannie Mae, Freddie Mac, and the major European banks rather than US major banks. Securitization involved lying and dissimulation at every stage, including homeowners, speculators, real estate brokers, mortgage brokers, commercial banks, and ratings agencies, but the assessment later in this chapter of the damage caused is that it was not great. Formal ratios of banking leverage did not increase over the period, but the underlying risk and illiquidity of bank assets did, and the breadth of banks' activities was such that regulators had little ability to assess them.

Scale was also vital to what caused the crisis. Rapid growth alone does not explain the largest problems. Poor neighborhoods may have had rapid subprime loan growth, but from a small base and taking out small loans. Subprime loans may have had the highest default rates but they only constituted 13% of home mortgages originated between 2002–07. CDOs may have been extreme concoctions but they were only 5% of all home mortgages or 25% of all private RMBS (in 2005 private RMBS reached 80%

of CDO collateral – see Chart 2.22). Highly leveraged corporate debt approached $4 trillion, equal to all forms of private RMBS outstanding. Commercial real estate debt was almost as large at $3.4 trillion, and leverage was as high as 70% for bank loans, REITs, and institutional property investments. Highly leveraged, illiquid assets may have offered unusual profit opportunities to bankers because of their intermediary position in asset flows, but there was a problem when these assets became multiples of banks' tangible common equity. Credit default swaps were written with leverage the equivalent of interest rate swaps that carried much less risk – leverage that resulted in massive collateral calls on AIG, Merrill Lynch, Citigroup, Morgan Stanley, and UBS when markets declined. Student debt began to assume large proportions.

The modern portfolio practices of state and local retirement funds, corporate pension funds, insurance companies, university endowments, and foundations contributed significantly to the crisis. Their large investments in private equity funds, hedge funds, commercial real estate, and special accounts run by aggressive investment managers created the shadow banking system that funded much of highly leveraged corporate debt and commercial real estate. The reasons these large investors made these choices lay in both their perceptions that traditional stock and bond investments could not meet the investment returns their operations needed and the belief that higher (hidden) leverage could produce higher returns.

The failure of Lehman Brothers in this broad picture does not loom as the tipping point in the crisis. Lehman Brothers' collapse was spectacular, but AIG, Merrill Lynch, Wachovia Corp., Citigroup, Countrywide, and WAMU were in distress at the same time. Lehman Brothers' failure can barely be identified as a factor in the economy's troubles and the decline in many financial markets. There was too much wrong with the housing markets and consumer leverage; too dramatic a drop in the prices of securitized mortgages of all types; too much highly leveraged private equity and commercial real estate; too many illiquid assets acquired by the largest commercial and investment banks; too much ill-informed leverage in credit derivatives; and too much tolerance of hidden leverage by the largest institutional investors to blame the crisis on Lehman Brothers' failure.

5.1 Consumer Credit and Home Mortgages

The leading cause of the crisis was the expansion in residential mortgage debt from 2002 to 2007 as housing prices rose, homeowners extracted their appreciating equity, and purchases of both second and investment homes

Chart 5.1

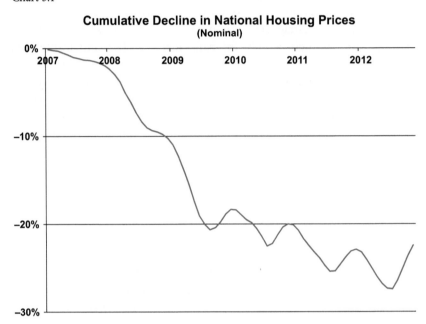

Cumulative Decline in National Housing Prices
(Nominal)

Source: Shiller (home page).

grew, especially in California, Nevada, Arizona, and Florida. Worries about consumer credit arose when housing prices nationwide had dropped 8% by August 2008. The financial community immediately began to project further declines that would in fact extend to 25% in 2012 (Chart 5.1). House prices in Las Vegas, Los Angeles, Miami and Phoenix dropped approximately 30% by the 3rd quarter of 2008, and, confirming predictions, 50% by 2011 (Chart 5.2).

The root of the credit problem was that as mortgage debt doubled from $5.3 to $10.6 trillion between 2001–07 (11% annually), $2.7 trillion of that increase was taken out for consumption. Home equity loans added $1.1 trillion to this mortgage debt. Existing homeowners also took on approximately $850 billion of incremental mortgage debt in 2004–07 as they traded up, accounting for approximately 25% of total home sales.[2]

Various parameters illustrate the extremes of this consumer borrowing. Household liabilities rose from 15% to 26% of net worth between 2000–08

---

[2] Assuming 40% 1st-time buyers, 33% investment/2nd home buyers, and that the 27% of buyers trading up bought a home priced 25% higher than the median, used a 70% mortgage, and previously had a median mortgage in 1996 of $110,000.

Chart 5.2

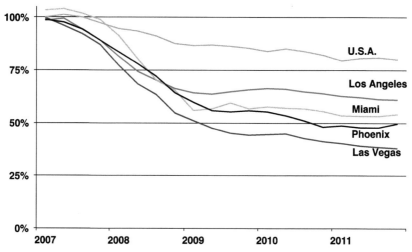

**Change in House Prices in Leading Cities
(4Q 2006 = 100%)**

Source: FHFA (house price index datasets).

(Chart 5.3). Debt service for those earning less than $200,000 a year reached 22% of disposable income in 2007.[3] Twenty-two percent understates debt service for actual borrowers. It could have been as high as 50%. It is not as if everyone jumped on the mortgage boom. Residential mortgages were only 38% of all households' nonfinancial assets (a proxy for home values). Thirty percent of homeowners didn't have a mortgage.[4] Plus, the huge increase in student debt as yet had almost no debt service requirements.

Real estate rose from 15% to 24% of household net worth between 2000–06 (Chart 5.4) because of both rising home prices and purchases of second and investment homes, but once home prices started to fall real estate dropped to 12% of household net worth.

As house prices declined, the financial community projected further declines. Deutsche Bank projected that prices would decline 42% nationally by 2011, and that 48% of homeowners would be "underwater" (i.e. where their mortgages exceeded their home's value).[5] A similar phenomenon of

---

[3] Federal Reserve debt service excluding interest expense and after-tax income of those earning over $200,000 annually according to IRS, Statistics of Income.

[4] *New York Times*, 1/16/2013, "Owning a Home, Mortgage Free," citing Zillow.

[5] *Reuters Business News*, 8/5/09.

Chart 5.3

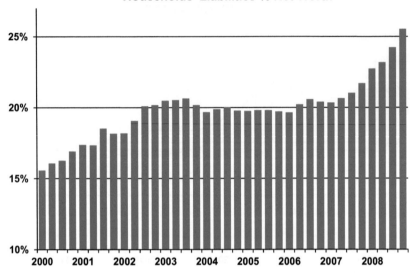

Households' Liabilities % Net Worth

Source: FRED.

Chart 5.4

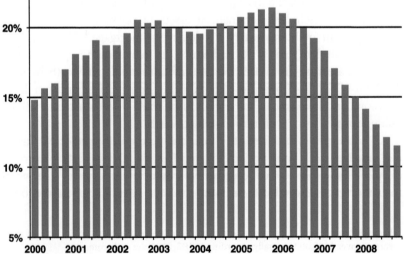

Real Estate % Household Net Worth

Source: FRED.

projecting further declines occurred in commercial real estate where commercial buildings with mortgages maturing in 2009 were thought to be 20% underwater, but those in 2010 34% underwater, those in 2011 50%, and those in 2012 63% underwater.[6]

The data on underwater residential borrowers in 2011 revealed the breadth of the mortgage credit problem. Purchases of second and investment homes were reflected in Deutsche Bank's projection that 90% of mortgages were underwater in Las Vegas and parts of Florida and California. This was also reflected in the PEW Organization's estimates of where home owners were furthest underwater – 63% in Nevada, 50% in Arizona, 46% in Florida, 36% in Michigan, 31% in California, and 30% in Georgia.

But buyers' credit and mortgage choices also indicated other factors at work. Deutsche Bank projected subprime borrowers would be 69% underwater by 2011, as might be expected, but they also projected Option ARMS borrowers would be 89% underwater, and jumbo borrowers 46%. At Fannie Mae and Freddie Mac, 41% of whose mortgages were underwater in 2011, the five most problematic states were Florida, California, Michigan, Illinois, and Georgia accounting for 52% of the total. This indicated a mix of both second and investment homes and generalized economic weakness.[7] A Census Report in 2009 illustrated even more complexity. It estimated that 11.6% of homeowners were underwater, 16% in the west and 7% in the east. The only significant racial difference was that Hispanics were double other racial groups with 21% underwater. Homeowners under age thirty-five were double those over age forty-five (19% vs 9%), adjustable mortgages were almost double fixed rate (22% vs 12%), and single homes (10%) were one-half of multifamily units (19%) and one-third of mobile homes (33%). However, underwater rates were comparable across all incomes and levels of education.[8]

Consumers' credit problems and the financial community's worst-case projection of the future were quickly transmitted to the mortgage-backed security markets.

---

[6] KBRA Credit Profile Report, Commercial RealEstate (sic) Direct, 6/29/11, citing Trepp LLC.

[7] *Reuters Business News*, 8/5/09, PEW Stateline Article, 7/8/11, and FHFA, "Review of Options Available for Underwater Borrowers and Principal Forgiveness," no date but probably in 2012.

[8] Carter (2009), appendix charts and tables.

5.2 Mortgage Securitization

Mortgage securitization was begun in the 1970s by Lewis Ranieri at Salomon Brothers as a solution to disintermediation of savings and loans that were funding long-term, usually fixed rate, mortgage loans with short-term deposits. Securitization also tried to address the flaw in state laws that give homeowners the free option to refund their mortgages when rates go down.

Mortgage securitization morphed in many ways between the 1970s and the crisis of 2008, generally in the direction of creating a scale of risks and higher returns so that investors could pick their own flavor. Mortgage payment streams were divided into interest-only and principal-only, early and later payments, different mortgage credits (FNMA and Freddie Mac, jumbo, Alt-A, subprime, home equity, and commercial real estate), different priority in late payments and defaults, differing margins of protection and third party guarantees, and ultimately CDOs that were secured by weaker combinations of these variations and varying corporate debt obligations. Naturally, investors' interest in these different variations changed from time to time as the economic outlook and the appetite for risk (the stretch for yield) varied.

Mortgage securitization ended up contributing to the crisis in numerous ways:

- All securitization (including Fannie Mae and Freddie Mac securitization) facilitated the expansion in consumer debt as consumers withdrew appreciated equity and used housing as a highly leveraged investment vehicle.
- All securitization (including Fannie Mae and Freddie Mac securitization) introduced risks of adverse selection, fraud, and lying that were controlled better when the institution creating the mortgages was the ultimate lender or at least continued to bear some significant portion of the risk.
- The complexity of private RMBS made investors reliant upon the ratings agencies which in turn made investors vulnerable to the ratings agencies' risk models as well as the agencies' difficulty in finding fault with a leading element of their income growth.
- The complexity of private RMBS concentrated market making in the original underwriters, eliminating liquidity if they ceased to make markets.
- Private RMBS were inherently volatile compared to traditional mortgage loans retained by the lender to maturity because the underlying

mortgages in private RMBS were in effect marked-to-market. Private RMBS prices therefore reflected anticipation of how bad things might get.

- Securitization turned the creation of residential mortgages into a business (rather than a portfolio investment) that the originators, brokers, underwriters, and mortgage servicers found difficult to reduce.

As total residential mortgage originations rose from $1 trillion in 2000 to over $3 trillion annually in 2003–06, the share of private mortgage securitization rose from 17% to 57%. Private securitization financed what Fannie Mae and Freddie Mac did not – 92% of prime jumbo fixed-rate originations, 64% of prime jumbo adjustable-rate originations, 89% of Alt-A originations, 97% of subprime jumbo originations, 80% of subprime fixed-rate originations, and 91% of subprime adjustable-rate originations.[9] The share of the weakest mortgage credits (subprime and Alt-A loans) rose from 12% of originations in 2000 to 33% in 2006. This understates the growth in weak credits because jumbo loans underwent a transformation to more speculative borrowers from what were originally loans to wealthier homeowners too large to qualify for Fannie Mae or Freddie Mac guarantees.[10] Including jumbo loans, weak credits expanded to 60% of all originations and 89% of all private securitizations.[11]

We should not lose sight of Fannie Mae and Freddie Mac's participation in the mortgage problems. Even in 2005–06 at the peak of private mortgage financing, Fannie Mae and Freddie Mac's share of prime fixed-rate mortgages (74%) and prime adjustable-rate mortgages (51%) was still dominant. Both agency and private RMBS participated in the trends to weaker borrower credit – financing homes at ever-higher prices, withdrawal of equity, and second/investment homes. There was no mystery about these flaws to market participants. Investors accepted them in the name of higher returns if one took higher risks and originators accepted them in the interest of keeping a good business going.

In principle, securitization introduced adverse selection in RMBS because few of the mortgages were retained in the portfolios of the originating parties. Less than 10% of 2005–06 originations were retained, whether prime or subprime, and even adjustable-rate mortgages (appropriate to

---

[9] Elul (2015-1), table 1.
[10] Thornburg Mortgage began buying wholesale loans in 2006 and basically went out of business in the spring of 2008.
[11] Inside Mortgage Finance (2012), volume 1, pp. 16–17, volume 2, pp. 2–3, 6–7.

banks with deposit liabilities) were retained only 14% of the time if conforming and 36% of the time if jumbo loans. But adverse selection, like basic credit deterioration, was no mystery and was accepted by market participants seeking higher returns. There has been research indicating that the data on adverse selection for private RMBS was mixed (Sean Chu, 2011; Agarwal, 2012; Elul, 2015-1), but commercial real estate mortgages show it clearly. Delinquencies were 9% on CMBS while they were only 0.3% on commercial real estate loans held by life insurance companies and 0.5% on CMBS apartment loans held by Fannie Mae and Freddie Mac. Banks averaged a 4% delinquency rate but this may have reflected that they also held loans that were interrupted on the way to securitization. Within the multifamily commercial sector, delinquency on CMBS rose to 15% in 2010 whereas Freddie Mac delinquencies were nearly zero.[12] Auto ABS also had losses on 2005–07 vintages of 13% versus 3.5% for the largest banks' own loans.[13]

Securitization also opened the lending process to unusual credit deterioration, lying, and fraud. Some standard measures of credit quality for private RMBS (FICO scores, loan-to-value ratios, junior liens) did not appear to deteriorate appreciably as securitization expanded, but others did. For subprime securitizations, bond insurance declined from 40% to 6%, debt-to-income rose from 35% to 41%, and interest-only rose from 0% to 28%. Full documentation dropped from 75% to 54%. For Alt-A securitizations, bond insurance dropped from 29% to 5%, debt-to-income rose from 19% to 29%, and interest-only rose from 0% to 61%. Full documentation dropped from 34% to 21%.[14] There was a similar decline in credit quality in the CMBS market where interest-only issues rose from 47% of loans in 2004 to 86% in 2007, "pro forma" ratios became prominent based on projections of rents rather than historical results, loan-to-value ratios did not drop despite escalating values. Levitin (2013) blamed CDO buyers of subordinated CMBS tranches for undermining underwriting standards.[15]

Consumers lied on a massive scale. Griffin (2015) found that 48% of privately securitized loans had one of three types of fraud (lying about owner occupancy, undisclosed second liens, or excessive appraisals). Mian (2015) found that income overstatement was rampant and related to low-

---

[12] Goldman Sachs (2016–1) exhibit 47.

[13] Goldman Sachs (2016–3) exhibit 3; Goldman Sachs (2016–4) exhibits 6–8, 10. Banks' own losses are the average for JP Morgan, Bank of America, Wells Fargo, and Citigroup in 2008.

[14] Ashcraft (2010), table 3.   [15] Levitin (2013), pp. 104–8.

income neighborhoods and high use of private securitization. It was commonplace for real estate brokers to lie about sales prices, for both buyers and sellers to accept the misrepresentations, for borrowers to be given credit for "sweat equity" that didn't exist, for borrowers to misrepresent their income and financial resources, for mortgage brokers to encourage borrowers to exaggerate, for appraisers to collude in raising valuations for sales or refinancings, and for loan officers to encourage justifications for higher loans. The term "liar loans" didn't apply just to borrowers.

Securitization facilitated the embrace of homes as a highly leveraged investment vehicle, a phenomenon also experienced in Europe. People bought vacation homes, potential retirement homes, and investment homes-to-rent or flip with a degree of leverage not available in other investments. The National Association of Realtors reported that second homes and investment homes reached a peak of 40% of home sales in 2005. Promotional real estate brokers acquired portfolios of homes that they managed for groups of retail investors. Investors who couldn't afford a complete home bought time-shares in vacation properties. Co-Star estimated in 2009 that there were seventeen million rental homes in the USA (Florance, 2010). The approximate value at $200,000 per home was $3.4 trillion. If mortgaged to 75% of value, this was 23% of the $11 trillion of all home mortgages outstanding in 2008 and 64% of the $4 trillion in privately securitized mortgages outstanding.

Among Alt-A borrowers, 22% of loans were for declared investment properties.[16] But lying was rampant because of the better mortgage rates for owner-occupied properties. Elul (2015-1) found that there were four times as many undeclared non-occupants as declared investors among jumbo borrowers.[17]

Second and investment home mortgages had greater credit risk. They were disproportionately financed with Alt-A mortgages with a disturbing credit feature – a borrower option of negative amortization that went from 2% of originations in 2003 to 30% in 2007.[18] Over one-third of second/ investment home mortgages were in Florida, California, or Arizona. In California and Arizona, as well as in Texas, lenders had no recourse beyond the value of the home itself so that investors found it easy to walk away from homes when their mortgages were underwater.

Collateralized Debt Obligations (CDOs) introduced impossible complexity into securitization and potentially no liquidity. CDOs were used to

---

[16] Mayer (2008), table 2, panel C, p. 32.   [17] Elul (2015-2), table 2.
[18] Mayer (2008), table 2, panel C, p. 32.

gather up the junior lien remainders of securitizations that were difficult to sell and higher yielding subordinated tranches of new loans. CDO collateral was concentrated in assets with a median rating of A-/A3. The senior portions of these CDOs were given AAA ratings under the rationale that diversification and superior liens protected lenders. The median real estate-based CDO had 900 tranches from previous securitizations. One issue had over 163,000 tranches.[19] This was an impossible analytical task for both investors and market makers other than the originators and the rating agencies. When it turned out that the rating agencies had given undue credit to CDOs for diversification (that didn't exist) and that cross-correlation was high under economic stress there was no alternative standard for valuations. The result was restricted liquidity for the issues and none if the originators stopped making markets.[20]

The model for private RMBS ratings originated in the 1970s when the rating agencies assigned Aaa/AAA ratings to monoline insurance companies' guarantees of municipal bonds that had extremely low default rates and implicit state protection. This philosophy crept into rating well-collateralized senior bonds on private residential mortgage pools on the basis of models that emphasized low historic default rates and broadly diversified mortgage pools that were not cross-correlated. Perhaps the high ratings were considered a social contribution that broadened the market for home ownership, but the ratings bore no relationship to the standards for Aaa/AAA ratings that governments and public companies had to meet.

For twenty-five years the Aaa/AAA RMBS ratings were not tested as interest rates declined, home prices rose, and homeowners repeatedly refinanced, but the credit deterioration among mortgagors was no secret in 2004–07. Moody's began a steep slide in ratings when it announced new standards in July 2007, but why did it take so long? The answers probably lie in Moody's stock price and an SEC rule in mid-2007 requiring rating agencies to eliminate conflicts of interest and "unfair rating practices." Moody's fees for rating structured securities grew to 70% of revenues between 2001–06 (Chart 5.5). After the change, Moody's ratings downgrades of RMBS (all types) increased steadily to a cumulative total of 75,000 by the 1st quarter of 2009. Its fees from structured products dropped to 43% of revenues and its stock price dropped 60% (Chart 5.6), although the declines in ratings, revenues, and stock price all had a common root in the excesses of the residential mortgage market.

---

[19] Owusu-Anah (2013), table 3, p. 10.   [20] Benmelech (2009), table 8, p. 183.

Chart 5.5

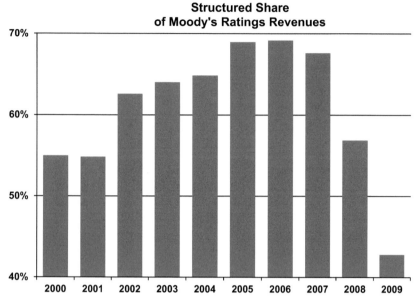

Source: Moody's Corporation 10-Ks.

Chart 5.6

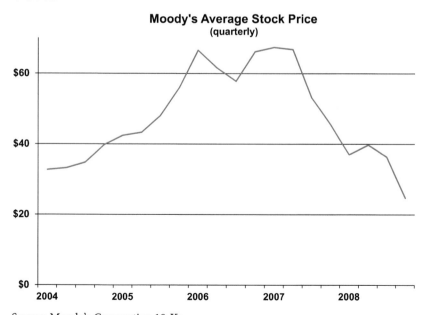

Source: Moody's Corporation 10-Ks.

Chart 5.7

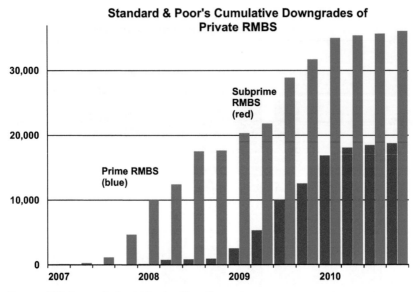

Source: ESF Quarterly Securitisation Data Reports.

Standard & Poor's ratings downgrades of both subprime and prime RMBS illustrate the deterioration in both sectors, and the persistence well into 2010 (Chart 5.7). Almost two-thirds of the prime downgrades were in 2009 but they continued into the 1st quarter of 2010. There is a tendency to assume the lag in prime downgrades reflected the feedback effect of the declining economy, but it could also have reflected that the continued decline in housing prices was raising prime mortgages' loan-to-value ratio. In due course, prime downgrades were 50% of subprime downgrades.

Standard & Poor's had only half of Moody's market share in rating private RMBS issues based on their cumulative downgrades (prime plus subprime). This may have led Standard & Poor's to give favorable ratings to CDOs because they ended up with a 25% higher share than Moody's in this smaller market. S&P's CDO downgrades skyrocketed in 2008–09 (Chart 5.8). CDO downgrades cumulatively of 25,000 were one-quarter of Moody's 100,000+ private RMBS downgrades reflecting that CDO volumes were only one-quarter of private RMBS. The timing of Standard & Poor's downgrades of CDOs matched Moody's private RMBS downgrades (Chart 5.9) despite the somewhat different collateral in CDOs.

Chart 5.8

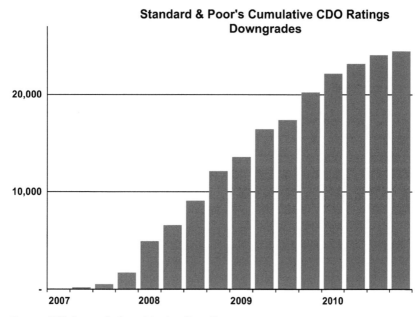

Source: ESF Quarterly Securitisation Data Reports.

Chart 5.9

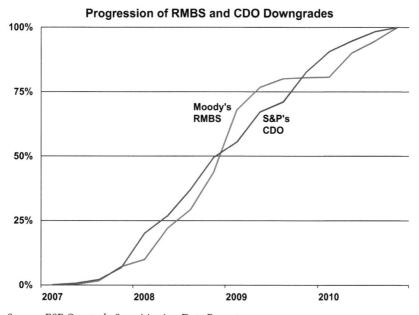

Source: ESF Quarterly Securitisation Data Reports.

Moody's and Standard & Poor's ultimately paid $2.4 billion in fines to the US government and various states to settle claims that they had inflated ratings leading up to the crisis.[21] Relative to the outstanding private RMBS and CDOs this was insignificant.

There were horrific market values for RMBS and CDOs in the crisis due to the acceleration of consumer credit problems, massive ratings down-grades, the problems inherent in securitization, and severe credit problems among financial intermediaries. Private RMBS indices were down 30–90%. The declines were a reflection of prices being marked down rather than high selling volume. Markets simply disappeared in subprime RMBS, other low-rated private RMBS, CMBS, CDOs, and CLOs. Complaints that there were no markets in these products were legion.

Table 5.1 broadly estimates the mark-to-market losses on residential mortgages based on private RMBS index values and the decline in housing prices. Prices reflect the worst of the crisis in the fall of 2008 and early 2009. The apparent losses in all residential mortgages were almost $5 trillion – 33% of GDP and 44% of Personal Disposable Income.

Table 5.1

RESIDENTIAL MORTGAGE LOSSES IN 2008			
	Outstanding ($ billions)	Prices	Losses ($ billions)
All residential mortgages:	11,030		
agency RMBS	4,965	0.75	1,241
private RMBS	4,061	0.25	3,046
unsecuritized	2,004	0.75	501
Total losses			4,788

Note on price assumptions:
1 Agency RMBS: 25% national home price decline, 50% "sand states" price decline; 75/25 proportions; 80% loan-to-value; 80% recovery on new value (equals 25% loss).
2 Private RMBS prices: AAA 35, A 15; proportions ¼ AAA-rated, ¾ A-rated (equals 25).
3 "Unsecuritized mortgages" same as agency.
Sources: Federal Reserve (Financial Accounts of the United States); public indices; author's estimates.

[21] Bloomberg 2/3/15 and Moody's Annual Report 2016, note 19, p. 107.

The US government absorbed Fannie Mae and Freddie Mac's losses beyond stockholders' 100% losses. It appeared as if the total losses might be as much as $1.2 trillion on almost $5 trillion of mortgages ($3 trillion at Fannie Mae and $1.8 trillion at Freddie Mac) if conditions did not improve. Fannie Mae and Freddie Mac combined had over $300 billion of nonperforming mortgages at the end of 2009 and foreclosed on approximately $600 billion in 2009–10 (their reporting is not consistent). They also had $400 billion of losses on $500 billion of private RMBS investments. The two agencies would actually report losing only $250 billion in 2008–11 with the benefit of flexible accounting and the recovery.

Private RMBS losses of $3 trillion were a blend of subprime, Alt-A, and jumbo losses. Subprime losses based on 1/3 of private originations would have been approximately $1 trillion or 21% of all residential mortgage losses.

The reader should be aware that these residential mortgage calculations were not accounting losses. Fannie Mae, Freddie Mac, commercial banks, savings and loans, and credit unions did not mark retained mortgages to market. Actual defaults turned out to be less than projected as not all underwater homeowners walked away from their mortgages. And market prices eventually recovered. Even before federal intervention, analysts repeatedly reported that market prices implied improbable rates of default and low recovery on defaulted property. But we know this with historical perspective and after massive federal intervention. The losses in Table 5.1 reflect the crisis atmosphere at its worst.

Securitization boomeranged on the very banks that created it as we saw in Chapter 4, Tables 4.13 and 4.14, because they invested in their own underwritings. They tended to hold the weaker tranches of what they had securitized and a mix of CDOs, SIVS, mortgage-servicing rights, mortgages en route to securitization, and mortgage residuals. The $466 billion held by the four largest investment banks (Goldman Sachs, Lehman Brothers, Merrill Lynch, and Morgan Stanley) would have lost $350 billion at crisis prices, half of all their losses, and substantially more than their $101 billion tangible common equity. The five leading commercial banks (Bank of America, Citigroup, JP Morgan, Wachovia, and Wells Fargo) held $453 billion of this mortgage mix that lost $340 billion at crisis prices, one-third of their total losses, and well in excess of their $231 billion of tangible common equity. These losses are overstated because the banks tried to hedge their trading positions but the hedges were invisible to the outside world.

Table 5.2

BANKS' MORTGAGE RESTITUTION						
($ billions)						
	2009	2010	2011	Total	Claims as of 2011	Total + claims
B of A (ML+Countrywide)	13	14	7	35	14	49
JP Morgan (WAMU)	8	8	2	17	3	21
Citigroup	5	3	2	10	1	12
Wells Fargo (Wachovia)	1	3	3	7	2	9
Ally Financial (GMAC)	1	3	3	6	1	8
				75	22	97

Source: Inside Mortgage Finance 2012.

The mortgage restitution and litigation costs that the leading commercial and investment banks had to pay after the crisis were only 9% of the broad market's losses on conforming and private RMBS in Table 5.1. Banks had to repurchase or make restitution for $75 billion of mortgages because they did not conform to the banks' representations at the time they were securitized. Banks also had claims for a further $22 billion from FNMA/FHLMC and other agencies and trustees between 2009–11 (Table 5.2) on similar grounds. The five banks with the largest liabilities accounted for 85% of these repurchases or restitutions. Bank of America bore the liability for Countrywide's and Merrill Lynch's misrepresentations. JP Morgan bore similar liability with respect to WAMU. Wells Fargo bore responsibility for Wachovia Corporation and Golden West Financial. Citigroup and Ally Financial (previously General Motors Acceptance Corporation) rounded out the five largest obligors.[22] The five banks' liability was 4½% of total private RMBS outstanding.

A broader measure of banks' liabilities was the cost of fines and litigation (Table 5.3). Moody's reported in 2017 that a broad group of banks that also included Goldman Sachs, Morgan Stanley, and the major European banks had paid or reserved $273 billion on their books for fines and litigation. This included public fines, private lawsuits, legal fees, and lesser fines for non-mortgage issues such as LIBOR manipulation. The bulk of the mortgage-related fines was for pushing inappropriate mortgages on low-income

[22] Inside Mortgage Finance 2012, volume 1, pp. 363–5.

1 The Wintel trio: Bill Gates (Microsoft), Michael Dell (Dell Computer), and Craig
Barrett (Intel) 2001.
Source: Getty Images/Mario Tama.

2 Steve Jobs presenting the Apple iMac 1998.
Source: Getty Images/Bernard Bisson.

3 Architects of the 1990s financial markets: Robert Rubin, Treasury Secretary, and Alan Greenspan, Chair of the Federal Reserve, preparing to testify before the House Banking and Financial Institutions Committee, September 16, 1998.
Source: Getty Images/Luke Frazza/AFP.

4 The attack on the World Trade Towers, September 11, 2001.
Source: Getty Images/Spencer Platt.

5 David Swensen, the venerated head of the Yale Endowment in his trading room.
Source: New York Times/Redux Alan S. Orling.

6 The People with the Power, September 18, 2008 at the height of the crisis: Rahm
Emanuel, Barney Frank, Ben Bernanke, Hank Paulson, Christopher Cox, Chris Dodd,
Richard Shelby, Spencer Bachus, Tom Coburn, Roy Blunt, Richard Durbin, Mitch
McConnell, Harry Reid, Nancy Pelosi, John Boehner, Steny Hoyer.
Source: Getty Images/Chip Somodevilla.

7 Ex-CEOs: Harley Snyder (Countrywide director), Angelo Mozilo (former Countrywide CEO), John Finnegan (Merrill Lynch director), Stan O'Neal (former Merrill Lynch CEO), Richard Parsons (Citigroup director), Charles Prince (former Citigroup CEO), before a Congressional hearing, March 7, 2008.
Source: Getty Images/Mark Wilson.

8 Richard Fuld, former CEO of Lehman Brothers and director Thomas Cruikshank, April 20, 2010.
Source: Getty Images/Chip Somodevilla.

9 The Government's team announcing financial stakes in banks totaling $250 billion, October 14, 2008: Ben Bernanke (foreground), (Chair of the Federal Reserve), Hank Paulson (Treasury Secretary), Sheila Bair (FDIC), Tim Geithner (Federal Reserve Bank of New York), John C. Dugan, (Comptroller of the Currency), Christopher Cox (Chair of the SEC), John M. Reich (Office of Thrift Supervision).
Source: Getty Images/Dominic Bracco li/The Washington Post.

10 The Bankers: Lloyd Blankfein (GS), Jamie Dimon (JP Morgan), Robert Kelly (BNY), Ken Lewis (BofA), Ronald Logue (State Street), John Mack (MS), Vikram Pandit (Citigroup), John Stumpf (Wells Fargo), February 11, 2009 before the House Financial Services Committee.
Source: Getty Images/Tom Williams.

11 Barack Obama, Sheila Bair, and Larry Summers addressing bankers – only one of them was on the side of saving the existing system, April 10, 2009.
Source: Getty Images/Chip Somodevilla.

12 Rep. Barney Frank (MA) and Senator Elizabeth Warren (MA) chat before a House Financial Services Committee hearing on TARP, July 22, 2009.
Source: Getty Images/Brendan Hoffman/Stringer.

13 Unfinished subdivision, Homestead, FL, 2009
Source: Getty Images/Joe Raedle.

14 Housing Eviction, Colorado Springs, CO, February 26, 2009.
Source: Getty Images/John Moore.

15 Foreclosed housing auction, Palmdale, CA, February 25, 2009.
Source: Getty Images/David McNew.

16 Two hundred and fifty homes at auction, Las Vegas, February 24, 2009.
Source: Getty Images/Ethan Miller.

Table 5.3

BANKS' RESERVES FOR FINES & LITIGATION 2017	
($ billions)	
Bank of America	73
JP Morgan/Chase	40
Royal Bank of Scotland	30
UBS, HSBC, Barclays	10
Citigroup	13
Wells Fargo	10
Deutsche Bank	7
Credit Suisse	5
Goldman Sachs	5
Total	193
Moody's Total	273

Source: Moody's, 7/19/17.

home owners, creating "toxic" securities, and improper foreclosure processes such as robo-signed affidavits, lack of accurate records, and failure to deal properly with defaulting home owners. Again, Bank of America and JP Morgan had the largest reserves. Boston Consulting Group similarly estimated in 2017 that US banks had been fined $204 billion between 2009–16 (85% from US regulators' legal claims) and European banks $118 billion (56% from US regulators' legal claims).[23]

The $370 billion total for mortgage restitution plus reserves for fines and litigation was 9% of the combined losses on agency and private RMBS in Table 5.1. It was also 81% of the tangible common equity of the thirteen largest US and European banks and investment banks at the end of 2006. Of course, by the time these charges were estimated, the $370 billion had already been charged against the banks' net worth and some of the reserves might never be required. Nonetheless, the comparison provides one

[23] Boston Consulting Group (2017), exhibit 4, p. 16.

illustration of the scale of the leading banks' culpable mistakes in mortgage origination and securitization.

There is no similar record of penalties borne by the liars.

5.3 Highly Leveraged Corporate Debt

Highly leveraged corporate debt had many forms – loans, high yield bonds, commercial real estate mortgages, highly leveraged financial corporations, and Baa-rated nonfinancial corporate borrowers. This sector lost $4 trillion based on crisis valuations (Table 5.4). These losses were only exceeded by the $4.8 trillion lost on all forms of home mortgages (Table 5.1).

Table 5.4

CORPORATE DEBT LOSSES IN 2008			
	Outstanding ($ billions)	Crisis prices	Losses ($ billions)
Corporate long-term debt	12,785		
commercial mortgages**	3,375		1,300
non-fin'l corporate:			
high yield	1,091	0.50	546
leveraged loans	2,600	0.60	1,040
remainder (BBB)	2,673	0.85	401
commercial banks*	1,426	0.75	357
finance companies	1,200	0.75	300
funding corps	420	0.65	147
Total losses			4,090

* includes holding companies.
** includes multifamily and noncorporate (REITs).
Note on prices: "remainder (BBB)" prices inferred from spreads off 10-year US treasuries; commercial banks and finance companies are each arbitrarily 0.10 lower than BBB, and funding corps a further 0.10.
Source: Altman (2012); Federal Reserve (Financial Accounts of the United States); BIS (2008); public indices; author's estimates and calculations.

Chart 5.10

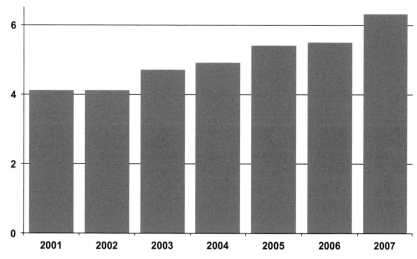

**Average Debt/EBITDA ratios
for LBOs**

Source: Altman (2007).

The best known of these highly leveraged sectors was corporate borrowers, principally for mergers and acquisitions. New highly leveraged corporate loan issues more than doubled between 2004 and 2007 to $1.1 trillion, creating significant risks compared to the past. The debt placed on leveraged buyouts by private equity firms rose from four times Earnings before Interest Depreciation and Amortization (EBITDA) in 2002 to over six times in 2007 (Chart 5.10) and the proportion of loans rated B or lower doubled to 40%. Similarly, B or lower rated high yield bond issues rose from 15% to over 50%.

The data on corporate loans can become confusing because of their terminology. Reference is often to syndicated term loans led by commercial banks that are easy to document. Nonbank investors took 57% of these loans. But investment banks led 62% of new highly leveraged corporate loans that were usually tied to acquisitions and more difficult to document. Nonbank lenders probably took even more of these issues. This was the real shadow banking system often referred to by regulators and academics, but little understood. Hedge funds alone took 35% of highly leveraged loans in 2007, plus they showed a marked appetite for junior debt, holding only 6% of senior debt, but 25% of mezzanine debt (BIS, 2008). The other nonbank lenders were mutual funds, insurance companies, investment managers, and foreigners.

Chart 5.11

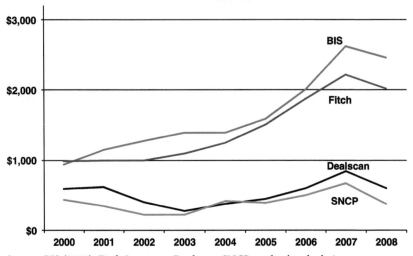

Highly Leveraged Corporate Loans Outstanding
($ billions)

Source: BIS (2008); Fitch Investors; Dealscan; SNCP; author's calculations.

Highly leveraged loans outstanding rose to $2.6 trillion in 2007 and perhaps higher in early 2008 before being affected by the crisis (Chart 5.11). This estimate is based on data from the Bank for International Settlements (BIS) with all of the caveats outlined in Chapter 2 about the inadequacy of estimates based on data from Fitch, Dealscan, and the Shared National Credit Program (SNCP) (Chart 2.39).

As the crisis developed, markets for all forms of highly leveraged corporate debt contracted. New issues of high yield bonds dropped to $1 billion in the 4th quarter of 2008 – only 4% of 4Q 2007 volume.[24] The market was already projecting 2009's 11% default rate. Prices for BB-rated bonds dropped to 60 and for B-rated bonds to 40 (Chart 5.12).[25] On $1 trillion of outstanding high yield bonds these prices created over $500 billion in losses. Goldman Sachs had categorized high yield bonds as potentially difficult to borrow against. Now there was a question whether they deserved collateral value at all.

Prices for highly leveraged loans fell by 35% based on CLO prices (Chart 5.13).[26] But these prices were almost certainly just for the senior tranches as they closely mirror the back-tested prices for S&P's LSTA US Leveraged

[24] SIFMA, Research Quarterly 4Q 2008, March 2009, p. 10.
[25] Based on changes in rates on B-rated corporate bonds, assuming a 20 basis-point change in yield translates to $1 in price for a 10-year bond.
[26] Prices were published by SIFMA, but not continuously.

Chart 5.12

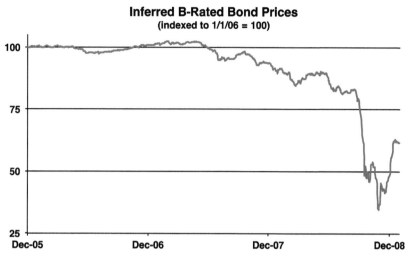

Source: FRED; author's calculations.

Chart 5.13

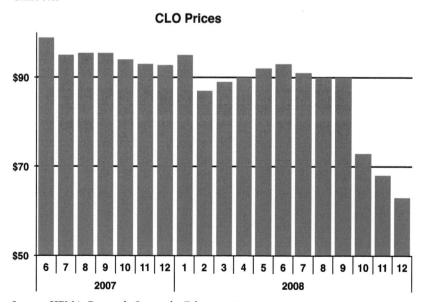

Source: SIFMA, Research Quarterly, February 2010.

Loan Index for senior secured loans. The prices for the 40% of these loans
that were rated B (covenant lite, subordinated, or mezzanine) had to be
much lower. SIFMA's 4Q 2008 Research Report said exchange-traded
closed end loan funds traded down 50% in 2008 (from $92 to $46).[27] The
composite price for all layers of highly leveraged corporate loans must have
been around $60, representing mark-to-market losses of over $1 trillion.
To the extent loans were in the hands of hedge funds, investment managers, mutual funds, SIVs, or held by banks in the process of distributing
them they had to be marked-to-market. Commercial banks could avoid
marking to market by taking the loans into their loan account, which some
did, but the prices for CLOs called into question the value of all corporate
loans since few were to high quality credits.

Highly leveraged corporate loans and high yield bonds do not encompass
all of the highly leveraged corporate debt market. The debt of commercial
banks, finance companies, and funding corporations (typically off-balance
sheet) was highly leveraged even if their bond ratings were investment grade.
Plus, nonfinancial corporations broadly gave up their Aaa/Aa/A ratings in
the last decade as they leveraged up for various strategic purposes. The
median rating for all corporate bonds was Baa – barely above a high yield
rating. Bond prices for financial issuers presumably dropped further than
BBB nonfinancial borrowers that dropped 15%.

5.4 Commercial Real Estate

Commercial real estate is included in the corporate losses in Table 5.4
(above). Commercial real estate carried debt similar to highly leveraged
corporate debt and its losses had an equal large impact. The REIT index
had a 14-year run in which it rose 668% by mid-2008 before it dropped by
two-thirds between early 2008 and March 2009. This was a good liquid
market indicator of commercial real estate prices where it could take
months or even years to sell a property. Using 2009 prices as an indication
of crisis period anticipations, office buildings dropped 52%, apartment
buildings 35%, and retail properties 30% (Chart 5.14).

This difficult environment translated into widespread losses on a mark-to-
market basis. Banks' commercial real estate delinquencies rose to 9% in 2009
(Chart 5.15) and were expected to rise for several years. CMBS issues came to
a halt as spreads rose to 800 basis points on AAA CMBS and 4,000 basis points
(no market) on A-rated CMBS. The apparent mark-to-market losses on

---

[27] SIFMA, Research Report, March 2009, p. 15.

Chart 5.14

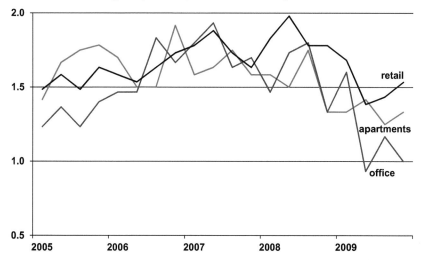

Commercial Real Estate Prices
(per square foot, indexed 1Q2001=1.0)

Source: MBA (2010); post 2006 MBA (2015).

Chart 5.15

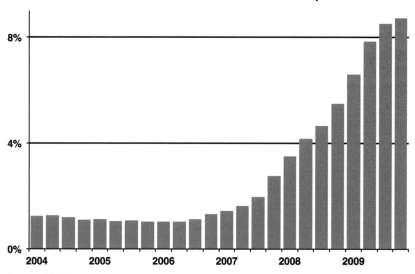

Banks' Commercial Real Estate Delinquencies

Source: FRED.

commercial real estate debt under these circumstances broke down approximately as follows.

- Commercial banks had $1.7 trillion in commercial real estate loans, many for construction. CLO senior debt pricing of $67 is probably an optimistic approximation of value, suggesting losses of $560 billion.
- Prices for $400 billion of A-rated CMBS fell to around $10 implying losses of $360 billion.
- Approximately $200 billion AAA-rated CMBS still existed with prices around 65 that implied losses of $70 billion.
- The balance of commercial real estate mortgages of approximately $1 trillion if priced at $67 (similarly to banks' loans) would imply losses of $330 billion.

These assumptions suggest that commercial real estate loans in aggregate had losses of $1.3 trillion on a mark-to-market basis, just slightly under the losses on high yield bonds and highly leveraged corporate loans.[28] This estimate could be low as the Federal Reserve's data may not include subordinated debt and debt of noncorporate structures such as limited partnerships and established real estate families.

Again, the $1.1 trillion estimate does not represent reported losses. Banks' accounting for loans was lenient if they were extended when a project was under construction, or interest rates were reduced, or terms were renegotiated, or partial payments were made. In addition, commercial real estate loans were broadly spread throughout the country. Community banks with assets of less than $1 billion had 31% of their loans in commercial real estate, but the crisis was not about them.

The aggregate mark-to-market losses of $4 trillion in the corporate debt markets in the midst of the crisis were equal to 28% of GDP. The mark-to-market losses of $9 trillion for combined residential mortgages and highly leveraged corporate debt paralyzed financial markets. As we shall see, the leverage of the country's principal financial institutions magnified their share of these losses many times beyond their tangible common equity.

---

[28] I have included all commercial mortgages as corporate debt even though the Federal Reserve's "Financial Accounts of the United States" only apportions one-third of the $3.5 trillion of commercial and multifamily mortgages to corporations. Much institutional and foreign real estate investment was through what the Federal Reserve may have considered noncorporate structures. Historically, established private families have had significant real estate ownership because of the tax advantages, but while their mortgage debt usually involved nonrecourse structures the Federal Reserve may have considered it noncorporate.

5.5 Financial Institutions' Leverage and Risks

The various financial intermediaries from Fannie Mae and Freddie Mac to the leading investment banks, commercial banks, and AIG were ill-prepared to handle the losses in housing, private RMBS, and highly leveraged corporate debt because of their leverage, illiquidity, and short-term borrowing. It is striking how a dozen large institutions concentrated the risks in these markets such that they threatened the whole financial system.

Fannie Mae and Freddie Mac

Fannie Mae and Freddie Mac participated in the rising risks that created the crisis as they guaranteed mortgages on rising home values, participated in the withdrawal of home equity, and (perhaps unwittingly) guaranteed highly leveraged mortgages on second/investment homes. They were also the largest investors in private RMBS and the most highly leveraged participants in the mortgage markets. Fannie Mae's common equity was 1% of its direct liabilities (mortgage guarantees plus debt) and Freddie Mac's ½% (Table 5.5). Such limited common equity left them in no position to weather the 25% decline in housing prices nationally, or the 50% decline for homes in the most active cities of Los Angeles, Las Vegas, Phoenix, and Miami.

Table 5.5

FANNIE MAE AND FREDDIE MAC 2007 LEVERAGE		
($ billions)		
	Fannie Mae	Freddie Mac
Total mortgage guarantees	2,307	1,739
Total debt	796	739
Total direct financial liabilities	3,103	2,478
Common equity	28	12
% of total direct financial liabilities	1%	0.5%

Sources: 2007 10-Ks.

Fannie Mae, the oldest and largest, illustrates the problems that the two companies had. Ninety-five percent of its mortgages had been originated since 2002, 64% were in the west or southeast, and 28% came from Countrywide. Twenty-five percent of its mortgages were at greater than 80% of value as of the end of 2007 when the decline in housing prices had barely begun. A year later housing prices were down 18%. Monoline insurers covered $116 billion of its mortgages that were originally greater than 80% loan-to-value.[29] It had investments of $750 billion in mortgages and securities, but $324 billion was in RMBS, $145 billion of them private RMBS that were about to drop over 50%. The decline in these private RMBS holdings alone could wipe out Fannie Mae's equity five times over.[30]

Fannie Mae and Freddie Mac's government regulator, the Office of Federal Housing Enterprise Oversight (OFHEO), made mechanical, politicized evaluations of the two agencies' capital adequacy such that OFHEO was about to declare them adequately capitalized just as Treasury Secretary Hank Paulson was about to take them over as bankrupt.[31]

In taking over the two agencies, the US government assumed direct financial liabilities of $5.6 trillion, dwarfing all other remedial measures. The two agencies lost $253 billion pre-tax in 2008–11 – six times their combined common equity in 2007.

Investment Banks

The leverage of investment and commercial banks also contributed greatly to the crisis, and, as with Fannie Mae and Freddie Mac, regulators had weak understanding of their finances and thus used standards that made the banks appear adequately capitalized. Ian Lowitt, Lehman Brothers' new CFO, was able to declare in the firm's 3Q 2008 conference call just before it collapsed:

Importantly, as we will discuss today, we ended the third quarter with a capital position and leverage ratios stronger than the second quarter. Total shareholder equity increased 8% to $28 billion; we reduced net leverage to 10.6 times from 12.1 times and our Tier 1 capital ratio is estimated at approximately 11% versus 10.7% last quarter.[32]

It is widely taken for granted that investment banks' became highly leveraged in the years leading up to the crisis. Total assets of the five largest investment banks grew from twenty-four times shareholders' equity in 2002 to thirty-one times in 2007 (Chart 5.16), but financial instruments

---

[29] Fannie Mae 2007 10-K, pp. 27, 126–7, 138–9.   [30] Fannie Mae 2007 10-K, p. 89.
[31] Paulson (2010), pp. 164–9.
[32] Lehman Brothers Press Release, 3rd quarter preliminary results, September 2008, p. 1.

Chart 5.16

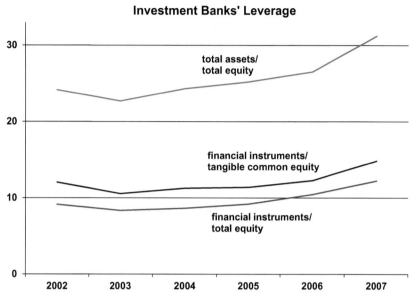

Investment Banks' Leverage

Source: Annual Reports.

only grew from nine times total equity to twelve times. An even more pertinent ratio, financial instruments to tangible common equity, was stable at eleven–twelve times from 2002 to 2006. Only in 2007 did it rise to fifteen times. Probably the most important measure was how fast financial instruments grew, averaging 19% compound annual growth from 2002 to 2007, inviting quality problems (Table 5.6). Goldman Sachs' financial instruments grew at a 28% rate, Bear Stearns at 25%, and Lehman Brothers at 22%.

Understanding the role of investment banks' leverage in the crisis requires analyzing more subtle aspects such as tangible common equity, long-term funding, dubious unspecified "Other Assets," and the quality of their illiquid investments. From a credit point of view, investment banks' shareholders' equity had to be adjusted for intangible assets, goodwill, and preferred stock as in Table 5.7. The resulting tangible common equity at the end of 2007 was 25% lower than total shareholders' equity.

Investment banks were not subject to standard capitalization ratios historically. Their brokerage subsidiaries had to follow SEC rules that established "liquidating equity in respect of securities positions" (not " total assets") and "net capital" available to meet obligations to customers (SEC rule 240.15c3-1). At the end of 2005 the holding companies became subject

Table 5.6

GROWTH in INVESTMENT BANKS' FINANCIAL INSTRUMENTS							
($ billions)							
	2002	2003	2004	2005	2006	2007	Growth rate
Bear Stearns	58	59	77	116	155	172	25%
Goldman Sachs	130	161	212	277	335	453	28%
Lehman Brothers	119	136	144	177	227	313	22%
Merrill Lynch	194	212	253	218	287	318	11%
Morgan Stanley	173	203	204	261	375	375	17%
averages	135	154	178	210	276	326	19%

Source: Annual Reports.

Table 5.7

INVESTMENT BANKS' TANGIBLE COMMON EQUITY in 2007				
($ billions)				
	Shareholder equity	Goodwill and intangibles	Preferred stock	Tangible common equity
Bear Stearns	11	1	1	9
Goldman Sachs	43	5	3	35
Lehman Brothers	22	4	1	17
Merrill Lynch	37	5	9	23
Morgan Stanley	31	4	1	26
	144	19	15	110

Source: Annual Reports.

to group wide SEC regulation and had to meet Basel II capital requirements monthly on a consolidated basis. The firms calculated their own risks ("Adjusted Assets") following SEC rules but the SEC had no authority over

Chart 5.17

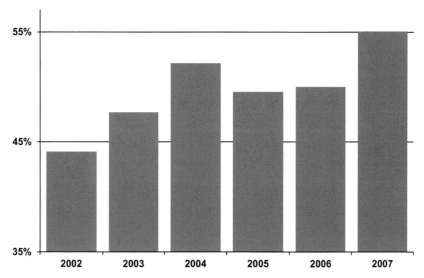

Leading Investment Banks' Tangible Common Equity plus Long-term Debt % of Financial Instruments

Note: Bear Stearns, Goldman Sachs, Lehman Brothers, Merrill Lynch, and Morgan Stanley.
Source: Annual Reports and author's calculations.

the vast majority of the holding companies' subsidiaries. SEC Chairman Christopher Cox testified soon after Lehman Brothers' failure that the SEC was not the regulator for 193 of its 200 subsidiaries.[33] The investment banks also internally adjusted their capital ratios for long-term funding. They were aware of their growing illiquidity and thus built up their tangible common equity plus long-term debt from under 45% of their Financial Instruments in 2002 to over 55% in 2007 (Chart 5.17).

In fact, even tangible common equity was less than it appeared. Any lender doing a cautious credit study of an investment bank would reduce tangible common equity by "Other Assets" because they had uncertain value, often dependent upon future earnings. This was similar to the Tier 1 equity calculation that the Federal Reserve imposed upon commercial banks, although complete deduction is more severe.

Goldman Sachs specified the elements of Other Assets in its 2007 annual report ($ millions):[34]

---

[33] Cox (2008), Christopher Cox testimony before the Committee on Oversight and Government Reform, US House of Representatives, 10/23/08.
[34] Goldman Sachs 2007 Annual Report, note 10, p. 121.

Property, leasehold improvements and equipment	$8,975
Goodwill and identifiable intangible assets	5,092
Income tax-related assets	4,177
Equity-method investments	2,014
Miscellaneous receivables and other	3,809
Total	$24,067

Table 5.8

INVESTMENT BANKS' "MARKET READY" EQUITY CAPITAL in 2007			
($ billions)			
	Tangible equity	Other assets	Tangible less other assets
Bear Stearns	10	9	1
Goldman Sachs	35	19	16
Lehman Brothers	17	5	12
Merrill Lynch	23	8	15
Morgan Stanley	26	9	17
Totals	111	50	61

Source: 2007 10-Ks.

Other investment banks also included interests in unconsolidated entities and conduits, pension fund surpluses, discontinued businesses, foreclosed real estate, securitization residuals, mortgage-servicing rights, loans in the transition to securitization, miscellaneous business assets, and claims against others. The problem was that Other Assets were large compared to tangible common equity, unknowable, and often dependent upon future profitability. Subtracting "Other Assets" as in Table 5.8 from the five leading investment banks' tangible common equity produced a sobering total of only $61 billion of "market ready" equity or what the SEC in its rule 240.15c3-1 governing capital requirements calls "liquidating equity."

The other aspect of leverage that was decisive in the crisis was the liquidity of investment banks' assets. Goldman Sachs presented this in its 2007 annual report:[35]

Certain financial instruments may be more difficult to fund on a secured basis during times of market stress. Accordingly, we generally hold higher levels of total capital for these assets than more liquid types of financial instruments. The table below sets forth our aggregate holdings in these categories of financial instruments:

Mortgage and other asset-backed loans and securities	$46 billion
Bank loans	$49 billion
High yield securities	$13 billion
Emerging market debt securities	$3 billion
Private equity and real estate fund investments	$16 billion
Emerging market equity securities	$8 billion
ICBC ordinary shares	$7 billion
SMFG convertible preferred stock	$4 billion
Other restricted public equity securities	$3 billion
Other investments in funds	$3 billion

Goldman Sachs did not add up this list but it came to $152 billion versus the firm's "financial instruments owned" of $553 billion, short-term borrowing of $137 billion, tangible common equity of $32 billion, and market ready equity of $13 billion, depending upon what metric one was evaluating. Nor did Goldman Sachs mention that these investments bore a higher level of risk than traditional publicly marketable securities and that a decline of 20% would wipe out the firm's tangible common equity and a decline of 10% would wipe out its market ready equity.

In September, the $61 billion of market ready equity in the four remaining large investment banks was the base financing $1.3 trillion in investment assets as we saw in Chapter 4 (Table 4.14). A 10% decline in the aggregate value of these investments would exceed these firms' shareholders' equity, an 8% decline would exceed their tangible common equity, and just 4% would exceed their market ready equity.

Bear Stearns

A distinguishing feature among the investment banks was how many got their investments wrong. Bear Stearns had the worst risk profile. Its tangible common equity at the end of 2007 was only $10 billion and that was without

[35] Goldman Sachs 2007 10-K, p. 98.

deducting $9 billion of "Other Assets." Bear Stearns had imposed two weak asset sectors on this equity base. It had $46 billion of whole mortgages and mortgage-backed securities. Of this, $15 billion was commercial mortgages concentrated in the resort industry where cap rates (risks) were highest.[36] Retained (unsalable) interests in old MBS accounted for another $8 billion. The remainder was in private RMBS and whole mortgages. Bear Stearns also held $35 billion of level 2 corporate debt of which $9 billion was high yield loans and $26 billion was unidentified corporate instruments. The latter was probably of a high yield nature. It also had $14 billion in unfunded highly leveraged corporate loan commitments.

Bear Stearns reported a 4th quarter 2007 loss after a $2.7 billion mortgage write-off and began losing both credit and clients.[37] James Cayne, CEO, resigned in January after selling stock (a Bear Stearns "sin"). In an important meeting that Bear Stearns held with hedge fund clients on February 20, 2008, John Paulson, who knew a great deal about the mortgage securities market at that time, asked the chief financial officer what the firm's level 2 and 3 assets were. When the reply was "I'll get back to you," Paulson said, "Well, I'll tell you what the number is. It's $220 billion. So what I'm seeing is that if you have $14 billion of equity … a small movement in the assets can wipe out your equity entirely."[38] When Moody's downgraded Bear Stearns' private MBS residual interests to junk status on March 11, both lenders and customers accelerated their withdrawal of funds. According to Bear Stearns' 1st quarter 10-Q:

A substantial number of prime brokerage clients have moved accounts to other clearing brokers. Customer margin balances were $66 billion at March 24, 2008, down 23% from $86 billion at February 29, 2008. Customer shorts at March 24, 2008 were $66 billion, down from $88 billion at February 29, 2008. Institutional equity and fixed-income commission and sales activity has declined precipitously to well less than 50% of activity levels in the first quarter of 2008.[39]

Bear Stearns' ability to borrow disappeared in mid-March when management put its needs at $60-$100 billion. Its advisor, Lazard Frères, estimated that a mere 2.5% decline in its securities holdings would wipe out its equity.[40]

---

[36] NAIC (2017–2), table 1, cited 2007 resort cap rates at 307 basis points over 10-year US treasuries vs 1 basis point for offices, 49 for multifamily, and 102 for retail; NCREIF (2018); Mellen (2019).

[37] William D. Cohan, *New York Times*, 4/14/16, "Bear Stearns Emails Show its Financing Breaking Away."

[38] Zuckerman (2009), p. 256.

[39] Bear Stearns 2007 10-K, p. 95; 1Q 2008 10-Q, pp. 39, 47, 66.

[40] SEC.gov, JP Morgan Chase & Co., Form S-4, April 11, 2008, p. 43.

Lehman Brothers

Lehman Brothers increased its risk profile and illiquidity recklessly in 2006–07. It had $71 billion in commercial real estate exposure (debt, equity, land, and lending commitments) at the end of 2007 versus $17 billion of tangible common equity. It ignored its own risk guidelines, exceeding them by multiples rather than percentages, when it joined Tishman Speyer in the acquisition of Archstone Realty, a public REIT that owned rental apartments. Lehman Brothers largely failed to syndicate this exposure to other investors. The deal exposed Lehman to a commitment of $11 billion. The Office of Thrift Supervision undertook an examination of the firm as a result and issued a report in early 2008 declaring that Lehman Brothers was "materially overexposed" to commercial real estate – a rare preemptive regulatory step. Lehman Brothers also expanded its leveraged loan exposure to almost $100 billion by the end of 2007 by broadly signing "covenant free" loans in pursuit of the accompanying merger business.[41]

Lehman Brothers made an effort to reduce its real estate and lending commitments in the first half of 2008 as Standard & Poor's downgraded the company's rating to A and Moody's announced a "negative outlook" for the company's A1 rating. For a company that was supposed to be in the business of making markets and underwriting, Lehman Brothers was simply too illiquid. It reported $269 billion in financial instruments of which only $68 billion was ready collateral. The rest was mortgage whole loans, securitization residuals, outright real estate, mortgage-servicing rights, highly leveraged corporate debt, derivative assets, private equity, and minority investments. The $68 billion of ready collateral was versus apparent short-term borrowing of $124 billion (its short-term liabilities were confusing). The company was able to sell $4 billion of common stock and $2 billion of preferred stock in 2008, but that would prove to be no help.[42]

Merrill Lynch

Merrill Lynch's CEO, Stan O'Neal, pushed for profits in what he seemed to think was the low-risk fixed-income business, promoting a London-based salesman, Osman Semerci, to run their CDO business free of any credit restraints.[43] Merrill Lynch reported 2nd quarter 2008 Total Capital equal

[41] Valukas (2010), pp. 108–13, 119–23, 296–302.
[42] Lehman Brothers 2Q 2008 10-Q, May 31, 2008, pp. 24–8, 33, 37, 51, 103.
[43] Farrell (2010), chapter 1.

to 12% of Risk-adjusted Assets, but it had $35 billion of unsalable CDOs coupled with $20 billion of derivative hedges that were mostly with monoline insurance companies and $175 billion of CMBS and other corporate loans and commitments with sharply falling values. Its losses in structured securities were $55 billion through the 3rd quarter of 2008, including $26 billion on CDOs. It sold $30 billion of CDOs in July 2008 at 22 cents on the dollar.[44] These losses were against tangible common equity of $23 billion.

Morgan Stanley

Morgan Stanley reported its 2Q 2008 Total Capital Ratio was 18.6% and Tier 1 Capital Ratio 12.4%. Both Moody's and Standard & Poor's downgraded its debt to A1/A+ although it earned over $1 billion in the quarter.[45] Morgan Stanley had engaged in high-risk efforts to create earnings that justified John Mack replacing its prior CEO, Phil Purcell, in 2005 after a rebellion by current and former Morgan Stanley executives. Its $25 billion of tangible common equity was exposed to $88 billion of real estate[46] and $94 billion of highly leveraged corporate debt.[47]

Commercial Banks

The largest commercial banks also needed government relief even while they were acknowledged as "well capitalized" by regulators. Bank of America outlined the regulatory standards in its 2007 Annual Report:

To meet minimum adequately capitalized regulatory requirements, an institution must maintain a Tier 1 Capital ratio of four percent and a Total Capital ratio of eight percent. A well-capitalized institution must generally maintain capital ratios 200 bps (basis points) higher than the minimum guidelines.

The five largest commercial banks averaged unvarying capital ratios of 8% Tier 1 and 12% Tier 2 from 2002 to 2007 (Chart 5.18), but in hindsight these ratios were meaningless. The banks had problems with tangible equity,

[44] Merrill Lynch 10-Q 6/30/08, pp. 38–9, 50, 69, 109; Benmelech (2009), table 1, p. 163.
[45] Morgan Stanley 2Q 2008 10-Q, pp. 1, 22, 92.
[46] $29 billion in commercial real estate, $28 billion in subprime, Alt-A, and jumbo mortgages, and $31 billion of VIE potential loss exposure. Morgan Stanley 2Q, 2008 10-Q, pp. 34, 72–6, 91.
[47] Morgan Stanley 2Q 2008 10-Q, p. 98. Includes unfunded commitments of $52 billion and estimated high yield bonds of $18 billion based on Goldman Sachs' percentage.

Chart 5.18

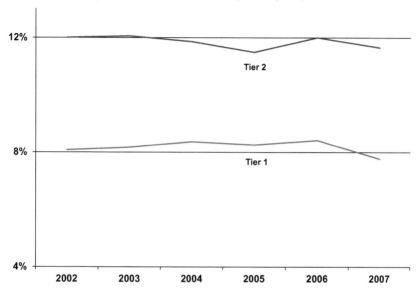

Leading Commercial Banks' Regulatory Capital Ratios

Note: averages for Bank of America, Citigroup, JP Morgan, Wachovia Corp., and Wells Fargo.
Sources: Annual Reports.

"market ready" equity, and poor assets similar to investment banks, albeit without the need to collateralize their deposits.

Greg Farrell in *The Crash of the Titans*, his story of the collapse of Merrill Lynch, had a revealing paragraph on the thinking of Bank of America as it suddenly found its credit challenged in 2008:

Lewis (BofA's CEO) and his management team had clung to the notion that Bank of America was well capitalized because its "Tier 1 capital ratio" was close to the industry norm, but in the harsh financial environment in which banks were now operating, the Tier 1 ratio – which regulators relied upon – was viewed as less pertinent than the real-world metrics of the tangible common equity ratio.[48]

Tangible common equity that excluded goodwill, other intangibles, and mortgage-servicing rights was less than half book common equity for the leading commercial banks (Table 5.9). Market ready equity that also

---

[48] Farrell (2010), p. 258.

Table 5.9

COMMERCIAL BANKS' EQUITY IN 2007				
($ billions)				
	Book equity	Tangible equity[1]	Other assets	Market ready equity
Bank of America	145	54	154	−100
Citigroup	114	50	169	−119
JP Morgan	123	63	74	−11
Wachovia	75	30	51	−21
Wells Fargo	47	34	37	−3
Totals	504	231	485	−254

[1] book equity less goodwill, other intangibles, and mortgage servicing rights.

Sources: Annual Reports.

excluded "Other Assets" was uniformly negative. Goodwill, intangibles, and "Other Assets" were particularly weak assets because of bank consolidation in the previous twenty years. Large elements of "Other Assets" and their valuations were inherited in these mergers and not subject to critical evaluation. These were especially vulnerable points at Bank of America and Citigroup because of their many acquisitions.

The banks' $231 billion of tangible common equity was the base financing almost $3 trillion of vulnerable financial assets (Table 4.13). A decline of just 7% would exceed the tangible common equity of Bank of America, Citigroup and Wachovia Corp., 10% for Wells Fargo, and 13% for JP Morgan.

These estimates exclude possible losses in the banks' derivatives portfolios. Traditional regulatory standards of capital adequacy were unable to deal with their derivatives businesses. The most active US banks in the derivative markets are outlined in Table 5.10. Goldman Sachs had the largest gross assets, while JP Morgan and Citigroup had the largest notional values by a wide margin. Table 5.10 does not include the European banks that had equally large derivatives books. While the banks reported

Table 5.10

INVESTMENT & COMMERCIAL BANKS' DERIVATIVES in 2007				
($ billions)				
	Gross assets	Gross liabilities	Net	Notional values
Bank of America	35	22	13	3,046
Bear Stearns	20	13	7	13,400
Citigroup	77	104	−27	36,714
Goldman Sachs	106	99	7	2,054
Lehman Brothers	41	29	12	738
Merrill Lynch	61	73	−12	4,563
JP Morgan	77	69	8	77,249
Morgan Stanley	77	72	5	7,120

Sources: Annual Reports.

relatively modest net assets or liabilities, their capital appeared meaningless versus their gross assets and liabilities.

Almost all of these derivatives were over-the-counter transactions for which the legal and economic structures had evolved over the years such that it was difficult for outside observers to have confidence in the documentation that established valuations, collateral requirements, counterparty offsets, credit risks, and enforceability. There were frequent media comments that banks' top executives had an inadequate grasp of their derivatives exposure.

Credit default swaps were particularly damaging for some of the banks. Their market value surged from $0.5 trillion at the end of 2006 to $5.6 trillion at the end of 2008, that meant that one side of these swaps was losing heavily. Their leverage (notional value/market value) shrunk from sixty-one times to seven times and meant huge margin calls. It is difficult to aggregate these effects, however, because reporting on credit default swaps differed from bank to bank. They spread losses and gains among derivatives accounts, fixed-income accounts, structured sales, and accrued liabilities. Sometimes losses occurred in off-balance sheet SIVs. Collateral calls

Table 5.11

THE LARGEST LOSERS TO CREDIT DEFAULT SWAPS			
($ billions)			
	Tangible 2007 equity	CDS 2008 losses	CDS 2007 losses	Monoline exposure
AIG	96	−29	−11	−36
Citigroup	50	−22	−22	−12
Merrill Lynch	23	−28	−8	−10
Morgan Stanley	26		−9	−12
UBS	21	−37	−21	−8
	216	−116	−71	−78

Sources: Annual Reports.

did not necessarily translate into realized losses but challenged the victims' liquidity.

Since one firm's loss was another's gain, the problems in the crisis occurred when the losses were concentrated, as for AIG, Citigroup, Merrill Lynch, Morgan Stanley, and UBS. These five companies combined had pre-tax derivatives losses in 2007–08 of $187 billion, equal to 87% of their tangible common equity (Table 5.11). Some of their credit default swaps were hedged but $78 billion with monoline insurance companies was of little value.

The monoline insurance companies used credit default swaps to guarantee various asset-backed securities based on private RMBS, CMBS, CDOs, and CLOs. AMBAC and MBIA, the principal insurers, had $175 billion of CDO and CLO guarantees.[49] All of the monoline insurance companies teetered on the edge of bankruptcy.

Commercial banks' stock prices appear to explain much of their risk behavior as Wachovia, Wells Fargo, and Bank of America were rewarded for their real estate concentration through 2007. Wachovia and Bank of America were punished for it in 2008 (Chart 5.19). Citigroup's weak stock performance throughout 2004–08 may explain its aggressive efforts to catch up.

[49] AMBAC 2008 Annual Report, p. 137; MBIA 2008 Annual Report, p. 11.

Citigroup's problems illustrated how important it was to understand the investments a bank was making and how it was financing them. Citigroup reported a 2Q 2008 Total Capital Ratio of 13%, but the bank had risks gone wrong on a scale that threatened the whole system. Its tangible common equity of $50 billion was only 2% of total assets and 4% of risk-adjusted assets (Table 5.12).

Table 5.12

CITIGROUP'S TANGIBLE EQUITY RATIOS 2007	
($ billions)	
Tangible equity	50
Total assets	2,188
Tangible equity % of total assets	2%
Risk-adjusted assets	1,253
Tangible equity % of risk-adjusted assets	4%

Source: Citigroup 2007 Annual Report; 2008 2Q.

Chart 5.19

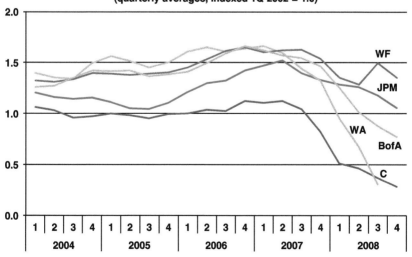

Source: Annual Reports.

Table 5.13

CITIGROUP'S MARKET EXPOSURE 2007	
($ billions)	
Private RMBS, CDOs, etc.	305
Conventional mortgages + home equity	268
Commercial real estate	87
Highly leveraged corporate debt	165
Public equities	107
Non-marketable equities	<u>22</u>
Total	954

Source: Table 4.13.

Citigroup had almost $1 trillion of serious market exposure at the end of 2007 supported by only $50 billion of tangible equity (Table 5.13). These commitments are not easy to untangle, because Citigroup was aggressive on many fronts, but also because of its weak disclosure. Various forms of residential mortgages accounted for 60% of the exposure. The combination of commercial real estate and highly leveraged corporate debt was 26% of the exposure. It also had the largest position in public equities at $107 billion although public equities were more easily hedged than other investments.

There was additional risk in other less market-oriented investments. It held $300 billion of foreign government, corporate, and other debt of which 75% had fair values that were levels 2 or 3. At least $40 billion was in Spain and Italy.

Citigroup procured its assets wholesale where credit controls were weakest. It doubled its loans on US consumer real estate between 2003–07. It doubled its 2007 provision for consumer loan losses to $16 billion on $63 billion of second mortgages, over half of which were originated through third parties.[50] The bulk of its highly leveraged corporate loan commitments were generated in the auction market to fund private equity transactions. It lost $20 billion pre-tax on subprime CDOs in the second half of 2007 that it bought in the open market.

---

[50] Citigroup 2007 10-K, pp. 7, 41, 48, 52, 54–5, 129.

Table 5.14

CITIGROUP'S BORROWING 2007	
($ billions)	
Total balance sheet borrowing:	1,271
Short-term debt	445
Unconsolidated VIEs	356
Unconsolidated SPEs	83
Tender Option bonds	50
% short-term	**53%**

Source: Citigroup 2007 Annual Report.

Fifty-three percent of Citigroup's $1.3 trillion of on and off-balance sheet borrowing was short term (Table 5.14). It had $146 billion of foreign deposits (up from $34 billion in 2005) that were vulnerable given its declining credit ratings. This short-term borrowing came under pressure during 2007 when it was already down $200 billion from its peak.[51] One of the pressures arose from Citigroup's aggressive use of off-balance sheet Special Purpose Entities (SPEs) and Variable Interest Entities (VIEs). It had $356 billion of unconsolidated VIEs at the end of 2007 of which $100 billion was funded with ABCP. It also had unconsolidated "Alternative Investments" that shifted from $114 billion at year-end 2006 to only $11 billion at the end of 2007. It had to consolidate most of this when forced to repurchase $25 billion of commercial paper in July 2007 that was funding SPEs and it effectively guaranteed $58 billion of SPE debt. It had also set up $50 billion of municipal Tender Option Bond Trusts with $50 billion of commercial paper funding.[52] Commercial paper funding for these various structured vehicles evaporated during 2007.

Citigroup was second only to JP Morgan in its notional derivatives contracts of $36 trillion. Within these contracts, it had $1.5 trillion of equity and commodities derivatives and $3.7 trillion of credit derivatives. These were not garden-variety interest rate swaps where parties exchanged interest rate differentials. Even netting out $2.5 trillion of credit default contracts where Citigroup was the beneficiary, there still remained $2.7 trillion of

[51] Citigroup 2007 10-K, p. 192.   [52] Citigroup 2007 10-K, pp. 86–7, 91–2.

high-risk exposure – over fifty times its tangible common equity.[53] What problems lurked within this enormous book could only be guessed at.

Citigroup posted a $17 billion pre-tax loss in the 4th quarter of 2007 and a 94% decline in pre-tax income for 2007. Its goodwill, intangible, and "Other Assets" suspiciously jumped $84 billion to $215 billion. The company cut its quarterly dividend from $0.54 to $0.32, and its stock closed 2007 at $29 versus a high of $56 in 2006. S&P cut Citigroup's rating in December to AA-, and Moody's cut its rating twice to Aa3.[54] In the first half of 2008 Citigroup had a pre-tax loss of $14 billion after increasing its provision for loan losses $8 billion (130%) and taking losses of $32 billion on subprime, Alt-A, and highly leveraged loans and its exposure to monoline insurers. It still had exposure to $38 billion of CDOs, $24 billion of highly leveraged loans, $16 billion of Alt-A loans, and $7 billion of monoline guarantees – $75 billion.[55]

Robert Rubin is a mystery in Citigroup's errant behavior. He was one of the most successful US Treasury Secretaries, retiring in 1999. Sandy Weill quickly persuaded him to join Citigroup as part of the three-man Office of the Chairman with a contract that promised $15 million a year and made him the second highest paid employee thereafter.[56] Later proxies listed him as Chairman of the Executive Committee. He became Chairman of the Board of Directors when Chuck Prince resigned in November 2007, but ceded the job to Sir Win Bischoff (Citigroup Europe) almost immediately. Rubin beneficially owned over five million shares of Citigroup worth $250 million at their high in 2007.[57]

Citigroup's trading activities were familiar to Rubin having run fixed income on his way to co-Senior Partner of Goldman Sachs. His early career in risk arbitrage was legendary. Few people in American understood risk better than he.

He had an important influence on Citigroup's strategies. The *New York Times* reported the following in April 2008.

Early in 2005, Citigroup's board asked the CEO, Mr. Prince, and several top lieutenants to develop a growth strategy for its fixed-income business. Mr. Rubin peppered colleagues with questions as they formulated the plan, according to current and former Citigroup employees. With Citigroup falling behind Wall Street rivals like Morgan Stanley and Goldman Sachs, Mr. Rubin pushed for the bank to increase its activity in high-growth areas like structured credit.[58]

---

[53] Citigroup 2007 10-K, p. 57.   [54] Citigroup 2007 10-K, p. 79.
[55] Citigroup 2Q 2008 10-Q, pp. 4, 7, 31, 47, 51.   [56] Citigroup 2005 Proxy, p. 48.
[57] Citigroup 2006 Proxy, p. 44.
[58] *New York Times*, April 27, 2008, "Where was the Wiseman?"

This was already late in the game. Did Rubin encourage Citigroup's risks in CDOs, CLOs, SIVs, subprime RMBS, and credit default swaps? Did he approve of the bank's leverage, short-term debt, and vulnerable international exposure? Did he have no objections to sourcing mortgages and consumer loans through brokers and buying CLOs in the open market? Where was the legendary Rubin discipline? Was his judgment overwhelmed by the trading legacy of Salomon Brothers at Citigroup? He reportedly told friends that he wasn't responsible for what was going on at Citigroup, which appeared inconsistent with his pay and titles.

Paulson and Geithner made no mention of him in their memoirs; yet Paulson grew up with Rubin at Goldman Sachs and was on the management committee with him. Geithner was a Rubin protégé in the Treasury and owed his job at the New York Federal Reserve to him. It is hard to believe that Paulson and Geithner were not regularly on the phone to him about Citigroup's problems unless he claimed he had a conflict in dealing with the government because of his past as Treasury Secretary. What explains their silence in their memoirs? Did they fear his disapproval? Most people sought it, if only because it was so hard to get. Yet his stature had been reduced after the Clinton era as a vague figure at Citigroup.

He resigned in January 2009, close on the heels of Vikram Pandit becoming CEO. The annual report did not have the usual notice of thanks to a highly placed executive. The 2009 proxy referred to him as a "former senior counselor." Did he leave amidst ill will at the worst possible moment for Citigroup? Was he bitter about his stock losses of over $200 million? Did he panic, fearing a depression? Did he think he was saving his good name and influence in Washington? His is an untapped story in the Citigroup debacle.

Wachovia Corp., an icon of the southeast establishment, was another example of the need to understand investments and funding rather than simple capital ratios. It reported Total Capital to risk-adjusted assets of 13%. It had committed heavily to aggressive California mortgage lending after it bought Golden West Financial in 2006 for $34 billion. Golden West's principal mortgage offering was "Pic-a-Pay" loans where the borrower could choose a minimum payment that retired no principal and allowed interest to be capitalized up to property value. Eighty-five percent of these loans were made under a "Quick Qualifier" program in which borrower documentation was minimized. By the end of 2007, its Pic-a-Pay loans were $120 billion, $71 billion of which were in California. Wachovia's total consumer real estate loans went from $51 billion in 2003 to $228 billion in 2007 and it also held $105 billion of private mortgage-backed and asset-backed securities. On the financing side, it had $50 billion of short-term borrowing through asset-backed commercial paper (ABCP), SIVs, and other more complicated off-balance sheet vehicles. Wachovia raised $12 billion in new equity early in 2008, but when housing values dropped this was offset by $33 billion of losses, mostly in the 3rd quarter, nearly wiping out its tangible common equity. Markets for its ABCP dried up and the bank began to lose deposits quickly. In its own words, there was "... a 47 percent decline in higher cost commercial money market accounts, which are more sensitive to the market turmoil." Unable to fund itself, it turned to the FDIC for assistance in arranging a merger with Citigroup, but that deal was topped by Wells Fargo when it agreed to acquire Wachovia without federal assistance.[59]

AIG, General Motors, and General Electric

AIG, General Motors' finance subsidiary GMAC, and General Electric resembled the banks in making poor investment decisions with high leverage. AIG had been an AAA-rated insurance company with a sophisticated reputation and a well-performing stock for a long time. It was not excessively leveraged in 2003 when it had $62 billion of debt and $71 billion of equity. However, in the low-rate environment of 2001–06 AIG earned only 5% on its aggregate investments and turned aggressively to securities lending, derivatives, and short-term borrowing. Worst of all, it focused on private RMBS. By August 2008, it had lent out $69 billion of its insurance subsidiaries' securities that had become a form of borrowing rather than lending because AIG had reinvested most of the cash collateral put up by borrowers in private RMBS. As a result, it held $141 billion of private RMBS and other asset-backed debt and $27 billion of high yield debt. A subsidiary, AIG Financial Products, had credit default swaps with a notional value of $149, a case in which the notional value was potentially the true risk exposure. And the consolidated company had $103 billion of short-term debt.

AIG came under pressure as the asset-backed markets collapsed in the summer of 2008. It published the data in Table 5.15 in its 2008 10-K to illustrate the declines in the securities it held or had guaranteed. On average, these prices dropped from 76% of par in 2007 to 39% in 2008.

AIG consistently argued that things were better than market prices indicated. Nonetheless, the loss at these prices on aggregate exposure of

---

[59] Wachovia Corp. 2007 Annual Report, pp. 30, 32, 37, 54, 87, 88; 2Q 2008 10-Q, p. 75; 3Q 2008 10-Q, pp. 3, 29, 37, 39.

Table 5.15

AIG ABS PRICES*		
	2008	**2007**
RMBS prime	50%	84%
RMBS Alt-A	32%	n.a.
RMBS subprime	29%	65%
CMBS	55%	93%
CDOs	18%	48%
Other	51%	92%
Average	39%	76%
*Average price at Dec. 31		

Source: AIG 2008 10-K.

$317 billion was over $120 billion versus its $87 billion of tangible common equity. The company had a profitable commercial and retail insurance business, but overall it lost $109 billion pre-tax in 2008. There was an aggregate cash demand by counterparties in September 2008 of $77 billion as private RMBS prices collapsed and the company's ratings dropped to A2/A-. Counterparties owing collateral to AIG held off tendering it in case AIG went bankrupt. Securities borrowers returned their securities and demanded their cash back, another form of cash drain. Regulators compounded liquidity difficulties by forbidding upstream lending to the parent by its insurance subsidiaries. AIG's commercial paper couldn't be sold and even the Export Credit Agency cut back AIG's borrowing. The company hired JP Morgan, Goldman Sachs, and Blackstone Group in quick succession to raise money, but as its stock fell from a high of $73 in 2007 to $4 in September 2008 the effort was unavailing and it needed to be rescued by The Federal Reserve Bank of New York.[60]

General Motors was a failing company that diverted GMAC, its auto finance subsidiary, into mortgages and also needed to be rescued by the government. GM's problems predated the financial crisis as its share of the

---

[60]　AIG 2003 10-K, p. 54; 2007 10-K, pp. 161, 248, 263; 2008 10-K, pp. 3–5, 14, 17–18, 23, 28, 36, 40, 130–1, 146, 248 (note a).

US vehicle market fell from 48% in 1960 to 24% in 2006 and its stock fell from a high of $66 in 2002 to $19 in 2006. The company suffered from inflated union costs, large unfunded postretirement benefits (493,000 retirees versus 280,000 working in 2006), low productivity, weak design, changing consumer tastes, and management more focused on finance than vehicles. Following the 2000–01 recession, the company leaned almost exclusively on its GMAC finance arm for earnings. Its automotive arm had pre-tax losses of $12 billion in 2004–06 while GMAC earned $2–3 billion each year. However, the secret behind GMAC's earnings was a plunge into nonconforming residential mortgage lending that made it the 7th largest originator in the USA. In 2003, GMAC's finance assets were 56% automotive and 44% mortgages. By 2007, its finance assets had flipped and were 37% automotive and 63% mortgages.[61] This was achieved by sourcing 83% of its mortgages through wholesale channels and making 75% of its loans on nonconforming mortgages. It was also providing warehousing for mortgage originators and land and construction financing to homebuilders and resorts.[62] Reacting to the developing mortgage problems, GM in its final act of dismemberment sold 51% of GMAC in November 2006 to a group led by Cerberus Capital Management, a specialist in distress investing that had previously acquired Chrysler Financial.

General Motors was crushed by the turn of events in 2008. Sales were down 25% from 2006 and market share from 24% to 21.5%. After losing $12 billion pre-tax in 2006–07, it lost $29 billion in 2008 and talk was widespread that it would declare bankruptcy. Its stock fell from a high of $43 in the 4th quarter of 2007 to $2 in the 4th quarter of 2008 (Chart 5.20). The company got $13 billion from the TARP at the price of a Viability Plan that undertook to lower costs by reducing wages and benefits to competitive levels, laying off 57,000 workers, closing 14 of 47 plants, closing one-third of its dealers, and tying pension and other retirement benefits to the future of GM's stock.[63]

GMAC lost $13 billion pre-tax in 2007–08 and also threatened bankruptcy. It was granted bank holding company status after it did a recapitalization at the end of 2008 in which the TARP contributed $5 billion, Cerberus and its partners put up another $2 billion, and debt holders exchanged

---

[61] Percentages are based on including securitized assets.
[62] General Motors 2003 10-K, p. 74; restated 2006 10-K, pp. 53, 56; 2008 10-K, p. 5; GMAC 2008 10-K, pp. 4, 19, 54–5, 70, 135, 143; Ally Bank 2008 10-K, p. 143.
[63] General Motors 2008 10-K, pp. 4, 6, 54–5, 57–60, 62.

Chart 5.20

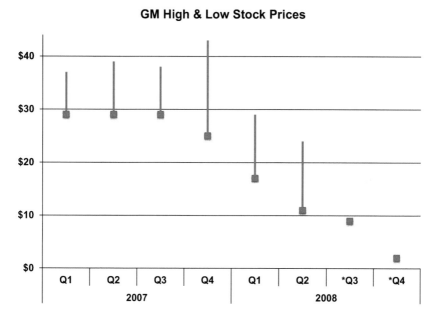

* low prices.
Source: General Motors 2008 10-K.

$21 billion of debt for $13 billion of debt, $2.6 billion of preferred stock, and $2.5 billion of cash. Still, both GMAC and GM struggled until GM went through a federally sponsored bankruptcy in June 2009 when TARP invested $50 billion in it and $17 billion in GMAC. As part of the transaction, GMAC was spun off by both Cerberus and GM and its successor, Ally Financial, became a bank holding company.

In contrast to General Motors, General Electric enjoyed acclaim throughout the 1990s under its CEO, Jack Welch. Its stock rose almost ten-fold, peaking at $60 in 2000, just before Welch's retirement. GE had traditional manufacturing businesses in electric turbines, airplane engines, medical equipment, and railroads, and Welch built up the financial side, GE Credit, to one-third of income. GE Credit did complex deals, often related to financing major equipment purchases, and had strong ventures in commercial real estate and insurance. It had over 500,000 business customers. It took full advantage of its parent company's AAA rating to incur $272 billion of debt by 2002 while the rest of GE had only $8 billion.[64]

---

[64] General Electric 2002 Annual Report, pp. 57, 183; 2009 Annual Report, p. 36.

In the recession following the hi-tech bubble, GE's manufacturing businesses came under pressure and its stock dropped over 50%. The company used GE Credit to help make up for the drop in manufacturing earnings. GE Credit's debt expanded from $272 billion in 2002 to $485 billion in 2007 and its debt rose from 6.5 times its equity in 2004 to 8.1 times. The stock market approved as GE's stock recovered from $20 to $40. GE Credit did not join the plunge into residential mortgage lending in any meaningful way. It divested its insurance business (Genworth) in 2006 and exited the US residential mortgage business in 2007. Its US consumer installment receivables of $28 billion and commercial real estate assets of $32 billion were only 15% of finance receivables.[65] Nonetheless, GE's stock dropped from $40 to $30 in mid-2008 along with financial stocks. In August–November, it dropped to $13 and GE sold $15 billion of new equity to sustain itself. It still had AAA/Aaa ratings, but both Moody's and S&P put it on CreditWatch with warnings of a "negative outlook" and "possible downgrades."[66] GE's problem was GE Credit's $192 billion of short-term borrowing. This was not only a large absolute sum but also an inappropriate amount for the specialized assets that GE Credit financed and their lack of near-term cash flows. GE Credit also made the mistake of pledging to post collateral on $20 billion of its debt if its ratings were reduced, and it guaranteed $15 billion for SPEs where collateral or cash could be called.[67]

GE Credit became a participant in most of the government's remedial financing programs. It used the Federal Reserve's commercial paper funding facility for $98 billion, and the FDIC's Temporary Loan Guarantee Program to sell $126 billion in bonds. However, GE didn't report a loss throughout 2007–09. Its profits dropped from $22 billion in 2007 to $11 billion in 2009 while GE Credit's profits dropped from $12 billion to $2 billion. GE Credit's "non-earning receivables" peaked in 2009 at 3.8% of assets – a financially sustainable level.[68]

5.6 Saving Lehman Brothers?

Many commentators have suggested that the bankruptcy of Lehman Brothers on September 15, 2008 was responsible for the crisis. On

---

[65] General Electric 2007 Annual Report, p. 67; 2008 Annual Report, pp. 35, 37.
[66] It was downgraded to AA-/Aa2 in March 2009.
[67] General Electric Annual Report 2008, pp. 38, 49, 53, 63, 97, 98, 100.
[68] General Electric Annual Report 2008, p. 38; 2009, pp. 34, 36, 43.

Saturday, September 13, Lehman Brothers was to be acquired by Barclays Bank for $3 billion while a Wall Street consortium acquired $40 billion of Lehman Brothers' worst assets. This appeared to be a workable plan in which the rest of Wall Street subsidized the transaction and Barclays gained access to the US investment banking industry. Barclays was to guarantee Lehman Brothers' operating liabilities during transition (as JP Morgan had for Bear Stearns), but to the surprise of those involved, this required a shareholders' vote under British law that would take too long and the British government refused to make an exception.[69] The transaction aborted and Lehman Brothers filed for bankruptcy early Monday morning, September 15.

Jean-Claude Trichet, President of the European Central Bank, said at the time that "... US officials had made a terrible mistake in letting Lehman fail, triggering the global financial crisis."[70] Christine Lagarde, French Economy Minister, similarly called the failure to save Lehman Brothers "horrendous" and said in a radio interview "... for the equilibrium of the world financial system this was a genuine error."[71] Numerous bankers, academics, and journalists have concurred. Laurence Ball has written a heavily researched book, The Fed and Lehman Brothers (Ball, 2018), which has given impetus to the argument that the Federal Reserve should have saved Lehman Brothers.

The practical answer to these criticisms is that financial officials were in nearly simultaneous efforts to "save" Fannie Mae and Freddie Mac (nationalized the week before), Lehman Brothers, AIG (pleading for help the week before), Merrill Lynch (being pressed by Paulson to merge with Bank of America the week before), Citigroup, Wachovia, GM, GMAC, Chrysler, Washington Mutual, and to a lesser degree Morgan Stanley, Goldman Sachs, and General Electric. The Federal Reserve was operating off the model of the strong acquiring the weak that was used to "rescue" Bear Stearns and Countrywide Financial earlier, Merrill Lynch and Washington Mutual contemporaneously, and Wachovia Corp. subsequently. There was

---

[69] Robert Diamond, who headed Barclays' acquisition team should have had this aspect cleared with the British government, but British officials also exhibited a curious detachment. The relevant politicians and regulators took their usual weekends in Scotland and Cornwall despite the fever pitch of crisis. Alistair Darling, British Chancellor of the Exchequer, complained about being "out of the loop" despite the fact it was his job to take charge of the UK side just as the US authorities took charge of theirs. Christopher Cox, Chairman of the SEC, bore some responsibility for not coordinating this issue with the UK but he just followed orders from others.

[70] Paulson (2010), p. 348.   [71] *Reuters*, Oct 8, 2008, French Radio interview.

not another option on the table for Lehman Brothers that weekend. Changing course would have required weeks.

Those arguing that the Federal Reserve should have lent Lehman Brothers enough to sustain it point to Section 13(3) of the Federal Reserve Act that permitted the Federal Reserve to lend in extreme situations on any collateral that it deemed adequate. This approach would have required the Federal Reserve to get Wall Street assistance evaluating Lehman's assets much earlier in the crisis. But that would have hurt the chances for the expected private sector solution. The evaluation could not have been done in secret. Federal Reserve staff had no experience relevant to evaluating Lehman Brothers' investments. Federal Reserve Bank of New York examiners had been on-site since March doing stress tests that contemplated Lehman Brothers' loss of repo borrowing, but they did not value its commercial real estate, private equity, and leveraged loan commitments – Lehman Brothers' greatest exposure.[72] This should be no surprise. The SEC regulated the investment banking industry – not the Federal Reserve. The Federal Reserve's own market expertise did not go beyond US treasuries and foreign exchange.

Officials' *ex post* arguments why Lehman Brothers could not be saved are simple and devoid of explicatory data. Hank Paulson argued that "... the toxic quality of Lehman's assets would have guaranteed the Fed a loss, meaning the central bank could not legally make a loan."[73] Tim Geithner claimed that, "We would only be lending into an unstoppable run."[74] Ben Bernanke in a November 4, 2010 letter to the Financial Institutions Inquiry Commission said that "... the credit relied on by Lehman to remain in operation was in the hundreds of billions of dollars...."[75] However, we will never know what valuations of Lehman Brothers' assets, what legal assumptions, what concern for the Federal Reserve's independence, what obeisance to public opinion, what political calculations (a presidential election was less than two months away), and what prejudices went into the thinking of the leading officials during the crisis. They were in a prolonged battle for months to save over a dozen companies. Paulson, who was the leader of the efforts, did most of his work face-to-face and on the telephone so he left few records. Lehman Brothers itself was in disarray and unable to provide much help having recently fired both its president and its chief financial officer.

[72] Valukas (2010), pp. 8, 68–9.   [73] Paulson (2010), p. 230.   [74] Ball (2018), pp. 125–6.
[75] Ball (2018), pp. 132–3.

Jean-Claude Trichet, Christine Lagarde, and other critics of Lehman Brothers failure appear to have believed that the Federal Reserve should "save" companies even if they are insolvent. But Section 13(3) of the Federal Reserve Act was intended to give the Federal Reserve power as a lender of last resort, not to have it bail out failed companies. The Federal Reserve earned approximately $40 billion each year that it turned over to the US Treasury. It had no accumulated earnings. A $200 billion loss (which is what occurred) if the Federal Reserve proceeded on its own would have forced it to appeal to Congress for large-scale support with unknown consequences.

It has historically been the job of national governments, not central banks, to bail out failed companies. This eventually happened systematically. The federal government took over Fannie Mae and Freddie Mac. When the Federal Reserve bailed out AIG it was only with the commitment from Hank Paulson that the Administration would seek Congressional approval of a broad relief effort (TARP) as it did two days later.[76] Federal Reserve authorities had repeatedly pressed for this help. TARP was used to sustain the equity of the nine largest banks. It was the federal authorities that guaranteed money market mutual funds, business bank deposits, and new long-term debt for the banks. Tim Geithner as Treasury Secretary publicly promised in the spring of 2009 that no more systemically important institutions would be allowed to fail. The rescues of GM, GMAC, and Chrysler were federal efforts. So were the federal rescue of Continental Illinois Bank and Trust in 1984 and the creation of the Resolution Trust in1991 to liquidate most of the savings and loans industry. In Europe, the UK government took over Northern Rock Bank, and central governments took over banks in Germany, France, Holland, Belgium, Ireland (attempted), and Iceland (attempted). The BIS identified sixteen governments that either injected capital into their banks or guaranteed their debts in the crisis.

Critics of the Federal Reserve ignore the depth of Lehman Brothers' problems. We now know that Lehman Brothers was a failed institution. In Tim Geithner's words, "Lehman Brothers looked insolvent in almost any state of the world."[77] Its nominal common equity position was $19 billion, but only $15 billion net of intangible assets and goodwill. This could not support market declines on the order of 30–80% on most of its $212 billion of "Financial Instruments" (excluding $47 billion of derivative assets).[78] The bulk of Lehman Brothers' so-called "Financial Instruments" was made

---

[76] Geithner (2014), p. 201. [77] Geithner (2014), p. 207. [78] As of May 31, 2008.

up of commercial real estate whole loans that couldn't be securitized, highly leveraged corporate loans, whole loan residential mortgages of the weak credit types in disfavor, RMBS residuals that were now of no value, mortgage-servicing rights that it had bought under the impression that they were undervalued, minority interests in real estate developers, equity in real estate properties, fourteen purchases that it made in 2007 of minority interests in private equity and hedge fund firms, and private equity limited partnerships. Forty-four percent of its real estate-related assets was foreign. Even apparently high-grade investments were not clean. Its \$27 billion of governments and agencies included \$16 billion of level 2 and 3 assets without public markets, presumably MBS residuals and developing countries' debt. Its \$5 billion of commercial paper when combined with \$2 billion of CDOs was valued by JP Morgan at less than \$2 billion just before Lehman Brothers failed.

By mid-2008, the values Lehman Brothers attached to its Financial Instruments were widely criticized. Its stock was the focus of well-advertised short selling by David Einhorn of Greenlight Capital (Einhorn, 2008). He accurately pinpointed that management set limits on write-offs, took value estimates from its traders and bankers, ignoring the values implied by public markets and indices for ABCP, CDOs, RMBS, CMBS, and CLOs – all facts eventually substantiated by Anton Valukas, the Examiner for the Bankruptcy Court. Analysts criticized Lehman Brothers for pricing its real estate equity and loan positions in the \$90s in its final 3Q 2008 report despite collapsing prices for comparable public indices.[79] Standard & Poor's calculated Lehman Brothers' \$2.3 billion equity in Archstone REIT at zero using a 7% cap rate, and the media declared Lehman Brothers' holdings of subordinated Archstone debt worthless.[80]

There is a litany of anecdotal evidence about Lehman Brothers' losses quoting Bank of America, Barclays Bank, and the Wall Street consortium, all working under intense pressure and never valuing everything. Bank of America, after a brief consideration of buying Lehman Brothers, told Valukas that Lehman had a "\$66 billion hole" in its valuations and that it "... did not want those \$66 billion in assets at any price . . .." This was without marking down Lehman's highly leveraged corporate loans and MBS residuals or valuing foreign assets.[81] Barclays estimated immediate write-downs of \$23–\$27 billion without valuing Lehman Brothers' highly leveraged corporate loans.[82] Perhaps importantly, the commercial banks

---

[79] Lehman Brothers 3Q conference call, September 10, 2008.
[80] Valukas (2010), pp. 231, 380.   [81] Valukas (2010), p. 209.   [82] Ball (2018), p. 67.

did not have to mark highly leveraged corporate loans to market when they took them onto their own loan books. The Wall Street consortium that had agreed to take on $40 billion of bad assets to assist the Barclays' acquisition estimated that real estate and private equity investments alone were overstated by $22–$25 billion.[83] It was widely known that Lehman Brothers took only minor charges for its $33 billion of highly leveraged corporate loans despite CLO prices around $60, and it took no charges for its $39 billion of unfunded highly leveraged corporate loan commitments.

But valuing Lehman Brothers' assets in September 2008 would have been highly uncertain for even the most knowledgeable experts because of the lack of public markets for a disproportionate share of its "Financial Instruments," the large foreign component, and the speed with which people were trying to assemble valuations. The most authoritative evaluation is the subsequent results of the bankruptcy process. They were disastrous.

The bankruptcy process was divided into two major proceedings – the holding company, Lehman Brothers Holding Inc. (LBHI), and the broker-dealer, Lehman Brothers Inc. (LBI). Alvarez & Marsal, consultants called in to manage the LBHI estate, in their first report two years after the crisis had accumulated only $21 billion in cash and estimated that final cash recoveries would be only $58 billion versus unsecured claims of $250–350 billion.[84] Recoveries ultimately rose to $121 billion in 2018 against allowed claims set in 2012 of $294 billion for a loss of $167 billion.[85] Present-valued to 3Q 2008 at 4%, recoveries were $97 billion for a loss of $197 billion.

Realizations by various unsecured creditors of the holding company and its many subsidiaries (twenty-three entities were involved) are outlined in Table 5.16. The holding company's direct lenders realized between 16–45% of their claims (not present-valued).

Lehman Brothers Inc. (LBI), the US brokerage subsidiary, went through bankruptcy proceedings under the Securities Investor Protection Act (SIPA) and was successful in transferring 100% of customers' accounts ($92 billion) to Barclays Bank in the USA, Nomura Securities in Europe and Japan, and through the sale of its Neuberger Berman investment management arm. However, LBI only paid $9 billion or 23% of allowed

---

[83] Ball (2018), p. 68.

[84] The initial unsecured claims were $1.2 trillion, but many were duplicative and this was Alvarez & Marsal's estimate of "realistic claims" (Alvarez, 2010), exhibit 99.1.

[85] Weil (2019), LBHI (chapter 11), p. 8, exhibit B.

Table 5.16

CREDITORS' LEHMAN BROTHERS HOLDING INC REALIZATIONS AS OF THE 15TH DISTRIBUTION (MARCH 29, 2018)	
LBHI:	
Senior	45%
Senior affiliate	36%
Senior affiliate g'teed	35%
General unsecured	42%
Other	16–33%
Lehman CP General and affiliates	66–81%
Lehman Special Financing	18–37%
Lehman Commodity Services	55–94%
Lehman OTC Derivatives	100%
Lehman Commercial Corp	100%
Various Lehman special purpose entities	36–100%
Various other claims	0%

Source: Weil (2019); LBHI (chapter 11).

unsecured claims after six–eight years, resulting in losses of $24 billion. $59 billion of unsecured claims were denied SIPA coverage, despite being customary liabilities such as repo borrowings, to-be-announced mortgage commitments, soft dollar brokerage claims, short sales positions, and foreign exchange balances.[86]

There was undoubtedly some destruction of value in the bankruptcy process. Default provisions in Lehman Brothers' derivatives contracts, joint ventures, Special Purpose Entities, and mortgage-servicing rights were sure to work against it. But rejected claims of $230 billion in LBHI and $59 billion in LBI represented huge liabilities that Lehman Brothers

---

[86] Hughes (2016), pp. 6, 16, 27.

did not have to meet. The estate also benefited by $68 billion beyond Alvarez & Marsal's original estimate of its value as markets improved.

Tim Geithner and Ben Bernanke appear justified in their estimations of Lehman Brothers' losses.

Little mention has been made of how much Lehman Brothers' lack of respect on Wall Street may have contributed to its demise. It was an outlier like Drexel Burnham that went bankrupt in 1990 without undue market disruption. Lehman Brothers had little franchise value despite its claim to longevity. It had a history of internal conflict, beginning in 1973 when Robert Lehman's successor, Fred Ehrman, was deposed by younger partners. In 1983, Lewis Glucksman forced out CEO Pete Peterson (who then cofounded The Blackstone Group) and subsequently sold the firm to American Express. Within American Express, Lehman Brothers was merged with Shearson Loeb Rhoades and E.F. Hutton before it was spun out again to become a public company in 1994. Its clients had gone through a roller coaster from which many defected.

When the New York Federal Reserve organized the consortium to take over Long-Term Capital Management's assets in 1998, Lehman Brothers pleaded inferiority and put up only $100 million while the leading firms put up $300 million. In the critical environment of mid-2008, its president and chief operating officer, Joseph Gregory, was forced out along with its CFO, Erin Callan.

The rest of Wall Street was a victim of the recklessness with which Lehman Brothers took on more risk in 2006–07 in the belief that it could take advantage of market dislocations.[87] Anton Valukas, the subsequent bankruptcy examiner, summed up this period as follows: "The evidence is that during the first eight months of Lehman's fiscal 2007, Lehman Brothers' leveraged loan business, like its commercial real estate business, was not subject to any limits."[88] He claimed that Lehman Brothers exceeded its risk limits at times by a factor of six.[89] Lehman Brothers' risk assets rose from $269 billion in 4Q 2006 to $373 billion in 4Q 2007 on a tangible common equity base of only $15 billion.[90] No other firm invested so recklessly in commercial real estate including resorts, land accumulation, minority interests in developers, and subordinated CMBS. To compete in the highly leveraged corporate loan market, Lehman offered no limit on bridge equity commitments for takeovers and "covenant lite" loans, abandoning "material adverse change" conditions, up-front syndication, and

---

[87] Valukas (2010), p. 45   [88] Valukas (2010), p. 176.   [89] Valukas (2010), p. 98.
[90] Valukas (2010), p. 57.

joint liability. Between August 2006 and July 2007, it entered into approximately thirty leveraged loans that exceeded the single transaction limit that had previously been adopted for these transactions, often by significant margins.[91]

Above all, Lehman Brothers lost trust. Wall Street couldn't trust its valuations, its quarterly maneuvers to temporarily take $50 billion of assets off its balance sheet (known as Repo 105), and its claims to liquidity. As late as its September 2008 conference call, it claimed that it had a liquidity pool of $45 billion when all but $2 billion was tied up as collateral with its clearing agents (mostly with JP Morgan for third-party repo financing and Citigroup and HSBC for London clearing).[92]

Lehman's lack of preparation for bankruptcy was the final straw. Its strategy appeared to be chaos if it was not rescued. Harvey Miller at Weil, Gotshal & Manges who oversaw the major part of the bankruptcy referred to the Chapter 11 filing as ". . . the most barebones Chapter 11 petition ever filed." He went on to say in a later speech at NYU's Stern School of Business, "The situation, in the face of total lack of preparation, was chaotic and completely novel in the world of bankruptcy."[93] Alvarez & Marsal, the bankruptcy management specialists, were not contacted until Sunday, September 15, the day before filing. This lack of preparation led to an unusual situation where Hank Paulson with his experience in finance and corporate crises pushed the Federal Reserve and the SEC to dictate that Lehman file for bankruptcy Sunday night so that all creditors would have to abide by the bankruptcy process and that smaller, less experienced, and foreign creditors would not be disadvantaged by a "rush to the courthouse."

Laurence Ball has argued that the Federal Reserve should have saved Lehman Brothers because it could have adequately secured a loan and then liquidated or restructured Lehman in an orderly way in a few months. This conclusion is wrong on several counts.

- Ball did not evaluate Lehman Brothers' assets, except anecdotally, but this was the whole issue. Alvarez & Marsal were in the best position to evaluate Lehman Brothers' assets as the manager of the holding company estate. In 2010 after some economic recovery, they estimated future cash flows would be $58 billion, implying a loss of

---

[91] Valukas (2010), pp. 96–7, 101, 176.   [92] Valukas (2010), pp. 10, 1066, 1082–3.
[93] Miller (2013), p. 11.

$236 billion versus allowed claims of $294 billion. These were the exceptional losses referenced by Paulson, Geithner, and Bernanke.

- Ball did not review Lehman Brothers' bankruptcy process that became the authoritative measure of Lehman Brothers' problems. Lehman Brothers Holding Inc. and Lehman Brothers Inc. combined ultimately paid out $130 billion versus allowed claims of $353 billion for a loss of $217 billion. This is without present-valuing the cash payments and without adjustment for the economic and financial recoveries that followed the crisis.

- Ball assumed that orderly liquidation or restructuring was possible when a $200 billion loss was impending, but it would have been little different from bankruptcy. The Federal Reserve had no power over Lehman Brothers' tens of thousands of contracts nor could it obviate bankruptcy laws in multiple countries that would govern privileged transfers as it liquidated. Senior management had to be replaced. Customers were fleeing, secured lenders would have taken over their collateral, counterparties would have claimed advantageous defaults, creditors would have fought and litigated, foreign securities authorities could claim jurisdiction, day-to-day operations would be obstructed by legal concerns, employees quit, and operations and information become muddled. This was Tim Geithner's "unstoppable run." It would have gotten worse as time went on and the time lapse would have been substantial as the sense of crisis did not even begin to dissipate for nine months. Real estate recovery took years. Commercial real estate spending was still down 2/3 in 2012, A-rated ABX index prices for RMBS were still under $10 in 2012 and house prices still down 30%–50% in the sand states. Consumer confidence remained depressed, unemployment near 10%, and financial stocks down 40%, although corporate earnings, the S&P 500, and many credit spreads had recovered. Unlike the Drexel Burnham bankruptcy in 1990, there were few bankruptcy investors anxious to pick up Lehman's assets.

Lehman Brothers' failure is not even a subtheme in this history. Chapters 4 and 6 document that the crisis began well before Lehman Brothers failed and was worse for months afterwards. Lehman Brothers was unconnected to Fannie Mae's and Freddie Mac's failures. Lehman Brothers was not a major underwriter in the private RMBS markets. It cannot be tied to consumers withdrawing $2.6 trillion in home equity through mortgage refinancing or the collapse in home prices that brought down private RMBS ratings and collapsed their prices. Lehman Brothers had nothing to do with the failures in 2007–08 of the aggressive low-credit lenders such as New Century Financial, Fremont General, Thornburg Realty, IndyMac, Countrywide, and Washington Mutual. Lehman Brothers was barely a factor in the credit default sector of the derivatives market where the contraction in leverage produced dramatic losses for AIG, Merrill Lynch, Morgan Stanley, Citigroup, and UBS. Lehman Brothers made bad decisions in commercial real estate and highly leveraged loans, but it had no connection with the bad decisions at Bear Stearns, Citigroup, Merrill Lynch, Wachovia, and the various European banks. Nor would saving Lehman Brothers have obviated that many of the largest commercial and investment banks had so many illiquid investments by 2007 that they were susceptible to collateral calls in the repo markets that they could not meet. It is a simplistic model of financial crises that suggests that saving one firm can save them all.

In evaluating the roles in the crisis of consumers' unusual leverage, the flaws in the securitization process, institutional investors' increased risk appetite, and financial intermediaries' illiquidity and bad investment decisions it should not be lost that America's penchant for gambling has risen sharply in recent decades. Gambling in the form of casinos, lotteries, and sports betting increased sixty times between 1962–2000 (Lambert, 2002). The stakes gambled in US casinos in 2016 approximated $1.6 trillion.[94] Some countries have a penchant for gambling, notably America and China, and this can be expected to influence investment decisions at both the individual and institutional levels. In some respects, the crisis was simply a bad pay-off.

---

[94] American Gambling Association (2017), pp. 9, 26. The approximation is based on a 4.3% casino take.

6

The Initial Obama Administration 2009

The state of our economy calls for action, bold and swift.
President Barack Obama's Inauguration Speech

6.1 The Continuing Crisis

The Obama administration had no honeymoon. Even before taking office it asked President Bush to release the second $350 billion of TARP funds. The financial industry continued to be troubled as Bank of America had to absorb a Merrill Lynch 4th quarter 2008 loss of $23 billion. A rescue package was put together similar to Citigroup's under which the Treasury, Federal Reserve, and FDIC protected an asset pool of $118 billion against losses.[1] Citigroup needed further assistance of $50 billion from TARP at the end of February and then in June the assistance had to be converted to common equity to prevent ratings downgrades and to keep the bank off the FDIC's troubled bank list. Either would have led to a run on its foreign deposits.[2] Credit default spreads for 6 large banks jumped back up to 375 basis points from 200 at the end of 2008.[3] AIG got $30 billion more from TARP in March to avoid ratings downgrades that would have accelerated collateral calls on it.

The sense of crisis was pervasive. There were doubts that the USA would continue to support Fannie Mae and Freddie Mac.[4] Housing prices reached a cumulative decline of 18% nationally, 55% in Las Vegas, 45% in Miami and Phoenix, and 35% in Los Angeles (Chart 6.1). Moody's ratings downgrades for private RMBS reached a peak of 25,000 tranches

---

[1] Federal Reserve Annual Report 2008, pp. 57–8. It was never used, however. See Bair (2012), p. 128.
[2] Bair (2012), pp. 168–74.   [3] Geithner (2014), p. 307.
[4] Goldman Sachs (2015), exhibit 3.

Chart 6.1

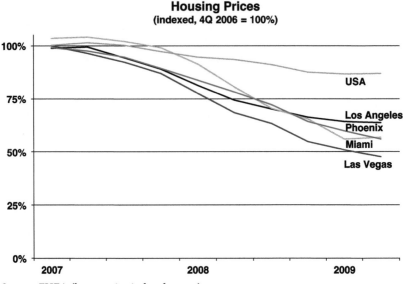

Housing Prices
(indexed, 4Q 2006 = 100%)

USA

Los Angeles
Phoenix

Miami

Las Vegas

Source: FHFA (house price index datasets).

in the 1st quarter of 2009 (Chart 6.2). CDO downgrades continued at near-record levels throughout all of 2009 (Chart 6.3).

The ABX AAA indices for subprime RMBS continued to decline into the spring when the index for mortgages originated in the second half of 2005 (2006–1) was down 40% and the 2006–2 index was down 70% despite still being rated AAA.[5] (Chart 6.4) This greatly understated the decline because AAA tranches that had been downgraded were removed from these indices and the 2006–1 and 2006–2 A-rated indices were around 10.

High yield default rates rose to 11% in 2009 (Chart 6.5) and high yield bond rates doubled. Rates on B-rated bonds reached 23% at the end of 2008 and were still as high as 18% in April. Higher quality BB rates peaked at 16% and were still 13% in April (Chart 6.6).

In May 2009, California couldn't sell $17 billion in municipal bonds and had to issue IOUs to pay its employees.

Credit conditions were highly restrictive. Seventy percent of banks were tightening loan standards in the 1st quarter and they were only barely letting up through June. Commercial bankruptcies surged. Bankruptcy filings greater than $100 million hit $100 billion in April (Chart 6.7).

---

[5] Stanton (2011), p. 18.

Chart 6.2

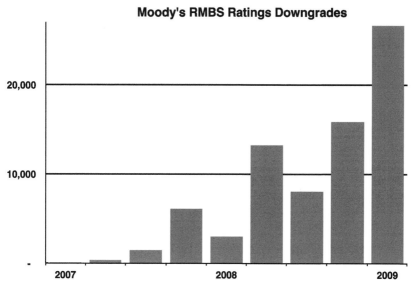

Source: ESF Quarterly Securitisation Data Reports.

Chart 6.3

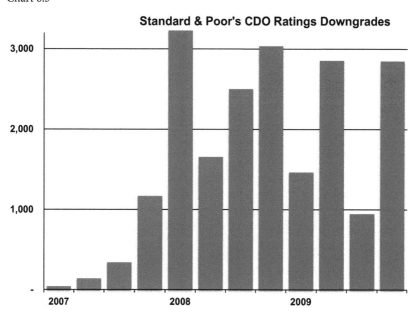

Source: ESF Quarterly Securitisation Data Reports.

Chart 6.4

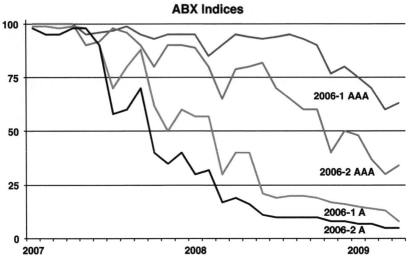

Source: Stanton (2011).

Chart 6.5

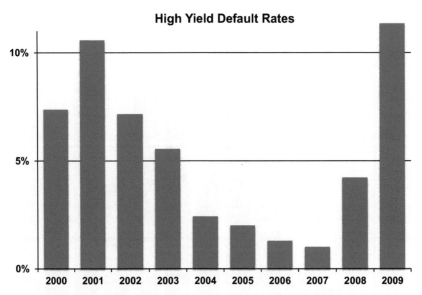

Source: Standard & Poor's Corp.

Chart 6.6

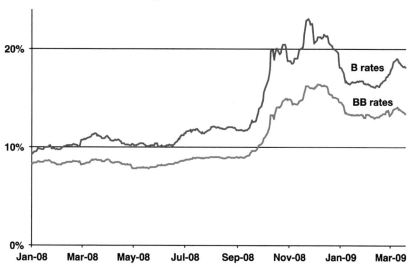

High Yield Bond Rates

Source: FRED.

Chart 6.7

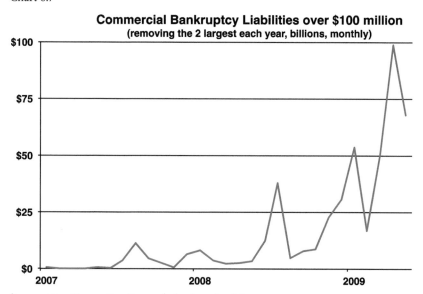

Commercial Bankruptcy Liabilities over $100 million
(removing the 2 largest each year, billions, monthly)

Source: New Generation Research, bankruptcydata.com.

Chart 6.8

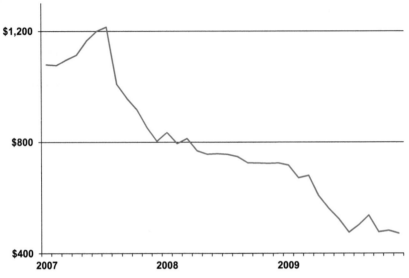

Asset-backed Commercial Paper Outstanding
($ billions)

Source: FRED.

This data removes the two largest bankruptcies each year to reveal the underlying trend.[6] Asset-backed commercial paper took another steep decline (Chart 6.8). Collateralized Loan Obligation (CLO) prices hovered around 70 through April. Mergers and acquisitions were around one-third of peak levels, in part because it was difficult to finance them.

Commercial real estate prices fell throughout 2009 as office, retail, and apartment properties reached low points that averaged a decline of 41% from their peaks (Chart 6.9). Cumulative downgrades of CMBS ratings more than quadrupled from 2008 to 1,300 tranches by the 4th quarter of 2009 (Chart 6.10). Issues originally rated AAA (39% of issues) had only modest downgrades, but one-third of those initially rated AA were downgraded two or more times and 70% of bonds originally rated BBB or lower were downgraded two or more times (Chart 6.11). Spreads on A-rated CMBS stayed elevated at 2,000 basis points (no market) above early 2008 levels. There were widespread fears that mortgages due in the next few

---

[6] New Century Financial and American Home Mortgage in 2007; Lehman Brothers Holding and Washington Mutual in 2008. The two largest bankruptcies in 2009 (General Motors and CIT Financial) were subsequent to April.

Chart 6.9

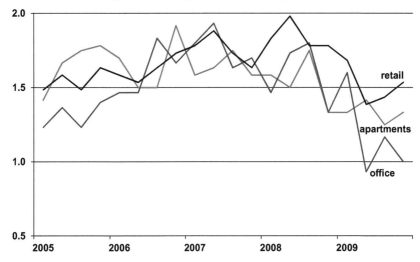

Commercial Real Estate Prices
(per square foot, indexed 1Q2001=1.0)

Source: MBA (2010).

Chart 6.10

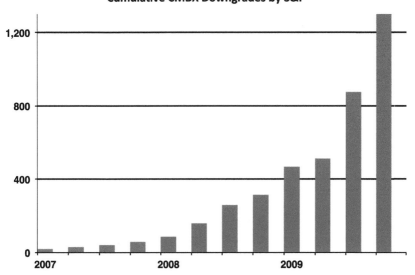

Cumulative CMBX Downgrades by S&P

Source: An (2014).

Chart 6.11

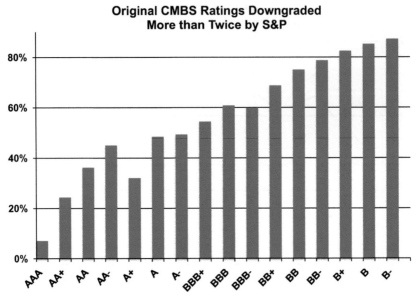

Source: An (2014).

years would not get refinanced successfully. Not surprisingly, commercial real estate construction collapsed, falling 38% in 2009 and a further 35% in 2010 (Chart 6.12). General Growth Properties, the second largest owner of US retail properties declared bankruptcy in April with $27 billion of debt. It was unable to refinance the $14 billion of debt it took on in 2004 when it acquired the Rouse Companies, the developer of Faneuil Hall in Boston.

The broad economic outlook was reflected in analysts' estimates of earnings for the S&P 500. Estimates for 2009 had dropped 24% in 2008 and estimates for 2010 dropped a further 9% through May 2009 (Chart 6.13). The S&P 500 dropped a further 25% between December 31 and March 15, leaving it 57% below its 2007 peak (Chart 6.14). The VIX for the S&P 500 was still elevated over 40 (Chart 6.15). Corporate stock repurchases completely dried up (Chart 6.16). As late as the end of June bank stocks were down 75% from the end of 2006 (Table 6.1), other financial stocks were down by two-thirds, and various durable industries by 50%. Technology and industries catering to consumer essentials were down 20% or less. Energy stocks held up because of a massive stimulus program in China that had high energy needs. Gold prices resumed their upward climb to just short of $1,000 in June (Chart 6.17).

The economy remained in free fall. Housing starts throughout 2009 were down 75% from 2005. Commercial real estate construction dropped

Chart 6.12

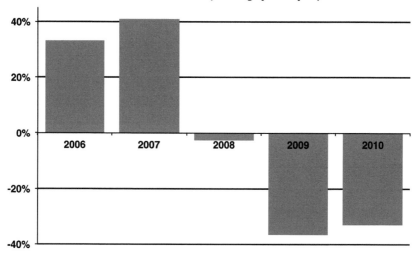

Commercial Real Estate Expenditures
(% change year-to-year)

Source: BEA (NIPA Accounts).

Chart 6.13

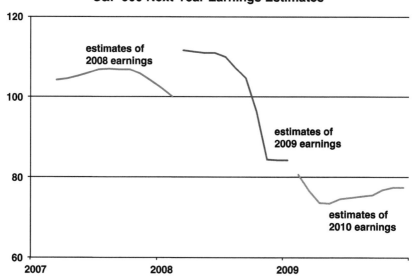

S&P 500 Next-Year Earnings Estimates

Source: Goldman Sachs.

Chart 6.14

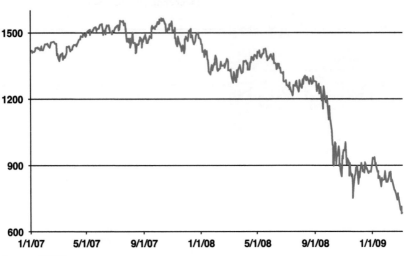

Source: FRED.

Chart 6.15

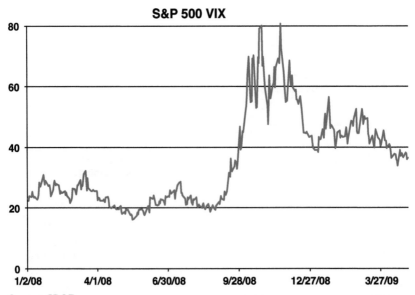

Source: CBOE.

Chart 6.16

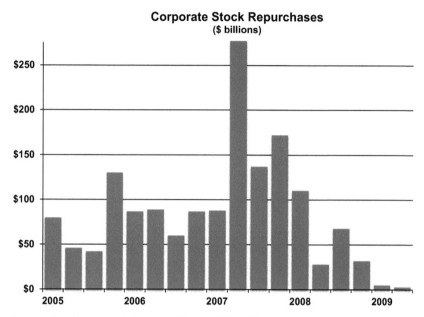

Corporate Stock Repurchases
($ billions)

Source: SIFMA Quarterly Research Report, 4Q 2009.

from 1.5% of GDP in 2007 to only 0.6% in 2010. Manufacturers' new orders were down 36% at mid-year. Industrial production was down 16% in June. Oil prices dropped to under $35 in February, a 75% decline from the middle of 2008. GDP in the 2nd quarter was down 4% from its peak in 2008.

The consumer was in a state of shock. Unemployment reached 10% in September and U-6 unemployment 18%. Delinquencies on all single-family mortgages escalated to 11½% at the end of 2009. Credit card losses rose $75 billion – three times the increase in 2004–07. The declining economy and its impact on employment and family income was adding to the default rates initially caused by excessive borrowing. Confidence in its various forms was shattered. The University of Michigan's Consumer Confidence Index dropped to 57 in the 1st quarter of 2009 and stayed in the 60s for most of the year, a stretch only matched by the agonies of 1979–82. The Index of Small Business Confidence hit a 25-year low in March (Chart 6.18). Retail sales continued to decline into the 2nd quarter, down 12½% versus mid-2008. The 3% decline in real consumer expenditures (Chart 6.19) was the largest decline since 1948.

Table 6.1

STOCK PERFORMANCE OF S&P INDUSTRIES 12/06 TO 6/09	
	Change
Banks	−74%
Insurance	−67%
Diversified financials	−65%
Real estate	−63%
Autos & components	−55%
Consumer durables	−50%
Media	−47%
Capital goods	−44%
Commercial & professional services	−43%
Retail	−35%
Semiconductors	−33%
Telecommunications	−33%
Materials	−29%
Heating & cooling equip't & services	−25%
Transportation	−24%
Utilities	−24%
Pharmaceuticals	−20%
Software	−19%
Consumer services	−19%
Energy	−18%
Household & personal products	−17%
Technology hardware	−14%
Food retail	−13%
Food & beverages	−7%

Source: Standard & Poor's Corp.

Chart 6.17

Source: FRED.

Chart 6.18

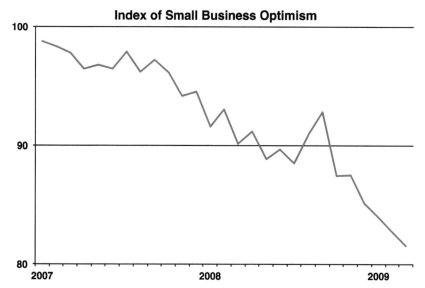

Source: National Federation of Independent Businesses.

Chart 6.19

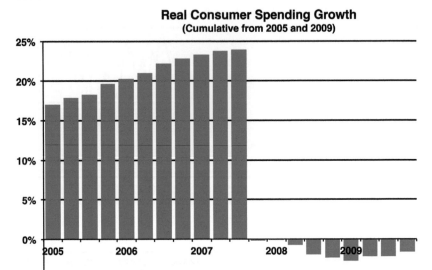

Source: FRED.

6.2 Fiscal Policy

The Obama administration inherited the responsibility for stimulating the economy to deal with the unrelenting financial distress. The administration's first step was the Treasury's "Stress Test" for whether the nineteen largest banks could withstand a further $600 billion loss from another economic shock. Developed by Tim Geithner once he became Secretary of the Treasury and implemented by the Federal Reserve Bank of New York, the test caused considerable stress itself until the Treasury made clear it would make sure that the banks had the necessary capital if they failed the test. The results were well received when Geithner announced them in May. Of the nineteen banks, nine needed no additional capital, seven needed a modest amount of new capital that the public markets could provide, Bank of America needed $34 billion that could follow the Citigroup model, and GMAC, which remained a mess, was outside the banking system.[7] With this good news in hand, fixing the banks went into mop-up mode.

Aside from restoring the financial system, the Obama administration faced a staggering loss of wealth in the country. Wealth had dropped almost

---

[7] Council of Economic Advisors, Economic Report of the President 2010, p. 540; Geithner (2014), pp. 345–50.

$23 trillion, over 150% of 2007 GDP and 200% of Disposable Personal Income. Stocks had lost $10 trillion, homes and residential mortgages of all types over $8 trillion, and corporate debt, including commercial real estate, over $4 trillion (Table 6.2).[8] Wealth could recover, but no one knew how much or how long it would take.

The immediate challenge facing the Obama administration was the debt loads accumulated by consumers and business. Consumers had increased their debt $6.5 trillion, mostly in the space of five years since 2002 (Table 6.3). The increase amounted to almost 150% of Disposable Personal Income. When home prices fell and mortgage defaults rose, this debt load produced America's first consumer-led recession. Prior recessions were the result of inflation, or dollar weakness, oil prices, defense contractions, savings and loan problems, the hi-tech bubble, or 9/11. Consumer spending represented 70% of the US economy, a problem on a scale with no historical precedent. By the spring of 2009, the problems with consumer leverage, the collapse in housing prices, and the leverage excesses in the financial markets were in a continual feedback loop with the declining economy that made restoring the country's purchasing power appear insurmountable.

Consumers defaulting on their debts were a heavy drag on the economy. Delinquencies on mortgages and other debts were almost $2 trillion (Table 6.4), 18% of Disposable Personal Income. Delinquencies went beyond residential mortgages. Credit card losses were escalating and would rise $75 billion by 2011 based on the difference in banks' net write-offs between 2004–07 and 2008–11 (Chart 6.20), leading banks to restrict consumer credit. Automobile loans were $800 billion in 2008 and severe delinquencies (ninety days) rose from 2% in 2005 to 5% in 2010, but, more importantly, auto loan maturities had been stretched from fifty-five to sixty-five months in 2004–07 creating a further $100 billion loss in purchasing power as people had to hold on to their cars longer.

Student loans were a largely unrecognized burden on consumer purchasing power as they almost doubled to over $600 billion between 2001–08 (Chart 6.21). Student loans grew a further 50% between 2008 and 2012 to just short of $1 trillion after Congress raised the limit on student loans twice in 2007–08. Most of this borrowing was done by students or their parents who had already made their education decisions in 2008. A study by AARP

---

[8] The losses of commercial real estate owners in Table 6.2 are difficult to assess on a mark to market basis. We have the REIT example where public prices fell 67%. In 2009 prices for apartment, office, and retail buildings averaged a decline of 39% from prior peaks. Averaging the two declines, institutional commercial real estate owners appear to have lost 53% or $441 billion on an estimated $833 billion of equity investments.

Table 6.2

2008 WEALTH LOSSES				
($ billions)				
	2007	2008	Prices	Losses
Housing value*	27,970	24,454	0.87	3,516
Inst'l commercial real estate equity	833	391	0.47	441
Stocks' value	25,196	15,190	0.60	10,006
Residential mortgages		outstanding		
agency RMBS		4,965	0.75	1,241
private RMBS		4,061	0.25	3,046
unsecuritized mortgages		2,004	0.75	501
Total residential mortgage losses				4,788
Corporate debt		outstanding		
commercial mortgages**		3,375	0.72	1,300
non-financial corporate				
high yield		1,091	0.50	546
leveraged loans		2,600	0.60	1,040
remainder (BBB)		2,673	0.85	401
commercial banks		1,426	0.75	357
finance companies		1,200	0.75	300
funding corporations		420	0.65	147
Total corporate debt losses				4,090
Total losses				22,842

*Financial Accounts of the United States, B.100.e "nonfinancial assets" of households.
**Including multifamily and noncorporate mortgages and REIT debt, L.220 and L.128, 3/8/12.
Sources: Federal Reserve (Financial Accounts of the United States); author's estimates from public prices and indices.

Table 6.3

INCREASE IN CONSUMER DEBT 2002 to 2008–2009			
($ billions)			
	2002	peak	% increase
Residential mortgages	6,434	11,324	76%
Home equity loans	213	612	187%
Consumer and auto loans	2,706	3,445	27%
Student debt	370	879	138%
Totals	9,723	16,260	67%
Disposable Personal Income		11,000	
% DPI		148%	

Note: Student debt is 2011 reflecting 4-year commitments that would have begun in 2007.
Sources: Federal Reserve System (mortgage debt outstanding); FRED; Looney (2018).

Table 6.4

Consumer Debt Delinquencies in 2009	
	($ billions)
Residential mortgages	1,265
Credit card delinquency increase	75
Automobile loan effect*	125
Student debt (if GAAP applied)	500
	1,965

*auto loans reflect longer maturities rather than delinquencies.
Sources: FRED; Looney (2018); author's calculations.

in 2019 found that between 2004 and 2018 the student loan debt of people over fifty had grown from $47 billion to $290 billion.[9]

Recognizing the impact of student debt on consumer purchasing power has been hindered by unusually poor government accounting. Only

[9] AARP.com, "Student Loan Debt Soaring Among Adults Over 50."

Chart 6.20

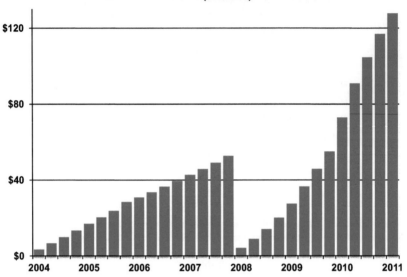

Banks' Cumulative Credit Card Charge-offs
($ billions)

Source: FRED.

Chart 6.21

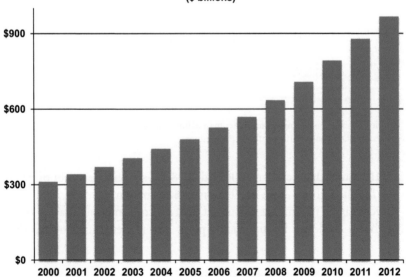

Student Loan Balances
($ billions)

Source: Looney (2018).

Chart 6.22

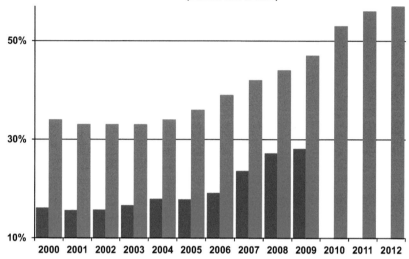

Students Owing More than Originally
2 Years After Repayment was to Begin
(default rate in blue)

Note: columns are for cohorts so students enrolling after 2009 do not begin repayment by 2012.
Source: Looney (2018).

recently has Looney (2018) done the appropriate vintage analysis for such a rapid expansion in debt. Looney found that 55% of borrowers who were supposed to begin paying off debt in 2011 (two years after graduating in 2009) had paid nothing and had actually increased their debt (Chart 6.22). One of the peculiarities of student loan data is that it takes so long to declare a student in default that only 28% of those who probably enrolled in 2005 were "in default" in 2011. In the AARP study, 29% of borrowers between 50–64 were in default based on being over 270 days past due. Sallie Mae, making private unguaranteed loans and subject to Generally Accepted Accounting Principles, treated borrowers as "final stage delinquent" 120 days after missing a scheduled payment.[10] If we assume 55% of 2012 student debt should have been written off (based on zero debt reduction per Looney (2018)), it represented a loss of $500 billion, one of the largest burdens on consumer purchasing power.

[10] Sallie Mae 2017 10-K, p. 63.

Table 6.5

INCREASE IN HIGHLY LEVERAGED CORPORATE DEBT 2002 to 2008–2009			
($ billions)			
	2002	peak	increase
High yield bonds (market value)	525	810	54%
Leveraged loans	1,275	2,625	106%
Commercial mortgages	1,343	3,407	154%
Asset-backed commercial paper	674	1,215	80%
Totals	3,817	8,057	4,240

Sources: Reilly (2009); BIS (2008); Federal Reserve System (mortgage debt outstanding); FRED; author's calculations.

Corporate recovery was also constrained by the growth in highly lever-aged corporate debt in its multiple forms (high yield bonds, highly leveraged corporate loans, commercial mortgages, and asset-backed commercial paper). It had grown by $4.2 trillion (111%) between 2002 and 2008/2009 (Table 6.5). While this increase was only two-thirds of the $6.5 trillion increase in consumer debt, its growth rate was higher at 12% annually.

The most important fiscal measure to counter the collapsing economy was the American Recovery and Reinvestment Act in mid-February 2009 that increased federal spending by $843 billion. This was equal to 2+% of GDP in 2009 and 2010, but it was not adequately targeted at consumers. The Act only provided $260 billion in personal tax cuts ($800 per couple in 2009 and 2010). An equal amount was approved for business tax cuts tied to spending for capital equipment, infrastructure programs, and increased R&D, plus $90 billion for new environmental technologies, $90 billion for homeowner help, unemployment insurance and welfare extensions, and $140 billion for state fiscal relief. There was a popular $3 billion program of "Cash for Clunkers" in June 2009 that temporarily stimulated new car purchases.[11] Various efforts were made to help troubled homeowners, the most important being the $75 billion Home Affordable Modification Program (HAMP) passed in March 2009.

---

[11] Council of Economic Advisors, Economic Report of the President 2010, pp. 53–4; 2011, pp. 41–2.

As the economy continued to struggle through 2009, unemployment benefits were further extended in November and small businesses were given tax refunds for current losses carried back against prior years' profits. The Tax Relief, Unemployment Insurance Reauthorization and Job Creation Act in December focused more on consumers. It extended the personal tax cuts into 2010 and 2011, the payroll tax was cut 2 percentage points ($112 billion), and unemployment benefits were extended through 2011.

Accepting the need for stimulus, the Obama administration did not reverse the Bush administration's tax cuts for capital gains, dividends, and estate taxes despite Democratic control of both houses of Congress. Estate taxes in 2010 dropped to zero, and when they were reinstated in 2011 it was with an increased exemption of $5 million.

It fell to the Obama administration to reorganize the auto industry. The TARP program provided loans of $25 billion over year-end 2008 to GM and Chrysler. In February, it became clear that General Motors was going to go bankrupt. It lost $31 billion in 2008 and was running out of cash. Both Congress and President Obama insisted that the company be reorganized as a condition of further support and its CEO, Rick Wagoner, was forced to resign. Chrysler and General Motors were sustained from April through June with a further $80 billion from TARP and federal guarantees of their vehicle warranties and supplier obligations while they proceeded toward forced bankruptcies that restructured their union contracts. For GM alone, the warranty program required a federal guarantee of up to $360 billion.[12] GM filed for preplanned bankruptcy reorganization in June. Chrysler was sold to Fiat. Ford, alone, refused assistance and remained solvent.

Between the administration's stimulus measures and the decline in government revenues, the federal deficit rose to an unprecedented (except in World War II) 10% of GDP (Chart 6.23). Federal debt expanded from 60% to 85% of GDP (Chart 6.24).

In June, the administration sent Congress a series of bills regulating the financial industry in response to the criticism of the role of large banks, investment banks, insurance companies, mortgage originators, and regulators in the financial crisis. Passed as the Dodd–Frank Act in July 2010, the Act forced banks to make "living wills" to show how they could be liquidated if they faced failure, required that they raise incremental capital, and severely limited their investments in hedge funds and private equity funds and their proprietary trading under the Volcker Rule. The Act required the registration

---

[12] Wikipedia, February 10, 2016, "General Motors Chapter 11 reorganization."

Chart 6.23

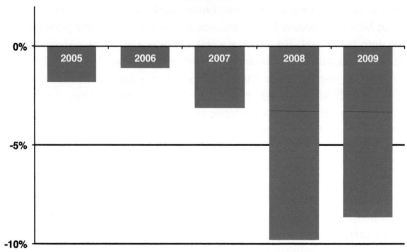

Source: FRED.

Chart 6.24

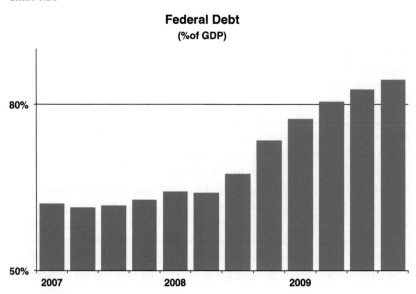

Source: FRED.

Table 6.6

FEDERAL RESERVE LOANS AND OTHER CREDIT EXTENSIONS							
($ billions outstanding)							
	Term Auctions	TALF	Dealers	AMLF	CP Funding	Total AIG	Totals*
2007	40						40
2008	450	48	37	24	334	74	967
2009	76	25			14	129	244
2010		9				115	124
2011		1				54	55
2012						15	15
*excluding central bank liquidity swaps							

Source: Federal Reserve Annual Report 2012.

of hedge fund and private equity advisors, but with little effect on the markets. It proposed that most derivatives be traded on public exchanges and centrally cleared but that has not happened. Regulation of rating agencies was introduced requiring clearer articulation of rating standards, but the effect has not been obvious. A Bureau of Consumer Financial Protection was established that Elizabeth Warren hoped to head, but President Obama failed to appoint her because she was too divisive a figure. She ran successfully for the US Senate in Massachusetts in November 2010.

6.3 Monetary Policy

The Federal Reserve Reserve's remediation efforts to fix or save the financial system (as distinct from traditional monetary policy measures) were extensive in 2008, amounting to almost $1 trillion (Table 6.6). They were cut back to $115 billion in 2009 and $9 billion in 2010 excluding the unusual deals with AIG to which the Federal Reserve was stuck like tar baby.[13]

---

[13] Federal Reserve Annual Report 2012, statistical table 6A.

Chart 6.25

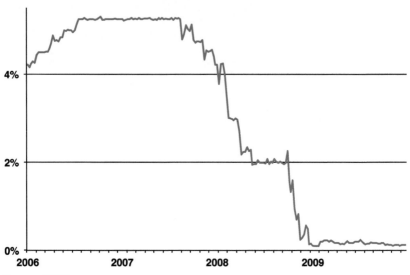

Source: FRED.

The Federal Reserve's traditional monetary programs late in 2008 were to cut the federal funds rate from 2% to virtually zero (Chart 6.25) and to announce at its November 25 meeting that it would buy $100 billion of federally sponsored housing agency bonds and $500 billion of AAA agency RMBS. It also set up a program to lend against new AAA asset-backed bonds (the Term Asset-Backed Securities Loan Facility – TALF). But beyond extending these programs, the Federal Reserve waited as the Obama administration came into office despite the dreadful economic data. The Federal Reserve made only minor open market transactions of any type in January and February and its balance sheet was almost 16% lower in mid-February 2009 than at the end of 2008 (Chart 6.26). M1 money supply growth dropped throughout 2009 from 15% to 6% and M2 growth from 9% to 2% (Chart 6.27).

It is possible that the Federal Reserve was influenced by poor estimates of what was happening to the economy. Census Department (Bureau of Economic Analysis) estimates of GDP went through huge revisions at this time (Chart 6.28). Each point along the line representing a quarter in 2008 indicates a revision in the BEA estimate. The eventual 3rd quarter 2008 estimate was 2 percentage points below the original estimate and the eventual 4th quarter estimate 5 percentage points below!

Chart 6.26

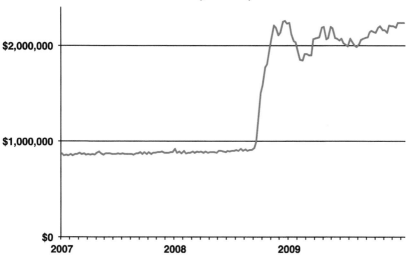

Federal Reserve Total Assets
(\$ millions)

Source: FRED.

Chart 6.27

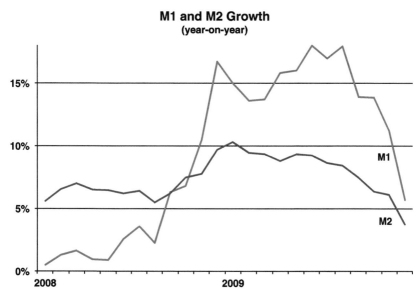

M1 and M2 Growth
(year-on-year)

Source: FRED.

Chart 6.28

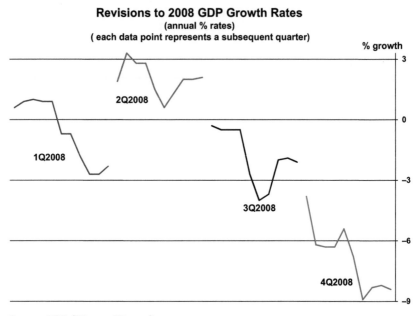

Revisions to 2008 GDP Growth Rates
(annual % rates)
(each data point represents a subsequent quarter)

Source: BEA (Vintage History).

The Federal Reserve was surprisingly ambivalent about further monetary stimulus. Although it kept fed funds and 2-year treasury rates low, it allowed 10-year treasury rates to rise from 2¼% to 3½% during 2009 (Chart 6.29). After its June 25, 2009 meeting, the FOMC announced that it was taking steps to wind down its special credit and liquidity programs; in August the FOMC decided to slow the pace of its bond purchases. At the November meeting the participants expressed concern that maintaining low interest rates would promote excessive risk-taking in financial markets (as indeed it had before the crisis). In January 2010 the swap lines with foreign central banks were allowed to expire. The Federal Reserve also began a test program to offer term deposits to banks so it could reduce their reserves when necessary. The 2009 Annual Report expressed the attitude that prevailed during the year:

... as the expansion (*sic*) matures, the Federal Reserve will need to begin to tighten monetary conditions to prevent the development of inflation pressures.
However, to help reduce the size of its balance sheet and the quantity of reserves, the Federal Reserve is allowing agency debt and MBS to run off as they mature or are prepaid. The Federal Reserve is rolling over all maturing Treasury securities,

Chart 6.29

Source: Federal Reserve.

but in the future it might decide not to do so in all cases. In the long run, the Federal Reserve anticipates that its balance sheet will shrink toward more historically normal levels and that most or all of its securities holdings will be Treasury securities. Although passively redeeming agency debt and MBS as they mature or are prepaid will move the Federal Reserve in that direction, the Federal Reserve may also choose to sell securities in the future when the economic recovery is sufficiently advanced and the FOMC has determined that the associated financial tightening is warranted.[14]

In March 2009, the Federal Reserve began purchasing large amounts of agency MBS so that its bond holdings expanded from $400 billion to $1.3 trillion at the end of 2009 (Table 6.7). This was helpful to the mortgage-backed markets, but the Federal Reserve's balance sheet didn't expand beyond its initial expansion in the crisis (previous Chart 6.26). It wasn't until August 2010 that the Federal Reserve announced it would re-invest MBS payments into longer-term treasuries in order to keep its portfolio constant (otherwise it would be tightening credit). Monetary policy in 2009 boiled down to keeping short-term rates low and helping the mortgage-backed securities market through open market purchases, but the Federal

[14] Federal Reserve, Annual Report 2009, pp. 36, 43, 45.

Table 6.7

FEDERAL RESERVE BOND PURCHASES IN 2009					
($ billions)					
	UST<10 years	UST>10 years	Agency Oblig'ns	MBS	Total	% MBS
Jan	0	0	10	7	17	44%
Feb	0	0	9	62	71	87%
Mar	15	3	14	168	199	84%
Apr	53	4	18	129	203	64%
May	45	10	12	62	128	48%
Jun	43	7	17	35	101	34%
Jul	39	9	10	81	138	59%
Aug	34	8	13	82	137	60%
Sep	20	2	13	67	102	66%
Oct	5	2	16	82	105	78%
Nov	0	0	8	78	86	91%
Dec	0	0	3	56	59	95%
Totals	253	44	142	908	1,346	67%

Sources: Federal Reserve, Annual Report 2009; Federal Reserve Open Market Transactions.

Reserve was surprisingly unaggressive about expanding its balance sheet and the money supply.

6.4 The Extent of Government Efforts

The extent of the government's financial remediation, monetary measures, and fiscal stimulus is not well understood. Tim Geithner, contradicting an early 2009 IMF estimate that the US government would end up spending nearly $2 trillion rescuing the financial system, estimated the "... combination of guarantees, capital injections, loans, and other support ..." would total nearly $7 trillion.[15] However, methodology is everything. The media, politicians, and government bodies tended to simply add up rescue expenditures, TARP expenditures, Federal Reserve bond purchases, and fiscal stimulus, but Generally Accepted Accounting Principles (GAAP) would require different numbers. For example, FNMA, FHLMC, and AIG would be consolidated in the government's accounts and their debts, mortgage guarantees, and derivatives liabilities reported by the government. Government guarantees of mortgages, bank deposits, bank debt, money market mutual funds, and auto warranties and liabilities to suppliers would be acknowledged in gross amounts, the related fees, losses, and recoveries estimated, and the time value of money acknowledged. The same formula would apply to the ring-fenced guarantees of asset pools to rescue Bear Stearns, AIG, Citigroup, and Bank of America. Federal Reserve purchases of long-term treasuries, agency bonds, and mortgage-backed securities would be acknowledged in gross amounts and then marked-to-market regularly to reflect losses or gains. The problem was that nowhere in the Treasury, the Federal Reserve, or the Congress was there the factual detail, the expert staff, the prior experience, or the will to cope with this. Such calculations were basic to selling insurance, guaranteeing mortgages, providing pensions, applying bond ratings, and buying private asset-backed securities or high yield bonds, but the government could not make them.

In estimating the scale of the government's remediation, we have to be content with consolidating Fannie Mae, Freddie Mac, and AIG and summing the gross amounts for the many federal guarantees. On this basis, the government's aggregate exposure to the financial system was $16 trillion (Table 6.8A) – more than double Tim Geithner's estimate and eight times the IMF's. The largest exposures were to Fannie Mae and Freddie Mac ($7.2 trillion), followed by the Money Market Mutual Fund guarantees ($3.2 trillion), the AIG rescue ($1.5 trillion), and the FDIC's expansion of deposit guarantees up to $250,000 ($1 trillion). The total extended for remediation was 110% of 2009 GDP. This was many multiples of the financial remediation in the Great Depression under President Roosevelt when it was only equal to 19% of GDP.[16]

The monetary measures in the crisis – most of them extraordinary except perhaps the central bank swap facilities – amounted to a further $3 trillion (Table 6.8B).

---

[15] Geithner (2014), pp. 369, 497.   [16] Wigmore (2010), p. 1.

Table 6.8A

AGGREGATE FORMS OF GOVERNMENT ASSISTANCE IN THE CRISIS OF 2008/2009		
Program	**$ billions**	**Institution(s)**
A. Financial Remediation:		
TARP	769	U.S. Treasury
Money Market Mutual Fund guarantees	3,200	U.S. Treasury
Temporary deposit guarantee expansion to $250,000	1,000	FDIC
Guarantees of new bank debt	618	FDIC
Bank transactions accounts guarantees	834	FDIC
Loss-sharing agreements	21	FDIC
FDIC representations and warranties on loan and servicing rights sales	184	FDIC
Bear Stearns acquisition	29	Federal Reserve Bank of NY
FNMA conservatorship incl. guarantees and derivatives liabilities	3,833	U.S. Treasury
FHLMC conservatorship incl. guarantees and derivatives liabilities	3,369	U.S. Treasury
AIG rescue incl. guarantees and derivatives liabilities	1,467	U.S. Treasury, Federal Reserve
Citigroup rescue	378	U.S. Treasury, Federal Reserve, FDIC
Bank of America rescue	164	U.S. Treasury, Federal Reserve, FDIC
Total	15,866	

Table 6.8B

AGGREGATE FORMS OF GOVERNMENT ASSISTANCE IN THE CRISIS OF 2008/2009		
Program	**$ billions**	**Institution(s)**
B. Monetary Policy:		
Purchases of MBS, Agency bonds, and US treasury bonds	1,346	Federal Reserve
CP funding facility (CPFF)	351	Federal Reserve
ABCP loan facility for MMMF (AMLF)	150	Federal Reserve
Central Bank swap facilities	583	Federal Reserve
Term asset backed lending facility (TALF)	46	Federal Reserve
Term securities lending facility (TSLF)	493	Federal Reserve
Primary dealer credit facility (PDCF)	147	Federal Reserve
Total	3,116	

The fiscal measures in Table 6.8C included a mix of traditional stimulus efforts as well as $425 billion for remediation of the auto industry. The total of the three tables amounted to over $20 trillion and 140% of GDP without including the extraordinary Federal Reserve efforts to stimulate the economy with QE-2 and QE-3.

Despite these massive efforts, there was little improvement in the economy during the rest of 2009. House prices and housing starts dropped to new lows and ABX prices didn't improve. Unemployment remained stuck at 10% and the U-6 rate at 17%. Manufacturers' new orders were down 35% and industrial production and retail sales at their bottom. Commercial real estate was still declining sharply.

Table 6.8C

AGGREGATE FORMS OF GOVERNMENT ASSISTANCE IN THE CRISIS OF 2008/2009		
Program	**$ billions**	**Institution(s)**
C. Fiscal Policy		
Bush 2% Temporary Tax Cut	96	U.S. Gov't
2009 American Recovery and Reinvestment Act	787	U.S. Gov't
"Cash for Clunkers"	3	U.S. Gov't
Home Affordable Modification Program	75	U.S. Gov't
2010 Tax Relief Act	112	U.S. Gov't
Auto relief, warranties, and supplier obligations guarantees	<u>425</u>	U.S. Gov't
Total	1,498	
Grand Total	20,480	
% of 2009 GDP	141%	

Sources: Wigmore (2010), except "Purchases of MBS, Agency bonds, and US treasury bonds" which is from Federal Reserve Annual Report 2009.

The one area of improvement was financial markets. The S&P 500 ended the year up 65% from its disastrous low in early March (Chart 6.30). S&P 500 volatility dropped back to the levels of early 2008 (Chart 6.31). Cautionary Money Market Mutual Fund balances dropped by $1 trillion to near their level in early 2007 (Chart 6.32). High yield bond rates dropped by over 50% as B-rated and BB-rated bonds converged around 9% after being as high as 23% and 16%, respectively (Chart 6.33). Ratings downgrades on private RMBS appeared to finally stop. Banks tightening their standards for commercial

Chart 6.30

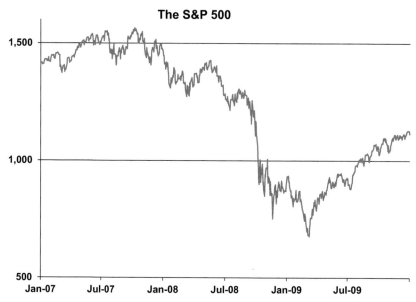

Source: Standard & Poor's Corp.

Chart 6.31

Source: CBOE.

Chart 6.32

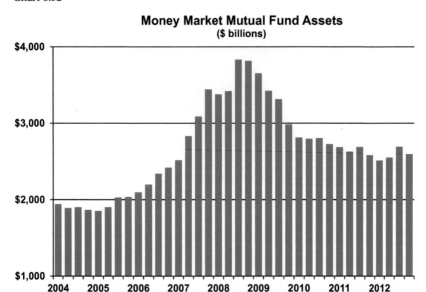

Money Market Mutual Fund Assets
(\$ billions)

Source: FRED.

Chart 6.33

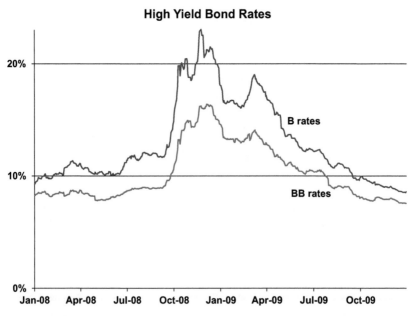

High Yield Bond Rates

Source: FRED.

loans dropped from 75% to 25%. Oil prices recovered to $75 and investment in oil and gas machinery was close to its 2007 record. Improvement in the broad economy would begin in 2010, but gold prices still flashed a signal of investor apprehension as they rose to $1,200 late in 2009.

7

Recovery 2010–2012

Money will always flow toward opportunity, and there is an abundance of that in America.

Warren Buffet, Berkshire Hathaway Annual Letter

7.1 Economic Recovery

Paul Krugman wrote in January 2009, "We're living in a Dark Age of Macroeconomics." The securities markets disagreed. The S&P 500 rose 80% from its early 2009 low to December 2010 (Chart 7.1). Clearly investors were looking ahead because all during 2009 analysts' earnings expectations for the next year remained dismal, but during 2010 their expectations for 2011 earnings rose 25% (Chart 7.2). The spread on high yield bonds dropped from its record 22% over treasuries (2200 basis points) at the end of 2008 to 7% in 2010. Large commercial bankruptcies over $100 million almost disappeared (Chart 7.3). Oil prices doubled from $40 to $80 by the beginning of 2010, although they weren't back to the $140 level in 2008.

The combined remedial, monetary, and fiscal policies of 2008–09 stimulated an economic recovery that began at the end of 2009. Retail sales began to grow again in the 4th quarter, but it wasn't until the end of 2010 that absolute sales exceeded 2007 (Chart 7.4).

There was a recovery in business inventories that contributed 3% to GDP growth in the 4th quarter of 2009 and the 1st quarter of 2010, a classic business cycle reaction, but it was a stimulus that wouldn't last. Exports grew back to 2008 levels thanks to a weak dollar and fiscal stimulus in China, India, South Korea, and Japan.[1] There was also incipient business

---

[1] Council of Economic Advisors, Economic Report of the President 2010, pp. 39, 44, 66, 98.

Chart 7.1

Source: FRED.

Chart 7.2

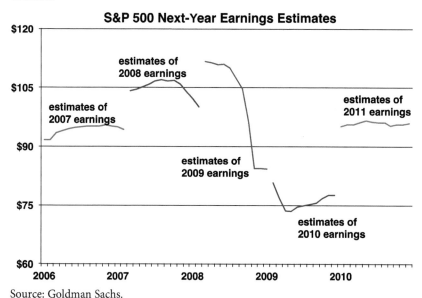

Source: Goldman Sachs.

Chart 7.3

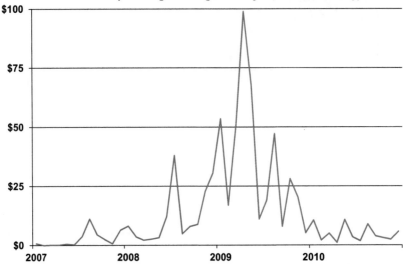

Commercial Bankruptcy Liabilities over $100 million
(removing the 2 largest each year, billions, monthly)

Source: New Generation Research, bankruptcydata.com.

Chart 7.4

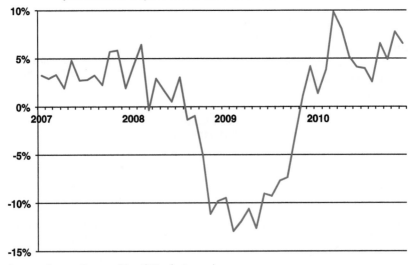

Retail Sales vs Year Ago
(nominal, no adjustments, incl. food and motor vehicles)

Source: Census Bureau (Retail Trade Survey).

Chart 7.5

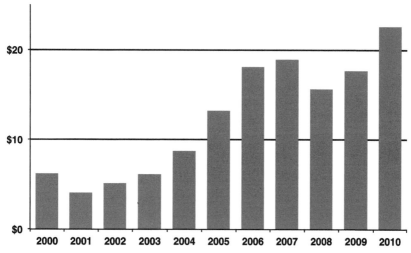

Investment in Oil & Gas and Mining Machinery
($ billions)

Source: FRED.

strength as private research and development in 2009 rose 25% above 2007.[2] Oil & Gas equipment spending was up almost 50% by 2010 (Chart 7.5) thanks to developments in seismology and horizontal drilling that were expanding production dramatically.

GDP growth in 2010 was around 2% (Chart 7.6) – less than the recoveries from previous recessions but not surprising in light of the shocks to the consumer and financial sectors. Economic growth got no help from small business, one of the most important sectors of the economy. Small business confidence remained mired in the doldrums as earnings continued to decline through 2010 (Chart 7.7). Note that earnings had not turned up in 2010 but rather stopped declining so sharply – down just 30%!

The consumer sector remained generally weak because of high unemployment and the troubled housing market. Unemployment stayed stuck near its peak of 10%. The U-6 measure of unemployment that took into account people leaving the workforce and unwillingly employed part-time was still 17%. Many people were not able to move to where the jobs were because they were stuck in their homes. In nine major cities where people might have

---

[2] National Science Foundation, Industrial R&D Information System, 2007 report, table no. 44 and National Center for Science and Engineering Statistics and US Census Bureau, Business R&D and Innovation Survey 2013.

Chart 7.6

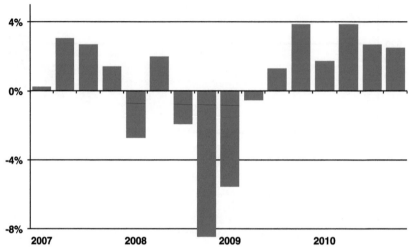

Source: FRED.

Chart 7.7

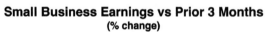

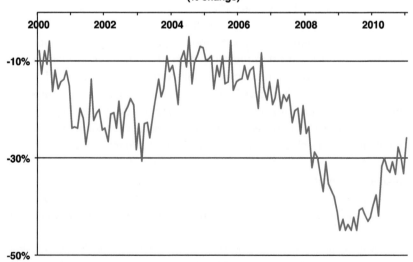

Source: National Federal of Independent Businesses.

Table 7.1

DECLINE IN HOUSE PRICES IN SOME MAJOR CITIES 2006–2011	
Sacramento	50%
Oakland	47%
Detroit	45%
Chicago	33%
Atlanta	29%
Charleston	29%
Minneapolis	28%
Providence	26%
Portland	25%

Source: FHFA (house price index datasets).

been expected to move out because of weak local economies, house prices were still down 25–50% at the end of 2011 (Table 7.1).

But it was not just prices that kept people stuck. In many cities, homes couldn't be sold. Sales of existing homes were 40% below 2005. Over 10% of all single-family homes had delinquent mortgages in 2010 and the number wasn't going down much. Negative equity in all homes with mortgages was estimated at $750 billion.[3]

A sense of how persistent the combination of weak housing prices, weak private RMBS markets, and mortgage distress was can be gathered from the 2006 ABX indices in Chart 7.8. Even private RMBS that were still rated AAA (and not many were) were valued at only 60 in 2010. Private RMBS that were A-rated were still valued at only 10–20.

Moody's downgrades of private RMBS dropped sharply in the last half of 2009, but there was some resurgence in 2010 as the weak economy affected homeowners in general. Consumer credit delinquencies were still double pre-crisis levels. Consumer confidence remained at the low level of 70

---

[3] Council of Economic Advisors, Economic Report of the President 2011, p. 35.

Chart 7.8

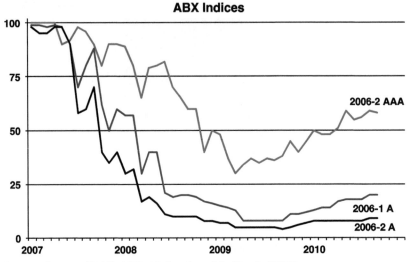

ABX Indices

Sources: Stanton (2011); 2009–10 data from MacKenzie (2012).

throughout 2009–10. Consumers cut back on their use of credit as debt other than student loans dropped 19% between 2007–13.[4]

The outlook was also complicated by a multi-year fiscal and banking crisis in Europe. Greece received its first bailout of $110 billion from the European Union and the IMF in May 2010. Ireland received €68 billion in November and its banks were reorganized. Bond markets indicated growing skepticism about the financial stability of Ireland, Portugal, Spain, Italy, and Belgium. The European Union set up a €500 billion lending facility for its member states and the European Central Bank began purchasing the bonds of its weaker member states.[5]

7.2 Fiscal and Monetary Policies

Consumer stagnation in 2010 and the building European financial crisis led both the Obama administration and the Federal Reserve to further stimulate the US economy. In December, President Obama signed the Tax Relief, Unemployment Insurance Reauthorization, and Job Creation Act

---

[4] Wolff (2017), table 9.
[5] Federal Reserve Annual Report 2010, "International Financial Markets," box 2, no page number.

that prevented scheduled individual tax increases from taking place for two years, extended unemployment benefits through 2011, took 2 percentage points off employees' payroll taxes ($112 billion), and offered companies 100% expensing of equipment purchases in 2011.[6] The administration felt restrained in going further as federal debt was projected to reach 100% of GDP in 2012 – up from 65% in 2008. The administration's signature policy focus became Obamacare.

The responsibility for further economic stimulus fell on the Federal Reserve. It announced in November 2010 that it would purchase $600 billion of longer-term treasuries in order to lower long-term interest rates, a policy quickly named QE-2 (the second quantitative easing after 2008). The move was immediately criticized by Nobel prizewinners Joseph Stiglitz and Paul Krugman as ineffective and was publicly opposed by many conservative economists and investors.[7] The Federal Reserve's policy statements also led markets to expect that the 0% federal funds rate would extend into 2012.[8]

As the European crisis worsened in 2011, Ireland, Portugal, Italy, and Spain lost access to public markets and fraught negotiations began with Greece for a second bailout package, finally agreed upon in February 2012. The European Economic Community began a series of measures to support its weakest members including increased scope and flexibility for the €440 billion European Financial Stability Facility, stepping up the implementation of the €500 billion European Stability Mechanism to July 2012, resumption of European Central Bank purchases of Spain and Italy's public debt, and €500 billion of 3-year financing for Europe's banks.[9]

In the USA, the Federal Reserve began a process in 2011 of overtly "jawboning" the markets to create expectations that it would do whatever was necessary to improve employment and the economy. It announced in August that it would keep rates low "at least through mid-2013," and then in January 2012 extended this "through late 2014." It switched its open market buying to more agency RMBS and announced that it was "prepared to adjust those holdings as appropriate to promote a stronger economic recovery." In September 2012, it announced QE-3, a program to buy $40 billion monthly of RMBS and three months later raised this to $85 billion. Federal Reserve assets grew to a peak of $4.5 trillion in the

---

[6] Council of Economic Advisors, Economic Report of the President 2011, p. 42.
[7] *The Wall Street Journal*, 11/15/10, "Open Letter to Ben Bernanke." Prominent signatories included Michael Boskin, Jim Chanos, William Kristol, Niall Ferguson, Seth Klarman, and Paul Singer.
[8] Federal Reserve Annual Report, 2010, "Monetary Policy Expectations and Treasury Rates."
[9] Federal Reserve Annual Report, 2011, pp. 30–1.

Chart 7.9

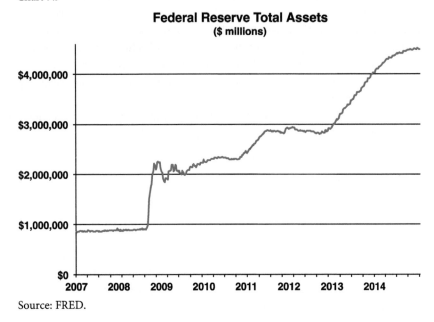

Federal Reserve Total Assets
($ millions)

Source: FRED.

fall of 2014 (Chart 7.9). Both in Europe and the USA, governments and their central banks were able to create expectations that they would do whatever was necessary to sustain failing institutions, stimulate economic growth, and grow employment.

Ten-year treasuries dropped under 2% in 2012 and 2-year treasuries under ½% (Chart 7.10). Thirty-year mortgage rates dropped under 3½% and under 2½% for floating rates (Chart 7.11).

Conservative observers criticized these policies as likely to cause inflation, leave a huge debt burden for later generations, and exhaust the authorities' remedial powers if another crisis developed, while the left wing criticized the authorities for not achieving enough growth and full employment. But the result was an environment of steady economic growth, modest wage pressures, improving corporate profits, and low inflation.

Retail sales exceeded pre-crisis 2008 levels by 6% in 2012 (Chart 7.12). Private equipment spending recovered to 2007's level. GDP growth was 2½% with only limited quarterly exceptions and there were no inflation pressures as CPI was mostly under 2%. Housing remained a drag on recovery as starts were mired at less than half the peak of 2006. Housing investment that had been 5% of GDP in 2000 before the housing bubble and 7% in 2005 was still at a post crisis low of 2½% in 2012.

Chart 7.10

Source: Federal Reserve.

Chart 7.11

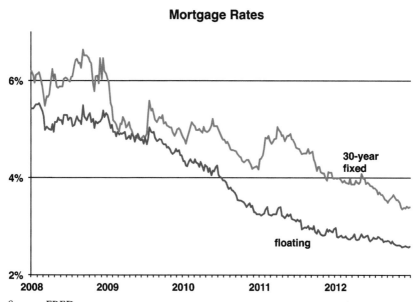

Source: FRED.

Chart 7.12

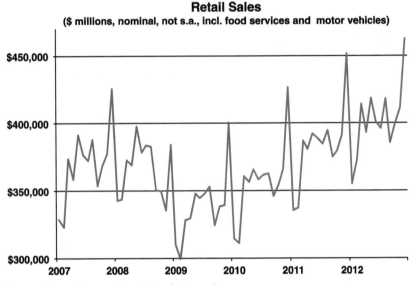

Retail Sales
($ millions, nominal, not s.a., incl. food services and motor vehicles)

Source: Census Bureau (Retail Trade Survey).

Still, there were uncertainties. Both the recession and the financial destruction were the worst since the 1970s. The effects were bound to linger. Unemployment only dipped below 8% at the end of 2012 – far from the Federal Reserve's target of under 6%. U-6 unemployment stayed over 14%. Mortgage problems hardly abated as delinquencies remained over 10%. Home prices nationally in 2012 were still down 18% from 2007. In the so-called "sand states" where building had been the most active, prices were still down 30–50% (Chart 7.13).

Consumer confidence stayed stuck below 75 and consumers steadily increased their savings until the personal savings rate reached 9% at the end of 2012 (Chart 7.14) – a level not seen since the early 1980s.

Small business optimism, a factor in half of the country's jobs and GDP, didn't improve at all (Chart 7.15). The Dodd–Frank Act appeared to have reduced the availability of loans to small business and inhibited business formation by raising the cost of regulatory compliance and reducing the incentives to make small loans (Bordo, 2018).

7.3 Securities Markets

In the face of the modest improvement in home prices and mortgage defaults in 2010–12, ratings downgrades of private RMBS almost came to

Chart 7.13

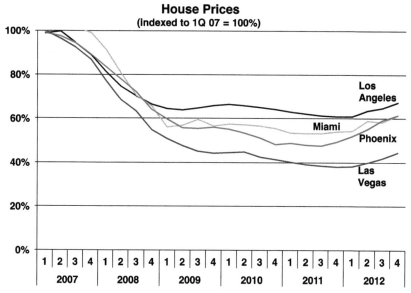

Source: FHFA (house price index datasets).

Chart 7.14

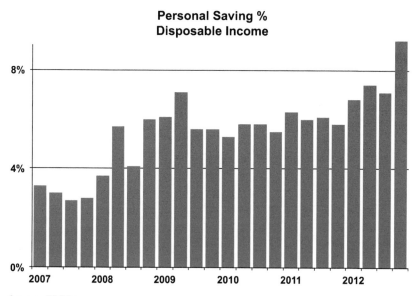

Source: FRED.

Chart 7.15

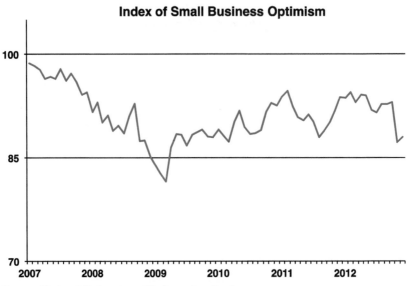

Source: National Federation of Independent Businesses.

a halt. Moody's downgrades mostly ran under 2,000 quarterly beginning in 2011 after being as high as 25,000 (Chart 7.16). CDO ratings downgrades virtually disappeared. The one disturbing feature was that Standard & Poor's downgrades of prime RMBS jumped to 5,000 in late 2012 after running near 1,000 quarterly for two years (Chart 7.17). On the positive side, Moody's began to upgrade some RMBS (not in a quantity that had much impact) (Chart 7.18). Standard & Poor's upgraded 300–600 CDO tranches quarterly in 2011–12, in part reflecting that these issues had other collateral than private RMBS (Chart 7.19).

The situation in commercial real estate was anomalous. The rating agencies continued to cut a high number of CMBS ratings throughout 2012, peaking cumulatively at 4,200 tranches (Chart 7.20) and A-rated CMBX spreads rose back to 3,000 basis points in 2011–12 (Chart 7.21) – a level that made most new CMBS issues impossible. Commercial real estate bad loans continued as a principal distress factor for banks around the country other than the largest that we have focused on (Antoniades, 2015). Commercial real estate construction dropped from 1.5% of GDP in 2007–08 to 0.65% in 2010–12 (Chart 7.22) – almost a 1% drag on GDP – and outstanding commercial mortgages in 2012 were $200 billion (13%) below their 2008 peak. Yet prices for both retail and apartment properties were

Chart 7.16

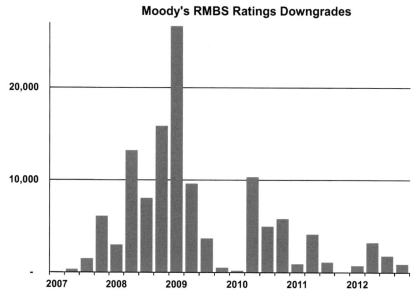

Source: ESF Quarterly Securitisation Data Reports.

Chart 7.17

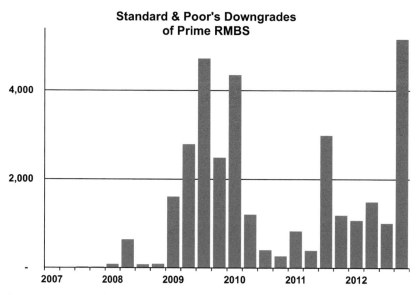

Source: ESF Quarterly Securitisation Data Reports.

Chart 7.18

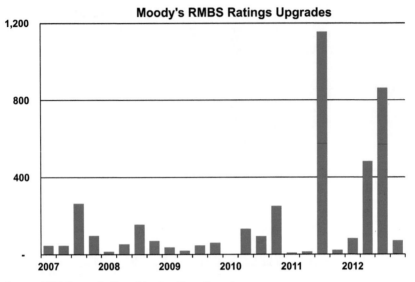

Source: ESF Quarterly Securitisation Data Reports.

Chart 7.19

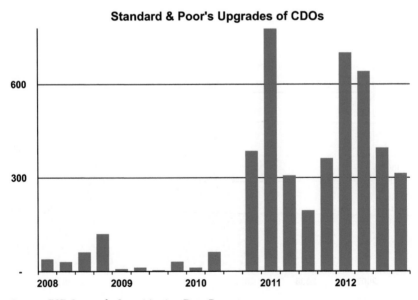

Source: ESF Quarterly Securitisation Data Reports.

Chart 7.20

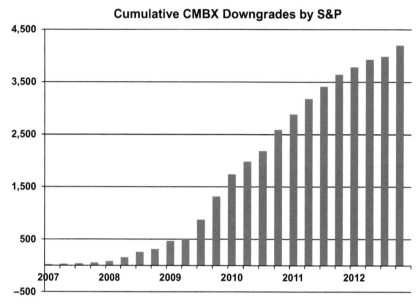

Source: An (2014).

Chart 7.21

Source: Bloomberg/GS Global Research.

Chart 7.22

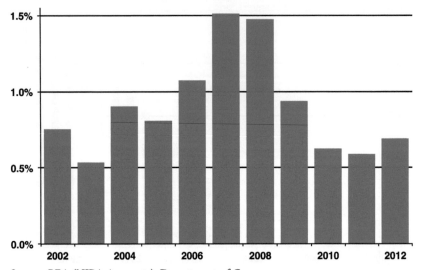

Commercial Real Estate Construction % GDP

Source: BEA (NIPA Accounts), Department of Commerce.

back above their 2007 peaks in 2012. Office property prices still lagged below (Chart 7.23). The recovery appears to have been due to institutions still stretching for yield as sales rebounded to $400 billion in 2013 (an appropriate look beyond 2012 given the long lead time for commercial sales). Sales in 2013 were two-thirds of 2007's peak activity (Chart 7.24).

The S&P 500 was up 16% in 2012 (Chart 7.25) and earnings estimates for 2013 were 10% above 2007's estimates for 2008 (Chart 7.26). Dividend increases resumed after the scarce years of 2008–10 (Chart 7.27). However, the S&P 500 still had not surpassed either 2007 or 2000 – a lean twelve years.

An epochal transition in equity valuations occurred in 2012 when dividend yields and 10-year US treasury rates converged for the first time since 1957 (Chart 7.28). Treasury rates had been at least double dividend yields in the intervening decades.[10]

There was wide variation in how the stocks of different industries performed in the recovery. Table 7.2 below lists the results between the end of 2007 and the end of 2012 for the twenty-four industries making up the S&P 500. Industries with stocks that rose 25% or more were

---

[10] The 10-year US treasury rate began to substantially exceed the S&P 500 dividend yield in the early 1960s.

Chart 7.23

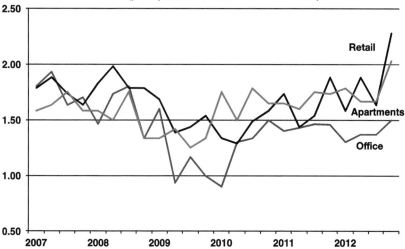

Commercial Real Estate Prices
(per square foot, indexed 1Q 2001 = 1.00)

Source: MBA (2010); post 2009 prices MBA (2015).

Chart 7.24

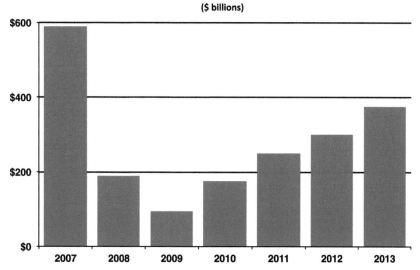

Commercial Real Estate Sales
($ billions)

Source: MBA (2018).

Chart 7.25

Source: FRED.

Chart 7.26

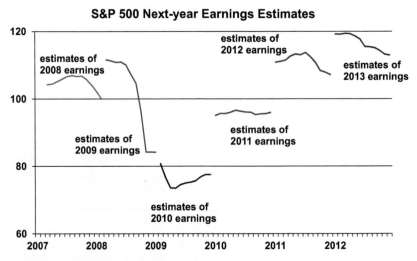

Source: Goldman Sachs.

Chart 7.27

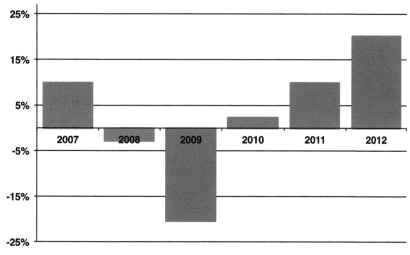

Source: FRED.

Chart 7.28

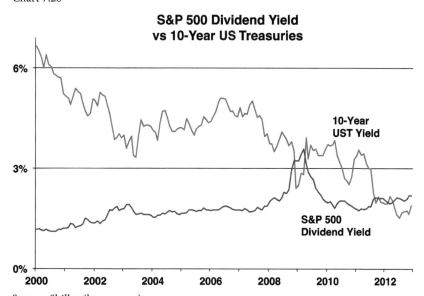

Source: Shiller (home page).

Table 7.2

STOCK PERFORMANCE OF THE S&P INDUSTRIES 2007–2012	
Diversified financials	−49%
Insurance	−45%
Banks	−42%
Semiconductors	−20%
Utilities	−18%
Commercial & professional services	−13%
Telecommunications	−13%
Capital goods	−13%
Energy	−12%
Materials	−9%
Autos & components	−8%
Household & personal products	1%
Healthcare equipment & services	2%
Real estate	7%
Software	11%
Pharmaceuticals	19%
Food retail	24%
Technology hardware	24%
Transportation	27%
Food & beverages	29%
Consumer services	38%
Consumer durables	40%
Media	49%
Retail	59%

Source: Standard & Poor's Corp.

concentrated in consumer sectors such as retail, food, technology, healthcare, and media. Financial industries were still down 40% in 2012, partly because the implementation of Dodd–Frank regulations threatened their profitability. The ramifications of the crisis continued to play out in the courts and government investigations, and the financial industries went through a major debt contraction as can be seen in Table 7.3. Banks in the S&P 500 contracted their outstanding debt 89% between 2007–12, insurance companies 63%, and diversified financial companies 62%.

The rise of technology, media, drug, and retail industries between 1990 and 2012 was reflected in the rising share of corporate profits in Gross Domestic Income from around 4% in the 1970s and 1980s to 7% in 2012 (Chart 7.29). The face of corporate America was changing, and profits with it. Seemingly unique business models existed at Microsoft, Google, Apple, Amazon (Facebook and Netflix were still to come), Costco,

Disney, Intuitive Surgical, and Nike. Duopolies were extensive between UPS/Fedex, Visa/Mastercard, L'Oréal/Estée Lauder, Pepsi/Coca-Cola, Kellogg/General Mills, Hershey/Mars, Home Depot/Lowe's, CVS/Walgreen's, Caterpillar/Deere, Boeing/Airbus, and Comcast/Time Warner. Oligopolies had developed among the major banks, investment banks, oil companies, railroads, airlines, and phone companies. All of these companies still had competition, but it tended to come from new companies taking advantage of technology.

Fiscal and monetary policies and troubles in Europe produced considerable variation in returns among the various sectors of the securities markets. S&P 500 total returns aggregated 36% for 2010 through 2012 making the USA the strongest equity market (Table 7.4). As interest rates came down, US treasuries and high yield bonds had equity-like returns of 47% and 39%. Commodities and cash, however, provided close to zero returns, and all bond rates looked non-compensatory going forward. Broad hedge funds lost their edge in the recovery.

After 2009, their returns were below the S&P 500, often substantially (Chart 7.30). Observers stretched to explain this weakness, highlighting the competition from so many funds, the difficulty in earning exceptional returns on very large portfolios, the low stock market volatility, and lack of return differentiation in stocks.

There were many indications during the recovery that markets still carried a burden of worry and residual asset destruction. The projected earnings yield on the S&P 500 remained far above historic norms at 400–500% of 10-year US treasuries (Chart 7.31). This relative yield had been in a range of 150% from 2000 to 2007. The higher spread implied either that investors treated the 1.8% rate on 10-year treasuries as artificially low

Table 7.3

CHANGE IN DEBT FOR THE S&P INDUSTRIES 2007–2012	
Banks	−89%
Autos & components	−75%
Insurance	−63%
Diversified financials	−62%
Real estate	−42%
Consumer durables	−31%
Commercial & professional services	−26%
Consumer services	1%
Household and personal products	9%
Food retail	22%
Utilities	28%
Retail	29%
Materials	30%
Telecommunications	37%
Technology hardware	39%
Transportation	40%
Capital goods	43%
Energy	49%
Media	60%
Food, beverages	95%
Software	99%
Pharmaceuticals	101%
Healthcare equipment & services	102%
Semiconductors	128%

Source: Standard & Poor's Corp.

and were discounting its rise to 4% (where the historic relationship would hold) or that the risk premium to hold equities had tripled, or some combination of the two.

Table 7.4

	S&P 500	MSCI EAFE	Emerging Mkts	U.S. Bonds	High Yield	Commodities	Cash
RETURNS FOR VARIOUS SECURITIES SECTORS 2010–2012							
2010	15%	8%	19%	9%	15%	9%	0%
2011	2%	–12%	–18%	30%	4%	–1%	0%
2012	16%	17%	19%	4%	16%	0%	0%
2010–2012	36%	11%	16%	47%	39%	8%	0%

Sources: Standard & Poor's Corp.; MSCI-EAFE; MSCI-EM; Barclays; Bank of America ML; Goldman Sachs Commodities Index.

Chart 7.29

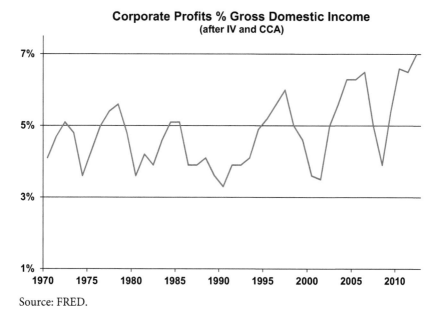

Corporate Profits % Gross Domestic Income
(after IV and CCA)

Source: FRED.

Worry was indicated when over $360 billion flowed out of domestic equity mutual funds between the 2nd quarter of 2011 and the 3rd quarter of 2012 after strong equity inflows in 2009 and 2010 (Chart 7.32). Baa

Chart 7.30

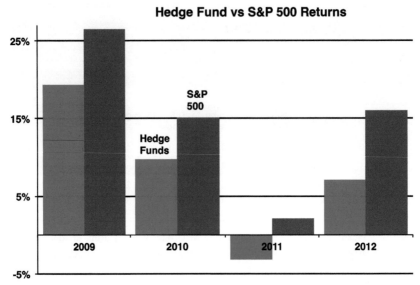

Source: Cambridge Associates (2011).

Chart 7.31

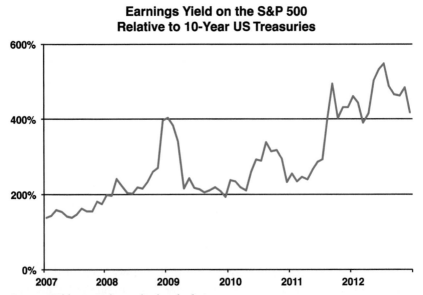

Source: Goldman Sachs; author's calculations.

Chart 7.32

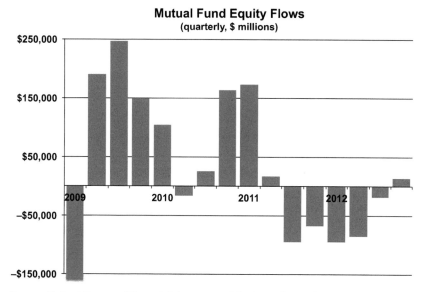

Mutual Fund Equity Flows
(quarterly, $ millions)

Source: Federal Reserve (Financial Accounts of the United States).

interest rates maintained a consistent 300 basis points spread that was almost as high as the stress period 2001–02. High yield rates were 600 basis points over treasuries – almost double the spreads in the recovery after the recession of 2001. Gold prices remained at a record $1,700. The dollar's weakness, down 30% from 2002 (trade weighted) and 8% from pre-crisis 2006, also suggested concern, especially when Europe was having such pronounced fiscal and financial problems. Merger activity only got back to 70% of levels in 2006–07.

The country had dealt with the worst of the crisis but was still proceeding unsteadily. It was uncertain how well the moderate policies of the Obama administration and the Federal Reserve would fare.

8

Epilogue 2012–2016

It ain't over 'til it's over.

Yogi Berra

By 2016 the policy makers in the Bush and Obama administrations and at the Federal Reserve must have felt vindicated in their understanding of the financial and economic world and the execution of their crisis policies. US economic growth, employment, wealth, and confidence had been achieved to a greater degree than in any other part of the developed world.[1] It was no coincidence, since US financial remediation and fiscal and monetary policies were more aggressive than anywhere else. There were still residual effects to be resolved, notably the high level of federal debt to GDP, the Federal Reserve's huge balance sheet, artificially low interest rates, and the status of Fannie Mae and Freddie Mac. But few could argue against the success of the recovery.

The Obama administration had followed a relatively conservative fiscal policy. Federal debt had reached 100% of GDP in 2013 (Chart 8.1). This landmark restricted further federal stimulus such that the federal deficit was constrained to 2–3% of GDP between 2013–16 and thus was a fiscal drag on growth (Chart 8.2).

The burden of stimulating the economy fell upon the Federal Reserve. It continued to expand its balance sheet to $5 trillion by 2014 under QE-3 (Chart 8.3) and held federal funds rates at virtually zero (negative if inflation is taken into account) (Chart 8.4). It was able to keep other treasury rates historically low through a combination of the influence of

---

[1] Goldman Sachs, Investment Management Division, (Un)Steady as She Goes, January 2018, reported that the length and magnitude of the US recovery was greater than any other developed country and nearing the longest since WW II (exhibits 1, 3, 6), as were corporate earnings and equity total returns (exhibits 7, 9, 10, 15).

Chart 8.1

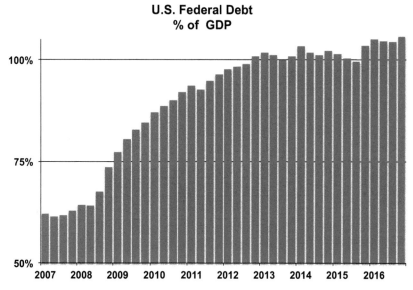

Source: FRED.

Chart 8.2

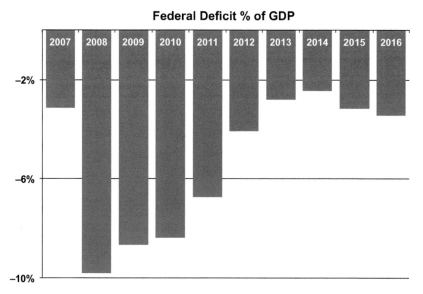

Source: FRED.

Chart 8.3

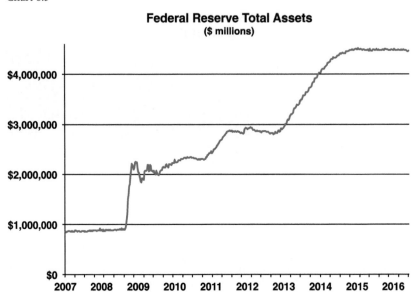

Source: FRED.

Chart 8.4

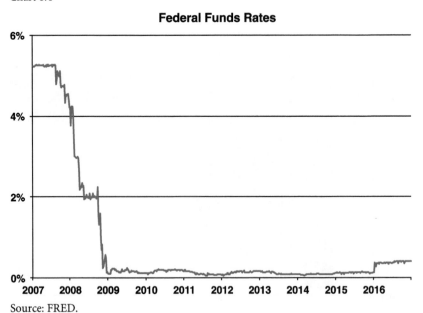

Source: FRED.

Chart 8.5

U.S. Treasury Rates

10-year

2-year

Source: Federal Reserve.

short-term rates, jawboning, and direct purchases of longer-term securities. Ten-year rates fell to 1½% in mid-2016 and 2-year rates stayed steadily under 1% (Chart 8.5).

In response to these policies, GDP grew through 2016 without a recession (Chart 8.6). The average growth rate of 2% was below the aftermath of prior recessions, but 2008–09 was unique in being a consumer-led recession. The damage to consumers' income, net worth, ability to borrow, and confidence plus the overbuilding in homes was such that an aggressive rebound could not be expected, especially when one added the effects of overbuilding in commercial real estate, the leverage built up in corporate debt, and the deleveraging of the financial industry. Inflation was constrained at 2% or less. If anything, there were worries that it was too low.

National housing prices finally recovered to 2006 levels in 2016 (Chart 8.7), and mortgage delinquency rates dropped from 11% to 4% (Chart 8.8). Housing prices were lifted by professional investors that came into the market in 2012 to take advantage of depressed prices and the need for rental homes. The two largest investors, Blackstone Group's Invitation Homes and American Homes 4 Rent, ended up owning over 120,000

Chart 8.6

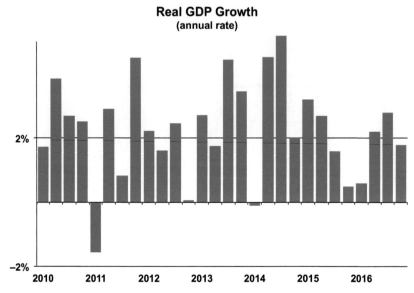

Source: FRED.

Chart 8.7

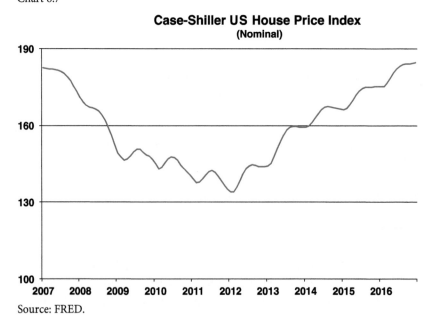

Source: FRED.

Chart 8.8

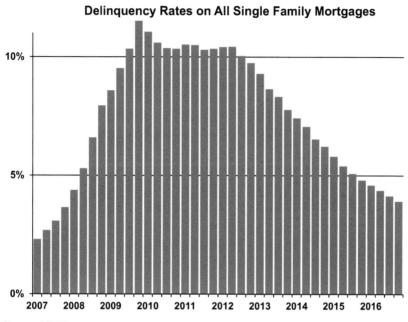

Delinquency Rates on All Single Family Mortgages

Source: FRED.

homes by 2018 at a cost of over $26 billion – an average price of $215,000. They had occupancy rates around 95%.[2]

Housing starts only recovered to 1.2 million units annually compared to twice that before the crisis (Chart 8.9). This was to be expected given the leverage involved in housing purchases, the damage to consumer finances in the crisis, and the overexpansion in speculative purchases and second homes. This level of housing starts constituted almost a 1% drag on GDP.

There was considerable differentiation in the rebound in commercial real estate prices. Young (2020) published the chart below that traced commercial real estate sector prices through 2014 (Chart 8.10). Apartment building prices in 2014 exceeded their 2007 peak by 14%, retail and industrial prices equaled 2007, office prices were lower by 2½%, and hotel/resort prices were lower by 16½%. Commercial real estate construction was almost back to its record 1½% of GDP in 2016 after being a 1%

---

[2] 2108 10-Ks.

Chart 8.9

Housing Starts
('000 units, annual rate)

Source: FRED.

drag on GDP growth for four years (Chart 8.11). Commercial real estate construction would set a new record in 2018 when it rose to 1.9% of GDP.

Industrial production did not recover beyond pre-crisis levels (Chart 8.12) because business equipment and consumer durable purchases (excluding autos) were stalled. Manufacturers' new orders (Chart 8.13) exhibited the same weakness. Both raised broad concern about the hollowing out of US manufacturing. Corporate capital spending indicated a stronger trend than production itself, as it recovered 20% beyond 2007, growing steadily until 2014 after which it leveled out (Chart 8.14).

The 50% decline in oil prices in 2014–16 was a factor in the industrial/manufacturing lag. Some of the industrial lag was centered in small businesses where earnings remained below the level in 2007. Small business optimism didn't improve until the election of President Trump when it surged to its highest level in a decade (Chart 8.15). The consumer recovered to a surprising degree as unemployment dropped steadily to under 5% in 2016 and U-6 to 9%. Consumer confidence recovered from its low of 65 to nearly 100 in 2015–16. Real retail sales in 2016 surpassed the levels of 2007 by 22% (Chart 8.16).

Chart 8.10

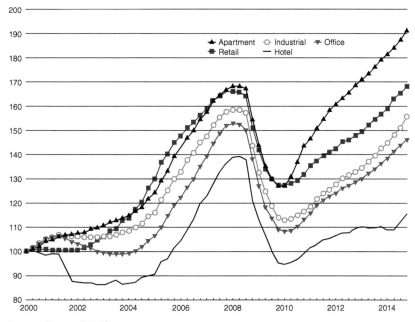

Indexed Market Value by Property Type 2001–14

Source: Young (2020).

The S&P 500 at the end of 2016 was triple its low in 2009 (Chart 8.17). This compared with its longest uninterrupted rises in the 1990s and 1920s. In 2018 it would exceed them. Next-year earnings estimates doubled versus 2009's estimates (Chart 8.18). Equity prices rebounded more than earnings because of lower interest rates, but also because there was a shift toward the hi-tech industry with its higher valuations. The earnings yield on projected earnings dropped to 250% of 10-year treasuries in 2016 (Chart 8.19), but it nonetheless remained elevated compared with 150% prior to the crisis.

The S&P 500 return of 133% between 2010–16 was superior to all of the other classic sector allocations, as can be seen in Chart 8.20. Long-term US treasuries and high yield bonds produced about half of that; other developed countries and emerging markets produced almost no return. Cash produced zero and commodities lost 47%.

The popularity of technology stocks reemerged beginning in 2012, as they rose 90% by 2016 (Chart 8.21). Technology infiltrated all parts of

Chart 8.11

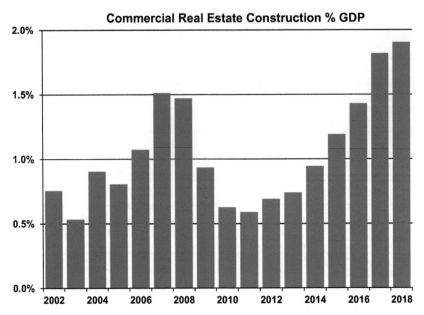

Source: BEA (NIPA Accounts).

Chart 8.12

Source: FRED.

Chart 8.13

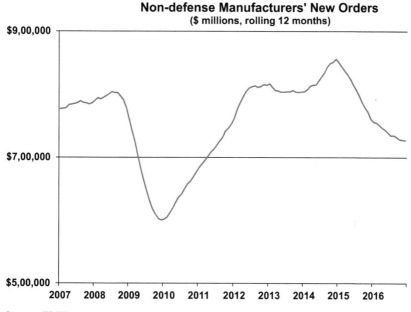

Non-defense Manufacturers' New Orders
($ millions, rolling 12 months)

Source: FRED.

life – cell phones (Apple), search (Google), retailing (Amazon), social media (Facebook), cloud computing (Amazon again), music (Apple), games (Microsoft, Nintendo, and Nvidia), streamed entertainment (Netflix), multimedia (Adobe), exchange-traded futures (CME), finance (Bloomberg), and travel (Priceline and others).

Biotechnology finally reemerged as a popular sector after a long slumber (at least twenty-five years) in which only Genentech and Amgen were significant companies (Chart 8.22). Andy Grove, Chairman of Intel, had mocked the industry in the 1990s for its lack of productivity and idiosyncratic standards. The Nasdaq Biotech Index more than tripled between 2012–15 as new drugs at companies such as Gilead (Hepatitis C), Biogen (Multiple Sclerosis), Celgene (Multiple Myeloma), and Regeneron (Retina disease) suddenly produced billions in sales and net income. Media enthusiasm for the potential from gene therapy and immune system treatments resulted in the public becoming the venture capital source for over one hundred biotech companies as they went public with no proven products and no sales.

Chart 8.14

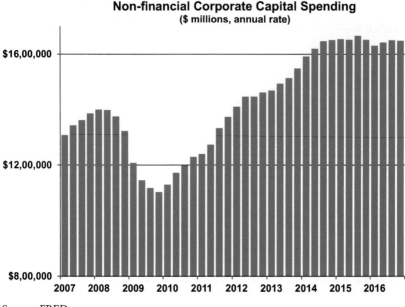

Non-financial Corporate Capital Spending
(\$ millions, annual rate)

Source: FRED.

Merger and acquisition activity came back to life, exceeding 2007's record level by over 50% (Chart 8.23). Prices in the merger market set records as the price-earnings ratios paid were 90% above the price-earnings ratio of the S&P 500 (Chart 8.24).

This time, private equity had less influence in the merger market as its fund raising only got back to 2007 levels (Chart 8.25).

Highly leveraged loan issues exceeded 2007 every year from 2013 to 2015 – in 2013 by over 50% (Chart 8.26).[3] Perhaps alarmingly, half of the loans were "covenant lite" (Chart 8.27) as lenders competed for deals in the atmosphere of very low interest rates. Estimated leveraged loans outstanding based on extrapolated data from the Bank for International Settlements and Fitch Ratings rose to almost \$6 trillion – double 2007 (Chart 8.28) and a level that was understated by the rating agencies and the media.

---

[3] Unfortunately, the BIS in reviewing leveraged loans in its September 2018 Quarterly Review used the S&P LCTA data that it disparaged in 2008. I have continued to adjust the post-2008 data published by Fitch Investors for the same higher proportion that the BIS found in its market-based procedure in 2008.

Chart 8.15

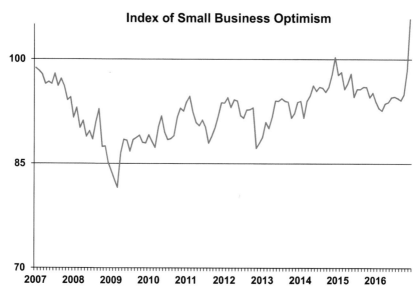

Index of Small Business Optimism

Source: National Federation of Independent Businesses.

Chart 8.16

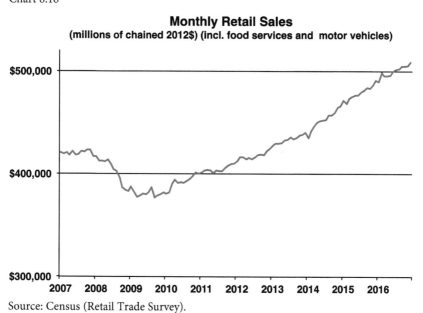

Monthly Retail Sales
(millions of chained 2012$) (incl. food services and motor vehicles)

Source: Census (Retail Trade Survey).

Chart 8.17

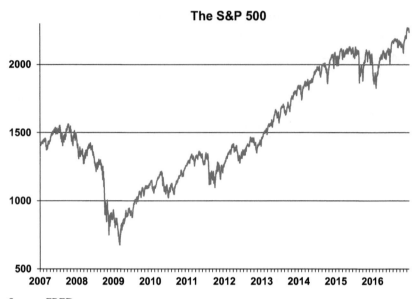

Source: FRED.

Chart 8.18

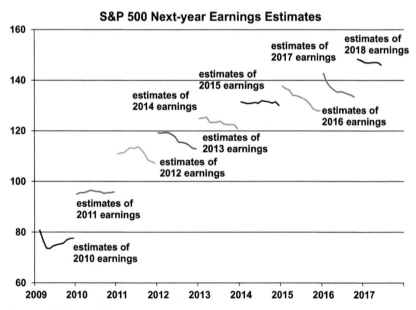

Source: Goldman Sachs.

Chart 8.19

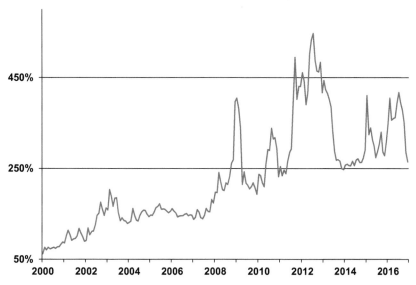

**Earnings Yield on the S&P 500
Relative to 10-Year U.S. Treasuries**

Sources: Goldman Sachs; author's calculations.

Some markets didn't recover. Private RMBS issues almost disappeared. So did credit default transactions that may have reflected that the Dodd–Frank Act tried to force speculative derivative transactions onto organized exchanges (Stout, 2011). The credit default swaps that remained were generally on single-name credits. Asset-backed commercial paper languished at one-quarter of its record level in 2007. Gold lost its charm as its price dropped from $1,800 to $1,130.

The continuity of Obama administration policies with the Bush administration's efforts in the crisis appeared vindicated. Remedial efforts for banks and other financial companies in distress had continued in the first term and there was no effort at retribution. Fiscal stimulation remained modest in the second term, arguably a drag of 1–3% on GDP growth in 2012–16. Reliance remained on the Federal Reserve and its QE-2 and QE-3 programs. It is not as if the Federal Reserve's purchases in 2012–16 could be said to have in themselves stimulated the economy. Interest rates did not go lower. They simply stayed low. Housing construction was not much stimulated, a traditional beneficiary of low interest rates. Consumer

Chart 8.20

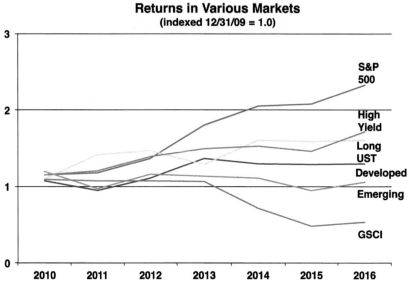

Sources: Standard & Poor's Corp.; MSCI-EAFE; MSCI-EM; Barclays; Bank of America ML; Goldman Sachs Commodities Index.

Chart 8.21

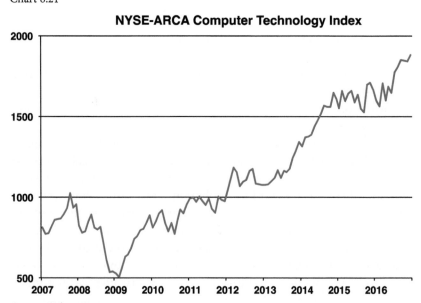

Source: Yahoo Finance.

Chart 8.22

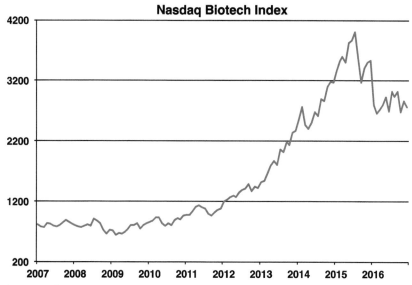

Source: Yahoo Finance.

Chart 8.23

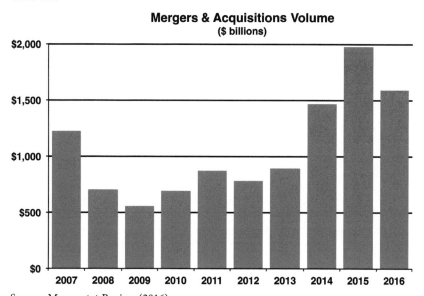

Source: Mergerstat Review (2016).

Chart 8.24

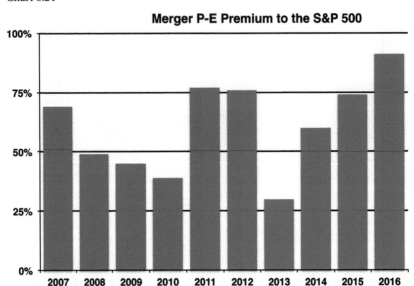

Source: Mergerstat Review (2016).

Chart 8.25

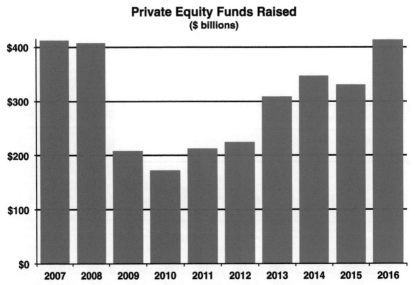

Sources: Prequin, "Private Equity Update"; KPMG Private Equity Forum, November 2016.

Chart 8.26

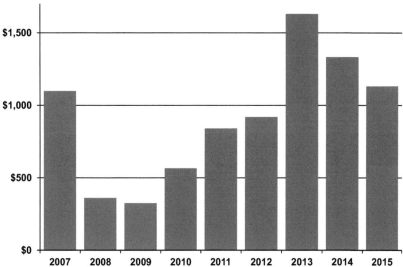

Highly Leveraged Loan Issues
($ billions)

Sources: BIS (2008); Fitch Ratings (2016).

Chart 8.27

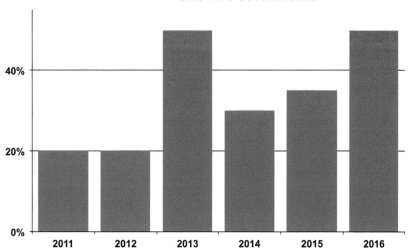

**Percent of Highly Leveraged Loans
that were Covenant Lite**

Source: BIS (2018).

Chart 8.28

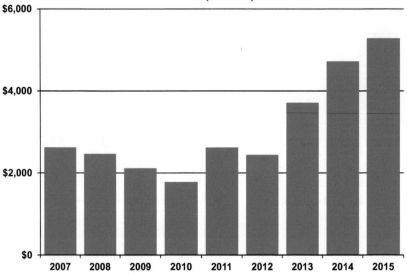

Highly Leveraged Loans Outstanding
(\$ billions)

Source: BIS (2008); Fitch Ratings (2016).

disposable income was little benefited by refunding home mortgages. They had already been refunded. It appears, rather, that federal policies that kept interest rates, inflation, and taxes low allowed native American acquisitiveness to grow on the consumer side and enterprise to flower in the business sector. The innovative motors of hi-tech, media, biotech, oil & gas, and commercial real estate were what stimulated the economy. The further effect was to create substantial wealth in the financial markets.

It is unclear whether any after-effects of the financial crisis affected Donald Trump's success in 2016 when he campaigned on an agenda of restructuring many of the country's key policies – foreign trade, corporate taxes, energy development, defense policy, healthcare, and environmental and other regulations.

Acknowledgments

This book would not have been possible without the FRED depository of financial and economic data maintained by the St. Louis Federal Reserve Bank. It is an easily accessible, *free* resource in standardized format from which data is easily downloaded. Whoever created this site deserves sainthood.

I am grateful to Michael Bordo, Rutgers University, for recommending the book for his economic series at Cambridge University Press. He has been a friend of long standing. I am most appreciative of the enthusiasm for the book shown by Robert Dreesen, my editor at Cambridge University Press, and the help of his assistant, Erika Walsh.

Andrei Shleifer (Harvard) and Craig Broderick (Goldman Sachs) provided unstinted advice and criticism although I had never met them previously. Richard Sylla (NYU) read the book twice and provided helpful comments. I deeply appreciate their generosity of time and spirit.

I am grateful to people at the following institutions for providing me with data: Jan Hatzius, Gene Sykes, and Marty Young at Goldman Sachs, James Bailey and Margaret Chen at Cambridge Associates, the investment management staff at the Metropolitan Museum, Reis Inc. (real estate data), and New Generation Research (bankruptcy data). Nor could this book have been completed without access to the work of the many scholars and institutions that make their data publicly available.

I am grateful to the following readers who also provided helpful advice: Nick Cancro, Forrest Capie, Russ Carson, Arthur Chu, Rodgin Cohen, Ira Crowell, Michael Cunningham, Barry Eichengreen, George Hodor, Steve Isenberg, Tony James, Hank Paulson, Roy Smith (deceased), Willard Taylor, Peter Temin, Eugene White, and three anonymous referees.

Charts

CHAPTER 1
The Heritage of the Hi-Tech Bubble 2000–2004

CHAPTER 2
The Stretch for Higher Returns 2004–2006

CHAPTER 3
The Impending Storm – 2007

CHAPTER 4
The Crisis – 2008

CHAPTER 7
Recovery 2010–2012

CHAPTER 8
Epilogue 2012–2016

Tables

CHAPTER 1
The Heritage of the Hi-Tech Bubble 2000–2004

CHAPTER 2
The Stretch for Higher Returns 2004–2006

CHAPTER 5
What Caused the Crisis?

CHAPTER 6
The Initial Obama Administration 2009

CHAPTER 7
Recovery 2010–2012

Acronyms

10-K	Public companies' annual financial filing with the SEC
10-Q	Public companies' quarterly financial filings with the SEC
Aaa/AAA	Moody's/S&P's highest rating
Aa/AA	Moody's/S&P's ratings
A/A	Moody's/S&P's ratings
Baa/BBB	Moody's/S&P's ratings
Ba/BB	Moody's/S&P's ratings
B/B	Moody's/S&P's ratings
Caa/CCC	Moody's/S&P's ratings
Ca/CC	Moody's/S&P's ratings
C/C	Moody's/S&P's lowest ratings
Aa3-,Aa- etc.	Moody's/S&P's gradations within a ratings category
ABCP	Asset-backed commercial paper
ABS	Asset-backed securities (mostly credit card debt, auto loans, receivables, and other short-term obligations)
ABX	A synthetic, tradable index referencing a basket of 20 subprime RMBS
Alt-A	Mortgages for which borrowers provided limited credit information
AMLF	ABCP loan facility for MMMF
ARMs	Adjustable rate mortgages
Basel II	Bank for International Settlements' capital regulations
BEA	The Bureau of Economic Analysis (part of the Census Bureau)
BIS	Bank for International Settlements, based in Basel, Switzerland

CALPERS	California Public Employees Retirement System
cap rates	the discount rate used to present-value commercial real estate cash flows
CDO	Collateralized debt obligation
CFMA	Commodities Futures Modernization Act
CFTC	Commodities Futures Trading Commission
CLO	Collateralized loan obligation
CMBS	Commercial mortgage-backed securities
CME	The Chicago Mercantile Exchange
CMO	Collateralized mortgage obligation
CP	Commercial paper
CPFF	CP funding facility
DPI	Disposable Personal Income
EAFE	An index measuring stock markets in Europe, Australia, and the Far East
EBIT	Earnings before interest and taxes (a stricter measure of cash flow)
EBITDA	Earnings before interest, taxes, depreciation, and amortization (a measure of cash flow)
ESF	European structured financing
FASB	Financial Accounting Standards Board
FDA	Food and Drug Administration
FDIC	Federal Deposit Insurance Corporation
FHLMC	Federal Home Loan Mortgage Association ("Freddie Mac")
FICO	Fair Isaac & Co. credit ratings
FIN 39	A FASB ruling allowing netting of derivatives contracts
FNMA	Federal National Mortgage Association ("Fannie Mae")
FOMC	Federal Open Market Committee
FRED	Federal Reserve Bank of St. Louis Economic Database
FSLIC	Federal Savings & Loan Insurance Corporation
GAAP	Generally Accepted Accounting Principles
GDP	Gross Domestic Product
GNMA	The Government National Mortgage Association
GSCI	Goldman Sachs Commodities Index
HAMP	The Home Affordable Modification Program
HERA	Housing and Economic Recovery Act
HUD	US Department of Housing and Urban Development
IBES	Institutional Brokers' Estimate System
IBES year-1	Estimate for the current year

IBES year-2	Estimate for the next year
IMF	International Monetary Fund
IPO	Initial public offering
LBHI	Lehman Brothers Holding Inc. (the parent company)
LBI	Lehman Brothers Inc. (the US brokerage subsidiary)
LIBOR	London inter-bank offered rate
LSTA	Index of public prices for syndicated loans originated by the Loan Syndications and Trading Association
LTCM	Long-Term Capital Management (a hedge fund)
LTD	Long-term debt
LTV	Loan-to-value ratio (for mortgages)
M&A	Mergers and acquisitions
M1	Money supply narrowly defined
M2	Money supply broadly defined
MBA	Mortgage Bankers Association
mid-cap	Public companies with stock market capitalizations between $2 and $10 billion
MLP	Master limited partnership
MMMF	Money market mutual fund
MSA	Metropolitan Statistical Area (a Census definition)
MSCI	Morgan Stanley Company index of worldwide stocks
MSCI–EM	Morgan Stanley Company index of emerging market stocks
MSCI–EAFE	Morgan Stanley Company index of stocks in Europe, Australia, and the Far East
NAIC	National Association of Insurance Commissioners
NAR	National Association of Realtors
NASDAQ	National Association of Securities Dealers Automated Quotations Index
NCREIF	National Association of Commercial Real Estate Investment Fiduciaries
NIPA	National Income and Product Accounts of the USA
NYSE	New York Stock Exchange
NYU	New York University
OECD	Organization for European Cooperation and Development
OFHEO	Office of Federal Housing Enterprise Oversight
OTC	Over-the-counter
PDCF	Prime dealer credit facility
P-E ratio	Price-earnings ratio

PEG	Private equity group
QE-1	Quantitative Easing program number 1
QE-2	Quantitative Easing program number 2
QE-3	Quantitative Easing program number 3
REIT	Real estate investment trust
Repo	Repurchase agreement (over-night borrowing)
RMBS	Residential mortgage-backed securities
S&P 500	Standard & Poor's index of 500 companies
S&P 600	The Standard & Poor's stock index of public companies with market capitalizations of less than $2 billion
Sallie Mae	Student Loan Marketing Association
SEC	Securities and Exchange Commission
SIFMA	Securities Industry and Financial Markets Association
SIPA	Securities Investor Protection Act
SIV	Structured investment vehicle
SNCP	Shared National Credit Program
SPE	Special purpose entity
STD	Short-term debt
TAF	Term auction facilities
TALF	Term Asset-Backed Securities Loan Facility
TARP	Troubled Asset Relief Program
TLGP	Temporary Liquidity Guarantee Program
Treasuries	US treasury debt (maturities vary)
tri-party	lenders, borrowers, and their intermediaries in the repo market
TSLF	Term Securities Lending Facility
UST	US treasuries
VIE	Variable interest entity
VIX	Volatility index on the Chicago Board of Options Exchange (CBOE)

Bibliography

Books

Acharya (2010), Acharya, Viral V., Richardson, Matthew, Van Nieuwerburgh, Stijn and White, Lawrence J., *Guaranteed to Fail*, Princeton University Press, Princeton, NJ, 08540.

Bair (2012), Bair, Sheila, *Bull by the Horns*, Free Press, Simon & Schuster, New York, NY, 10020.

Ball (2018), Ball, Lawrence M., *The Fed and Lehman Brothers*, Cambridge University Press, New York, NY.

Bernanke (2013), Bernanke, Ben S., *The Federal Reserve and the Financial Crisis*, Princeton University Press, Princeton, NJ.

Bernanke (2015), Bernanke, Ben S., *The Courage to Act*, W.W. Norton Company, New York, NY, 10110.

Bernanke (2019), Bernanke, Ben S., Geithner, Timothy F. and Paulson, Henry M., Jr., *Firefighting, The Financial Crisis and its Lessons*, Penguin Group (USA), Inc., New York, NY, 10014.

Blinder (2013), Blinder, Alan S., *After the Music Stopped: The Financial Crisis, the Response, and the Work Ahead*, Penguin Group (USA), Inc., New York, NY, 10014.

Eichengreen (2016), Eichengreen, Barry, *Hall of Mirrors*, Oxford University Press, New York, NY, 10016.

Farrell (2010), Farrell, Greg, *The Crash of the Titans*, Crown Publishing Group, a division of Random House, New York, NY.

Geithner (2014), Geithner, Timothy F., *Stress Test*, Crown Publishing Group, a division of Random House, New York, NY.

Gennaioli (2018), Gennaioli, Nicola and Shleifer, Adrei, *A Crisis of Beliefs*, Princeton University Press, Princeton, NJ, 08540.

Greenspan (2007), Greenspan, Alan, *The Age of Turbulence*, Penguin Group (USA) Inc., New York, NY, 10014.

Krugman (2009), Krugman, Paul and Wells, Robin, *Macroeconomics*, Worth Publishers, New York, NY, 10010.

Lewis (2010), Lewis, Michael, *The Big Short*, W. W. Norton & Company, Inc., New York, NY, 10110.

McLean (2010), McLean, Bethany and Nocera, Joe, *All the Devils are Here*, Penguin Group (USA), Inc., New York, NY, 10014.

Mian (2014), Mian, Atif and Sufi, Amir, House of Debt, The University of Chicago Press, Chicago, IL, 60637.

Morgenson (2011), Morgenson, Gretchen and Rosner, Joshua, *Reckless Endangerment*, Henry Holt and Company, LLC, New York, NY, 10010.

Paulson (2010), Paulson, Henry M., Jr., *On the Brink*, Hachette Books Group, 237 Park Ave., New York, NY, 10017.

Paulson (2015), Paulson, Henry M. Jr., *Dealing with China*, Hachette Book Group, 1290 Avenue of the Americas, New York, NY, 10104.

Reinhart (2009), Reinhart, Carmen M. and Rogoff, Kenneth S., *This Time is Different: Eight Centuries of Financial Folly*, Princeton University Press, Princeton, NJ, 08540.

Shiller (2013), Shiller Robert J., Irrational Exuberance, Princeton University Press, Princeton, NJ, 08540.

Sorkin (2009), Sorkin, Andrew Ross, *Too Big to Fail*, Penguin Group (USA), Inc., New York, NY, 10014.

Swensen (2009), Swensen, David, *Pioneering Portfolio Management*, Free Press, a division of Simon & Schuster, Inc., New York, NY.

Tett (2009), Tett, Gillian, *Fool's Gold*, Free Press, a division of Simon & Schuster, Inc., New York, NY, 10020.

Zuckerman (2009), Zuckerman, Gregory, *The Greatest Trade Ever*, Crown Publishing, a division of Random House Inc., New York, NY.

Articles

Agarwal (2012), Agarwal, Sumit, Chang, Yan and Yavas, Abdullah. "Adverse Selection in Mortgage Securitization," *Journal of Financial Economics*, 105(3), September.

Altman (2005), Altman, Edward, I., Brooks, Brady, Resti, Andrea and Sironi, Andrea. "The Link between Default and Recovery Rates: Theory, Empirical Evidence, and Implications," *The Journal of Business*, 78(6), 2203–28.

Altman (2007), Altman, Edward I., "Global Debt Markets in 2007: New Paradigm or the Great Credit Bubble?", *Journal of Applied Corporate Finance*, 19(3), Summer.

Altman (2012), Altman, Edward I. and Kuehne, Brenda J., "Special Report on Defaults and Returns in the High Yield Bond and Distressed Debt Market: The Year 2011 in Review and 2012 Outlook," NYU Salomon Center, February.

Amromin (2010), Amromin, Gene and Paulson, Anna L., "Default Rates on Prime and Subprime Mortgages ...", Profitwise, September, Federal Reserve Bank of Chicago.

An (2014), An, Zudong and Nichols, Joseph, "The Upgrade and Downgrade of CMBS Credit Ratings," 1/29/14. No publisher cited.

Antoniades (2015), Antoniades, Adonis, "Commercial Bank Failures During the Great Recession: The (Real) Estate Story," *BIS Working Paper*, 530.

Ashcraft (2010), Ashcraft, Adam, Goldsmith-Pinkham, Paul, and Vickery, James, "MBS Ratings and the Mortgage Credit Boom," Federal Reserve Bank of New York Staff Report No. 449, May.

Atkinson (2019), Atkinson, Robert D. and Lind, Michael, Debunking the Myth of Small Business Job Creation, The MIT Press Reader, posted May 30.

Benmelech (2009), Benmelech, Efraim and Dlugosz, Jennifer, "The Credit Rating Crisis," NBER Macroeconomics Annual.

Bhaskar (2010), Bhaskar, Rajeev R., Gopalan, Yadav K. and Kliesen, Kevin L., Federal Reserve Bank of St. Louis, "Commercial Real Estate: A Drag for Some Banks but Maybe Not for the Economy," January 1.

Blundell-Wignall (2008), Blundell-Wignall, Adrian, Hu, Yu-Wei and Yermo, Juan, "Sovereign Wealth and Pension Fund Issues," Financial Market Trends, OECD, ISSN 1995–2864.

Bolton (2011), Bolton, Patrick and Oehmke, Martin, "Should Derivatives be Privileged in Bankruptcy?", NBER Working Paper No. 17599, 11/11.

Bord (2012), Bord, Vitaly M. and Santos, João A.C., "The Rise of the Originate-to-Distribute Model and the Role of Banks in Financial Intermediation," FRBNY Economic Policy Review, July.

Bordo (2018), Bordo, Michael and Duca, John V., "The Impact of the Dodd–Frank Act on Small Business," NBER Working Paper No. 24501.

Boston Consulting Group (2017), Boston Consulting Group, Staying the Course in Banking, March.

Boyd (2008), Boyd, Roddy, "Mortgage Mess Socks Ex-Goldman Sachs Stars," Fortune, February 29.

Cambridge Associates (2011), Cambridge Associates, "Still Nursing the U.S. Private Equity Overhang Hangover," May.

Carter (2009), Carter, George R. and Gottschalk, Alfred O., "Drowning in Debt: Housing and Households with Underwater Mortgages," U.S. Census Bureau, Appendix Charts and Tables.

Copeland (2010), Copeland Adam, Martin, Antoine and Walker, Michael, "The Tri-Party Market before the 2010 Reforms," Federal Reserve Bank of New York Staff Report no. 477, November.

DeFusco (2017), DeFusco, Anthony A., Nathanson, Charles G. and Zwick, Eric, "Speculative Dynamics of Prices and Volume," NBER Working Paper, May.

Domanski (2008), Domanski, Dietrich, "Government-Led Bank Rescue Initiatives," *BIS Quarterly Review*, December 2008.

Duca (2020), Duca, John V. and Ling, David C., "The Other (Commercial) Real Estate Boom and Bust: the Effects of Risk Premia and Regulatory Capital Arbitrage," *Journal of Banking and Finance*, 112(C), 2–16.

Edelman (2013), Edelman, Daniel, Fung, William and Hsieh, David A. "Exploring Uncharted Territories, *Journal of Financial Economics*, 109(3), 734–58.

Einhorn (2008), Einhorn, David, "Private Profits and Socialized Risk," Grant's Spring Investment Conference, April 8.

Elul (2015–1), Elul, Ronel, "Securitization and Mortgage Default," Federal Reserve Bank of Philadelphia Working Paper No. 15-15, February 19.

Elul (2015–2), Elul, Ronel and Tilson, Sebastian, "Owner Occupancy Fraud and Mortgage Performance," Federal Reserve Bank of Philadelphia Working Paper No. 15–45, December.

Fender (2008), Fender, Ingo and Scheicher, Martin, "The ABX: How Do the Markets Price Subprime Mortgage Risks?", *BIS Quarterly Review*, September.

Florance (2010), Andrew C., Miller, Norm G. and Spivey, Jay, "Slicing, Dicing, and Scoping the Size of the U.S. Commercial Real Estate Market," *Journal of Real Estate Portfolio Management*, 16(2).

Forbes (2007), 400 Richest Americans, September 20.

Goldman Sachs (2014), Goldman Sachs & Co., "2015 US Equity Outlook: Low Return and Low Dispersion," November 19.

Goldman Sachs (2015), Goldman Sachs & Co., The Mortgage Analyst, January 9.

Goldman Sachs (2016–1), Credit Strategy Research. "US Housing and Mortgage Outlook."

Goldman Sachs (2016–2), Credit Strategy Research. "Tracking Liquidity Using Trading Volume Data," February 18.

Goldman Sachs (2016–3), Goldman Sachs & Co., "Subprime Auto ABS vs. Subprime Mortgage Loss Comparison," March 11.

Goldman Sachs (2016–4), Goldman Sachs & Co., "Assessing Risk in the Auto Loan Market," March 15.

Goldman Sachs (2016–5), Goldman Sachs & Co., "Deteriorating US Credit Quality: Looking Under the Hood," October 6.

Gorton (2010–1), Gorton, Gary and Metrick, Andrew, "Haircuts," May 12, ssrn.com/abstract-1447438

Gorton (2010–2), Gorton, Gary and Metrick, Andrew, "Securitized Banking and the Run on Repo," November 9, ssrn.com/abstract-1440752

Greenlaw (2008), Greenlaw, David, Hatzius, Jan, Kashyap, Anil K. and Shin, Hyun Song, "Leveraged Losses: Lessons from the Mortgage Meltdown," Proceedings of the U.S. Monetary Policy Forum 2008, The University of Chicago Graduate School of Business.

Griffin (2015), Griffin, John M. and Maturana, Gonzalo, "Did Dubious Mortgage Origination Practices Distort House Prices?", Working Paper, May.

Harris (2014), Harris, Robert S., Jenkinson, Tim and Kaplan, Steven N., "Private Equity Performance: What Do We Know?", *Journal of Finance*, 69(5), October.

Kaplan (2009), Kaplan, Steven N. and Strömberg, Per, "Leveraged Buyouts and Private Equity," *Journal of Economic Perspectives*, 23(1), Winter.

KPMG Private Equity Forum (2016), November.

Lambert (2002), Lambert, Craig, "Trafficking in Chance," Harvard Magazine, July–August.

Levitin (2013), Levitin, Adam J. and Wachter, Susan M., "The Commercial Real Estate Bubble," *Harvard Business Law Review*, 3.

L'Her (2016), L'Her, Jean-François, Stoyanova, Rossitsa, Shaw, Kathryn, Scott, William and Lai, Charissa, "A Bottom-Up Approach to the Risk-Adjusted Performance of the Buyout Fund Market," privatecapital.unc.edu/ . . . /L'Her_FAJArticle_2016%20

Longinetti (2009), Longinetti, Christopher, "The Credit Crisis in Commercial Real Estate," Center for Real Estate, Quarterly, 3(2).

Looney (2018), Looney, Adam and Yannelis, Constantine, "Borrowers with large Balances: Rising Student Debt and Falling Repayment Rates," Brookings Institute, February.

Marsh (2011), Marsh, Tanya D., "Understanding the Commercial Real Estate Debt Crisis," *Harvard Business Law Review Online*, 33.

Mayer (2008), Mayer, Christopher J. Pence, Karen M., and Sherlund, Shane, "The Rise in Mortgage Defaults," Finance and Economics Discussion Series, Federal Reserve Board 2008-59, November.

MacKenzie (2012), MacKenzie, Donald, "Knowledge Production in Financial Markets: Credit Default Swaps, the ABX and the Subprime Crisis," *Economy and Society*, 41(3), published online, doi.org/10.1080/03085147.2012.661635

McDonald (2015), McDonald, Robert and Paulson, Anna, "AIG in Hindsight," *Journal of Economic Perspectives*, 29(2), Spring 2015.

Mellen (2019), Mellen, Suzanne R., "Hotel Cap Rates Hold Steady – Values Under Pressure," 1/16/19, HVS.com accessed 2/12/20.

Mian (2015), Mian, Atif R. and Sufi, Amir, "Fraudulent Income Overstatement on Mortgage Applications During the Credit Expansion of 2002 to 2005," May 15, 2015, Kreisman Working Papers Series in Housing Law and Policy No. 21, ssrn.com/abstract=2561366

Miller (2013), Miller, Harvey R. and Maurice Horowitz, Maurice, "Resolution Authority: Lessons From The Lehman Experience," April 11, presentation at NYU Stern School of Business.

Owusu-Anah (2013), Owusu-Anah, Yaw, "What Went Wrong? Examining Moody's Rated CDO Data," Economics Department, Columbia University, December 1.

Reilly (2009), Reilly, Frank K., Wright, David J. and Gentry, James A., "Historic Changes in the High Yield Bond Market," Exhibit 2, *Journal of Applied Corporate Finance*, 21.

Sean Chu (2011), Sean Chu, Chenghuan; "Adverse or Maybe Not-so-adverse Selection in the Commercial Mortgage-backed Security Market," Federal Reserve Board of Governors, June.

Shampine (2006), Shampine, Allan and Hal Sider, Hal, "Boom and Bust in Network Industries: Rising from the Ashes," 6th Global Conference on Business & Economics, October 15–17, Gutman Conference Center.

Stanton (2008), Stanton, Richard and Wallace, Nancy E., ABX.HE Index Credit Default Swaps and the Valuation of Subprime MBS," February 15.

Stanton (2011), Stanton, Richard and Wallace, Nancy E., "The Bear's Lair: Index Credit Default Swaps and the Subprime Mortgage Crisis (2011)," *Review of Financial Studies*, 24(10), October, 3250–80.

Stout (2011), Stout, Lynn A., "Derivatives and the Legal Origin of the 2008 Credit Crisis," *Harvard Business Law Review*, 1.

Stulz (2010), Stulz, Renée M., "Credit Default Swaps and the Credit Crisis," *Journal of Economic Perspectives*, 24(1), Winter.

Telegeography (2002). telegeography.com

Totten (2015), Totten, Mark, "The Enforcers & the Great Recession," 36 Cardozo L. Rev. 1611.

Vickery (2013), Vickery, James and Wright, Joshua, "TBA Trading and Liquidity in the Agency MBS Market," FRBNY Economic Policy Review, May.

Wigmore (1990), Wigmore, Barrie A., Financial Analysts Journal, "The Decline in Credit Quality of New Issue Junk Bonds 1982–1988," Sept/Oct.

Wigmore (2010), Wigmore, Barrie A., "A Comparison of Financial Remediation in the Great Depression and 2008–2009," *Research in Economic History*, 27, Emerald Group Publishing.

Wolff (2017), Wolf, Edward N., "Household Wealth Trends in the United States . . . .", NBER Working Paper No. 24085, November.

Yannelis (2018), Yannelis, Constantine, personal website people.stern.nyu.edu/Data/Student Loan Data, downloaded March 10.

Young (2020), Young, Michael S., Fisher, Jeffrey, D. and D'Alessandro, Joseph, New NCREIF Value Index and Operations Measures, Exhibit 5, Indexed Market Value Index by Property Type, Revised 8/28/2016, NCREIF.org/Academic Papers, accessed 1/6/20.

US and Other Government and Related Institutions

BIS (derivatives) Bank for International Settlements, "Statistical release: OTC derivatives market statistics," various years.

BIS (2008), Bank for International Settlements, Committee on the Global Financial System, "Private equity and leveraged finance markets," CGFS Papers No. 30, July.

BIS (2018), Bank for International Settlements, Quarterly Review 9/18.

Federal Reserve Board of Governors of the Federal Reserve System, Annual Reports.

Federal Reserve (Factors Affecting Reserve Balances), Board of Governors of the Federal Reserve System, Factors Affecting Reserve Balances, H.4.1.

Federal Reserve (Financial Accounts of the United States), Board of Governors of the Federal Reserve System, Financial Accounts of the United States.

Center for Disease Control (2003), MMWR weekly, June 13.

Council of Economic Advisors Economic Report of the President, various years.

Cox (2008), Cox, Christopher, testimony before the House Committee on Oversight and Government Reform, 10/23/08.

BEA (Vintage History) Department of Commerce, Bureau of Economic Analysis, "Vintage History of Quarterly Gross Domestic Product (GDP) and Gross Domestic Income (GDI) Estimates."

BEA (NIPA Accounts) Department of Commerce, Bureau of Economic Analysis, NIPA Accounts, "Investment in Private Fixed Asset Types."

BLS Department of Commerce, Bureau of Labor Statistics, various years.

Census (Residential Vacancies) Department of Commerce, U.S. Bureau of the Census, "Quarterly Residential Vacancies and Home Ownership," Table 4.

Census (Retail Trade Survey) Department of Commerce, U.S. Bureau of the Census, "Monthly Retail Trade Survey."

FDIC.gov "Temporary Liquidity Guarantee Program," accessed 3/02/18.

FDIC (Annual Report) Federal Deposit Insurance Corp., Annual Report, various years.

Federal Housing Finance Agency "Review of Options Available for Underwater Borrowers and Principal Forgiveness," no date but probably in 2012.

Federal Reserve Bank of New York (2012), "Liberty Street Economics," "Forecasting the Great Recession: DSGE vs Blue Chip," April 16.

FHFA (house price index datasets), Federal Housing Finance Agency, house price index datasets from 100 largest MSAs.

FRED Federal Reserve Bank of St. Louis, FRED Economic Data.

IRS Internal Revenue Service, Statistics of Income, various years.

National Science Foundation (2007), Industrial R&D Information System, 2007 report, table no. 44 and National Center for Science and Engineering Statistics and U.S. Census Bureau Business R&D and Innovation Survey 2013, p. 447.

SNCP Board of Governors of the Federal Reserve System, Shared National Credit Program.
The President's Working Group on Financial Markets (2008), "Policy Statement on Financial Market Developments," March.
Treasury Agency Financial Reports, 2009–2012.

Court Filings & Congressional Testimony

Alvarez & Marsal (2010), Alvarez & Marshal Holdings LLC, "Lehman Brothers Holdings Inc. The State of the Estate," dex991.htm, exhibit 99.1, September 22, Sec.gov/Archives/edgar/data/806085
Complaint no. 08-CV-08060-PGG, 1/05/2010, SOUTHERN DISTRICT OF NEW YORK. Cannot find on-line but citation number is correct. Also, SEC Plaintiff, Case 1:09-md-02011-PGG, filed 11/25/09
Fcic-static.law.stanford.edu.cdn_media/fcic-testimony/2010–0701-Goldman-AIG-collateral-timeline.pdf, table 18.
Hughes Hubbard & Reed (2016), Hugh Hubbard & Reed, LLC, In re: Lehman Brothers Inc., Case No. 08–01420 (SCC) SIPA, "State of the Estate, August 16, 2016."
Public Law 110–289 – 110th Congress, July 30, 2008/H.R. 3221, "Housing and Economic Recovery Act of 2008," 42 USC 4501.
Valukas (2010), Valukas, Anton R., U.S. Bankruptcy Court, Southern District of New York, In re: LEHMAN BROTHERS HOLDINGS INC. et al., Debtors, Chapter 11 Case No. 08-13555 (JMP), REPORT OF ANTON R. VALUKAS, EXAMINER, March 11.
Viniar (2010), Viniar, David, testimony before the Senate Permanent Subcommittee on Investigations, 4/27/10.
Weil, Gotshal & Manges (2019), Weil, Gotshal & Manges, LBHI (Chapter 11), Case No. 08-13555 (JMP), 15 notices of distribution on Lehman Brothers Holding, Case #08-13555, dm.epiq11.com. Also, Doc 59597, filed 3/28/19.

Databases and Rating Agencies

Barclayhedge.com "Hedge Fund Assets Under Management."
Cambridge Associates (2006), Trends in the Hedge Fund Industry, Cambridge, MA.
Dealogic dealogic.com
Fitch Ratings (2016), The Annual Manual, U.S. Leveraged Finance Primer, June.
IBES Institutional Brokers Estimate System, refinitiv.com
Inside Mortgage Finance (2012), Mortgage Market Statistical Annual 2012, 1 and 2.
Mergerstat Review (2006), (2007), (2012), (2016).
Moody's Analytics, CLO Vintage Analysis (2005–14) (2015), 3 March. moodysanalytics.com
New Generation Research bankruptcydata.com
Shiller (home page) Shiller, Robert J., home page of, Online Data, econ.yale.edu, long-term stock, bond, interest rate, and consumption data 1871–present, and U.S. Home Prices 1890–present. www.econ.yale.edu/~shiller/data.htm

Trade Organizations

American Council of Life Insurers (2007), Fact Book.

American Gambling Association (2017), 2017 State of the States, AGA Survey of the Casino Industry.

European High Yield Association (2008), "European Quarterly High Yield and Leveraged Loan Report," fourth quarter.

European Securitisation Forum Quarterly Securitisation Data Reports. SIFMA.org

IMF (2009), Global Financial Stability Report, Responding to the Financial Crisis and Measuring Systemic Risks, April.

International Swaps & Derivatives Association (2004), (2006), (2010), "ISDA Operations Benchmarking Survey."

Investment Co. Institute (2016). Fact Book.

MBA (2010, 2015, 2018), Mortgage Bankers Association, Commercial Real Estate/ Multifamily Financing Quarterly Databooks Q.

NAIC (2011–1), National Association of Insurance Commissioners, Capital Markets Special Report, "Securities Lending in the Insurance Industry—part 2," July 11.

NAIC (2011–2), National Association of Insurance Commissioners, Capital Markets Special Report, Schedule BA-Private Equity and Hedge Funds, September 23.

NAIC (2012), National Association of Insurance Commissioners, Capital Markets Special Reports, "The Insurance Industry's Exposure to Commercial Mortgage Lending and Commercial Real Estate Investments: An Overview," 10/26/2012.

NAIC (2016), National Association of Insurance Commissioners, Capital Markets Special Report, 26 January.

NAIC (2017–1), National Association of Insurance Commissioners, Capital Markets Special Report, May.

NAIC (2017–2), National Association of Insurance Commissioners, Capital Markets Special Report, "U.S. Commercial Real Estate Valuation Trends," 6/01/2017.

Nareit, National Association of Real Estate Investment Trusts, ReitWatch, various issues.

National Association of Realtors (2017), Investment & Vacation Homebuyer's Survey.

National Federation of Independent Businesses Small Business Optimism Index, various years.

NCREIF (2018), National Association of Commercial Real Estate Investment Fiduciaries, NCREIF.org, "Quarterly Highlights," 3Q.

SIFMA, Securities Industry and Financial Markets Research Quarterlies, various years.

Index

Abacus 2007 AC1, 150–2
ABCP. *See* Asset-backed commercial paper
    (ABCP)
ABN AMRO Mortgage Group, 67–8, 150
Abu Dhabi Investment Authority, 68
ABX indices
    crisis, during, 154, 156, 157, 183–5
    early Obama Administration, during,
        282, 284
    leadup to crisis, during, 118–20
    recovery, during, 321–2
Ackman, William, 132–3
Adjustable Rate Mortgages (ARM), 53
Adobe, 349–56
Advanced Semiconductor, 91–2
AIG
    generally, 180, 207
    bank run theory and, 3, 221–2
    beginning of crisis, losses during, 160–2
    Blackstone Group and, 267
    bond rating, downgrading of, 160–1
    cost of remediation measures, 309
    credit default swaps and, 80, 142, 179–80,
        223, 260
    downgrading of, 169
    Federal Reserve and, 171, 216, 218, 219, 267,
        303
    Goldman Sachs and, 125, 127, 129–30,
        153, 267
    government rescue of, 273
    government taking control of, 3
    increase in debt, 114
    JP Morgan Chase and, 267
    leadup to crisis, problems during, 125, 127
    Lehman Brothers situation compared,
        179–80, 223, 271–2, 279–80

losses during crisis, 3–4, 266–7
    margin borrowing by, 112
    poor management, 5–6
    private equity, investing in, 86
    repo market and, 111, 174
    role in crisis, 266–7
    securities lending and, 111, 112
    stock prices, 84, 162, 170, 207
    subprime mortgage guarantees, 133
    TARP and, 273, 281
    Treasury and, 219
    uncertainty at, 212–13
AIG Financial Products (AIGFP), 160–1
Airbus, 337
Albertson's, 91–2
Alcatel SA, 17–18
Allison Transmission, 163
Ally Financial, 238, 268–9
Alt-A mortgages
    credit deterioration in, 230
    defaults in, 154–6
    increase in debt, 115
    insurance companies guaranteeing, 131–2
    leadup to crisis, during, 63
    lying and fraud and, 231
    mortgage rates, 231
    second and investment homes and, 231
    shift to, 56–9
Alternative investments
    derivatives (*See* Derivatives)
    insurance companies investing in, 114
    search for higher returns and, 34, 35, 41–4
    2004–2006 period, during, 114
Alvarez & Marsal, 275, 278–9
Amaranth Advisors, 107, 349–56
Amazon, 156, 337

Federal Home Loan Mortgage Company
 (Freddie Mac)
 alternative investments and, 114
 bank run theory and, 3–4, 221–2
 beginning of crisis, losses during, 162–3
 capital flows and, 1–2
 CMBS and, 102, 229–30
 containment of crisis, belief in, 144
 cost of remediation measures, 309
 equity raised by, 150
 government taking control of, 3, 169–70,
  216, 217, 218, 248, 273
 highly leveraged debt and, 5, 222, 247–8
 Housing and Economic Recovery Act and,
  162–3
 housing bubble and, 2
 increase in debt, 114
 insurance companies and, 131
 leadup to crisis, problems during, 131, 153
 Lehman Brothers situation compared,
  179–80, 271–2, 279–80
 leveraged debt and, 5, 222, 247–8
 long-term status of, 342
 losses absorbed by government, 237
 low-income home ownership and, 7, 62, 64–7
 mortgage securitization versus, 229
 oversight of, 6
 remediation measures and, 7
 risks and, 247–8
 RMBS and, 52–3, 64–7, 68–9, 115, 222
 role in crisis, 229, 247–8
 stock prices during crisis, 207
 subprime mortgages, as buyer of, 6
 underwater mortgages held by, 227
Federal National Mortgage Association
 (Fannie Mae)
 alternative investments and, 114
 bank run theory and, 3–4, 221–2
 beginning of crisis, losses during, 162–3
 capital flows and, 1–2
 CMBS and, 102, 229–30
 containment of crisis, belief in, 142, 144, 153
 cost of remediation measures, 309
 Countrywide Financial and, 248
 derivatives and, 78
 equity raised by, 150
 government taking control of, 3, 169–70,
  216, 217, 218, 248, 273
 highly leveraged debt and, 5, 222, 247–8
 Housing and Economic Recovery Act and,
  162–3

housing bubble and, 2
increase in debt, 114
insurance companies and, 131
leadup to crisis, problems during,
 131, 153
Lehman Brothers situation compared,
 179–80, 271–2, 279–80
leveraged debt and, 5, 222, 247–8
long-term status of, 342
losses absorbed by government, 237
low-income home ownership and, 7, 62,
 64–7
mortgage securitization versus, 229
oversight of, 6
remediation measures and, 7
risks and, 247–8
RMBS and, 52–3, 64–7, 68–9, 115, 222
role in crisis, 229, 247–8
stock prices during crisis, 207
subprime mortgages, as buyer of, 6
underwater mortgages held by, 227
Federal Open Market Committee (FOMC),
 116–17, 142–4, 164, 306
Federal Reserve. *See also* Monetary policy
 generally, 216–17
 ABCP Money Market Mutual Fund
  Liquidity Facility, 218
 AIG and, 171, 216, 218, 219, 267, 303
 asset holdings, 149, 166–7, 323–4, 342–5
 Bank of America and, 182
 bank run theory and, 221–2
 bond holdings, 307–8
 Bush Administration, changes under, 24
 Citigroup and, 181–2
 Commercial Paper Funding Facility, 219
 containment of crisis, belief in, 142–4,
  145–9, 153
 federal funds rate (*See* Federal funds rate)
 Federal Open Market Committee (FOMC),
  116–17, 142–4, 164, 306
 foreign exchange swaps and, 218
 on GDP, 166–8
 General Electric and, 270
 "Goldilocks" economy and, 9
 highly leveraged corporate debt and, 303
 on housing prices, 116
 indecision in, 164
 on inflation, 9–11, 37, 145–7, 166–8
 Lehman Brothers and, 272, 273, 279
 as lender of last resort, 3
 on leveraged debt, 135

Index

Robert L. Hetzel, *The Monetary Policy of the Federal Reserve: A History* (2008)

Caroline Fohlin, *Finance Capitalism and Germany's Rise to Industrial Power* (2007)

John H. Wood, *A History of Central Banking in Great Britain and the United States* (2005)

Gianni Toniolo (with the assistance of Piet Clement), *Central Bank Cooperation at the Bank for International Settlements, 1930–1973* (2005)

Richard Burdekin and Pierre Siklos, Editors, *Deflation: Current and Historical Perspectives* (2004)

Pierre Siklos, *The Changing Face of Central Banking: Evolutionary Trends since World War II* (2002)

Michael D. Bordo and Roberto Cortés-Conde, Editors, *Transferring Wealth and Power from the Old to the New World: Monetary and Fiscal Institutions in the 17th through the 19th Centuries* (2001)

Howard Bodenhorn, *A History of Banking in Antebellum America: Financial Markets and Economic Development in an Era of Nation-Building* (2000)

Mark Harrison, Editor, *The Economics of World War II: Six Great Powers in International Comparison* (2000)

Angela Redish, *Bimetallism: An Economic and Historical Analysis* (2000)

Elmus Wicker, *Banking Panics of the Gilded Age* (2000)

Michael D. Bordo, *The Gold Standard and Related Regimes: Collected Essays* (1999)

Michele Fratianni and Franco Spinelli, *A Monetary History of Italy* (1997)

Mark Toma, *Competition and Monopoly in the Federal Reserve System, 1914–1951* (1997)

Barry Eichengreen, Editor, *Europe's Postwar Recovery* (1996)

Lawrence H. Officer, *Between the Dollar-Sterling Gold Points: Exchange Rates, Parity and Market Behavior* (1996)

Elmus Wicker, *The Banking Panics of the Great Depression* (1996)

Norio Tamaki, *Japanese Banking: A History, 1859–1959* (1995)

Barry Eichengreen, *Elusive Stability: Essays in the History of International Finance, 1919–1939* (1993)

Michael D. Bordo and Forrest Capie, Editors, *Monetary Regimes in Transition* (1993)

Larry Neal, *The Rise of Financial Capitalism: International Capital Markets in the Age of Reason* (1993)

S. N. Broadberry and N. F. R. Crafts, Editors, *Britain in the International Economy, 1870–1939* (1992)

Aurel Schubert, *The Credit-Anstalt Crisis of 1931* (1992)

Trevor J. O. Dick and John E. Floyd, *Canada and the Gold Standard: Balance of Payments Adjustment under Fixed Exchange Rates, 1871–1913* (1992)

Kenneth Mouré, *Managing the Franc Poincaré: Economic Understanding and Political Constraint in French Monetary Policy, 1928–1936* (1991)

David C. Wheelock, *The Strategy and Consistency of Federal Reserve Monetary Policy, 1924–1933* (1991)